Blockchain Technology and Applications for Digital Marketing

Rohit Bansal
Department of Management Studies, Vaish College of Engineering, India

Pacha Malyadri
ICSSR, Center for Economic and Social Studies, India

Amandeep Singh
Chitkara Business School, Chitkara University, Punjab, India

Asif Pervez
Jamia Millia Islamia University, India

A volume in the Advances in Marketing, Customer Relationship Management, and E-Services (AMCRMES) Book Series

IGI Global
PUBLISHER of TIMELY KNOWLEDGE

Published in the United States of America by
IGI Global
Business Science Reference (an imprint of IGI Global)
701 E. Chocolate Avenue
Hershey PA, USA 17033
Tel: 717-533-8845
Fax: 717-533-8661
E-mail: cust@igi-global.com
Web site: http://www.igi-global.com

Library of Congress Cataloging-in-Publication Data

Names: Bansal, Rohit, 1982- editor. | Malyadri, Pacha, 1958- editor. | Singh, Amandeep, 1982- editor. | Pervez, Asif, 1988- editor.
Title: Blockchain technology and applications for digital marketing / Rohit Bansal, Pacha Malyadri, Amandeep Singh, and Asif Pervez, editor.
Description: Hershey, PA : Business Science Reference (an imprint of IGI Global), [2021] | Includes bibliographical references and index. | Summary: "The main objective of the book is to provide insights on the blockchain technology and its applications in digital marketing to allow professionals and researchers gain comprehensive understanding of how this technology can influence the future of the digital marketing industry"-- Provided by publisher.
Identifiers: LCCN 2021008449 (print) | LCCN 2021008450 (ebook) | ISBN 9781799880813 (hardcover) | ISBN 9781799880820 (paperback) | ISBN 9781799880837 (ebook)
Subjects: LCSH: Internet marketing. | Blockchains (Databases)
Classification: LCC HF5415.1265 .B574 2021 (print) | LCC HF5415.1265 (ebook) | DDC 658.8/720285574--dc23
LC record available at https://lccn.loc.gov/2021008449
LC ebook record available at https://lccn.loc.gov/2021008450

This book is published in the IGI Global book series Advances in Marketing, Customer Relationship Management, and E-Services (AMCRMES) (ISSN: 2327-5502; eISSN: 2327-5529)

British Cataloguing in Publication Data
A Cataloguing in Publication record for this book is available from the British Library.

Advances in Marketing, Customer Relationship Management, and E-Services (AMCRMES) Book Series

ISSN:2327-5502
EISSN:2327-5529

Editor-in-Chief: Eldon Y. Li, National Chengchi University, Taiwan & California Polytechnic State University, USA

MISSION

Business processes, services, and communications are important factors in the management of good customer relationship, which is the foundation of any well organized business. Technology continues to play a vital role in the organization and automation of business processes for marketing, sales, and customer service. These features aid in the attraction of new clients and maintaining existing relationships.

The Advances in Marketing, Customer Relationship Management, and E-Services (AMCRMES) Book Series addresses success factors for customer relationship management, marketing, and electronic services and its performance outcomes. This collection of reference source covers aspects of consumer behavior and marketing business strategies aiming towards researchers, scholars, and practitioners in the fields of marketing management.

COVERAGE

- Social Networking and Marketing
- Relationship Marketing
- Ethical Considerations in E-Marketing
- E-Service Innovation
- Online Community Management and Behavior
- Mobile CRM
- CRM strategies
- Customer Retention
- CRM and customer trust
- Telemarketing

IGI Global is currently accepting manuscripts for publication within this series. To submit a proposal for a volume in this series, please contact our Acquisition Editors at Acquisitions@igi-global.com or visit: http://www.igi-global.com/publish/.

The Advances in Marketing, Customer Relationship Management, and E-Services (AMCRMES) Book Series (ISSN 2327-5502) is published by IGI Global, 701 E. Chocolate Avenue, Hershey, PA 17033-1240, USA, www.igi-global.com. This series is composed of titles available for purchase individually; each title is edited to be contextually exclusive from any other title within the series. For pricing and ordering information please visit http://www.igi-global.com/book-series/advances-marketing-customer-relationship-management/37150. Postmaster: Send all address changes to above address.

Titles in this Series

For a list of additional titles in this series, please visit: http://www.igi-global.com/book-series

Developing Successful Global Strategies for Marketing Luxury Brands
Fabrizio Mosca (University of Turin, Italy) Cecilia Casalegno (University of Turin, Italy) and Rosalia Gallo (Universitat Autònoma de Barcelona, Spain)
Business Science Reference • © 2021 • 351pp • H/C (ISBN: 9781799858829) • US $225.00

Insights, Innovation, and Analytics for Optimal Customer Engagement
Samala Nagaraj (Woxsen University, India)
Business Science Reference • © 2021 • 334pp • H/C (ISBN: 9781799839194) • US $195.00

New Techniques for Brand Management in the Healthcare Sector
Ana Pinto Borges (European Business School and Research Group, ISAG (NIDISAG), Portugal) and Paula Rodrigues (Lusíada University of Porto, Portugal)
Business Science Reference • © 2021 • 244pp • H/C (ISBN: 9781799830344) • US $225.00

Impact of ICTs on Event Management and Marketing
Kemal Birdir (Mersin University, Turkey) Sevda Birdir (Mersin University, Turkey) Ali Dalgic (Isparta University of Applied Sciences, Turkey) and Derya Toksoz (Mersin University, Turkey)
Business Science Reference • © 2021 • 357pp • H/C (ISBN: 9781799849544) • US $195.00

Building Consumer-Brand Relationship in Luxury Brand Management
Paula Rodrigues (Lusíada University of Porto, Portugal) and Ana Pinto Borges (Instituto Superior de Administração e Gestão, Portugal)
Business Science Reference • © 2021 • 318pp • H/C (ISBN: 9781799843696) • US $225.00

Innovations in Digital Branding and Content Marketing
Subhankar Das (Duy Tan University, Vietnam) and Subhra Rani Mondal (Duy Tan University, Vietnam)
Business Science Reference • © 2021 • 311pp • H/C (ISBN: 9781799844204) • US $195.00

IGI Global
PUBLISHER of TIMELY KNOWLEDGE

701 East Chocolate Avenue, Hershey, PA 17033, USA
Tel: 717-533-8845 x100 • Fax: 717-533-8661
E-Mail: cust@igi-global.com • www.igi-global.com

Editorial Advisory Board

Table of Contents

Detailed Table of Contents

The proliferation of information and communication technology and online business platforms joined together with smartphone technology and thereby changed the business-to-consumer business landscape, restructured organizations, and refurbished the process of value creation. Thus, it facilitates the businesspeople to reach a wider customer base by the customized customer targets; in so doing, it increases customers' trust and loyalty towards a brand. The internet-enabled technologies help the businesspeople to develop new digital markets and to make new demands for their products and services. Thus, the internet-enabled technologies are contributing a lot to the market engagement and customer target. Inline, a new technology called blockchain has transformed the digital marketing process completely and helps to do the business effectively with accurate and up-to-date data. With this backdrop, this chapter is designed to demonstrate how blockchain technology acts as a cutting edge technology in the consumer-centric pattern.

This chapter explores the role of cryptocurrency in digital marketing. Throughout the most recent years, cryptocurrency has developed, both in worth and ubiquity. Indeed, numerous industry leaders trust that cryptocurrency can change money and promote it until the end of time. In any case, as computerized cash, bitcoin turns out to be more ordinary ; cryptocurrency may introduce a few issues for advertisers hoping to gather shopper information. The cryptocurrency market is an appropriate environment dependent on the distributed network innovation. Decentralization is a distinguishing characteristic of this framework, and it is an impression of how there is no national bank or another case that authorizes power over the organization. The exchanges are led and checked to employ an appropriated blockchain system that relies upon clients' assets called diggers.

The tourist activity realized early on the advantages in the adoption of technology for the performance of its activities. With the emergence of the technological environment provided by Industry 4.0, blockchain technology emerges as the most disruptive and consequently more challenging technology for the tourism industry, since it has excellent potential to leverage innovation in this activity, whether in terms of products, processes, management, marketing, or institutionally. A bibliometric analysis was carried out to investigate affected studies in the tourism area, including the hotel, restaurant, marketing, and other sectors. Application of blockchain technology may be the key to boost tourism since its applicability presents several opportunities for tourism stakeholders, adds security and confidence in business transactions, can influence changes in the tourism value system, in terms of the value creation for customers, value creation for business, and in the tourism distribution chain.

Digitalization uses digital technology to change a business model and provide new revenue models and value-producing opportunities. Blockchain is a type of database that stores various kinds of information in blocks that form a chain of information. It is one of the secured ways of transferring and storage of data. Blockchain is helping in creating trust for digitalization among its users. This research aims to study the impact of trust in blockchain by analyzing the privacy and security concerns that can impact the user attitude and its intention to the adoption process. For this structure, literature review is performed. Five variables are used, and they are attitude, privacy, trust, security, and intention. A questionnaire is developed for survey-based research in the software firms, banking sector, and digital marketing companies. For analysis, exploratory factor analysis and structural equation modeling are used. A model is developed that shows a good fit, and the parameters are satisfied.

A family health management system deals with a safe and secure way of managing family member health details such as illness diagnosis, treatment, medical prescriptions, medical reports, and life insurance policies. All health records are encrypted and stored in chronological order utilizing blockchain technology so that authenticity, integrity, security, and privacy of the records are safeguarded. All stages of medical treatment are documented and stored for ease of future reference by the family. This becomes very handy if a person changes doctors and/or relocates to some other place/country for varied reasons. All the necessary health reports are shared with the life insurance company so that insurance claims become hassle free, if applicable. Medicine details are cross-verified with the manufactures to avoid fake drugs. This chapter explores the compatibility of using ethereum with the interactive MyEtherWallet to implement the proposed model.

Blockchain (BC) is a collective, indisputable ledger that makes easy the course of action of recording dealings and footpath possessions in an industry system. On the other hand, BC is significant in business that sprints on information. A BC network can follow instructions, expenditure, financial records, manufacture, and many more. Yet, the difficulties of BC in industry like mindfulness and getting, association, culture, cost and proficiency, regulation and administration, and security and protection must be properly dealt with to gain the advantages fully. Hence, the objectives of this chapter are to investigate various applications of industries that involve BC technology, the challenges, evolution of BC in industry applications, and its need, types of BC, and networks for industries and comparison. Further,

Quantum leaps in technology affect all phases of business models over numerous industries and are the fundamental characteristic of any technological revolution. Emerging technologies provide new avenues for industries to increase their competitive advantage and enhance the economic progression. The aim of this study is to advance a theoretical model on motivating antecedents and consequences of blockchain technology in insurance industry based on the evidence from past literature. This chapter is approached from the theoretical viewpoint, so it meticulously assesses and examines the prior literature to debate on the role of blockchain technology in the insurance industry. The outcome of the present study is dispassionate and corresponding to the conclusions of the prior literature. Blockchain helps in achieving innovation, augmenting transparency, refining data standards, and advancing an integrated approach for quality service. Thus, the espousal of blockchain in insurance is developing very quickly, and it has become the default platform for the complete insurance industry.

Preface

The rapid adoption and future prospects of Block Chain technology in digital marketing have been the reason and source of motivation for editors for the selection of topic for this edited book. Marketing has changed a lot in the past decade, but it's about to go through another revolution, thanks in large part to the blockchain. After being introduced in 1991 by *Stuart Haber* and *W. Scott Stornetta*, the concept of Block chain technology was first used by *Satoshi Nakamoto* to introduce a cryptocurrency, *Bitcoin*. Now, the block chain technology is being used for new ways of digital marketing for building more trust of consumers. Yes, while most of us associate digital marketing with things like AI and analytics, blockchain may be the most disruptive technology yet to hit marketers in every industry.

The importance of Block Chain Technology in digital marketing has become very well founded all over the world. This field is witnessing rapid development forcing researcher, academicians and practising managers to keep them updated on the latest advances in the field of digital marketing. Blockchain has brought a drastic change to the technology in the last few years and it is referred as Distributed Ledger Technology (DLT), makes the historical backdrop of any computerized resource unalterable and straightforward using decentralization and cryptographic hashing. In a time when digital marketing seems to be changing and growing by the moment, blockchain is changing digital marketing in disruptive, perhaps even irreversible ways.

We are sure that this book will be useful to the Researchers, academicians and practicing managers to update them with recent development in the area of digital marketing and to deal with the challenges of the dynamic marketing management. We hope that the book will provide proper insights of Blockchain technology to the students and creates a topical interest.

We appreciate the efforts put in by the researchers in terms of quality research work done by them. We express our gratitude to the reviewers of the various articles for giving their valuable contribution in the form of comments and suggestions for the enrichment of this edited book. We are also thankful to IGI Global for publication of this book.

We hope our commitment to the cause of promoting high quality research work in the area of Marketing management will contribute to enlighten our readers in the time to come.

Chapter 1: Blockchain Technology and Its Brunt on Digital Marketing

The proliferation of information and communication technology and online business platforms joined together with Smartphone technology and thereby changed the business-to-consumer business landscape, restructure organizations, and refurbished the process of value creation. Thus, it facilitates the business people to reach a wider customer base by the customized customer targets, in so doing it increases customers' trust and loyalty towards a brand. The internet-enabled technologies help the business people to develop new digital markets and to make new demands for their products and services. Thus, the internet-enabled technologies are contributing a lot to the market engagement and customer's target. Inline, a new technology called Blockchain; has transformed the digital marketing process completely and helps to do the business effectively with accurate and up-to-date data. With this backdrop this chapter designed to demonstrate how blockchain technology acts as a cutting-edge technology in the consumer-centric pattern.

Chapter 2: Applications of Blockchain Technology for Digital Marketing – A Systematic Review

Using blockchain technology in digital marketing is still a budding concept. Hence, this proposed chapter will aim to do a systematic review of research published on this topic from 2015 to 2021 (Q1). The chapter will look to uncover the various impacts of using blockchain technology on digital marketing. Impacts include (but are not limited to) improving digital marketing security, countering click fraud, developing trust and transparency and creating loyalty programs. Moreover, the chapter will also present future research propositions to further investigate blockchain applications in the realm of digital marketing.

Chapter 3: Blockchain Towards Decentralized Digital Marketing

Blockchain is a decentralized digital technology that is growing and standing out in digital marketing. The potential use of blockchain technology (BCT) will help affected companies create secure digital records and will also allow secure storage of data. During this chapter, we will try to understand the meaning of the concept of blockchain technology, its operating principle as well as its different types and sectors of applications, to make the relationship between blockchain technology and other emerging technologies such as big data, AI and smart contracts and to review the positive impact of blockchain technology on the e-commerce sector and in particular on customer relationship management.

Chapter 4: AIC Algorithm for Online Purchasing Intention

In recent years, the Internet market in Vietnam has developed strongly, leading to many forms of electronic business being born and with rapid growth. Online shopping is seen as the solution to cost-effective, fast, and convenient shopping. This paper was based on concepts and theoretical grounds related to behavior intention to accept and apply new technology to form the proposed research model. Consists of four independent factors: (1) Utility Perception, (2) Trust, (3) Social Influence, and one dependent factor Online Purchasing Intention. Previous studies revealed that using linear regression. This study uses the optimal choice by the AIC algorithm.

Chapter 5: Role of Cryptocurrency in Digital Marketing

This chapter explores the role of Cryptocurrency in digital marketing. As throughout the most recent years, Cryptocurrency has developed, both in worth and ubiquity. Indeed, numerous industry leaders trust Cryptocurrency can change money and promote it until the end of time. In any case, as computerized cash, as Bitcoin turns out to be more ordinary, Cryptocurrency may introduce a few issues for advertisers hoping to gather shopper information. The Cryptocurrency market is an appropriate environment dependent on the distributed network innovation. Decentralization is a distinguishing characteristic of this framework, and it is an impression of how there is no national bank or another case that authorizes power over the organization. The exchanges are led and checked to employ an appropriated Blockchain system that relies upon clients' assets called diggers.

Chapter 6: Blockchain Technology in Tourism Management – Potentialities, Challenges, and Implications

The tourist activity realized early on the advantages in the adoption of technology for the performance of its activities, with the emergence of the technological environment provided by industry 4.0, Blockchain technology emerges as the most disruptive and consequently more challenging technology for the tourism industry, a since it has excellent potential to leverage innovation in this activity, whether in terms of products, processes, management, marketing and institutionally. A bibliometric analysis was carried out to investigate affected studies in the tourism area, including the hotel, restaurant, marketing, and other sectors. Application of Blockchain technology may be the key to boost tourism since its applicability presents several opportunities for tourism stakeholders, adds security and confidence in business transactions, can influence changes in the tourism value system, in terms of the value creation for customers, value creation for business, and in the tourism distribution chain.

Chapter 7: Developing a Model to Highlight the Relation of Digital Trust With Privacy and Security for the Blockchain Technology

Digitalization uses digital technology to change a business model and provide new revenue models and value-producing opportunities. Blockchain is a type of database that stores various kinds of information in blocks that form a chain of information. It is one of the secured ways of transferring and storage of data. Blockchain is helping in creating trust for digitalization among its users. This research aims to study the impact of trust in blockchain by analyzing the privacy and security concerns that can impact the user attitude and its intention to the adoption process. For this structure literature review is being performed. Five variables are being used and they are attitude, privacy, trust, security, and intention. A questionnaire is being developed for survey-based research in the software firms, banking sector, and digital marketing companies. For analysis, exploratory factor analysis and structural equation modelling is being used. A model is being developed which shows a good fit and the parameters are satisfied.

Chapter 8: Design Family Health Management System Based on Ethereum Blockchain Interacting With MyEtherWallet Using Solidity

Family health management system deals with safe and secure way of managing family member's health details such as illness diagnosis, treatment, medical prescriptions, medical reports and life insurance policies. All health records are encrypted and stored in the chronological order utilizing block chain technology so that authenticity, integrity, security and privacy of the records are safe guarded. All stages of medical treatment are documented and stored for ease of future reference by the family. This becomes very handy if a person changes the doctor and/or relocates to some other place/country for varied reasons. All the necessary health reports are shared with the life insurance company so that insurance claim becomes hassle free, if applicable. Medicines details are cross verified with the manufactures to avoid fake drugs. It explores the compatibility of using Ethereum with the interactive MyEtherWallet to implement the proposed model.

Chapter 9: Investigation on Industry Applications of Blockchain Technology

Blockchain (BC) is a collective, indisputable ledger that makes easy the course of action of recording dealings and footpath possessions in an industry system. On the other hand, the BC is significant in Business that sprints on information. A BC network can follow instructions, expenditure, financial records, manufacture, and many more. Yet, the difficulties of BC in industry like mindfulness and getting, association, culture, cost and proficiency, Regulation and administration and security and protection which must be properly dealt to gain the advantages fully. Hence, the objectives of this chapter are to investigate various applications of industries that involve BC technology, the challenges, Evolution of BC in industry applications and its need, Types of BC and Networks for Industries and comparison. Further, the proposed chapter discusses how to manage the hyper connected supply chain in terms of industrial applications in terms of scalability, integrity and legacy.

Chapter 10: Risk-Resilient Supply Chain Using Blockchain Technology

Recently, Blockchain technology has been recognized for other industries than finance, proving it's potential other than cryptocurrencies and Bitcoin. Supply chain is one of the exponentially growing industries which needs to undergo through changes in order to survive in tomorrow's economy. There are many risks involved in current supply chains which can be potentially eliminated with the implementation of blockchain. This chapter analyses the various aspects of blockchain technology and how other technologies can be integrated with it to deliver exceptional solutions. Various risks present in the current system are discussed and how those risks can be handled using blockchain, contributing towards building a risk resilient supply chain.

Chapter 11: Role of Cryptocurrency in Digital Marketing – Cryptocurrency and Digital Marketing

Today, world has become a digital platform where technology has become an important part of day-to-day life. The world is growing at a rapid pace where there is a new innovation every other day. As days are passing every aspect of life has become online. Companies have also identified the scope and opportunity of digital marketing. This paper discusses how cryptocurrency is a challenge for digital marketing. This study is an exploratory study which involves secondary data collection. The objective of the research is to identify the influence of cryptocurrency on digital marketing. The findings of the study suggest that digital marketing is a data-driven marketing techniques and cryptocurrency is a payment mode which hides data, thus, popularity of cryptocurrency as mode of payment is a challenge for digital marketing.

Chapter 12: The Integration of the Blockchain Technology Into Wine Tourism

The aim of this study is to offer some suggestions to both the tourism industry and the practitioners in terms of making wine tourism and wine supply chain more transparent and traceable. From this point of view, in the current study, in which the block chain technology in wine supply chain is examined, first the technology of block chain has comprehensively been assessed and later the operational principles of block chain technology are discussed. Afterwards the block chain technology was attempted to be integrated into wine tourism and wine supply chain. Hence, a new model was proposed. In this respect, the outputs that can be obtained via the use of block chain technology in wine tourism and wine supply chain are revealed in this study.

Chapter 13: Adoption of Blockchain Technology – A Case Study on Walmart

In today's world society has become totally digitalized where technology is playing very important role in everyone's life. . Blockchain is a method which is useful in recording information and makes its difficult of change, hack or fraud with the system. A blockchain is fundamentally a digital ledger of volume of transactions that is distributed across the overall network of IT system on the blockchain. This technology act as a reliable layer in the evolution of E-commerce. Walmart has been working with IBM on a food safety blockchain solution to add transparency to the decentralized food supply ecosystem by digitizing the food supply chain process.1.This chapter will cover the concept & origin/emergence of Blockchain technology.2.Implications of Blockchain technology in supply chain (Walmart)3.The Significance and role of blockchain technology for the users and the stakeholders 4.The implications for the users.5.Challenges faced by Walmart during the Adoption of Blockchain Technology.6.The Approachability of Walmart to the IBM for the implication of blockchain to their organization

Chapter 14: Impact of Blockchain on E-Commerce – A SCOT Analysis: Mathematical Analysis to Study the Impact of Blockchain

The current disruption has created many challenges for all businesses in the short run, but it has created many opportunities for a long time. By helping in crisis and recovery, Blockchain can play a prominent role in accelerating post-crisis digital transformation initiatives. Trade has become more efficient, more inclusive, and less costly through Blockchain. These innovative technologies in the Fourth Industrial Revolution are transforming the world by making the processes more inclusive and efficient.

Chapter 15: Analytical Impact of Technology on the COVID-19 Pandemic

Covid-19 has totally changed the way that we live earlier and it also changed the way of our work. It changed the way of all the businesses that they run in the past. Many of the businesses today either shutdown due to lack of technological performance or the others moves towards the online mode to sustain in the market. During the time of this pandemic the businesses have no choice rather than shift to online mode. Some of the businesses that operate offline and it was not possible for them to shift online mode in a very short time due to lack of technology with them, lack of knowledge etc they faced much difficulty to operate their business smoothly like Dairy stores, Small wholesales markets, and daily need basic products shops. So, the impact of technology during the Covid-19 pandemic plays a very important role throughout the world. When this pandemic was on their peak technology became as a lifeline of the human beings. this research paper shows the trend of digital technology during Covid-19 pandemic and some innovations during this pandemic.

Chapter 16: Blockchain and Future of Digital Marketing

Blockchain is an amazing new technology and the way facts are stored and shared electronically. Blockchain in digital advertising reflects clarity, security, and access to waft revenue and stream flow. It can promote digital advertising to consumers, companies that are profitable in spending big money on digital advertising campaigns. With this new technology, consumers can share and improve their statistics simultaneously with advertisers and advertisers. Blockchain technology can be considered to restore data control to statistical owners focused on digital advertising. Today's society has grown into a very digital one where local technology plays a major role Participate in everyone's lives. Moreover, society is advancing rapidly, at an alarming rate Innovation in every corner and additional business made online. The authors of the concept chose to find out how the blockchain works could affect the use of big facts in digital advertising. The concept is set out for both selecting challenges issues and useful opportunities when applying blockchain on digital marketing content.

Chapter 17: Motivating Antecedents and Consequences of Blockchain Technology in the Insurance Industry

Quantum leap in technology affects all phases of business models over numerous industries and it's the fundamental characteristic of any technological revolution. Emerging technologies provide new avenues for industries to increase their competitive advantage and enhance the economic progression. The aim of this study is to advance a theoretical model on motivating antecedents and consequences of blockchain technology in insurance industry based on the evidence from past literature. This paper is approached from the theoretical viewpoint, so, meticulously assesses and examines the prior literature to debate on the role of blockchain technology in insurance industry. The outcome of the present study is dispassionate and corresponding to the conclusions of the prior literature. Blockchain helps in achieving innovation, augmenting transparency, refining data standards and advancing an integrated approach for quality service. Thus, the espousal of blockchain in insurance is developing very quickly and it has been putative to become the default platform for complete insurance industry.

Rohit Bansal
Pacha Malyadri
Amandeep Singh
Asif Pervez

Chapter 1
Blockchain Technology and Its Brunt on Digital Marketing

Dhanabalan Thangam
https://orcid.org/0000-0003-1253-3587
Acharya Institute of Graduate Studies, India

Anil B Malali
Acharya Institute of Graduate Studies, India

S.Gopalakrishnan Subramaniyan
https://orcid.org/0000-0002-2158-7483
Acharya Institute of Graduate Studies, India

Sudha Mariappan
Acharya Institute of Graduate Studies, India

Sumathy Mohan
Bharathiar University, India

Jin Yong Park
Konkuk University, South Korea

ABSTRACT

The proliferation of information and communication technology and online business platforms joined together with smartphone technology and thereby changed the business-to-consumer business landscape, restructured organizations, and refurbished the process of value creation. Thus, it facilitates the businesspeople to reach a wider customer base by the customized customer targets; in so doing, it increases customers' trust and loyalty towards a brand. The internet-enabled technologies help the businesspeople to develop new digital markets and to make

DOI: 10.4018/978-1-7998-8081-3.ch001

new demands for their products and services. Thus, the internet-enabled technologies are contributing a lot to the market engagement and customer target. Inline, a new technology called blockchain has transformed the digital marketing process completely and helps to do the business effectively with accurate and up-to-date data. With this backdrop, this chapter is designed to demonstrate how blockchain technology acts as a cutting edge technology in the consumer-centric pattern.

INTRODUCTION

Consumer-oriented marketing practices are the important ones for the business people who are in the B2C milieu to expand their existing market and to survive in the market (Sheth et al., 2000). Marketing plays a major role in recognizing and enlightening the value that the consumers are willing to attain from the consumption of goods and services (Lariviere et al., 2013). Communication plays a predominant role in understanding the consumers, for the same companies will be using a different form of communication modes and it would differ from company to company. The onset of the internet and digital technologies has made some insightful and astonishing things on communication and it is being an opportunity for the companies to increase their customer base. Thus the new generation of digital technologies offers lots of benefits to business people and consumers in various forms. Moreover, such kind of new generation technologies is also affordable to all type of industries especially for the micro, small and medium size of companies. Thereby these types of companies can improve their competitive advantage and sustain themselves in the markets (Rishel and Burns, 1997). Moreover, such kinds of technologies have been developed automation technologies and their solutions with the help of Industry 4.0 inputs like Artificial Intelligence, Internet of Things, and Big Data, and so on. Its a result, the marketing field is also becoming fully systemized with automation technology, and it influenced the marketing firms positively the way those firms attain and retain their consumers (Cvitanovi, 2018). Like the marketing automation technologies redesign the firms' outreach one side, and increase the consumers' purchase intention on the other side, thus the new generation marketing technologies shifting the customer-company relations to the new horizons (Treiblmaie, 2018).

In the global market economy, firms should concentrate more on various consumer engagement methods and techniques to attract new customers, retain the existing customers, expand the current market, and compete with the competitors. Thus a firm can strengthen its competitive advantage in all the aspects by deploying various consumer engagement methods (Santomier, 2008). Firms in the recent days investing more on the different portfolio of technologies for utilizing different types of media and sales promotional methods to place their products and services in the minds of the consumers (McAllister and Turow, 2002). Digital marketing is supporting lot to this process by promoting new channels along with the social network platforms such as Facebook, Whatsapp, Twitter, and so on. All these kinds of social media or social network platforms offering new, ground-breaking, gainful, and prominent support to the firms to attract and engage with the consumers (Melewar et al., 2017). The growth and development of internet technologies have replaced the conventional marketing mix considerably. The recent internet technology called Big Data analytics aids the business to process the millions of million data related to the consumers and thereby provides accurate data to attain more consumer insights towards the business (Stone and Woodcock, 2014). Similarly, wholesalers, retailers, and e-tailers have been investing more and more on social network platforms to promote their marketing practices and to strengthen their competitive advantages (Vend, 2018).

Thus, DeMers (2016) estimated that online businesses having the possibility to increase in the future with more consumer propensity to purchase the goods and services online. As the estimation made by DeMers (2016) the performance of the online business has been increasing in the recent days like anything. Moreover, the recent internet technologies are also concentrating more on consumers' data security, and privacy. By ensuring these things digital technologies also increases the consumers' trust towards online shopping and augment business transparency. Because, while consumers are engaging in the online business they are recording their various personal data such as goods what they purchased, what preferred, debit and credit card details, price range what they preferred, and other confidential data. However, the privacy of the consumers' data became the big question mark in the online business, since the data collection methods have turned into handy and ever-present.

This is because of the failure in following the regulatory activities, and numerous privacy leaks, all these factors made an impact on the trust of the consumers (Ingram et al., 2018; Martin, 2018; Bodoni, 2019). It results in consumers having more doubts regarding data privacy; it induces consumers' awareness to be safe in providing the data. Thus, consumers are very careful nowadays in using personal data for buying or selling goods in online business (Norman et al., 2016). But still, the privacy regulations are not followed properly in many developing countries. Hence, online traders should ensure consumers' data security by administering new data security regulations. Thus, online traders should comprehend the expectations of the consumers and maintain advanced technologies enhancing consumers' data, for the same the systems should be designed with an inbuilt concept called "privacy-by-design". The same has been now realized with a technology called Blockchain. This technology has established its positive as well as powerful outcomes in various fields of the business such as banking and finance, Medical and healthcare, travel and tourism, real estate, supply chain management, and marketing is no exemption. In the beginning, it was used in bitcoin for supporting cryptocurrency, the first and foremost facet of blockchain technology is to ensure peer-to-peer communication without third party involvement, thus this technology removing the needless interest of the third parties in controlling the course of business (Yli-Huumo et al., 2016). Such an innovative and efficient blockchain technology is defined as a digital ledger that records the business transactions are arranged in a chronological sequence to generate everlasting and unaltered records (Treiblmaier, 2018). The specialty of this technology is, it can be configured for any business for addressing issues or problems existing in it, and it can be rectified by its manifold technologies and methods (Rejeb, Keogh & Teriblmaier, 2020). Thus, marketing managers, as well as business people, should comprehend the potential of blockchain technology since it is switching the internet information into customers' trust and value. As a consequence, blockchain technology has changed the way of doing online business and communication by ensuring customers' data security and privacy (Twesige, 2015; Zamani and Giaglis, 2018). With is backdrop, the present work has made an attempt to explain what is blockchain technology, how it works, what the blocks are doing in this technology, brunt of this technology on digital marketing, and feature of this technology with the detailed review in the following sections.

WHAT IS A BLOCKCHAIN TECHNOLOGY?

Blockchain can be explained as, it is a technology that records and holds consumers' digital transaction details along with data security, privacy, and transparency, without the involvement of third parties. Moreover, the collected information or the data would be stock up as blocks, and those blocks can be guard by no one. Since it a disseminated recorder, it is entirely open for all individuals who are on the digital network or online marketing. Once the data are stored in this blockchain, it is not possible to alter or modify later, accordingly, this technology safeguards the interest of the consumers' by ensuring data privacy and security. Moreover, the records of each online transaction would be secured by a digital signature mode and thereby it also establishes its genuineness and legitimacy. As a result, the stored data on the blockchain cannot be changed or tamper-proof. This technology also enables online customers to move with an agreement called a consensus. It means online customers' data would be recorded and stored on a blockchain digitally, and its history would be accessible for online customers. By this method, blockchain technology ensures consumers' data privacy and security by reducing the chances of deceptive doings and duplication of the transactions by eliminating or avoiding the role of third-party. Since the blockchain database is scattered public no one controls records and the information. While the customers' data and transaction details are not stored in a particular place, there's no possibility for the corruption or hacking of data (Business.com, 2020).

HOW DOES BLOCKCHAIN TECHNOLOGY WORKS?

Every block of a blockchain would contain different data along with the hash of its prior block. Hash is one of the components in blockchain technology, and it is functioning with a distinctive mathematical code. Thus each hashes having its unique codes. If any recorded data is modified in a block, automatically the hash of the block will also be changed. Thus the connection of each block is ensured through the hash codes and thereby the entire blockchain is becoming safe. When the online business transactions are taking place on a blockchain, those transactions will be validated through the nodes of the network. These network nodes are also called miners in the bitcoin-enabled blockchain, and they are used as proof of work to validate and approve the business transactions in the online environment. For validating each transaction, the hash of every block should be referring to its preceding. If the hash is correct and matches with its preceding block, then only the transaction would take place. Even if a hacker attempt to break the network and collapse the data of any particular block, the hash associated with the particular block will also get into change. Thus the breach of network or the system can be identified easily if a hash is not match up with the original one. Thus the hash is ensuring that the blockchain unchangeable, since any changes made in a block of a chain, would be replicate the same in the entire blockchain and it can be identified simply (Abraham, 2021). Figure 1 explains how the blockchain technology works in the digital marketing.

HOW THE BLOCKS DO WORK IN BLOCKCHAIN?

Further, this technology also ensures authentication and providing access for storing and retrieving data with the help of cryptography and digital signature technology. These technologies are safeguarding the stored data from corruption. The mathematical codes make sure that the nodes incessantly accept the transactions and enter each one in the ledger. While the transactions are recording in the blocks, it would be collecting the information such as transaction data, time, amount of purchase, and parties involved. Thus each node in the network should collectively consent that the particular transaction has happened on the mentioned date and time unless it won't be stored in the blockchain. Since every block restrains a hash of the prior block, the data can be verified by anyone at any time in the transaction history.

Nodes on the network contend to authenticate the business transactions by mining and establishing that the buyer and seller have done the transactions correctly in the first place (Newman, 2019).

Figure 1. Mechanism of blockchain technology
Source: *www.tripsinterview.com*

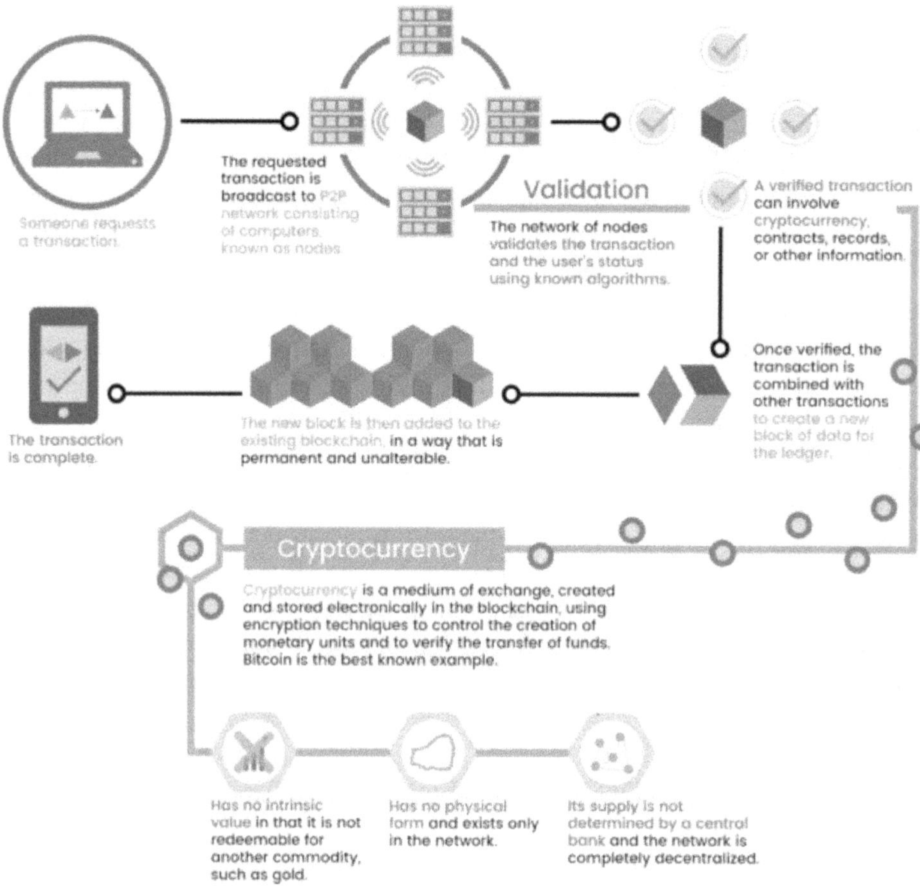

BRUNT OF BLOCKCHAIN TECHNOLOGY ON DIGITAL MARKETING

The recent advancements of industry 4.0 technologies such as artificial intelligence, the internet of things, machine learning, big data analytics, and other related technologies have remodeled the existing business process in various industries. Blockchain technology has also joined in the same line and establishing itself by changing the way of doing business in various industries and processes. Where marketing is one of the fields that are estimated to get more benefits from the application of blockchain technology. Finance and cryptocurrencies are the most benefitted fields by the application of this technology, and the kind of benefits is expected to rise in the marketing field also. Since this technology ensures the business transaction between the parties without the involvement third-party. Technologies like artificial intelligence and business analytics have offered more benefits to the business enterprises than the customers; on the other hand blockchain technology provides more benefit to the consumers by giving rights over their data. Thus, in many ways, blockchain technology provides benefits to firms as well as customers (Pärssinen et al., 2018). Here are some of the ways hoe blockchain technology made an impact on digital marketing:

Figure 2. Mechanism of blocks in blockchain technology
Source: *www.tripsinterview.com*

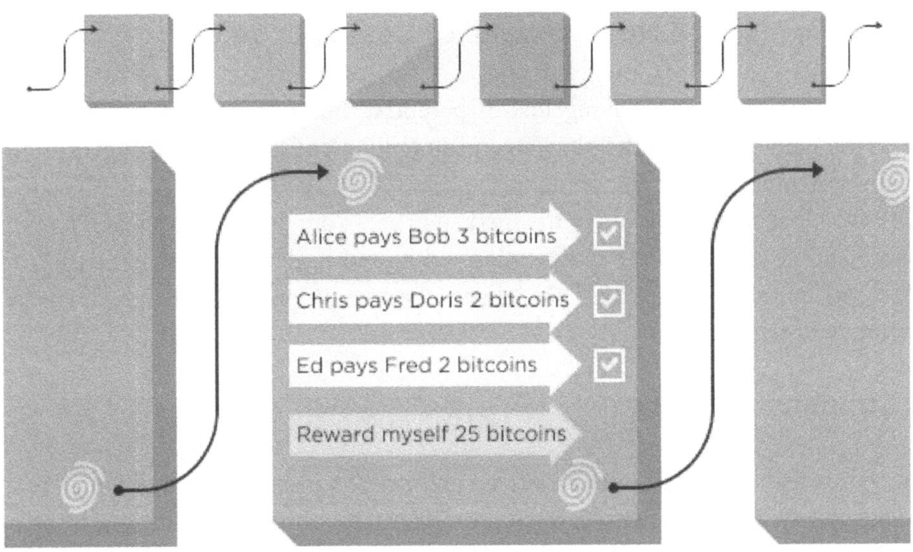

Blockchain Technology Expands Global Markets

Blockchain technology offers more benefits to the digital marketers with the help of cryptocurrency concept. Yes, when the marketing efforts directed towards the use of crypto to purchase the goods and services by means of bitcoin e-wallets, it expands the global markets. This is possible because of the crypto payments, and it can be performed between two countries with no exchange and processing cost. This type of perks will encourage the customers to purchase more goods and services from the international firms and it is an impressive way through the marketers can use to their plus (Tribis, Bouayad, & El Bouchti, 2018).

Augment the Transaction Transparency and Brand Trust

In some cases blockchain technology can be used for finding solutions to various marketing related services such as while using this technology to supervise the delivery related to a purchase made by a consumer, it allows the buyer and seller to look into the parcel's journey. Thus, it has built and increase consumers' trust over the business and brand, thereby marketers can get the benefit simultaneously. Moreover this technology can also be used to record and store companies' data, since many of the customers are concerned seriously about the usage of the data. It should be highlight by the marketers when they are using customers for marketing the goods and services (Pareek, 2019).

It Aids to Manage Huge Volume of Data with Safety

Blockchain and bigdata having lots of potential, but still it is not utilized fully. With the help of bigdata the blockchain can predict and analyze to discover future business trends, price fluctuations and the value of the goods and services. Moreover, with the blockchain technology the marketers can store huge volumes of data with safety and no one can do any alterations in it, and it also prevents the data from loss, corruption, and hacking. Thus it keeps the data properly and thereby it ensures accuracy of the results.

It Condenses Costs

Since this technology is a decentralized and peer-to-peer, a huge amount of costs associated with the business can be controlled by eliminating the third parties from the transactions. Thus it ensures smart agreement between buyer and seller, and the buyer will be paying to the seller only when the terms and conditions of the agreement are fulfilled. This type of practice enables the customers to pay the amount without any third parties. However, there are costs such as infrastructure, installation, and transaction associated with the blockchain, but they are nil almost.

It Targets the Customers Accurately

The successful marketing of goods and services is depends upon the promotional activities followed by the firms. Where advertisement plays a major role in attract and retain the customers, however many of the firms getting failure in this process by the horrible results of the marketing operations. Though the advertisement elements such as advertisement copy, its format, visual effects, and the target audience are arranged in a manner, it won't get success sometimes. These issues can be eliminating or avoiding with blockchain technology by decentralizing the advertising network, marketers can get right media to propagate the message to the target audience.

It Amplifies the Business Efficiency

Blockchain improves the business efficiency by reducing the process time consumption. Further, it also avoids middleman thereby it speedup the disbursement of the payment. Thus it speedup the business transactions in real time by avoiding third parties. The data can be accesses by both the parties in this technology; hence, there is no need to have detached records. Moreover, this technology also helps to execute smart agreements for the instant payment as quickly as the conditions in the contract are met.

Decentralized Applications

When it comes to traditional mobile apps, the rules are dictated by the Play Store or App Store. The same goes for any platform that has a single authority that controls the entire platform. Since no single authority governs decentralized apps, there is no my way or the highway approach. We saw how Steem enables brands to create apps and provides them with an opportunity to monetize and build a community. Similarly, Ethereum, EOS, NEO, Tron, Cardano, etc. are some platforms that enable you to build apps on their platforms. The absence of a single authority allows you to connect with your target audience directly.

Management of Business Content

Business Content is an important for any business to attract, attain and retain the customers. It should be managing effectively since it is more data-driven. As it is a data-driven it can be consistent with Blockchain. Thereby, the Content development, dissemination, monetization, personalization, innovation and creation will be easier task for the digital marketers who are using blockchain technology in their business (Pareek, 2019).

BLOCKCHAIN TECHNOLOGY AND ITS FUTURE IN BUSINESS LANDSCAPE

Business analysts and marketing experts mentioned that the future of marketing is in the clutch of blockchain technology. Because. It has predicted that by 2023almost 30 percent of the social media marketing activities will be authenticated by this technology. By 2025 world's 50 percent of the population is expected to have Smartphones, thereby it is also expected that conventional banking practices will be replaced by this technology. By 2023, it is also expected that various technical standards of blockchain technology will replace the third party enabled contract, by developing and deploying the smart contracts in a decentralized manner. Right from logistics to the internet of things, from marketing to money banking, from the government to private, almost in all the business fields, it is expected that the blockchain technology likely to do persistent involvement and renovate them for the enhanced position shortly. Moreover, the present business world has realized a lot from the blockchain technology developments and it will transform the present business patterns so that it is expected that in 2023, the ordinary blockchain platforms will be functioning in an easy way to use, access data, and will also hold up to the trustworthy business transactions with the data security that consumers and the companies want. Even though the market analysis augur that within 2025, this technology will be utilized to influence the use cases with remarkable business and societal values, such as serving to impede the stretch of bogus reports and content, and supports to extent the digital commerce and banking products and services to digitally excluded population (Sahu, 2020). To accomplish this market extension, first, this technology should get mature enough. So that it can be served better for the visibility and utility of this technology. However in some cases, this technology is not lived up to the mark due to some reasons as it is not support for building business and social models, and still, in most of the business units, this technology is under experiment mode only. The business and technical experts have named this stage a "trough of disillusionment". Still, this trough of disillusionment doesn't call for a cause for depression. Many of the reports prepared by Gartner stating that this "trough" issue may be solved by 2023 since the blockchain technology having advancements in its operations and realistic uses. Further, this technology is the source of advantages in various ways such as transaction precision, safety and security of data, information devolution, haste, and controlling the cost as well. Thus this technology is functioning like a pioneer in the modern business and transforms the way of doing business globally. This technology is being a common platform to the business units and helps to avoid problems, easy to use and access the data; thereby it gamely maintains confidential business transactions with the data privacy and security. To make the blockchain a dominant and potential one for normal usage, business people need not worry about deciding the right platform, because of the appropriate system concatenation, the suitable chic agreement language, or the suitable agreement algorithms. The back end of the blockchain technology shouldn't substance to punters, because it is just like various internet protocols and it is not such a matter to users of the web. Every web user are much caring about their internet-based relevancies. But, every blockchain customers have to mind about their scattered relevancies and e-contracts. The perfect use of blockchain technology and its application in across sector are yet to become extensive, meantime there is some notable and optimistic growth are already taking place in various industries. As per a market report, it is expected to happen by 2022 that the famous online business platforms such as Facebook, Twitter, Uber, Amazon, Airbnb, PayPal, Alibaba, eBay, and some other online business companies have planned to offer mobile-enabled online business services to more than 750 million new customers. Thus it could understand from this fact that the growth of the online business will pave the way for the massive utilization of blockchain technology (Focalpoints, 2020).

CONCLUSION

The growth of internet technologies lead to technological developments and the growth of online business and online marketing, and these developments have wrought the value creation process considerably. Lots of business units and industries have depended upon the technologies heavily, for producing the goods and services to their customers and to face the competitors. The recent technologies have the potential to design the products and services according to the taste and preference of the market, helps to improve the data quality, and redesign the production process in a most economical and receptive manner (Felix, Rauschnabel, & Hinsch, 2017). Thus the emerging technologies have reshaped the marketing landscape significantly by changing the conventional marketing pattern and strategies. In recent years companies are concentrating more on technologies to expand their markets by piercing new markets and creating a new customer base. At this juncture, the information and communication technologies have supported a lot to the marketers to attain consumers with well-equipped internet communication modes (Pawczuk, Massey, & Holdowsky, 2019). In the meantime, consumers have turned into more clued-up about the available products and services, and their various offers and thus they are making the right decisions to what to buy and what not (Wang, Luo, & Lee, 2019). On the other side, with the data mining system and big data analytics business units have taken smart and accurate decisions about the needs and wants of the consumers. Analyzing a huge volume of data would support the business units to get various useful insights through prognostic analytics. Some methods and technologies have been used in data analytics; however, blockchain technology is having more advanced futures than the other techniques. Thus this technology is providing accurate results to the business people to consider and attract a new customer base. At present online marketing is full of intermediaries, and they are controlling the buyer and seller relationship significantly. By doing this, intermediaries are slowdown the inventiveness of business and remove the direct marketing benefits to the consumers. In this worst situation, blockchain technology plays a major role to avoid business intermediaries and facilitates the consumers to do the transactions in a straight line without the role of intermediaries. In this way, this technology creates a new way of doing business by improving the trust over the business, data privacy, and transparency, consequential in more trusted business operation with more customer-oriented (Langan, Cowley, & Nguyen, 2019). Furthermore, the high-tech features and advancements of blockchain technology have established feasibility for caring for consumers' solitude and improve digital marketing security. This technology also helps to avoid prevalent click fraud issues, thus this technology is generating a better marketing landscape for the business, consumers, and other members concerned with the process of value creation and delivery. From a business point of view, instituting consumer loyalty is habitually a difficult task, because consumers at all times think about the costs and benefits in their purchase and always ready to switch to other brands for the same (Joshi, & Marthandan, 2019). But this issue can be avoided with the help of blockchain technology and its rehabilitated move towards designing, incorporating, and supporting well-designed loyalty plans. Blockchain-supported recompense programs permit business people and consumers to achieve benefits from their loyalty plans, ensuing in higher brand attachment and sustainability.

REFERENCES

Abraham. (2021). *How an uncertain economic environment can be the biggest driver of innovation.* yourstory.com

Bodoni, S. (2019). *Mastercard Alerts Privacy Watchdogs After Loyalty Program Leak.* Bloomberg.Com. Available online at: https://www.bloomberg.com/news/articles/2019-08-23/mastercard-tells-belgian-german-privacy-watchdogs-ofbreach

Business.com. (2020). *How Will Blockchain Impact Digital Marketing?* Available online at: business.com

Cvitanovi´c, P. L. (2018). New technologies in marketing as competitive advantage. *2018 ENTRENOVA Conference Proceedings*, 294-302.

DeMers, J. (2016). *New Technologies Shaping Online Marketing for the Better*. Academic Press.

Felix, R., Rauschnabel, P. A., & Hinsch, C. (2017). Elements of strategic social media marketing: A holistic framework. *Journal of Business Research*, *70*(C), 118–126. doi:10.1016/j.jbusres.2016.05.001

Focalpoints. (2020). *The impact of blockchain in digital marketing*. Available online at: https://www.mediaupdate.co.za/marketing/147788/the-impact-of-blockchain-in-digital-marketing

Forbes. (n.d.). https://www.forbes.com/sites/jaysondemers/2016/

Gialis. (2018). Future challenges on the use of blockchain for food traceability analysis. *Trends Anal. Chem., 107*, 222–232. doi:10.1016/j.trac.2018.08.011

Ingram, D., Panchadar, A., & Auchard, E. (2018). *Facebook Privacy Scandal Widens as Data Leak Hits 87 Million Users*. CIO. Available online at: https://www.cio.com.au/article/635768/facebook-privacy-scandal-widensdata-leak-hits-87-million-users/

Joshi, P. L., & Marthandan, G. (2019). The Hype of Big Data Analytics and Auditors. *Emerging Markets Journal*, *8*(2), 1–4. doi:10.5195/emaj.2018.153

Langan, R., Cowley, S., & Nguyen, C. (2019). The State of Digital Marketing in Academia: An Examination of Marketing Curriculum's Response to Digital Disruption. *Journal of Marketing Education*, *41*(1), 32–46. doi:10.1177/0273475318823849

Larivière, B., Joosten, H., Malthouse, E. C., Van Birgelen, M., Aksoy, P., Kunz, W. H., & Huang, M.-H. (2013). Value fusion: The blending of consumer and firm value in the distinct context of mobile technologies and social media. *Journal of Service Management*, *24*(3), 268–293. doi:10.1108/09564231311326996

Martin, K. (2018). The penalty for privacy violations: How privacy violations impact trust online. *Journal of Business Research*, *82*, 103–116. doi:10.1016/j.jbusres.2017.08.034

McAllister, M. P., & Turow, J. (2002). New media and the commercial sphere: Two intersecting trends, five categories of concern. *Journal of Broadcasting & Electronic Media*, *46*(4), 505–514. doi:10.120715506878jobem4604_1

Melewar, T. C., Foroudi, P., Gupta, S., Kitchen, P. J., & Foroudi, M. M. (2017). Integrating identity, strategy and communications for trust, loyalty and commitment. *European Journal of Marketing*, *51*(3), 572–604. doi:10.1108/EJM-08-2015-0616

Newman. (2019). *How Blockchain Is Changing Digital Marketing*. Available online at: https://www.forbes.com/sites/danielnewman/2019/09/18/how-blockchain-is-changing-digital-marketing/?sh=7f60417816eb

Norman, G., Pepall, L., Richards, D., & Tan, L. (2016). Competition and consumer data: The good, the bad, and the ugly. *Research in Economics*, *70*(4), 752–765. doi:10.1016/j.rie.2016.09.002

Pärssinen, M., Kotila, M., Cuevas Rumin, R., Phansalkar, A., & Manner, J. (2018). Is Blockchain Ready to Revolutionize Online Advertising? *IEEE Access: Practical Innovations, Open Solutions*, *6*, 54884–54899. doi:10.1109/ACCESS.2018.2872694

Pawczuk, L., Massey, R., & Holdowsky, J. (2019). *Deloitte's 2019 Global Blockchain Survey: blockchain gets down to business* [Report]. Deloitte.

Rejeb, A., Keogh, J. G., & Treiblmaier, H. (2020). How Blockchain Technology Can Benefit Marketing. *Six Pending Research Areas. Front. Blockchain*, *3*, 3. doi:10.3389/fbloc.2020.00003

Rishel, T. D., & Burns, O. M. (1997). The impact of technology on small manufacturing firms. *Journal of Small Business Management*, *35*, 2–10.

Sahu. (2020). *Why is Blockchain the Future? Future Prospects, Expectations & Current Scenario.* Available online at: https://www.upgrad.com/blog/why-is-blockchain-the-future/#:~:text=According%20to%20Gartner%2C%20the%20world,with%20the%20data%20confidentiality%20enterprises

Santomier, J. (2008). New media, branding and global sports sponsorship. *International Journal of Sports Marketing & Sponsorship*, *10*(1), 9–22. doi:10.1108/IJSMS-10-01-2008-B005

Sheth, J. N., Sisodia, R. S., & Sharma, A. (2000). The antecedents and consequences of customer centric marketing. *Journal of the Academy of Marketing Science*, *28*(1), 55–66. doi:10.1177/0092070300281006

Tipsinterview. (2018). *Blockchain technology and its impact on digital marketing in 2018 revealed*. Available online at: https://tipsinterviews.blogspot.com/2017/11/blockchain-and-its-impact-on-digital.html

Treiblmaier, H. (2018). The impact of the blockchain on the supply chain: A theory-based research framework and a call for action. *Supply Chain Management*, *23*(6), 545–559. doi:10.1108/SCM-01-2018-0029

Treiblmaier, H. (2018a). The impact of the blockchain on the supply chain: A theory-based research framework and a call for action. *Supply Chain Management*, *23*(6), 545–559. doi:10.1108/SCM-01-2018-0029

Tribis, Y., Bouayad, H., & El Bouchti, A. (2018). Supply chain management based on blockchain: A systematic mapping study. *MATEC Web of Conferences, 200*, 1-8. 10.1051/matecconf/201820000020

Twesige, R. L. (2015). *A Simple Explanation of Bitcoin and Blockchain Technology*. Available online at: https://www.researchgate.net/profile/Richard_Twesige/publication/270287317

Wang, L., Luo, X., & Lee, F. (2019). Unveiling the interplay between blockchain and loyalty program participation: A qualitative approach based on Bubichain. *International Journal of Information Management*, *49*, 397–410. doi:10.1016/j.ijinfomgt.2019.08.001

Yli-Huumo, J., Ko, D., Choi, S., Park, S., & Smolander, K. (2016). Where is current research on blockchain technology? - A systematic review. *PLoS One*, *10*(10), e163477. doi:10.1371/journal.pone.0163477 PMID:27695049

Zamani, E. D., & Giaglis, G. M. (2018). With a little help from the miners: Distributed ledger technology and market disintermediation. *Industrial Management & Data Systems*, *118*(3), 637–652. doi:10.1108/IMDS-05-2017-0231

Chapter 2
Applications of Blockchain Technology for Digital Marketing:
A Systematic Review

Kazi Turin Rahman
Coventry University, UK

ABSTRACT

Using blockchain technology in digital marketing is still a budding concept. Hence, this chapter aims to do a systematic review of research published on this topic from 2015 to 2021 (Q1). The chapter will look to uncover the various impacts of using blockchain technology on digital marketing. Impacts include (but are not limited to) improving digital marketing security, countering click fraud, developing trust and transparency, and creating loyalty programs. Moreover, the chapter will also present future research propositions to further investigate blockchain applications in the realm of digital marketing.

INTRODUCTION

Blockchain technology has taken the world by storm with its ability to disrupt business operations as we know it (Nowiński and Kozma, 2017). Seemingly, it has gained the attention of practitioners, lawmakers and academics everywhere. The origins of blockchain can be traced back to 2008, when Bitcoin was launched. In the following years, many studies acknowledged the potential of blockchain to radically alter business processes across various industries (Antoniadis et al., 2018).

DOI: 10.4018/978-1-7998-8081-3.ch002

Marketing in general, including digital marketing, has been affected by blockchain technology as well. It has dramatically changed the way marketers interact with their stakeholders and manage digital marketing campaigns. The existing online advertising and digital marketing landscape is quite competitive for companies and marketers (Antoniadis et al., 2019).

Moreover, famous companies like IBM and Walmart have already integrated blockchain technology into their business functions, including marketing. Additionally, Facebook is planning to integrate its own cryptocurrency system within its network of social media platforms (Andriotis et al., 2019). Certainly, the marketing mix will never be the same again, courtesy of blockchain.

Unfortunately, despite the game-changing potential of blockchain technology, very little research has been done regarding its applications for digital marketing. Therefore, this chapter will aim to uncover the possible uses of blockchain technology in digital marketing. A systematic review of the current literature will reveal the potential applications and pave the way for future research in this field.

METHODOLOGY

Search Strategy

The systematic review was developed as per the guidelines of PRISMA (Preferred Reporting Items for Systematic Reviews and Meta-Analyses). The objective was to methodically search and include past research papers involving the terms' blockchain' and 'digital marketing'. Moreover, scholarly search engines were used to find said papers like EBSCO, ProQuest and Google Scholar.

Furthermore, the past studies were critically analyzed to uncover the current standing on the topic and subsequent literature gaps for future research.

Inclusion Criteria

In order to include the latest studies on applications of blockchain technology for digital marketing, the following inclusion criteria were adopted:

- The research papers must be authored in English
- The papers can be quantitative, qualitative or mixed in nature.
- Studies published from January 2015 to January 2021 were included. Blockchain technology emerged in 2008 with Bitcoin and its applications spread to various sectors recently. Therefore, research into the application of this technology in digital marketing is likely to appear post 2015.

- The systematic review focused on past studies dealing with various impacts of using blockchain technology on digital marketing. Impacts included (but not limited to) promoting digital marketing security, reducing click fraud, strengthening trust and transparency and enabling loyalty programs.

Additionally, more relevant applications were also uncovered along the course of this review. They have been grouped under specific themes and presented accordingly in the next section.

Search and Screening

Eventually, few papers were found that matched the inclusion criteria perfectly. This further confirms that research into applications of blockchain technology for digital marketing is minimal. Most papers dealing with blockchain focuses on its applications for digital currency and hence were excluded. Moreover, many duplicate studies were also discarded that appeared more than once.

Further exclusions are outlined below:

- Non-English papers.
- Studies older than 2015.
- Papers with inconsistent titles, abstracts and full-texts.
- Multiple instances of the same study appearing elsewhere.
- Research dealing with implications of blockchain in areas other than digital marketing.

RESULTS

Detailed research regarding blockchain applications for digital marketing is very scarce. However, the benefits of this disruptive innovation are indisputable (Ghose, 2018). Essentially, the foundation of blockchain technology consists of a peer-to-peer communication network. Said network ensures the removal of many intermediaries who stand between the business and consumer. Hence, it grants companies the ability to foster consumer relationships and maintain a high level of transparency, privacy and security (Rejeb et al., 2020). In the following sections, various digital marketing applications of blockchain technology will be discussed.

Developing Trust and Transparency

As per the existing literature, consumer trust and confidence in brands are eroding at a steady pace (Jones, 2018). It is no secret that brands need to regain that trust and establish themselves as worthy of consumer confidence. Nowadays, transactions happen without physical contact owing to the internet. Hence, companies need to maintain a high level of trust and transparency online to uphold their brand image (Tapscott and Tapscott, 2016). Moreover, the type of technological infrastructure they invest in can play a huge role in strengthening their relationships with customers. Blockchain is one such technology that can enhance the trustworthiness of brands through transparent digital marketing efforts.

According to Rejeb et al. (2020), blockchain technology can establish a system of trust with its characteristics of transparency, consistency and immutability. This trust protocol or 'trust by design', guarantees that both brands and their customers (potential and existing) will behave with integrity and honesty. Ultimately, blockchain has the power to create a transparent digital marketing ecosystem where consumers, brands and marketers can exist in harmony (Chapron, 2017). A harmony that is safe, secure and long-lasting.

That's not all; blockchain can end malicious marketing of duplicate products that violate the intellectual property rights of brands and manufacturers. This is possible due to the end-to-end product traceability and strict monitoring that blockchain provides (Galvez et al., 2018). Consequently, consumers have greater verifiability and visibility over the brand claims. For instance, if a brand claims to be sustainable or halal, a potential customer can crosscheck and verify whether this is true or false. It's not just about product certifications; blockchain can even help detect the authenticity of a company's business practices and even their commitment to corporate social responsibility (Treiblmaier, 2020). All of this is possible through a digital marketing platform built on the foundation of blockchain technology.

By promoting such a high level of transparency, marketers will be able to signal many positive traits, highlighting their selfless motive to look out for the best interest of consumers. The New York Interactive Advertising Exchange (NYIAX) is a prime example of using blockchain technology to stimulate a transparent marketplace, where a matching engine pledges a fair exchange of future premium advertising inventory as guaranteed contracts (Epstein, 2017). Overall, blockchain-based transparency fuels trust among consumers. In this context, blockchain-enabled trust is both a precursor and a consequence of consumer-centric transparency in digital marketing.

Reinforcing Security

According to Humayun et al. (2020), 'cyber security is concerned with the security and privacy of digital assets-everything from networks to computing devices and information that is processed, stored or exchanged by internetworked information systems'. This particular study also stresses the importance of developing a reliable information security system to keep both the organization and its customers safe from external cyber-attacks. Information security is a must-have feature for businesses since they are responsible for safeguarding consumers' personal data. Companies must engineer preventative measures to boost the transaction security of customers. Otherwise, it will be difficult for said businesses to develop trust among consumers while delivering their services online. Greenlow (2018) refers to this as 'marketing security', which is the prevention of consumer data abuse or leakage through a robust system of real-time management.

Previous research has proved that information security issues are a big barrier to digital marketing since sensitive customer data (home address, credit card details, etc.) is involved. Unsurprisingly, consumers are concerned about potential credit card information theft, identity theft, unauthorized account access, content manipulation, and cookies misuse. Speaking of cookies, they are susceptible to being tracked by third parties that compromise customer privacy (Lee et al., 2019). Behavioral targeting via a cookies-based approach is a common strategy for malicious parties to clone and misappropriate consumer data. In 2021, various forms of cybercrimes are expected to cost the world a staggering $6 trillion annually (Wertheim, 2020). However, being the gatekeeper of consumer data is no easy task for companies. They need to establish a sophisticated and expensive technological infrastructure that mitigates security loopholes and boosts consumers' trust in the digital marketing landscape. In this regard, blockchain technology can prove to be an effective and affordable solution to combat security threats posed to brands and consumers. The decentralized and distributed data management ensures an exceptional security level in the digital marketing environment (Yanik and Kilic, 2018).

To be more specific, the appropriate storage and overall management of large sums of customer data can be secured using multiple safety mechanisms like digital signatures, asymmetric encryption and access control. Integrating these safety protocols of blockchain with digital marketing will promote information reliability and accountability, something that consumers are desperately demanding (Rejeb et al., 2020). Blockchain technology entails self-organizing and decentralizing of business functions. It can also help with integrating and synchronizing digital marketing-based information across the entire network of stakeholders. Eventually, decentralization can usher in a new era of economic prosperity and security for all stakeholders through superior product listings, pricing policies, advertisements, marketing plans, discounts or promotional benefits and outcomes of market research (Epstein, 2017). So, how will security be enhanced exactly?

For example, customers will have precise insights into a company's traits, values and principles. The very same customers would also regain more control over their personal data, without worrying about security breaches. That's not all; the decentralized nature of a blockchain-based digital marketing system will allow brands to eliminate single points of failure and achieve a higher resistance level against DoS attacks (Helebrandt et al., 2018). In case of misappropriation and errors, information availability and ubiquity facilitated by blockchain technology increase accountability and provide more accurate evaluation and monitoring (Omran et al., 2017). This implies that said technology can provide customers and companies with some leverage and counteract measures in worst-case scenarios. For instance, promoting marketing convenience and new secure models of advertisements, Keybase is a blockchain platform developed to verify the integrity of social media users' signature chains and identify malicious attempts (Keybase, 2019).

Enhancing Privacy

Online privacy is a complicated issue that is of great concern to consumers of digital services. It is no secret that they are fueled by anxiety regarding their transaction confidentiality and anonymity. According to research, 78% of U.S. consumers believe it is imperative for companies to have secure data management. However, only 20% of these consumers completely trust companies with their personal data (IBM, 2018). Organizations possess data collection and mining techniques that enable them to identify, track, collect and manipulate customer information. Naturally, there is a risk of this information being improperly obtained and ethically misused. Some consumers try to counter this threat by supplying false information to websites to block online-ad targeting systems. But, that is not a long-term, transparent solution.

Many of the privacy concerns can be eliminated by adopting a digital marketing system that is powered by blockchain technology. For instance, online shoppers can entrust their personal information to a blockchain-based platform since interactions are routed through random points in the network. Hence, real identities are safe from being misused or manipulated (Jesus et al., 2018). Online privacy of customers can be sufficiently managed within blocks. Transactions are private, but simultaneously, they are authenticated by a community of participants in the shared network. Furthermore, blockchain technology can be an effective privacy-by-design or privacy-enhancing system as it appeals to the technological prowess of digital customers by enabling them to encode their credentials resiliently (like usernames, passwords and other electronic information). Consequently, customers can assume more control over their personal data in digital marketing since their data cannot easily be commercialized (Kosba et al., 2016).

That's not all; customers can depend on the blockchain platform's transactional history to get detailed analytics and precise predictions regarding their tastes, perceptions and brand expectations. Besides, customers have even more opportunities to effectively and securely share their personal data with companies (Travizano et al., 2018). Ultimately, the threat of website cookies unethically capturing information can be mitigated through a robust digital marketing system supported by blockchain technology.

Reducing Click Fraud

The internet is the premier digital marketing channels and advertising platform for companies to showcase their services and establish relationships with their clients. It is also an effective communications medium that enables them to inform customers of latest developments and offerings. Even though having an online presence is unquestionable, the advertising and marketing industry has always been mired by an endless cycle of scandals, fraud, and fraudulent campaigns. One such botheration for companies is click fraud. Mouawi et al. (2019) state that this is an act of illicitly clicking on pay-per-click ads to intensify site revenue or to drain a rival firm's advertising budget. This can be done by an individual or a rival organization to hurt a business intentionally. It is no secret that click fraud significantly diminishes the credibility of the online marketing landscape. According to Juniper Research (2020), companies have suffered losses worth $17 billion in 2020 due to online click fraud. The forecast is bleak as losses from click fraud are expected to surpass $25 billion in 2024. That's an estimated 52% increase in losses over the next 4 years caused by this online menace.

Combatting click fraud is no easy task and many suggested counter measures have fallen short. Such recommended measures included selling a specific percentage of all ad-views to marketers or the introduction of pay-per-click advertising models. The prevalence of click fraud is due to the absence of intermediaries who monitor online advertising and offer third party solutions capable of resolving issues and establishing trust. Evidently, advertisers need to engage with independent solution providers to mitigate click fraud. Although this is beneficial, it can also be unreasonably expensive for small and medium firms. Unfortunately, all these solutions are failing to give advertisers control over their online advertisements. The marketing and advertising industry is paying the price since click fraud compromises promotional effectiveness of targeting customers and potentially satisfying their needs (Kshetri and Voas, 2019). Additionally, increasing advertising losses are a serious threat to businesses since click fraud generates unreliable, inadequate, and dubious analytical data. Botnets (a term derived from 'robot' and 'network') are another big challenge for organizations. These happen to be collections of internet-based devices operating code or 'bots' primarily with a devious intent. It is estimated that advertising losses triggered by a fraudulent botnet activities amount to $100,000 per day. Particularly, peer-to-peer botnets, which use an overlay network to exchange and control data, inflict financial and reputational damage to businesses (Alauthaman et al., 2018). Hence, companies need to embrace a robust defense mechanism to combat these threats as the digital marketing ecosystem is rife with sophisticated botnets.

Blockchain technology can alleviate many risks associated with click fraud by developing a secure digital marketing environment for customers and brands alike. The proposed blockchain-based system can persuade stakeholders in the digital marketing industry to function in a collaborative environment where each party upholds integrity and honesty (Chartier-Rueg and Zweifel, 2017). For instance, information asymmetry can mitigate click fraud in a blockchain ecosystem. More specifically, controlled supervision over advertisement publishers can be reinforced by harnessing the extensive analysis of qualifications, credibility and transaction information. This is possible owing to the auditable and transparent nature of transactions over blockchain technology. At this point, some noteworthy efforts against click fraud need mentioning. Firstly, there is the blockchain-based 'AdChain' platform that allows advertisers to benefit from real-time tracking and campaign auditing (Goldin et al., 2017). Secondly, there is 'Ubex', an advertising platform that combines blockchain with AI to offer precise digital marketing data for consumers, publishers and advertisers (Ubex, 2019). Both models are powerful in eliminating irrelevant ads and promoting better management of impressions, and revenues for each user in the ecosystem, thus helping marketers optimize their advertisement budgets.

Apart from promoting transparency, click fraud prevention allows advertisers to assess consumers' habits online more effectively. The traceability features of the technology guarantee genuine customer visits (Alvarenga et al., 2018). Essentially, this is achievable by assigning customers to verified profiles on the blockchain network. This eliminates the possibility of using device emulation software and will result in higher accuracy in targeting and personalization due to real-time traceability. This approach allows marketers to obtain reliable data, generate more enhanced analytics, and thus to craft compelling marketing campaigns. One such example is Lucidity's blockchain pilot with the Japanese car manufacturer Toyota, which resulted in a 21% surge in campaign performance (Lucidity, 2018). Similarly, Pinmo integrates blockchain infrastructure into its overall media advertising strategy aimed at better campaign tracking and more precise analytics (Pinmo, 2019). These examples illustrate the blockchain's potential to prevent click fraud and promote enhanced trust and transparency in the digital marketing ecosystem.

Reforming Loyalty Programs

Companies need to ensure customers stay loyal to their product or service offerings in a relentlessly competitive marketing environment. To promote customer retention, said companies have been systematically gathering and storing their personal information (e.g., purchasing habits, transactional history, and product preferences) through a series of loyalty programs. Such programs aim to reduce price sensitivity, increase brand loyalty, encourage word of mouth, and enlarge a brand's consumer base. Furthermore, loyalty programs are being implemented across various industries to boost sales and generate more profit for respective brands (Cvitanovic, 2018).

Companies are continuously on the hunt for tactics that are ideal for reaching customers like, reward schemes. Technological developments have made it possible for them to collect personal data and tailor effective loyalty programs for each individual customer. Presently, a multitude of technologies promotes the dissemination of loyalty programs like database management and mobile marketing. These allow for a customer-centric approach where they are systematically tracked and informed about loyalty programs. In addition, the internet has also been a favorable breeding ground for such programs. Potential online customers are increasingly becoming interested to know more about loyalty reward systems, even though their personal information might be at risk. Speaking of the internet, existing participants of loyalty programs tend to paint a very different picture (Lee and Jung, 2018).

Although loyally schemes are deemed to be customized to an individual, they tend to feature limited program components. Focusing only on customer retention, brands often ignore the need to diversify their reward programs. Evidently, consumers want flexible and attractive rewards programs for their brand loyalty but, end up being drawn into a lackluster retention cycle. As per Bond Brand Loyalty (2020), companies with innovative reward programs can drive 47% higher brand engagement. However, a mere 25% of customers believe that loyalty schemes make them feel special and recognized. These figures emerged from an examination of 1000 reward programs experienced by 68,000 customers across 4 continents, courtesy of Bond Brand Loyalty. Such statistics are proof that loyalty programs are not living up to the hype. Moreover, low customer satisfaction leads to unused reward points across said programs. The low rates of redemption are a result of stringent, time-based procedures to claim rewards. This policy invokes a state of considerable frustration among loyal customers, mainly when a potential reward expires (Colman, 2015). Consequently, information about customer attitudes toward the reward schemes is not considered by brands, which hinders the development of loyalty programs. For the reasons stated above, many scholars in marketing have begun to question the overall efficiency of loyalty programs in consumer retention (Magatef and Tomalieh, 2015). There needs to be a way to improve existing programs.

In the realm of digital marketing, blockchain technology has the inherent ability to redesign how loyalty schemes are developed, tracked and disseminated to customers. Inside a blockchain-based digital marketing ecosystem, every stakeholder like marketers, customers, information technology managers, customer support and sales outlets are all efficiently interlinked and integrated. Instead of a fragmented system, all parties concerned with loyalty programs can work synergistically to upgrade customer experience and entice various customer segments. For instance, blockchain technology can rectify compatibility issues plaguing loyalty programs and promote increased channel harmony and fluid customer experience. There is also a massive opportunity for loyalty program facilitators to actively collaborate and use the interactive technology to jointly design loyalty programs that have an inter-convertible reward points system. Real-time access to customer profiles, accumulated points, buying behavior, transaction history, and promotion responses will help marketers to engineer more authentic, valuable, and personalized loyalty schemes. Consider American Express's example; they have successfully incorporated a blockchain-based ledger that rewards points to customers based on their service consumption. Previously, they would be awarded on their spending behavior at a specific branch (Coleman, 2018). Besides, blockchain's decentralized nature also enables customers to track and trade their reward points, freeing them and brands from physically possessing coupons. The technology appeals for both B2C and B2B loyalty programs as rectifiability of transactions and information is necessary to curtail dubious activities and promote consumer advocacy. Overall, blockchains can foster a more interoperable and secure environment that is unachievable through traditional, centralized loyalty schemes (Zhang et al., 2017).

Championing Disintermediation

Previously, companies needed to rely heavily on many intermediaries or middle-men, to disburse their goods and services. However, the advent of digitalization has reduced dependency on such traditional intermediaries and launched new forms of electronic intermediaries. Moreover, the internet is championing a new age of disintermediation, where a vast range of online intermediaries offer better products and services. The value chain will never be the same again with the emergence of digital services like online search capabilities, information brokering, communication, advertising and trust provision (Rejeb et al. 2020).

Subsequently, brands need to engage with their customers on social media channels like Facebook, Twitter, and YouTube. They need to depend on revenue through data and targeted advertisements while they are deprived of income from the customers directly. While it is true that these social media channels are helping brands reach their audiences, they are also locking said brands into a cycle beyond their control (Nieves and Diaz-Meneses, 2016). Moreover, companies also rely on intermediaries to recognize their impact of blockchain on digital marketing. These intermediaries have a wealth of information regarding the demand for goods and services. This means that, companies are not in control of their dissemination decisions. They are silently held hostage to intermediaries who hinder their ability to generate new prospects and target offerings (Tönnissen and Teuteberg, 2020). Additionally, customers also dislike their data being monetized by electronic intermediaries. It is clear that an intermediated channel prevents companies from directly connecting with customers and establishing co-creation, customer-centric support, and dynamic personalization. So, what is the solution?

For mitigating these existing concerns, blockchain technology can be an auspicious tool that enables brands to bypass intermediation and create stronger ties with consumers. By engineering a blockchain-based digital marketing system, companies can improve their customer targeting capabilities, expand their online advertising campaigns and enhance service responsiveness. Besides, brands need to pay credit card companies various fees like sales commissions and processing charges (Harvey et al., 2018). Blockchain can help in eliminating these costs and reducing dependency on the layer of intermediation.

Through blockchain-based digital marketing, brands can take control and be in charge. They can offer incentives to consumers for sharing information through cryptocurrency rewards, micropayments, and cash-backs. Developing such a loyalty rewards program will potentially strengthen the direct relationship between companies and consumers. Alternatively, via this enhanced interaction model, consumers themselves can reap benefits by responding to digital marketing campaigns with a verified product review (Rejeb et al., 2020).

FUTURE RESEARCH DIRECTIONS

The systematic review has yielded the current standing on applications of blockchain technology in the digital marketing sector. Subsequently, numerous research propositions can now be presented as follows:

- Investigating how blockchain can develop trust and transparency in the digital marketing ecosystem
- Reinforcing digital marketing security through a robust blockchain-based platform
- Enhancing privacy of consumers using blockchain-based digital marketing efforts

- Uncovering blockchain platforms that mitigate click fraud in the digital marketing environment
- Reforming loyalty programs to offer consumers an authentic, personalized experience
- Championing disintermediation using blockchain to develop stronger consumer-brand relationships

All of these aforementioned propositions need a thorough investigation to establish a more robust research base on blockchain technology applications for digital marketing.

Future studies also need to explore and analyze the barriers to blockchain adoption in digital marketing. The suggested research propositions provide starting points for further investigations into the matter. More examination is needed to identify enablers, precursors and impacts of blockchain applications in digital marketing. Another area of interest relates to the immutability and personal data management of blockchain technology. Some officials are exploring consumer-based policies where consumer rights need adequate protection. Additionally, researchers could explore confidentiality in the context of blockchains to satisfy changing regulatory requirements.

CONCLUSION

This chapter has systematically unearthed the current standing on research into blockchain technology applications for the digital marketing landscape. Moreover, the future research propositions will help in furthering knowledge in this field. The existing digital marketing environment is plagued with electronic intermediaries failing to satisfy brands and consumers adequately. Their limited potential hampers the ingenuity of brands and deprives customers of direct engagement. In this regard, blockchain technology promises to develop trust and transparency, resulting in more genuine campaigns and consumer-centricity. Simultaneously, the sophistication embedded in blockchain is capable of upholding customer privacy and reinforcing digital marketing security. That is not all; the technology can aid in combating the ubiquitous phenomenon of click fraud, thus fostering a sustainable digital marketing space for all stakeholders. Moreover, blockchain-based loyalty programs and disintermediation enables consumers to be rewarded handsomely for their brand loyalty.

Blockchain is an incremental innovation that can lead to substantial changes in the realm of digital marketing. The cumulative benefits of this technology can significantly reshape existing business functions and improve digital marketing practices. However, new technologies can have disruptive effects on organizations depending on their values, processes, and resources. Thus, if not strategically approached and cautiously embedded in the organizational infrastructure, said technologies can lessen brands' competitiveness in general and shrink their marketing acumen in particular.

REFERENCES

Alauthaman, M., Aslam, N., Zhang, L., Alasem, R., & Hossain, M. A. (2018). A P2P Botnet detection scheme based on decision tree and adaptive multilayer neural networks. *Neural Computing & Applications*, *29*(11), 991–1004. doi:10.100700521-016-2564-5 PMID:29769759

Alvarenga, I. D., Rebello, G. A., & Duarte, O. C. M. (2018, April). Securing configuration management and migration of virtual network functions using blockchain. In *NOMS 2018-2018 IEEE/IFIP Network Operations and Management Symposium* (pp. 1-9). IEEE. 10.1109/NOMS.2018.8406249

Antoniadis, I., Sariannidis, N., & Kontsas, S. (2018). The effect of bitcoin prices on US dollar index price. In *International Conference on Applied Economics* (pp. 511-521). Springer. 10.1007/978-3-030-02194-8_34

Antoniadis, I., Spinthiropoulos, K., & Kontsas, S. (2019). Blockchain applications in Tourism and Tourism marketing: A short review. *Proceedings of ICSIMAT*.

Bond Brand Loyalty. (2020). *The Loyalty Report: State of Loyalty*. Author.

Chapron, G. (2017). The environment needs cryptogovernance. *NATNews*, *545*(7655), 403. PMID:28541332

Chartier-Rueg, T. C., & Zweifel, T. D. (2017). Blockchain, leadership and management: Business as usual or radical disruption? *EUREKA: Social and Humanities*, *4*(4), 76–110. doi:10.21303/2504-5571.2017.00370

Coleman, L. (2018). *American Express Gives Loyalty Program a Blockchain Upgrade*. https://www.ccn.com/american-expresstaps-hyperledger-blockchain-for-rewards-program-revamp

Colman, A. M. (2015). *A dictionary of psychology*. Oxford quick reference.

Cvitanović, P. L. (2018, September). New technologies in marketing as competitive advantage. *2018 ENTRENOVA Conference Proceedings*.

Epstein, J. (2017). *Blockchain and the CMO*. Whitepaper. Availble online at: https://s3.us-east-2.amazonaws.com/brightline-website/downloads/reports/Brightline_Epstein_Blockchain-and-the-CMO_Blockchain-Research-Institute.pdf

Galvez, J. F., Mejuto, J. C., & Simal-Gandara, J. (2018). Future challenges on the use of blockchain for food traceability analysis. *Trends in Analytical Chemistry*, *107*, 222–232. doi:10.1016/j.trac.2018.08.011

Ghose, A. (2018). What blockchain could mean for marketing. *Harvard Business Review*, *5*, 2–5.

Goldin, M., Soleimani, A., & Young, J. (2017). *The Adchain Registry*. Whitepaper. Available online at: https://blockchain-x.eu/wp-content/uploads/2018/02/The_adChain_Registry_ENG.pdf

Greenlow, M. (2018). *Marketing Security: The Phrase Every Executive Needs to Understand in 2019*. https://www.martechadvisor.com/articles/marketing-analytics/marketing-security-the-phrase-every-executiveneeds-to-understand-in-2019/

Harvey, C. R., Moorman, C., & Toledo, M. (2018). *How blockchain can help marketers build better relationships with their customers*. https://hbr.org/2018/10/how-blockchain-can-helpmarketers-build-better-relationships-with-their-customers

Helebrandt, P., Bellus, M., Ries, M., Kotuliak, I., & Khilenko, V. (2018, November). Blockchain adoption for monitoring and management of enterprise networks. In *2018 IEEE 9th Annual Information Technology, Electronics and Mobile Communication Conference (IEMCON)* (pp. 1221-1225). IEEE. 10.1109/IEMCON.2018.8614960

Ho Lee, S., & Jung, K. S. (2018). Loyal customer behaviors: Identifying brand fans. *Social Behavior and Personality*, *46*(8), 1285–1303. doi:10.2224bp.6482

Humayun, M., Niazi, M., Jhanjhi, N. Z., Alshayeb, M., & Mahmood, S. (2020). Cyber security threats and vulnerabilities: A systematic mapping study. *Arabian Journal for Science and Engineering*, *45*(4), 3171–3189. doi:10.100713369-019-04319-2

IBM. (2018). *Cybersecurity and Privacy Research*. IBM.

Jesus, E. F., Chicarino, V. R., de Albuquerque, C. V., & Rocha, A. A. D. A. (2018). A survey of how to use blockchain to secure internet of things and the stalker attack. *Security and Communication Networks*, *2018*, 2018. doi:10.1155/2018/9675050

Jones, K. (2018). *How Much Will Blockchain Really Affect Digital Marketing?* https://www.forbes.com/sites/forbesagencycouncil/ 2018/10/04/how-much-will-blockchain-really-affect-digital-marketing/

Juniper Research. (2020). *Online Payment Fraud: Emerging Threats, Segment Analysis & Market Forecasts 2020-2024*. Author.

Keybase. (2019). *Server*. https://keybase.io/

Kosba, A., Miller, A., Shi, E., Wen, Z., & Papamanthou, C. (2016, May). Hawk: The blockchain model of cryptography and privacy-preserving smart contracts. In 2016 IEEE symposium on security and privacy (SP) (pp. 839-858). IEEE.

Kshetri, N., & Voas, J. (2019). Online advertising fraud. *Computer*, *52*(1), 58–61. doi:10.1109/MC.2018.2887322

Lee, W. B., Chen, H. B., Chang, S. S., & Chen, T. H. (2019). Secure and efficient protection for HTTP cookies with self-verification. *International Journal of Communication Systems*, *32*(2), e3857. doi:10.1002/dac.3857

Lucidity. (2018). *Lucidity's Blockchain Pilot with Toyota Results in 21% Lift in Campaign Performance*. https://www.prnewswire.com/news-releases/luciditys-blockchain-pilot-with-toyota-results-in-21-lift-in-campaign-performance-300731983.html

Magatef, S. G., & Tomalieh, E. F. (2015). The impact of customer loyalty programs on customer retention. *International Journal of Business and Social Science*, *6*(8), 78–93.

Mouawi, R., Elhajj, I. H., Chehab, A., & Kayssi, A. (2019). Crowdsourcing for click fraud detection. *EURASIP Journal on Information Security*, *2019*(1), 1–18. doi:10.118613635-019-0095-1

Nieves, J., & Diaz-Meneses, G. (2016). Antecedents and outcomes of marketing innovation. *International Journal of Contemporary Hospitality Management*, *28*(8), 1554–1576. doi:10.1108/IJCHM-11-2014-0589

Nowiński, W., & Kozma, M. (2017). How Can Blockchain Technology Disrupt the Existing Business Models? *Entrepreneurial Business and Economics Review*, *5*(3), 173–188. doi:10.15678/EBER.2017.050309

Omran, Y., Henke, M., Heines, R., & Hofmann, E. (2017). *Blockchain-driven supply chain finance: Towards a conceptual framework from a buyer perspective*. Academic Press.

Pinmo. (2019). *How Pinmo Will Utilize Blockchain to Revolutionize the Advertising Industry*. https://pinmo.ca/

Rejeb, A., Keogh, J. G., & Treiblmaier, H. (2020). How blockchain technology can benefit marketing: Six pending research areas. *Frontiers in Blockchain, 3*, 3. doi:10.3389/fbloc.2020.00003

Tapscott, D., & Tapscott, A. (2016). *Blockchain revolution: how the technology behind bitcoin is changing money, business, and the world*. Penguin.

Tönnissen, S., & Teuteberg, F. (2020). Analysing the impact of blockchain-technology for operations and supply chain management: An explanatory model drawn from multiple case studies. *International Journal of Information Management, 52*, 101953. doi:10.1016/j.ijinfomgt.2019.05.009

Travizano, M., Minnoni, M., Ajzenman, G., Sarraute, C., & Della Penna, N. (2018). *Wibson: A decentralized marketplace empowering individuals to safely monetize their personal data*. White paper.

Treiblmaier, H. (2020). Toward more rigorous blockchain research: Recommendations for writing blockchain case studies. In *Blockchain and Distributed Ledger Technology Use Cases* (pp. 1–31). Springer. doi:10.1007/978-3-030-44337-5_1

Ubex. (2019). *Artificial Intelligence in Advertising*. https://www. ubex.com

Wertheim, S. (2020). Tips for Fighting Off Cybercrime in 2020. *The CPA Journal, 90*(3), 64–66.

Yanik, S., & Kiliç, A. S. (2018). A framework for the performance evaluation of an energy blockchain. In *Energy Management—Collective and Computational Intelligence with Theory and Applications* (pp. 521–543). Springer. doi:10.1007/978-3-319-75690-5_23

Zhang, P., White, J., Schmidt, D. C., & Lenz, G. (2017). *Applying software patterns to address interoperability in blockchain-based healthcare apps*. arXiv:1706.03700.

Chapter 3
Blockchain Towards Decentralized Digital Marketing

Nozha Erragcha
Higher Business School of Tunisia, Tunisia

Hanene Babay
The Fashion Institute of Monastir, Tunisia

ABSTRACT

Blockchain is a decentralized digital technology that is growing and standing out in digital marketing. The potential use of blockchain technology will help affected companies create secure digital records and will also allow secure storage of data. During this chapter, the authors will try to explain the meaning of the concept of blockchain technology, its operating principle, as well as its different types and sectors of applications to make the relationship between blockchain technology and other emerging technologies such as big data, AI, and smart contracts and to review the positive impact of blockchain technology on the e-commerce sector and in particular on customer relationship management.

INTRODUCTION

In a world where the use of digital platforms has become essential and the volume of data continues to increase, Big data has become essential for companies wishing to properly manage their relationship with the environment. The importance of big data today is primarily due to its impact on the commercial performance of these

DOI: 10.4018/978-1-7998-8081-3.ch003

companies, in particular by disrupting their customer relationship management practices and tools. The issues that companies face in relation to the retention of their customers in a dynamic and hypercompetitive environment are commonly accepted. Nevertheless, interest is increasingly directed towards finding practical and fruitful solutions allowing these companies to ensure their sustainability and achieve their profitability and development objectives, by using technology to better manage their activity. Achieving these objectives is inevitably linked to better knowledge of customers in order to offer a customer experience that is both attractive and loyal, but also to better monitoring of the market to spot new trends. To do this, businesses need to store, manage and transmit the collected data securely. These constraints have linked the success of Big data to the emergence of another technology, relating to data storage and analysis, namely the Blockchain (De Meijer, 2019). The potential use of blockchain technology (BCT) will help affected businesses create secure digital records and build their decisions based on incorruptible data.

Thus, this chapter will first be devoted to the presentation of this Blockchain technology, its operating principle, its characteristics and benefits as well as its different types and fields of application. It will also draw up the relationship of the blockchain with other emerging technologies (Big Data, Artificial Intelligence, etc.). Then, this chapter will place particular emphasis on the contributions of blockchain applied to the "e-commerce" sector, by placing itself at the heart of managers' concerns in relation to the management of their relationship with customers.

Therefore, the objectives of the chapter are to

- understand the meaning of blockchain technology's concept, its operating principle as well as its different types and sectors of applications
- understand the main characteristics of blockchain technology and the main advantages it offers to users
- make the relationship between blockchain technology and other emerging technologies such as big data, AI and smart contracts
- review the positive impact of blockchain technology on the e-commerce sector and in particular on customer relationship management

BLOCKCHAIN, A SHARED AND SECURE CHAIN OF INFORMATION

Overview of Blockchain Technology

Definition of the Blockchain

The blockchain is defined as "A register, a large database which has the particularity of being shared simultaneously with all its users, all of whom are also holders of this register, and who also all have the capacity to register data, according to specific rules set by a very secure computer protocol thanks to cryptography". (Source: National Assembly report on blockchain and its uses, published in December 2018)

More specifically, blockchain is considered to be a technology for storing and transmitting information that allows its users - connected in a network - to share data without an intermediary. This technology operates without a central control body, which allows it to offer a very high level of transparency and security.

Principle of Operation

As a technology, blockchain is a revolutionary invention that has captured the attention of businesses and governments around the world. This technology has been around for almost two decades. However, it grew exponentially in 2008 (Nakamoto, 2008) as a disruptive technology innovation with the Bitcoin cryptocurrency (Bohme, Christin, Edelman, & Moore, 2015).

The blockchain operates on a "distributed ledger system". It is a decentralized network topology with an increased level of security (Khalifa, 2019) where all transactions are stored in individual blocks. Each new transaction is recorded in a new block which must be validated by the users connected to the network. Figure 1 illustrates the six stages of active exchange between two economic actors using Blockchain technology.

In practice, the operation of a blockchain is based on the following foundations:

- Each user of the blockchain is identified using a cryptographic process.
- Data integration occurs chronologically and indelibly.
- The blocks created on the blockchain are linked to each other and a copy of the data is automatically transmitted to all "nodes" of the network.
- The history of transactions made is accessible and can be viewed at any time by all stakeholders.
- Data security is managed in a decentralized manner, eliminating the possibility of tampering.

Figure 1. The stages of operation of the blockchain

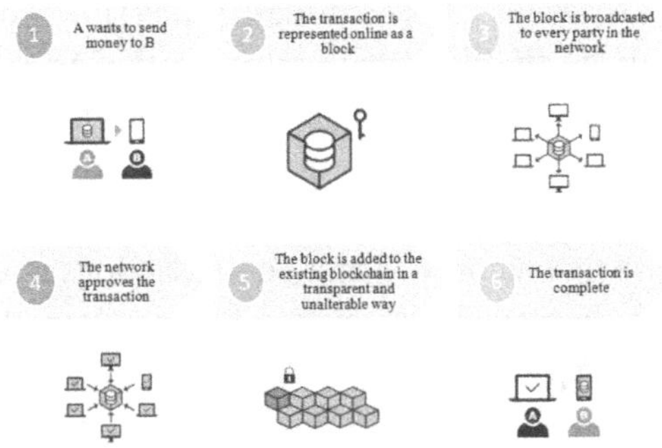

Source: Adapted from Coinmama (2018)

This operating principle emits both characteristics and advantages of the Blockchain as summarized in the following section.

Characteristics and Advantages Offered by the Blockchain

The Characteristics of the Blockchain

Blockchain technology admits three essential properties: decentralization, immutability and integrity.

Decentralization

In blockchain, decentralization refers to the transfer of control and decision-making from a centralized entity (individual, organization or group thereof) to a distributed network. This is because Blockchain is a technology that does not operate in a central perspective where all data should be gathered, but rather in a decentralized way where data can be analyzed "directly at the edge of individual devices". Decentralization has the merit of reducing the ability of participants to exercise authority over the data, since each member of the network has access to a shared, real-time view of the data. Thus, in decentralized networks, it is not imperative that participants acquire a high level of trust in each other to ensure the proper functioning of the network. It is the architecture of this network that supports it.

Immutability of Data

Data immutability is very important for companies concerned with Big Data. Indeed, if the data that should be analyzed can be altered in some way then the value of the resulting analyzes will be of minimal value. From this perspective, the contribution of the blockchain around the immutability of the data recorded therein is extremely valued. The blockchain is designed to secure the data that flows between stakeholders. Indeed, being decentralized, the blockchain optimizes the security of data and makes it completely immutable. Immutability means that once recorded, the data cannot be changed. And even if a transaction record contains an error, a new transaction must be added to correct the error and both transactions will be visible. Blockchain is a distributed database that records economic transactions in such a way that they cannot be changed. The recorded information remains immutable as long as the network exists. Each general ledger entry (each "block") contains the complete transaction history for that entry and this history is searchable by all stakeholders, making it nearly impossible for any user to change this information.

Data Integrity

Like immutability, data integrity is highly demanded by businesses. Indeed, these seek to protect their data against the risks of falsification and malicious manipulation (hacking, data leakage, etc.). The blockchain makes it possible to fight against these abuses thanks to the fact that it operates in a decentralized manner. Indeed, this digital network is not controlled by a central organization, but managed and duplicated simultaneously by several entities which may have divergent interests. This decentralization makes it possible to certify that the practices of an entity will not adversely affect the integrity of the data. Thus, the recorded information is listed in a tamper-proof manner, so it is considered to be of great integrity and reliability.

The Benefits of Blockchain

The blockchain provides its users with a set of advantages including:

Ensure the Security of the System

By managing a decentralized ledger, the blockchain makes it possible to carry out data integrity and audit trails. Indeed, the data can be validated by all users of the system. These users are not only different but are not meant to know each other. That said, the data is all the more secure, especially against any malicious attempt that may be practiced by these users. Information security is the biggest advantage that Blockchain technology offers. This advantage is all the more valued since the players work in open, diverse IT environments that are threatened by fraudulent activities. It also serves to simplify the task of businesses who can now verify and validate identities and transactions without having to resort to cumbersome and tedious blacklists.

Improve the Quality of Data

Blockchain brings innovations to data storage. Indeed, by replacing traditional storage methods with blockchain technology, companies can access data that is not only complete but also structured and therefore of high quality. Thus, the integration of the blockchain in a Big Data analysis procedure is likely to reinforce the precision and the rigor of this analysis and allows the company to provide reliable solutions. When the data captured by large companies is more secure, more reliable and more accessible, it will become easier for these companies to reduce the risk of making bad decisions based on bad data.

Prevent Fraud

The Blockchain makes it possible to overcome the difficulties of fraud detection and risk assessment. Indeed, unlike the old methods of detection and evaluation, blockchain technology makes it possible to verify each transaction in real time. So instead of analyzing records of fraud that has already occurred, financial institutions are able to identify risky or fraudulent transactions as they arise, identify suspicious patterns and prevent fraud altogether.

Streamlining of Big Data

By storing data in a decentralized ledger, big data companies could process all data much faster and more efficiently than centralized solutions. It will also speed up the transaction process (making it almost instantaneous) and lower the cost of money transfers by removing the security and risk control barriers involved.

Facilitate Data Access

Another way blockchain can power big data and analytics is by streamlining data access. This simplifies the work process and also shortens the cycle of data access and analysis time. By storing the database in a blockchain, a single, immutable source of information is being developed where all who are allowed to obtain particular information. As part of the blockchain, one may need multiple "signatures" or authorized permissions from other parts of a network to access records. This will ensure that all will receive the precisely measured information necessary to perform their role.

Discover Insights in Real Time

Given the value of real-time information and its impact on decision-making, it is of the utmost importance to use technologies to access and analyze huge amounts of data to derive insight., in near real time. The marriage of blockchain and big data will help businesses make real-time analytics much more feasible and reliable.

"Since the blockchain has a database record for every single transaction, it provides a way for institutions to mine for patterns in real-time." Abhinav Vankat of Noah Data

Even better, expanding blockchain to other areas such as AI, new data analytics, and specialized forms of data intelligence will better meet these information needs and also make it easier to operate in real time.

Save on Costs

Financial transactions are expensive and their cost weighs heavily on businesses and consumers alike. This cost is partly inflated by the fees relating to the payment. Indeed, traders, especially in the United States, pay banks around 3% commission for bank card transactions. These charges are likely to increase the price of goods and are very often passed on to the consumer, which has forced many traders to reduce the purchase amounts for this type of settlement to avoid altering their profitability because of these charges. In the face of these challenges, the contribution of blockchain is proving to be considerable. In fact, it is now possible to transfer money via a blockchain rather than by credit card, which will reduce the cost of transactions to practically zero. Financial organizations such as Mastercard or Visa have already implemented this modality, thus taking advantage of the enhanced security and transparency of the blockchain.

In addition, the adoption of blockchain technology as part of big data analytical models can significantly reduce storage costs. Immutable information becomes a business asset because it can be used over a long period of time and enable long-term business decisions.

Ultimately, the blockchain generates multiple gains, especially in terms of productivity, efficiency and costs. Indeed, thanks to this technology, it is possible to mitigate transaction costs including financial costs, control costs and the remuneration of intermediaries and service providers involved in the exchange. These costs are significantly lower compared to those generated by traditional systems.

The Different Types of Blockchain

Blockchain exists in many forms and can be applied differently depending on its purposes of use. It exists:

Public Blockhains

This is an "open source" network, that is, one in which anyone can participate (Rennock et al., 2018). This form is based on the anonymity of the participants and on an online payment logic based on banking disintermediation. The Bitcoin blockchain is the best example of a public blockchain.

Private Blockchains

Unlike public blockchains, this form refers to databases whose access and use are limited to a certain number of actors. These databases are based on authorized validators and administrators; they are not designed for decentralized digital assets. The private blockchain architecture is in fact more faithful to the structure described by Stornetta and Haber in 1991.

Consortium Blockchains

This type is an extension of private blockchain technology. A consortium blockchain brings together several private actors who have an interest in working together. The blockchain consortium preselects several nodes to which permissions are granted (Sankar et al., 2017). This type is the preferred choice by banking and insurance players and by governments since they adapt well to regulated contexts and to control over the transmission of information.

Table 1. The three types of blockchain technology

Type	Principle	Examples
Public Blockchain	- Free access / pseudonyms - Decentralized network: operating P2P - Transactions recorded and validated by a network	Bicticoin, Ethereum
Private Blockchain	- Low decentralization: The blocks are validated by a central agent - The central agent modifies the blockchain protocol - The entries can be altered by its owner.	IBM
Consortium Blockchain	Validation of blocks by the most important members - A decentralized system with modifiable writing rights -Nodes are private, no user can question them	Quorum, Hyperledger, Corda

Blockchain Technology Applications Sectors

Blockchain technology is therefore used in many sectors: commercial and non-commercial, public and private. Many industries also plan to use it in the years to come. The authors describe in the following some applications of this technology specific to certain fields:

- *In the banking industry,* it is now possible to validate transactions without resorting to the intermediation of a clearing house. This validation by the blockchain would allow the certification of operations more quickly. In addition, by resorting to the use of blockchain, competing banking institutions can manage common instruments and share information without compromising the confidentiality of their own business data.
- *In the insurance industry*, blockchain allows a lot of paperwork to be reduced and customer reimbursement procedures to be automated. However, to reap these benefits, the conditions for compensation should be clearly and explicitly established.
- *In the logistics sector*, the use of blockchain offers several advantages including: providing traceability of exchanges, safeguarding data relating to interventions that take place on a production and / or distribution chain, reducing formalities and define the conditions under which the actors of a sector can cooperate. From this perspective of use, the blockchain can be used, in particular, in the agro-food sector, in particular to create food traceability. This use of the blockchain is very interesting, especially in the case of a health crisis.
- *In the energy sector*, blockchain makes it possible to set up local networks making it possible to produce and exchange energy, without going through a central body to manage these exchanges. These networks are created taking into account the technical capacities of the players in the exchange and with a view to ensuring a balance between energy supply and demand.

Besides these areas, other sectors are now affected by the use of blockchain technology. Indeed, this technology can be used in the health sector, the real estate sector, luxury goods, e-commerce, etc. The blockchain seems to be involved in rebuilding the relationship with customers but also with suppliers. Experts today are talking about the GRC and SRM revolution in the blockchain age.

Explicitly, the PricewaterhouseCoopers report in 2008 showed that 77% of respondents out of a set of 600 blockchain-savvy executives recognize that their companies are involved in blockchain technology projects. There are plenty of examples. In China, giant Alibaba relies heavily on blockchain. During the Chinese version of Black Friday, the blockchain allowed this company to trace 400 million cross-border products, to finance its supply chain, to certify the authenticity of its products and to facilitate the management of suppliers thanks to digital identities. Another example is the Taiwanese Start Up BioIPSeeds based on blockchain technology to help biomedical researchers to exchange ideas freely.

BLOCKCHAIN AND COMPLEMTENTARY TECHNOLOGIES

Principle of Complementarity

Blockchain is a digital technology, it can be used as a general-purpose technology (GPT). This technology works in complementarity with other technologies which:

1. define and support it. Indeed, the blockchain is made up of several technologies, such as encryption technology used to protect data security.
2. allow its implementation. Indeed, to achieve the decentralization of online transactions, extensive technical requirements are imposed on the blockchain such as the implementation of transaction-sharding to increase the speed of transaction processing (Liu et al., 2019), and
3. allow for social, political and economic transformations (Chen et al., 2020). For example, blockchain is likely to promote the development of cryptocurrencies including Bitcoin, and this cryptocurrency technology transforms the traditional economic model (Berg, 2020; Schilling and Uhlig, 2019).

Blockchain and Big Data

Blockchain and Big Data are among the emerging technologies that feature high on the agendas of many companies. Both are expected to radically transform the way businesses and organizations are run in the years to come. Distributed ledgers are increasingly expected to help companies finally get to grips with big data, which so far faces a number of challenges. They are both powerful on their own, but when combined, they can offer a great number of opportunities. Some even say that blockchain and big data are made for each other.

Big Data is an incredibly profitable business, with revenues expected to grow to $ 203 billion by 2020. The data within the blockchain is predicted to be worth trillions of dollars as it continues to make its way into banking, micropayments, remittances, and other financial services. In fact, the blockchain ledger could be worth up to

20% of the total big data market by 2030, producing up to $ 100 billion in annual revenue. Chris Neimeth, COO of NYC Data Science Academy.

Currently, The rise of big data has presented a host of challenges for large businesses and consumers. Some of these major issues relate to data management and analysis. Indeed, companies face the risk of using so-called dirty data, of being forced to use inaccessible data and / or of overcoming data confidentiality issues. In this regard, and as big data grows in size and the web of connected devices explodes, companies are increasingly faced with potential security holes in the data they use.

With the advent of Big Data, managing data quality is both more important and more difficult than ever. Businesses dealing with large data sets need to ensure that the data is clean, secure, and unaltered, and comes from a genuine source. Make sure that the latest version is synchronized between all data centers in real time. It is also important to ensure that this data is accessible. For the most part, however, data silos remain a major issue, and a complete enterprise-wide digital transformation is still more of a concept than a reality.

To overcome all these constraints, it was necessary to consider these two technologies as complementary. Indeed, when the blockchain focuses on recording validation data, big data lends itself to analyzing this data to make useful predictions. In this regard, blockchain can serve big data by ensuring the integrity of the data to be analyzed. The confidence provided by this technology is likely to increase the value of the predictions estimated by big data.

However, the supposed complementarity of these two technologies does not imply that they are substitutable. The essence of each technology testifies to their different vocation. Indeed, while the blockchain acts on the management of data between users, big data transforms the nature of this data with a view to exploiting value. Combining big data and blockchain could therefore offer a lot of interesting opportunities. There are several ways that blockchain can be useful for big data management, in particular, data analysis. This technology has the most potential in data quality. This means that the data captured and validated by large companies on the blockchain will become much more valuable to businesses.

If there is a 'sweet spot' for blockchain, it will likely be the ability to turn ideas and questions into assets. Blockchains will give you greater confidence in the integrity of the data you see. Immutable inputs, audit trails, and certainty as to the origin of data (for example, a sensor or kiosk) are all areas where you will see improvement as blockchain technology becomes more and more current. VentureBeat

Blockchain and Artificial Intelligence

Since its emergence, artificial intelligence (AI) has been seen as capable of transforming the world and reinventing the way companies operate and evolve. Indeed, to support scientific progress, companies are increasingly using technologies based on artificial intelligence, such as "Machine Learning", for example. However, to use it, companies need to build large databases that encompass very high quality data in order to be able to conduct training or prediction on that data. Otherwise, the simulation of some AI solutions will become unimaginable, which will undoubtedly influence the possibility of using such solutions or at least affect their performance. The constraints raised here in relation to the use of artificial intelligence seem to generate disparities between companies according to their size and their ability to use AI. Worse still, even for companies with sufficient resources, the development of AI systems through the constitution of large databases remains a heavy financial investment and difficult to manage.

In addition, if we take the systemic approach, it is clear that it is difficult for a company to unilaterally design a complete and effective solution to problems where several stakeholders are involved, especially if these stakeholders belong to different environments.

In this context, the Blockchain provides a miraculous solution to these challenges, in particular by making it possible to collect and analyze data, not only in large volumes but also sufficiently representative. This technology also allows the companies involved to share this data and use it to perform the required training of AI models as quickly as possible. This ease in collecting and sharing data will necessarily reduce the resulting financial cost and have a positive impact on the profitability of these companies.

Blockchain and Smart Contracts

Blockchain technology also relies on a feature called smart contracts. The functionality of smart contracts is very useful for automatically settling transactions in a network. This type of contract is self-executing and self-executing and consists of programmed code that creates an agreement between several parties (Boucher, Nascimento, & Kritikos, 2017). Smart contracts are able to influence companies because they are able to ensure a higher level of disintermediation (reduced need for intermediaries).

Smart contracts can also help businesses automatically place orders, complete transactions, and issue payments without the need for approval. Through the use of the escrow features of these contracts, two unknown parties can enter into a transaction. Developers can encode payment details such as wallet address, bank account information, and payee details. When transactions are executed, they can be validated by users connected to the network and settled automatically. This implies that blockchain technology allows transparent transactions since all actions and activities are visible to all users. They do not need a third party to perform these activities (Revfne, 2018). This technology operates as a peer-to-peer network, ie without a central authority.

The use of smart contracts can be widespread across many industries. In the context of e-commerce, in particular, smart contracts allow transactions to be carried out with confidence and limit all kinds of disputes. For example, if a user orders an item from an online store, developing a smart contract will guarantee a secure purchase.

This contract is established between the e-merchant, the carrier and the customer. Its operating principle is as follows:

- If the package is delivered to the customer, the e-merchant and the carrier will be paid.
- If the package is lost or damaged by the carrier, the customer is reimbursed and the carrier will owe compensation to the e-merchant.
- Smart contracts will allow the customer to feel at ease with every transaction.

Platforms using Blockchain Technology: Some Examples

The blockchain industry is already very active in this area. Blockchain developers are building decentralized data markets that are now starting to emerge. These marketplaces are platforms that use the peer-to-peer connectivity possible through blockchain technology to connect data sellers with data buyers.

The common goal of these platforms is to offer services that store this data on decentralized networks, instead of central servers, in which third parties do not have access to the data stored on the network. Some of these platforms even offer services, which allow users to rent their unused storage capacity, in exchange for ordinary money or cryptocurrency.

Here are a number of networks that are using some sophisticated blockchain technology developments to address the challenges of big data decentralization. However, these are just a few of many other blockchain platforms that can be used by businesses. They increasingly need to use quality data for the management of their activities as well as to get rid of their dependence on intermediary institutions and to regain control of the market.

Streamr

One example is the Big Data Streamr Marketplace, which collects data from both individual users and IoT devices. In an increasingly connected world, IoT devices contain large amounts of data about how we use our home electronics. Streamr exploits "sharding," a process by which a blockchain ledger is divided into smaller pieces so that each node in the network does not need to bear the weight of the entire database, to create a fast network that includes all of those data.

ReBloc

Another example is ReBloc, a data marketplace for the real estate industry. This sector currently suffers from a lack of transparency and trust in its data. Real estate transactions usually depend on many and different parties including insurers, land registers, surveyors, mortgage companies, etc. Therefore, reliable data is essential to a real estate sale. ReBloc uses a validation protocol to ensure the accuracy and reliability of the data on its platform. Each data transaction is done through a smart contract, and before the data is released to the interested user, it is executed through a validation protocol that compares it to other datasets to judge its accuracy. Once they have passed the validation protocol, the buyer can be sure that the data is valid, regardless of the supplier. The data is automatically transmitted to the buyer and the payment is sent to the seller.

Endor Protocol

Founded by researchers Alex 'Sandy' Pentland, and Yaniv Altshuler, the Endor protocol enables organizations to analyze large volumes of data and generate automated and accurate business predictions using AI. These instant predictions help find patterns in customer behavior, which can be exploited for multiple cases and within a variety of industries ranging from retail to fintech.

BLOCKCHAIN TECHNOLOGY IN THE E-COMMERCE SECTOR

Focusing in particular on the possible impact of blockchain on the commercial performance of companies, the authors will focus in this section on the place of blockchain technology in the e-commerce sector and the changes produced by this technology in the customer relationship management. This section will open up some very interesting perspectives towards the spread of the use of this technology by commercial companies in all sectors.

What Contributions of Blockchain in the E-Commerce Sector?

Blockchain technology now offers companies working in e-commerce the possibility of managing their activities more profitably and optimizing the experience of customers in e-commerce sites in order to retain them. . Indeed, technology allows these companies to analyze the data collected on the market to design appropriate and reliable solutions. It also allows them to place the management of their relationship with customers (as well as that with suppliers) in a long-term perspective and to build relationships of trust based on mutual respect for each other's interests.

Explicitly, all the advantages offered by the blockchain are valid to face the risks and constraints that have led to slow down the development of e-commerce. In this regard, the authors come back to the benefits of blockchain in the e-commerce sector with a view to highlighting the development prospects of this sector which will now be possible thanks to this technology. Indeed, in relation to e-commerce, the blockchain allows:

Alternative Payment Methods

The contribution of blockchain to the development of e-commerce lies first of all in the use of an alternative currency: Bitcoin. Indeed, by substituting cryptocurrencies for traditional currency, the blockchain has made alternative payment methods available to customers that offer more convenience, especially to unbanked or under-banked people. Now, customers can pay for their purchases in bitcoin just as they can choose PayPal, Stripe, or any other online payment method. Best of all, using bitcoin is all the easier since transferring money is as easy as scanning and sharing a QR code.

Accelerated and Less Expensive Transactions

In traditional systems, developing business transactions involves up to 16 different steps and involves charging between 2% and 6% in total fees. These fees are mostly due to the number of stakeholders involved as intermediaries in the execution of these transactions. And the more we go through intermediaries, the more the process becomes more complex and more expensive. The blockchain then simplifies the transaction process and benefits both sellers and customers by allowing transactions to be carried out on a single network, which reduces or even eliminates the need for intermediaries. Thanks to the blockchain, transactions can be carried out at a more accelerated pace. This pace will primarily depend on the speed of the network and the time it takes to create new blocks or nodes. The acceleration of transactions in the blockchain age is phenomenal. Indeed, the Lightning Network, for example, is now capable of processing millions of transactions per second.

Highly Secure Payments

In order to strengthen their relationship with customers, companies have an interest in using blockchain technology to build a climate of trust around transactions. Indeed, individuals have long shown resistance to online shopping, in particular because of the lack of security in payments but also because they prefer to protect their personal data. In fact, in 2015, for example, out of more than 100 billion transactions carried out by bank card, 31.8 million American consumers were victims of theft of their card number.

To combat these risks, the blockchain ensures the confidentiality of personal data through the use of bitcoin-type currencies. These currencies can be compared to cash and allow the customer who uses them to no longer display their bank card number. The buyer only needs to authorize a transfer of money from their personal "wallet" to that of the seller. These portfolios are distinguished via unique identifiers generated at random.

However, the blockchain offers the e-commerce sector the possibility of operating within a fast network that ensures the confidentiality and integrity of data, which allows users to guarantee secure processing of their payments online.

Well-Processed Orders

In the context of e-commerce, one of the most important benefits of blockchain is to create a visible chain of all events related to the fulfillment process of an order. Each step is represented as a block of data and linked to the other steps, themselves represented by corresponding blocks. When a customer places an order on a merchant site using blockchain technology, an order processing process is triggered to record stakeholder interventions with great precision.

A practical example is presented here to explain this process which involves the steps relating to the processing of the order from the validation of the basket to the delivery of the goods. The blockchain is based on the identification of a block for each of these stages while accurately providing information related to the corresponding stage (date, time, speaker, etc.). Indeed, to buy online, the customer is supposed to first select one or more items by adding them to the basket and entering the shipping address to which he wishes to receive his order. The Blockchain network generates a block at this stage that states that an order has actually been launched. Then, as soon as the customer goes to payment for the chosen items, the platform generates another block to prove the payment sent to the seller. For his part, the seller receives the two blocks relating to the order and the payment. He then ships the products. The platform generates at this level a third block intended to record the processing and shipping of the order. The chain relating to this transaction may also include other movements or stages relating to the intervention of other actors such as the transport company. In this case, the blockchain generates a fourth block relating to this intervention.

By making unalterable records of all steps undertaken between stakeholders, blockchain technology paves the way for building trusting relationships between all of these parties. All stakeholders would benefit from using this kind of network to profit, in particular by reducing the risk of litigation concerning payments and details relating to the management of orders. From this perspective, the virtues offered by the blockchain are likely to arouse the interest of managers and customers and the use of this technology seems to be in perpetual development. Predictions estimate that by 2025, activities conducted using blockchain are expected to generate around 10% of global GDP.

Financial institutions around the world are likely to exploit this technology to redesign future transactional exchanges. In fact, there are already plenty of examples. Indeed, Mastercard has since developed its own blockchain to process payments. Its vice-president Justin Pinkham sees this technology as an interesting alternative for managing movements relating to the exchange of various products, including luxury items and diamonds.

Thus, we can admit that the blockchain is on the way to redesigning e-commerce, all products combined, even if it is still early to assume that cryptocurrencies have succeeded in establishing themselves in the same way as traditional currencies.

Blockchain and Customer Relationship Management (CRM)

The atmosphere of transparency and security established by blockchain technology is exemplary in encouraging managers to invest more in the development of privileged and lasting relationships with the various partners. Indeed, trust is the keystone for the development of lasting and favorable relationships with stakeholders, in particular with customers. The development of relationships of this type is the concern of many managers who aim to ensure their competitiveness in a hypercompetitive environment where the retention of current customers is much more advantageous and less expensive than the conquest of new customers.

The operation of the blockchain can be easily adapted to the world of customer relations. Indeed, it suffices to take advantage of the speed of the flow of information, the principle of disintermediation, the guaranteed integrity of the data and the convenience provided by the blockchain to create an atmosphere of trust favorable to loyalty and to achieve greater satisfaction of these customers.

A concrete example of the successful intervention of blockchain in the insurance sector could illustrate the benefits of this technology to better serve the customer. Indeed, unlike traditional circuits that may confront the customer with the difficulties of being reimbursed in the event of a flight delay or cancellation, a customer who has suffered a flight delay will be automatically reimbursed without waiting for prior notice from the airline. insurance or the airline but simply on the basis of a delay detection established on the blockchain.

Effectively, it is thanks to the development of a smart contract that the customer is reimbursed very quickly and that neither the company nor the insurer have the possibility of contesting this reimbursement.

In addition, companies could exploit the blockchain system as part of their loyalty programs. This is because companies can use bitcoin to convert customer loyalty points into virtual currency. They can also reward their customers by granting them rewards for making a transaction directly on the company's site.

By using blockchain, companies can also allow their customers to access databases, especially to deliver their documents directly to these platforms, instead of going to the corporate office. This method would make it possible to feed these databases while reducing the time required for updating customer files. These will support this update, which will positively affect the productivity of customer services. In addition, blockchain technology is likely to add value to customer relations, in particular by improving the customer experience or outright by making it possible to create new digital customer experiences (helping Internet users to manipulate unique digital objects and promote their sale or exchange between members of a community on the web). Thus, extending to several sectors, the blockchain is on the way to revolutionize the relationship between the company and its customers and to break with all the procedural constraints that can attenuate the level of customer satisfaction.

Ultimately, the contributions of blockchain in the commercial context are due to the fact that it helps promote the performance of companies that register for it. Indeed, blockchain allows these companies to build privileged and lasting relationships with their customers by focusing on fundamental values such as transparency, fairness and security. The blockchain can vouch for this transparency and security as well as fair treatment for customers. The blockchain also helps optimize the experience of customers who visit business sites adopting this technology. It will therefore promote the satisfaction of these customers with the online shopping experience as well as develop their confidence in their service provider. Therefore, the blockchain is likely to have a positive effect on the quality of the relationship between the company and its customers and consequently promote the loyalty of these customers.

CONCLUSION

Blockchain is a technological revolution that will disrupt our economies and our systems of governance. Indeed, thanks to its decentralized architecture, the blockchain guarantees its users (organizations, companies and individuals) a level of transparency and security that is not formidable. Moreover, because it can be carried out in various sectors, this technology makes it possible to give birth to new forms of more open and collaborative organizations, but also to the development of privileged partnership relations based on the common good. In the market context in particular, blockchain offers companies, all sectors combined, the possibility of serving their market by optimizing the customer experience and promoting customer satisfaction and loyalty. Indeed, the blockchain allows customers to carry out more secure transactions but also to live more user-friendly and more satisfying consumer experiences. Thus, thanks to this technology, the exchanges that take place between companies and their customers will take place in a climate of mutual trust, which will give rise to more favorable and lasting relationships between the parties concerned. On the other hand, and thanks to the digitization of currency by the blockchain, this technology could also serve as a miraculous solution for people without bank accounts or without an identity card (these number around 5 million people in the world) or for the three billion people considered to be underbanked (that is to say in particular those who are subject to severe restrictions on currency transfers). For all these reasons, it is expected that blockchain technology will be increasingly adopted by individuals and organizations and that the number and value of merchant exchanges occurring using this technology will increase dramatically. In addition, and outside the commercial context, the use of blockchain seems to be promising, in particular to improve public services. Indeed, many states in the world recognize the need to modernize administrations and public services, taking advantage of technological advances. Thus, taking advantage of the possibility of recognizing the digital identity of people, several services could operate more efficiently thanks to the blockchain (in particular to deliver more quickly and without causing congestion of gray cards or medical files, etc.) and allow a greater citizen participation for the benefit of better governance.

REFERENCES

Berg, A. (2020). The identity, fungibility and anonymity of money. *Economic Papers*, *39*(2), 104–117. doi:10.1111/1759-3441.12273

Bohme, R., Christin, N., Edelman, B., & Moore, T. (2015). Bitcoin: Economics, technology, and governance. *The Journal of Economic Perspectives, 29*(2), 213–238. doi:10.1257/jep.29.2.213

Chen, Y., Li, Y., & Li, C. (2020). Electronic agriculture, blockchain and digital agricultural democratization: Origin, theory and application. *Journal of Cleaner Production, 268*, 122071. doi:10.1016/j.jclepro.2020.122071

Coinmama. (2018). *What is the blockchain?* Retrieved February, 25, 2001, from https:// www.coinmama.com/guide/what-is-the-blockchain

De Meijer, C. R. W. (2019). *Blockchain and big Data: A great marriage.* Retrieved February, 22, 2021, from https://www.finextra.com/blogposting/16596/blockchain-and-big-data-a-great-mariage

Hervey, A. (2017). *Blockchain is A new model that makes the existing model obsolete.* Retrieved January 30, 2021, from https://medium.com/future-crunch/blockchain-is-a-new-model-that-makes-the-existing-model-obsolete-8671ee6dd252

Khalifa, E. (2019). Blockchain: Technological Revolution in Business and Administration. *American Journal of Management, 19*(2).

Liu, C. C., Xiao, Y. H., Javangula, V., Hu, Q., Wang, S., & Cheng, X. (2019). NormaChain: A blockchain-based normalized autonomous transaction settlement system for IOT-based E-commerce. *IEEE Internet of Things Journal, 6*(3), 4680–4693. doi:10.1109/JIOT.2018.2877634

Nakamoto, S. (2008). *Bitcoin: a peer-to-peer electronic cash system.* Retrieved February 2, 2021, from https://bitcoin.org/bitcoin.pdf

Rennock, M. J. W., Cohn, A., & Butcher, J. R. (2018). *Blockchain technology and regulatory investigations*. Academic Press.

Sankar, L. S., Sindhu, M., & Sethumadhavan, M. (2017). Survey of consensus protocols on blockchain applications. In *4th international conference on advanced computing and communication systems* (pp. 653-657). Piscataway, NJ: Institute of Electrical and Electronics Engineers.

Schilling, L., & Uhlig, H. (2019). Some simple bitcoin economics. *Journal of Monetary Economics, 106*, 16–26.

Wong, D. R., Bhattacharya, S., & Butte, A. J. (2019). Prototype of running clinical trials in an untrustworthy environment using blockchain. *Nature Communications, 10*(917), 917. Advance online publication. doi:10.103841467-019-08874-y PMID:30796226

Chapter 4
AIC Algorithm for Online Purchasing Intention

Bui Huy Khoi
Industrial University of Ho Chi Minh City, Vietnam

ABSTRACT

In recent years, the internet market in Vietnam has developed strongly, leading to many forms of electronic business being born and with rapid growth. Online shopping is seen as the solution to cost-effective, fast, and convenient shopping. This chapter was based on concepts and theoretical grounds related to behavior intention to accept and apply new technology to form the proposed research model. It consists of three independent factors—(1) utility perception, (2) trust, (3) social influence—and one dependent factor, online purchasing intention. This study reveals the optimal choice by the AIC algorithm.

INTRODUCTION

Vietnam is currently considered one of the fastest-growing e-commerce markets in Southeast Asia, second only to Indonesia. With high and continuous growth from 2015 up to now, many people believe that in 2020 the scale of Vietnam's e-commerce market is likely to reach 13 billion USD. According to the DataReportal (2020) report, Vietnam has more than 68.17 million Internet users in January 2020, an increase of 6.2 million (up 10%) as of January 2019. In Google and Temasek (2020) on the e-commerce market in Southeast Asia shows that Vietnam's Internet economic market is considered to have a scale of 12 billion USD in 2019 with a growth rate of 38% from 2015 to 2019, ranking 2nd in Southeast Asia, behind a market worth 40 billion USD in Indonesia. Abuodha (2020) identifies factors that influence

DOI: 10.4018/978-1-7998-8081-3.ch004

college students' online purchases. The study was guided by three specific goals, which include: Assessing the benefits of shopping online, examining risk levels, and evaluating psychological factors. However, with the strong development of the online commerce landscape over the years, the research papers that go ahead still lack other influencing factors to update and in-depth study of the factors that affect online shopping behavior in Vietnam, particularly in Ho Chi Minh City.

LITERATURE REVIEW

Consumer Behavior Intention

The typical concept in behavioral intent studies is the definition of Ajzen (1991). Research suggests that individual behavioral intent is the degree of willingness to try it out on the fastidious and the degree to which individuals intend to commit a behavior. Ajzen (1991) also shows that the individual's intention to perform the behavior is the predictor of whether they proceed to perform the behavior explaining an individual's behavioral intent is driven by motivational factors that include subjective attitudes and norms. These factors indicate that people are willing to make such an effort how much effort to make the act. Ajzen (1991) states that the stronger the behavioral intention, the higher the efficiency of the individual performing the act. Ajzen's concepts of personal behavioral intentions have paved the way for later studies of consumer behavioral intent in many different economic sectors.

In the field of technology, the Davis (1989) study explained: "the common factors that determine computer adoption, which lead to the interpretation of technology user behavior on a broader scale. ". Venkatesh et al. (2003) argue that consumer behavioral intent will be examined by "the perception of the usefulness and ease of use of that technology". At the same time, behavioral intent can help predict actual emerging technology adoption.

Utility Perception

According to Forsythe et al. (2006) and Abuodha (2020) study the development of a scale to measure the utility and risks that the perceptions of online shopping establish that the Internet has revolutionized the international business market, connecting the whole world into a dynamic market. Abuodha (2020) defines Utility Perception as consumers' confidence in how much better they feel when shopping online. This utility is subjective and is determined by the customer's response to the stimuli and actions of the online supplier or seller (Tandon et al., 2016). Hence Utility Perception is the sum of the advantages that doing online shopping leads to customer satisfaction (Abuodha, 2020). Arora and Aggarwal (2018) and Rungsrisawat et al. (2019) specify that Utility perceptions are price benefits, convenience benefits, and product diversity benefits. Nayak and Debashish (2017) and Abuodha (2020), which conducted a study of young consumers' online shopping, showed that Utility perceptions are convenience, time efficiency and cost, availability of product information, and website interface. According to Jadhav and Khanna (2016), it is determined that the main influence of factors on online such as availability, low price, promotion, sense of time, trust, and finding diversity. Katta and Patro (2017), research on the influence of website attributes on consumer purchases reveals that they seek convenience, innovation, diversity, and attitudes toward online advertising. Factors that moderately affect consumer intentions are security, services, and discounts (Abuodha, 2020). Therefore, Utility Perception is the fact that the customer is interested in the product being sold. Trust is provided with sufficient reliability (Bilgihan, 2016), besides the utility that customers perceive when buying online is the time and place of sale (Meixian, 2015) and the product must be sold on a high-quality web (Rungsrisawat et al., 2019).

Perceived Risk

Ariffin et al. (2018) identified that there are some perceived risks from the consumer's point of view. The perceived risks are financial risk, product risk, security risk, time risk, and social risk. These risks occur mainly because buyers do not see the actual product image and do not have direct contact with sales staff. Furthermore, all customer transactions are done through the website, not directly as in traditional transactions (Lester et al., 2006). A customer's online purchase intention is influenced by many factors, of which the risk factor is considered to be an important factor (Pavlou, 2003). Therefore, perceived risk is the customer's perception of the ability to gain and lose in the results of an e-commerce transaction (Yang et al., 2015). According to Abuodha (2020), the factor that is concerned is that personal information can be compromised and leaked. The perceived risk identifies the risk of transporting the goods that could damage or delay the intended receipt of the goods (Abuodha, 2020) and according to Tanadi et al. (2015), it is difficult to determine whether the quality of the product matches the description or not because there is the limited direct interaction between the product and the customer so there is a high chance of being affected by the authenticity of the product information.

Trust

Psychological factors that influence a person's behavior are classified as consumer motivations, expectations, training, and beliefs. According to Chen (2009), trust is a big influence on consumer behavior in both online and traditional shopping. Individuals may have attitudes about specific products or services that affect their behavior towards goods and services (Oh and Jeong, 2015). Marketers are concerned with the beliefs people form about specific products and services because these beliefs make products and brand image influence purchase intention (Abuodha, 2020). If certain beliefs are false and negatively affect the purchase, the marketer must launch a campaign to correct them; trust can be based on knowledge, belief, or rumor (Oh and Jeong, 2015). Trust creates a positive image in the mind of customers about a product/service, about companies trading in the form of e-commerce. Therefore, trust is also considered as a factor driving online shopping intent when customers perceive benefits (Corbitt et al., 2003) and product information integrity (Pavlou and Fygenson, 2006). According to Jarvenpaa et al. (2000), belief is the expectation of individuals or companies who interactively act ethically, reliably, following social norms, and will show commitments that individuals/companies make.

Social Influence

According to Kelman (1974), the term social influence is used to refer to "the change in behavior of an individual caused by the influence of society (a person or group of others)." This impact can come from "leader opinion, superiors, or personal interactions with online communities" Castle et al. (2014). The concept indicates that photo

Social beneficiaries can guide or change an individual's behavior when they come into contact with other individuals or groups. The impact comes from the individual receiving an opinion or suggestion by a person or group of others through a certain type of behavior, communication. The newly offered behavior "does not have to be implemented immediately, but it may challenge an individual's current beliefs, opinions, or opinions" (Kelman, 1974). The internal association is defined as "the degree to which an individual perceives others around them to believe they should use new technology because it can meet their needs (Wang and Lin, 2011), including family members with that individual referred (Pavlou and Fygenson, 2006).

Methodology

Sample Approach

The object of the research is people over 18 years old, have experience buying online, living, or working in Ho Chi Minh City. The author selected survey subjects over 18 years old because according to regulations, individuals over 18 years old can work and earn income to spend on shopping. Because survey subjects are not identical in terms of age, gender, occupation, income, the author chooses a convenient sampling method used by the author through online surveys on the Internet through Google Docs. Combining two sampling methods (Worthington and Whittaker, 2006; Tabachnick et al., 2007), to meet the suitable sample size for factor analysis method, the author chose size as 200 respondents to study for results showed a high level of statistical significance. Table 1 describes statistics of sample characteristics.

Table 1. Statistics of sample

Characteristics		Sample size	
		Amount	**Percent (%)**
Sex	Male	73	36.5
	Female	127	63.5
	18-24	145	72.5
	25-35	43	21.5
	36-49	7	3.5
	Above 50	5	2.5
Monthly Income	Below 3 million VND	81	40.5
	3-7 million VND	65	32.5
	8-10 million VND	24	12.0
	11-15 million VND	22	11.0
	Over 15 million VND	8	4.0
Online Purchasing Experience	Never bought	19	11.3
	Buying	153	76.5
	Bought	28	13.8

There are 19 unsuitable respondents. We use the 5-point Likert scale to evaluate the level of consent for the related factors for 201 respondents. Therefore, this paper also uses the 5-point Likert scale to evaluate the level of consent for all observed variables, with 1: Disagree... and 5: Agree in table 2.

Blinding

For the duration of the study, all study staff and respondents were blinded. No one from the outside world had any contact with the study participants.

Table 2. Factor and item

Factor	Code	Item
Utility Perception	PB1	When I purchase online, I worry about the credibility reliability of product information
	BP2	When I purchase online, I am not concerned about the time
	BP3	When I purchase online, I only buy at a high-quality website
	BP4	When I purchase online, I don't worry about shopping space
Perceived Risk	PR1	When shopping online, personal information can be compromised and leaked
	PR2	When shopping online, the buyer may not receive the product
	PR3	When shopping online, product quality does not match the product description on the website
	PR4	When shopping online, there is a risk that the merchandise will be damaged during delivery
Trust	TR1	I believe that website X is always oriented towards the best interests of customers
	TR2	I believe the X website provides truthful information about the product
	TR3	I believe that the X website is trustworthy
Social influence	SI1	People I know say that buying online at website X meets their needs
	SI2	Most people I know influence my intention to shop online
	SI3	Most of the people I refer to recommend/encourage me to buy online
	SI4	Comments/comments made by individuals on the internet that affect my X shopping
Online Purchase Intention	OPI1	I intend to continue buying online for the next time
	OPI2	I plan to buy online the next time
	OPI3	I will recommend other people to shop online

RESULTS

Akaike Information Criterion Selection

AIC (Akaike's Information Criteria) was utilized to choose the best model by R software. AIC has been used in the theoretical context for model selection. And when multicollinearity occurs, the AIC approach can handle multiple independent variables. As a regression model, AIC can be applied, estimating one or more dependent variables from one or more independent variables. An essential and useful measurement for deciding a complete and straightforward model is the AIC. Based on the AIC information standard, a model with a lower AIC is selected. The best model will stop when the minimum AIC value (Burnham and Anderson, 2004;

Khoi, 2021). R reports show every step of searching for the optimal model. The first step stop with 3 independent variables with AIC = -342.07 for OPI = f (UP, SI, TR)

All variables have a P-value lower than 0.05 (Hill et al., 2018), so they are correlated with Online Purchase Intention, which is in table 3. Utility Perception (UP), Social influence (SI), Trust (TR) impact Online Purchase Intention (OPI).

Table 3. The coefficients

MA	Estimate	Std. Error	T	P-value	Decision
Intercept	0.42458				
UP	0.42297	0.05540	7.635	0.000	Accepted
SI	0.25054	0.05405	4.635	0.000	Accepted
TR	0.23358	0.04813	4.853	0.000	Accepted

Table 4. Model test

<table>
<tr><td rowspan="2">VIF</td><td colspan="2">UP</td><td colspan="2">SI</td><td>TR</td></tr>
<tr><td colspan="2">1.345039</td><td colspan="2">1.130910</td><td>1.311276</td></tr>
<tr><td rowspan="2">Heteroskesdaticity</td><td rowspan="2" colspan="2">Breusch-Pagan test</td><td>chi2</td><td>df</td><td>p</td></tr>
<tr><td>5.0952</td><td>3</td><td>0.165</td></tr>
<tr><td rowspan="2">Autocorrelation</td><td rowspan="2" colspan="3">Durbin-Watson = 1.8842</td><td colspan="2">test for autocorrelation</td></tr>
<tr><td colspan="2">p-value = 0.212</td></tr>
<tr><td>Model Evaluation</td><td>Adjusted R-squared 0.5498</td><td colspan="3">F-statistic
73.87</td><td>p-value:
0.00000</td></tr>
</table>

Variance Inflation Factor

The multicollinearity phenomenon occurs when there is a high degree of correlation between the independent variables in the regression models. Gujarati and Porter (2009) showed some signs of multicollinearity in the model when the VIF coefficient is greater than 10.

According to table 4, VIF (Variance inflation factor) for the independent variables is smaller than 10 (Miles, 2014), so there is no collinearity between the independent variables.

Heteroskesdaticity

One of the fundamental assumptions of the classical linear regression model is that the random error must have a constant (Homoskedasticity). Obviously, in practice, this assumption is unlikely to exist. On the contrary, if the variance of the random error for each observation is different, we meet heteroscedasticity.

Breusch-Pagan test shows that P-value = 0.165 and greater than 0.05 (Breusch and Pagan, 1979), so it can be concluded that there is no heteroskedasticity in table 4.

Autocorrelation

Durbin-Watson Test shows that there is no autocorrelation from the model in table 4 because p-value = 0.212 is greater than 0.05 (Durbin and Watson, 1971).

Model Evaluation

According to the results from table 4, Utility Perception (UP), Social influence (SI), Trust (TR) impact Online Purchase Intention (OPI) is 54.98% in table 4. The above analysis shows the regression equation below is statistically significant (Greene, 2003).

$$OPI = 0.42458 + 0.42297UP + 0.25054SI + 0.23358TR$$

SOLUTIONS AND RECOMMENDATIONS

The results of the AIC Algorithm for the Online Purchase Intention (OPI) showed that 3 independent variables Utility Perception (UP), Social influence (SI), Trust (TR) have a positive impact on the Online Purchase Intention (OPI) because their p-value is greater than 0.05. Compare the impact level of these 3 variables on the dependent variable Online Purchase Intention (OPI) in descending order as follows: Utility Perception (0.42297), Social influence (0.25054), Trust (0.23358).

CONCLUSION

Online Purchase Intention (OPI) showed that it was influenced by Utility Perception (UP), Social influence (SI), Trust (TR) impact Mall Online Purchase Intention (OPI). Accordingly, all 3 factors mentioned above have a positive impact on the Online Purchase Intention (OPI). Besides, the AIC Algorithm also shows the influence of

3 independent factors on the dependent factor. The results of the study analysis are quite similar to the results of some previous studies.

ACKNOWLEDGMENT

This research is funded by the Industrial University of Ho Chi Minh City, Vietnam.

REFERENCES

Abuodha, K. (2020). *Factors Influencing Online Buying Behavior among University Students: A Case Study of United States International University Africa*. United States International University-Africa.

Ajzen, I. (1991). The theory of planned behavior. *Organizational Behavior and Human Decision Processes*, *50*(2), 179–211. doi:10.1016/0749-5978(91)90020-T

Ariffin, S. K., Mohan, T., & Goh, Y.-N. (2018). Influence of consumers' perceived risk on consumers' online purchase intention. *Journal of Research in Interactive Marketing*.

Arora, N., & Aggarwal, A. (2018). The role of perceived benefits in formation of online shopping attitude among women shoppers in India. *South Asian Journal of Business Studies*.

Bilgihan, A. (2016). Gen Y customer loyalty in online shopping: An integrated model of trust, user experience and branding. *Computers in Human Behavior*, *61*, 103–113. doi:10.1016/j.chb.2016.03.014

Breusch, T. S., & Pagan, A. R. (1979). A simple test for heteroscedasticity and random coefficient variation. *Econometrica*, *47*(5), 1287–1294. doi:10.2307/1911963

Burnham, K. P., & Anderson, D. R. (2004). Multimodel inference: Understanding AIC and BIC in model selection. *Sociological Methods & Research*, *33*(2), 261–304. doi:10.1177/0049124104268644

Castle, N. W., Combe, I. A., & Khusainova, R. (2014). Tracing social influence in responses to strategy change in an online community. *Journal of Strategic Marketing*, *22*(4), 357–375. doi:10.1080/0965254X.2013.876081

Chen, L. (2009). *Online consumer behavior: An empirical study based on theory of planned behavior*. The University of Nebraska-Lincoln.

Corbitt, B. J., Thanasankit, T., & Yi, H. (2003). Trust and e-commerce: A study of consumer perceptions. *Electronic Commerce Research and Applications*, *2*(3), 203–215. doi:10.1016/S1567-4223(03)00024-3

DataReportal. (2020). *Digital 2020 in Vietnam*. Author.

Davis, F. D. (1989). Perceived usefulness, perceived ease of use, and user acceptance of information technology. *Management Information Systems Quarterly*, *13*(3), 319–340. doi:10.2307/249008

Durbin, J., & Watson, G. S. (1971). Testing for serial correlation in least squares regression. III. *Biometrika*, *58*(1), 1–19. doi:10.2307/2334313

Forsythe, S., Liu, C., Shannon, D., & Gardner, L. C. (2006). Development of a scale to measure the perceived benefits and risks of online shopping. *Journal of Interactive Marketing*, *20*(2), 55–75. doi:10.1002/dir.20061

Google & Temasek. (2020). *E-Conomy SEA 2019*. Author.

Greene, W. H. (2003). *Econometric analysis*. Pearson Education India.

Gujarati, D. N., & Porter, D. (2009). *Basic Econometrics. McGraw-Hill.*

Hill, R. C., Griffiths, W. E., & Lim, G. C. (2018). *Principles of econometrics*. John Wiley & Sons.

Jadhav, V., & Khanna, M. (2016). Factors influencing online buying behavior of college students: A qualitative analysis. *Qualitative Report*, *21*(1), 1.

Jarvenpaa, S. L., Tractinsky, N., & Vitale, M. (2000). Consumer trust in an Internet store. *Information Technology and Management*, *1*(1), 45–71. doi:10.1023/A:1019104520776

Katta, R. M. R., & Patro, C. S. (2017). Influence of web attributes on consumer purchase intentions. *International Journal of Sociotechnology and Knowledge Development*, *9*(2), 1–16. doi:10.4018/IJSKD.2017040101

Kelman, H. C. (1974). Social influence and linkages between the individual and the social system: Further thoughts on the processes of compliance, identification, and internalization. In J. Tedeschi (Ed.), Perspectives on social power. Academic Press.

Khoi, B. H. (2021). *Factors Influencing on University Reputation: Model Selection by AIC. In Data Science for Financial Econometrics*. Springer.

Lester, D. H., Forman, A. M., & Loyd, D. (2006). Internet shopping and buying behavior of college students. *Services Marketing Quarterly*, *27*(2), 123–138. doi:10.1300/J396v27n02_08

Meixian, L. (2015). Convenience and online consumer shopping behavior: A business anthropological case study based on the contingent valuation method. *The Anthropologist*, *21*(1-2), 8–17. doi:10.1080/09720073.2015.11891788

Miles, J. (2014). Tolerance and variance inflation factor. *Wiley StatsRef: Statistics Reference Online*.

Nayak, P., & Debashish, S. (2017). Young consumers' online shopping decision influencers: A study on university students of Odisha. *Effulgence*, *15*(1), 45–50. doi:10.33601/effulgence.rdias/v15/i1/2017/45-50

Oh, J.-S., & Jeong, D.-Y. (2015). The effects of consumers' beliefs about TV home shopping advertising on attitude and purchase intention. *Indian Journal of Science and Technology*, *8*(14), 1.

Pavlou, P. A. (2003). Consumer acceptance of electronic commerce: Integrating trust and risk with the technology acceptance model. *International Journal of Electronic Commerce*, *7*(3), 101–134. doi:10.1080/10864415.2003.11044275

Pavlou, P. A., & Fygenson, M. (2006). Understanding and predicting electronic commerce adoption: An extension of the theory of planned behavior. *Management Information Systems Quarterly*, *30*(1), 115–143. doi:10.2307/25148720

Rungsrisawat, S., Joemsittiprasert, W., & Jermsittiparsert, K. (2019). Factors Determining Consumer Buying Behaviour in Online Shopping. *International Journal of Innovation. Creativity and Change*, *8*(8), 222–237.

Tabachnick, B. G., Fidell, L. S., & Ullman, J. B. (2007). *Using multivariate statistics* (Vol. 5). Pearson Boston.

Tanadi, T., Samadi, B., & Gharleghi, B. (2015). The impact of perceived risks and perceived benefits to improve an online intention among generation-y in Malaysia. *Asian Social Science*, *11*(26), 226. doi:10.5539/ass.v11n26p226

Tandon, U., Kiran, R., & Sah, A. N. (2016). Understanding online shopping adoption in India: Unified theory of acceptance and use of technology 2 (UTAUT2) with perceived risk application. *Service Science*, *8*(4), 420–437. doi:10.1287erv.2016.0154

Venkatesh, V., Morris, M. G., Davis, G. B., & Davis, F. D. (2003). User acceptance of information technology: Toward a unified view. *Management Information Systems Quarterly*, *27*(3), 425–478. doi:10.2307/30036540

Wang, S., & Lin, J. C. C. (2011). The effect of social influence on bloggers' usage intention. *Online Information Review*, *35*(1), 50–65. doi:10.1108/14684521111113588

Worthington, R. L., & Whittaker, T. A. (2006). Scale development research: A content analysis and recommendations for best practices. *The Counseling Psychologist*, *34*(6), 806–838. doi:10.1177/0011000006288127

Yang, Q., Pang, C., Liu, L., Yen, D. C., & Tarn, J. M. (2015). Exploring consumer perceived risk and trust for online payments: An empirical study in China's younger generation. *Computers in Human Behavior*, *50*, 9–24. doi:10.1016/j.chb.2015.03.058

Chapter 5
Role of Cryptocurrency in Digital Marketing

Hardik Bharatbhai Bhadeshiya
https://orcid.org/0000-0002-9907-8056
The Maharaja Sayajirao University of Baroda, India

ABSTRACT

This chapter explores the role of cryptocurrency in digital marketing. Throughout the most recent years, cryptocurrency has developed, both in worth and ubiquity. Indeed, numerous industry leaders trust that cryptocurrency can change money and promote it until the end of time. In any case, as computerized cash, bitcoin turns out to be more ordinary ; cryptocurrency may introduce a few issues for advertisers hoping to gather shopper information. The cryptocurrency market is an appropriate environment dependent on the distributed network innovation. Decentralization is a distinguishing characteristic of this framework, and it is an impression of how there is no national bank or another case that authorizes power over the organization. The exchanges are led and checked to employ an appropriated blockchain system that relies upon clients' assets called diggers.

CRYPTOCURRENCY: PROLOGUE

Throughout the most recent couple of years, the digital currency has developed, both in worth and prominence. As an arising social marvel, cryptographic money has pulled in incredible examination considerations and begins to frame another exploration zone in the previous decade (Guo & Donev, 2020). Numerous industry chiefs accept the digital currency can change money and advertising for eternity. Be that as it may, as computerised cash, as bitcoin, turns out to be a more normal

DOI: 10.4018/978-1-7998-8081-3.ch005

spot, cryptographic money may introduce a few issues for advertisers hoping to gather customer information. What makes computerised cash unique concerning the conventional financial framework getting utilised today? The exchanges are made, checked, got, and authorised on a decentralised record. The strange idea of digital currency is the thing that may shape the fate of advertising and how online media can impact its development (*Cryptocurrency: Social Media Influence and Digital Marketing Pitfalls*, n.d.). Market-molding research expects that organizations are the essential entertainer to lead, oversee, and react to business sectors' arrangement. This perspective is progressively being tested; however, exact bits of knowledge clarifying the jobs, assets, and entertainment activities other than firms moulding markets stay restricted (Breidbach & Tana, 2021). The selection of these trendy innovations is relied upon to affect the results for firms and clients. Notwithstanding, these are powerfully developing advances that have not yet been totally investigated and whose maximum capacity presently cannot seem to be uncovered (Kumar et al., 2021). There is a critical interest in developing and advancing digital currencies, the most striking ones being Bitcoin and Ripple. Worldwide exchanging these cryptographic forms of money has prompted exceptionally theoretical and "bubble-like" value developments. Since these cryptographic forms of money exchange like stocks give a plausible option in contrast to gold and value during questionable occasions, it tends to be theorized that their costs are incompletely controlled by the worldwide stock files, gold costs, and dread checks, for example, the VIX and the US Economic Policy Uncertainty Index (Malladi & Dheeriya, 2021). Cryptographic money has influenced a great deal—speculation, funds, and even medical services. One thing that did not have any acquaintance with it influenced was computerized promoting. This second, the web-based business industry is taking off, and individuals are purchasing and selling merchandise on the web continually (*The Impact of Cryptocurrency on Digital Marketing - Digiperform*, n.d.). The sequencing of empowering innovations and ensuing promoting apparatuses shows the need to adjust showcasing and IT to configuration new advertising instruments that can be applied to client associations and encourage advertising control (Philipp et al., 2020). An exchange that happens through blockchain exists just between two gatherings. The information is secretly shared, and just the two who share the blockchain realize it occurred. Outsider organizations can just think about what went on earlier, during and after the exchange. Alternatively, even whether it occurred by any stretch of the imagination (*What Cryptocurrency Means for Digital Marketers*, n.d.). Blockchain and digital money have given customers the way to place exchange security in their own hands. As it constructs validity and turns out to be more far and wide, advertisers and the organizations they elevate should acclimate to new strategies (Carreira et al., 2020). Digital currency is the primary fruitful use of blockchain innovation and can be utilized as the worldwide cash move network's principal fuel.

Blockchain is a progressive innovation that can change the world with its comfort, straightforwardness, precision, speed, and cost-effectiveness. The development of blockchain utilization in money relies upon additional acclimation and trust acquired by an expanding number of demonstrated fruitful use cases and tributes just as proper authoritative changes (Mohammad et al., 2019). Morals of blockchain and its applications are fundamental for innovation appropriation. There is a void of examination on blockchain morals (Yong et al., 2019). Digital currencies keep on drawing a ton of consideration from financial backers, business people, controllers and the overall population. Much ongoing public conversations of digital forms of money have been set off by the generous changes in their costs, guarantees that the market for cryptographic forms of money is an air pocket with no principal esteem, and worries about avoidance of administrative and legitimate oversight. These worries have prompted calls for an expanded guideline or even an absolute boycott. Further discussions concern entomb-Alia: the classification of digital currencies as products, cash or something different; the possible improvement of cryptographic money subordinates and of credit contracts in digital currency (Giudici et al., 123 C.E.). Blockchain and digital money are two interesting issues that are acquiring gigantic ubiquity in this day and age because of their protection and may different benefits over the cash that is available today. Blockchain is suspected to assume control over the charge later on for each exchange, installment while the cryptographic money will be the main essence of the cash later on. The subject of blockchain and digital currency is so hot these days, nonetheless, hardly any individuals haven't knew about the blockchain or about the cryptographic money. In the event that you are one of such individuals, this article is about you just We will disclose to you everything about the blockchain and its effect and future in advanced promoting. We will likewise enlighten you concerning the digital currency and what potential cryptographic money hold for what's to come (*The Ultimate Guide to Blockchain Marketing and Cryptocurrency - Blog - Creative Bear Tech*, n.d.). Digital money is one of the ways, blockchain is utilized in this day and age. Cryptographic money is a kind of cash that is absolutely computerized. There is no actual money or coins needed in the digital currency. The cryptographic money is more similar to a computerized wallet that utilizes blockchain as its major base. They are utilized as government cash and are utilized as a mechanism of trade in this day and age. The strategies for working for the digital currency is basic. It chips away at the ground of blockchain. At whatever point an exchange demand is made through bitcoin, a square is produced by a P2P organization. The exchange is then moved to the ideal individual who checks the bock. When the square is confirmed the square is added to the current rundown of blockchain. At that point the exchange is made between two clients. Assuming the square is not checked, the exchange is declined for the individual. Like the blockchain, there are numerous benefits of cryptographic money like straightforwardness security, and so on the digital currency has no actual structure and requires no centre specialist like banks. The method of cryptographic trading money is secure and solid.

CRYPTOCURRENCY V/S DIGITAL CURRENCY: A DIFFERENCE

It is a time of the fast change of a computerized economy where everything is coordinated into bits. Any movement done in the computerised stage circle can be shared, gotten to, and engendered into a simple structure. The effect was not too extreme, yet the revelation of the computerized cash astounded many residents. That is the way the term Digital Currency appeared on the scene designated into its units. Since the advancement of advances decentralized money traded stage, the appearance of Cryptocurrency is not new. Digital currency utilizes solid cryptography, regularly a blockchain with regards to serving economic data set trades. On the off chance that they misjudged their jobs and work, this is an ideal opportunity to investigate significant contrasts

Figure 1. Digital currency vs. cryptocurrency
(Source: Difference Between Digital Currency Vs Cryptocurrency, n.d.)

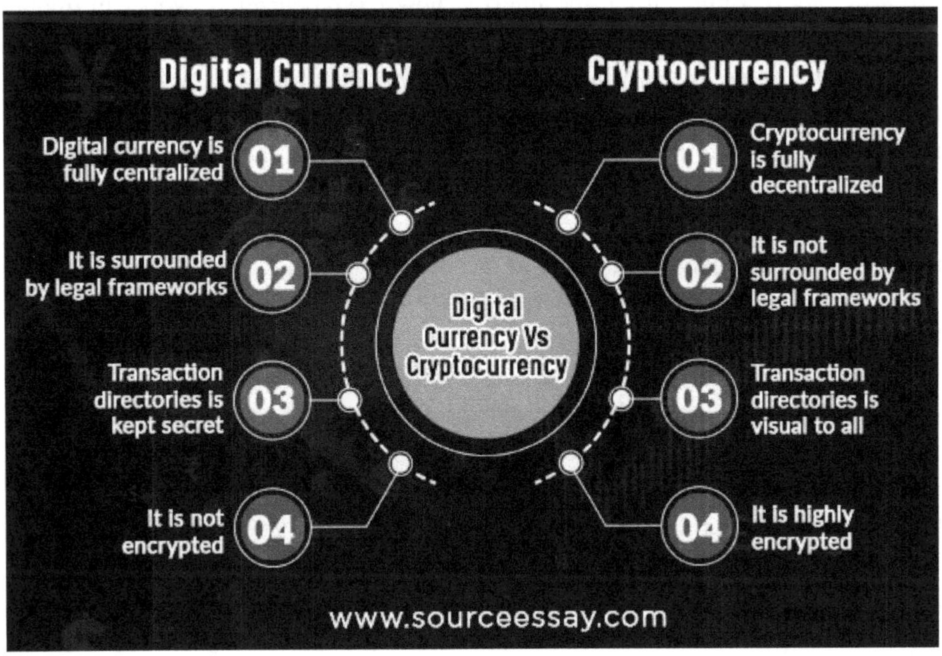

Table 1. Conceptual difference between digital currency and cryptocurrency

Digital Currency	Cryptocurrency
According to the European Central Bank, a Unified Electronic Cash is the computerized portrayal of the money recorded electronically into charge or Mastercards. Computerized monetary forms display comparable properties as actual monetary forms utilized and acknowledged by the virtual boards of trustees individuals. Over 100 years prior, when paper dollar note sponsored by the silver coins, nobody could gauge the impact of computerized money at a particularly colossal level. The advanced cash turned into an open-wellspring of contactless instalment passages between the dealers in the current environment. Subsequently, it guarantees the immaterialness of the cash that can save into electronic wallets after that. Even though these monetary forms exist in the advanced world, they can be traded in the money mode. Accordingly, there is exciting counsel on computerized cash given by task help benefits that can use for a superior comprehension of the subject.	An Encrypt Form Of Digital Currency The previously decentralized cryptographic money(Bitcoin) made by Developer Satoshi Nakamoto in 1990 that pre-owned cryptography hash work. Co-informant fabricated a correlation for Australia to break down cryptographic money strength; it found this is the most gotten, scramble, calculation fueled cash dependent on the blockchain innovation. Blockchain is pathways that keep up the respectability of the exchange stream. It is lauded for its freedom, movability, swelling opposition, and got doors. These absolute highlights of digital currencies and their security headway impact the clients generally. There are suitable around 2000 most well known digital forms of money, including Bitcoin, Ethereum, XRP, and Litecoin, which urged designers to deal with digital money. On the off chances of finding out about bitcoin history, paper composing helps administration accessible over the web.

MECHANISM OF CRYPTOCURRENCY IN DIGITAL MARKETING

From the above figure, it can be inferred how Cryptocurrency works in digital transactions. For example, Mr A has purchased some goods or services from Mr B, and for the same, Mr A wants to pay Mr B. Now the transaction will take place through the 'block'. The block will broadcast to every participant of the transaction of the network. The next move will take place from the end of the network participant. The participant who approves the transaction will be considered valid. The block can then be added to the chain, as shown in the above image in step 5, which provides an indelible and transparent transaction record.

At last, the money will be transferred from A to B. Digital money can be acquired the majority of similar ways different kinds of monetary standards can. One can trade products and enterprises for cryptographic money; one can exchange dollars for digital currencies or exchange cryptographic forms of money for other digital currencies. Exchanging is by and large done using specialists and trades. Dealers are outsiders that purchase/sell cryptographic money; trades resemble online stock trades for digital currency. One can likewise exchange cryptographic forms of money straightforwardly between peers. Distributed trades can be interceded by an outsider or not. If it is not too much trouble, know that cryptographic money costs will be unpredictable. One should slide into digital currency contributing and exchanging and be prepared to lose all that they put in (*How Does Cryptocurrency*

Work? (For Beginners) - CryptoCurrency Facts, n.d.). Cryptographic money is one of the ways blockchain is utilized in this day and age. Cryptographic money is a kind of cash that is simply advanced. There is no actual money or coins needed in digital currency. Cryptographic money is more similar to a computerized wallet that utilizes blockchain as its central base. They are utilized as government money and are utilized as a trading vehicle in this day and age. The strategies for working for cryptographic money is straightforward. It chips away at the ground of blockchain. At whatever point an exchange demand is made through bitcoin, a square is produced by a P2P organization. The exchange is then moved to the ideal individual who confirms the bock. When the square is checked, the square is added to the current rundown of blockchain. At that point, the exchange is made between two clients. On the off chance that the square is not checked, the exchange is declined for the individual. Like the blockchain, there are numerous benefits of digital currency like straightforwardness and security. Digital money has no actual structure and required no centre specialist like banks. The method of trading the digital currency is secure and dependable (*The Ultimate Guide to Blockchain Marketing and Cryptocurrency - Blog - Creative Bear Tech*, n.d.).

Figure 2. The working model of cryptocurrency in digital transaction
(Source: Onecoin-Steps-to-Protect-Your-Digital-Currencies-9-638.Jpg (638×479), n.d.)

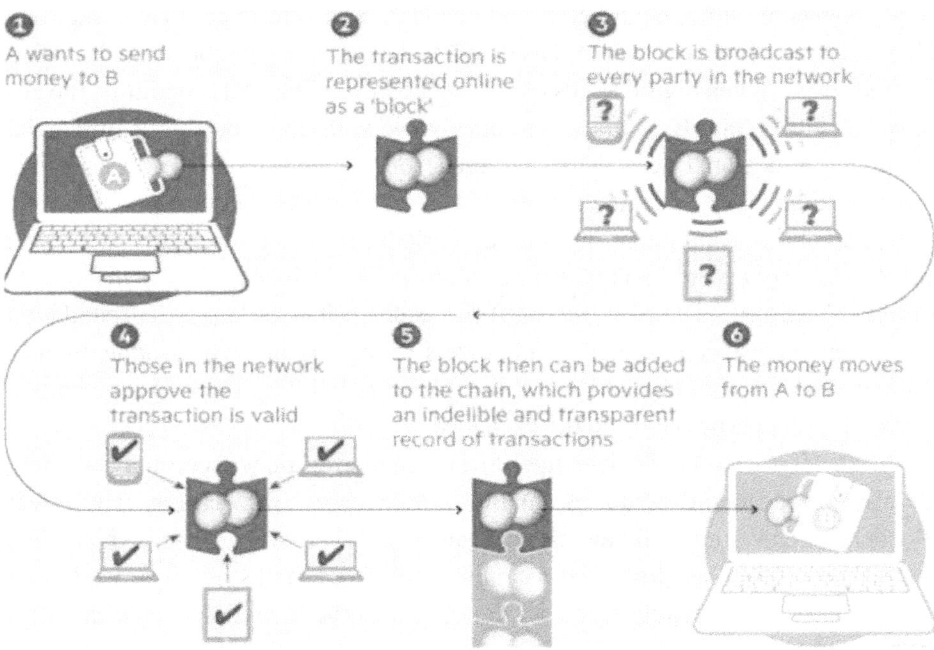

CRYPTOCURRENCY: A GAME-CHANGER FOR DIGITAL MARKETING

Because of the decentralized distributed organization, blockchain, and cryptographic money support, advertisers will think it is more challenging to gather shopper information. Also, without wealth and timely customer information, computerized advertising methodologies can be complicated to target. Utilizing digital money is likewise another progression toward online secrecy, something numerous web clients are taking a stab at. As per Pew Research Center, "86% of web clients have made strides online to eliminate or veil their computerized impressions — going from clearing treats to scrambling their email, from abstaining from utilizing their name to utilizing virtual organizations that cover their web convention (I.P.) address." The more modest the advanced impressions, the less purchaser information advertisers can incorporate to recognize crowd portions and key socioeconomics, anticipate customer conduct, test promotions, and that is just the beginning. Digital currency exchanges permit customers to buy items and administrations namelessly and safely. While that can be incredible for purchasers, it has prompted some genuine hiccups for advertisers — and will keep on doing as such as computerized cash acquires force (*Cryptocurrency: Social Media Influence and Digital Marketing Pitfalls*, n.d.). Stages like eBay help the web-based business cause and acquire their benefit by charging expenses to the purchasers and merchants who utilize the stage. By and large, ledgers of both the purchaser and vendor are utilized to confirm exchanges. They likewise affirm that the purchaser and dealer are both genuine individuals and that they exist. When digital forms of money are infused into this condition, the go-between is taken out. Exchanges are conceivable without an outsider commercial centre, and it does not need the requirement for a ledger—killing most exchange charges all the while. Indeed, even worldwide buys, which frequently incorporate additional charges and longer holding up periods, are made more expensive with the utilization of cryptographic forms of money (*The Impact of Cryptocurrency on Digital Marketing - Digiperform*, n.d.). Blockchain innovation is the foundation of the shared advanced exchange and powers wellspring of cryptographic money. Without the dark chain innovation, it is difficult to build up the exchange among the two players participating in the exchange.

While it is difficult to deviate, the Blockchain innovation will certainly be going to influence different territories, mainly computerized showcasing. The effect Blockchain innovation will have on computerized advertising can be both positive and negative. It implies proficient computerized showcasing specialists need to set up their missions to exploit Cryptocurrency just as the blow they would get from the disturbed on the lookout (*How Cryptocurrency Will Affect Digital Marketing?* -, n.d.). Although Blockchain has been around digital forms of money and account, there is no denying that fundamental innovation could be gigantic for advertising. At its centre, Blockchain empowers smooth exchanges without including any outsider delegates. Besides, it is unchanging and straightforward nature guarantees that information put away on an appropriated record remains got. Dissimilar to A.I. and ML that are perceived as changing organizations, Blockchain, then again, is changing the advanced advertising space for the better by giving the force of information back in possession of buyers (*Scope of Blockchain in Digital Marketing* -, n.d.).

1. This Will Make it Difficult to Get Purchaser Information

Cryptographic money affects the advanced world by making it effectively harder for advertisers to get data from shoppers. Also, organizations like Google and Facebook are no particular case here. It will be difficult for states to gather and offer purchaser data to promoting companies. In the most recent couple of years, the instances of media observing have practically multiplied. It has carried organizations to the computerized breadcrumbs. It joins how individuals respond to a specific item, what they need, what they purchase and how they share data with others across the web-based media stages. All these were online promotions crusades; however, Cryptocurrency has changed the entire situation. Cryptocurrency utilizes cryptography to make the client information unknown and private. Cryptocurrency is pushing forward to make the stage safer, making organizations face web showcasing business challenges.

2. Cryptography Engages Buyers

The expanding utilization of Cryptocurrency will at last power advanced advertisers to pay the purchasers for the data. As referenced above, exchanges are done on the Blockchain innovation will be noticeable to everything except the start to finish clients will remain unknown. In this way, publicists cannot discover any information on the clients. Moreover, Cryptocurrency clients will be more invulnerable to promoting advertisements.

3. End of the Centre Man

It is probably the most significant effect of Cryptocurrency on advanced promotion. Thus the term centreman, we are alluding to banks, information organizations like Facebook, Google and insurance agencies. In the current situation, we take help from the outsiders to make the exchanges, yet with the Cryptocurrency, the centre man will be disposed of, and a significant lump of cash would be saved. So, advanced advertising will unquestionably exploit the moving advances, and there is no uncertainty that Cryptocurrency will get upheaval in the computerized world.

4. Examine the Industry Results

If one needs to decide the precise length for the internet searcher result page, utilize their objective catchphrase to look through the top outcomes in Google search. Examine the word check by utilizing instruments like SEMrush and Aherfs of different sites. Record the outcomes for later reference. The outcome conveyed by these devices probably will not be exact, yet it can give a thought for the beginning stage.

5. Quality and Quantity

Assuming dissect the primary page of any SERP, more likely than not saw that Google offers an inclination to a long and more exhaustive substance. However, this does not imply that one needs to add an excessive amount of stuff to their substance. One should maintain their emphasis on the nature of a substance. There is no compelling reason to surge after the word tally and backlink numbers. Recognize the need of the crowd and request their criticism. One can utilize their input for making content as per their necessities.

6. Keeping up and Upgrading Content

One's errand does not end whenever they have assembled a vital substance for the site—redesigning the new just as existing substance by reinforcing their length is additionally significant. It is the quickest method of improving positioning. Eliminate all the exhausting web journal and article post from the site. Everyone needs to peruse new and new material. Keeping up the SEO of the site is not a simple undertaking. If one needs to make long haul progress, one should consider finding support from computerized showcasing specialists. Qdexi innovation is the most notable organization in this field that gives the best advanced promoting answers for the business site. This organization has a group of web designers, computerized advertising specialists, SEO specialists that are consistently prepared to help. Do not hesitate to get in touch with us for more data.

7. Upgraded Consumer Security and Privacy

Information penetrating is an enormous issue for each of the individuals who bargain online as there are ongoing changes of data fraud and bargain of money related data. Accordingly, to manage this, Blockchain can help in checking every exchange. Albeit every exchange is openly noticeable, the people included are anonymous. Moreover, it gives the force back to the client who can choose what information they might want to share and so forth.

8. Straightforwardness and Authenticity

Because of its decentralized nature, Blockchain can help purchasers sort out all subtleties identified with a particular item, such as where the item was produced, who made it, and so on. With the coming of Blockchain, end-clients can acquire total straightforwardness and know every insight concerning the items and, in this manner, can settle on an educated decision.

9. Annihilates Fake Actors

Albeit online is acquiring a great deal of public consideration, it is likewise evident that it includes many phoney entertainers like, for instance, counterfeit devotees, fake likes, and surprisingly counterfeit items, which is the reason purchasers struggle confiding in commercials. With no outsider association, one can manage distributors; subsequently, promoting will be more compelling.

10. Engages People

Perhaps the most energizing reasons why the extent of Blockchain is thriving is that it gives the estimation of information back in possession of purchasers. Organizations that keep on pulling clients' information have profited by selling their data, for example, email addresses, contact subtleties, and others. Blockchain can change and patch up the promoting business. Fearless program is one of the Blockchain programs, changing how clients connect with web-based publicizing. It offers another method of review advertisements while giving a profound degree of safety and security assurance. Besides, it permits clients to acquire and remunerate their number one distributers with Blockchain-based tokens. BitClave, an internet searcher, utilizes brilliant agreements to connect clients to organizations. Clients may procure serious motivators and advantages for sharing their outcomes. However, they have the certainty that the arrangements they get are both valid and transparent regarding how their information is utilized. Need to get familiar with Blockchain Technology and become a Certified Blockchain Exert? Look at Blockchain Council.

11. Encouraging quicker and simpler exchanges

Digital forms of money work their cycles utilizing innovation. It implies that one can get to advanced monetary forms utilizing a cell phone, P.C., or any computerized gadget associated with the Internet. They utilize a particular stockpiling called a computerized wallet to progressively get, send, and track crypto assets. Electronic business stages can utilize cryptographic forms of money to give a quicker and more practical instalment alternative for their clients. With only a couple of taps on a portable wallet, instalments can be made in a flash—no compelling reason to visit instalment focuses or banks and sit tight for extensive preparing times. Entrepreneurs can get crypto instalments whenever, and clients can make crypto instalments anyplace—unquestionably a mutually beneficial arrangement! What is more, digital currency and blockchain selection are reliably on the ascent. That is why it will not shock anyone that innovation and crypto nerds in the advanced promoting circle are bound to help such spearheading endeavours and tries.

12. Giving Less Expensive and Borderless Instalments

It is entirely appropriate for advanced worldwide advertisers. Finishing cross-line exchanges utilizing fiat monetary standards accompany significant expenses for move measures and other potential reasons. With cryptographic forms of money, one does not need to stress over such things! Digital currencies are decentralized, which means they are not worked or upheld by any focal power to run their tasks and cycles. This exciting element prepares for instalment exchanges to move all through a nation's boundaries at lower costs. Entrepreneurs can certainly and effectively get instalments without agonizing over changing the BTC instalments over to their nearby cash. They need to search for computerized wallets or cryptographic money commercial centres and trades to do the wizardry. Straightforward and simple, isn't that so?

13. Boosting Brand Acknowledgement through Straightforwardness

Digital currencies utilize an incredible innovation called blockchain, a dispersed record innovation (DLT) that safely records and stores data. It utilizes complex frameworks that make it troublesome and almost difficult to be hacked, changed, or fashioned. Simply envision having a profoundly gotten journal where record day by day expenses, for instance. Since the blockchain is a computerized public record, everybody in the organization can see records. Be that as it may, nobody will want to adjust them with its robust security frameworks. Cryptographic forms of money like BTC and thousands more can help advanced advertisers and vendors assemble buyer trust in their presenting brands. Utilizing blockchain-based arrangements permits progressive organizations to give more straightforwardness and responsibility to their clients. Due to robust digital currency frameworks, exchanges on the blockchain are affirmed and checked before being recorded on the standard record.

14. Killing the Utilization of Outsider Stages

Exiting go-betweens or outsider stages is perhaps the main effect of cryptographic forms of money in advanced advertising. These outsider stages incorporate monetary organizations like banks, instalment focuses, information organizations, and other monetary assistance goliaths in the web-based business industry. Arbiters fill in as the layer that affirms whether the purchaser or vendor exists and is genuine. These outsider stages likewise acquire benefits from advanced advertisers by confirming exchanges. Cryptographic forms of money take out the utilization of these stages by permitting customers and crypto clients to straightforwardly purchase merchandise and enterprises from another individual or business while keeping the exchange free from all harm.

15. Fortifying Purchaser Security

For online organizations that run entirely on advanced, instalments in digital currencies are snappier and more helpful than fiat cash instalments. While cryptographic forms of money may support specific organizations and firms utilizing blockchain-based answers for administrations and items, they can likewise influence advanced advertisers on an altogether different note. Computerized advertising utilizes outsiders in the internet business industry to access and accumulate notable data about their objective business sectors. The data and information gathered are regularly used to enhance business procedures and strategies, set up goals, and make an examination. On the other side, exchanges with digital currencies are made straightforwardly—with no arbiter or outsider. Due to the shortfall of such stages, advertisers and promoters will think it is hard to accumulate such data and information from purchasers.

16. Restricting the Effect of Online Notices

Social affair individual data on the Internet is accessible, however not for exchanges made with digital forms of money. Since they give higher purchaser protection levels, it very well may be precarious for promoters to make or arrive at their objective business sectors. As a result of the untraceable and direct crypto instalments, web-based business stages may struggle drawing in clients through online media, messages, SMS, and other computerized advertising channels.

17. Advancing Customer Mindfulness

As we referenced before, it very well may be trying to gather the individual information of buyers who utilize decentralized digital currencies like Bitcoin. Individual subtleties, like name, date of birth, residence, or telephone number, will not be gathered when making instalments in crypto. One needs the wallet address where one will send or get the BTC instalments. Individual information will not be accessible for Bitcoin exchanges since everything on the blockchain is encoded. Customers currently have command over the measure of information they are willing to share or whether they are willing to give out such close to home information or not.

18. Modifying the Expenses of Advanced Publicizing and Advancements

Most organizations depend on media checking to accumulate essential data required for promoting purposes. While this may, in any case, work for specific organizations, the reception of cryptographic money instalments in various businesses is developing comprehensively and rapidly. This reality leaves advanced, showcasing organizations without hints of individual information. For online organizations that rely upon shopper information following, this will push them to recruit advanced publicizing organizations that will accumulate the data they need for running advertising methods. However, stop and think for a minute: this methodology does not come for anything. Web-based business stages and undertakings may need to bring out heaps of money to have the essential assets and advances they need to accomplish their business objectives and arrive at more clients. Organizations that acknowledge digital currency instalments may require publicizing specialists to focus on business sectors and contact them. Doing so can carry a chance to straightforwardly connect with clients and track their buy exercises through various channels and stages. It incorporates blog or site remarks, item or administration audits, and reactions to web-based media posts. However, of course, this can set back a ton of cash.

CRYPTOGRAPHIC MONEY IN DIGITAL MARKETING: A WAY FORWARD

The computerized advertising traps cryptographic money presents are constraining advertisers to go straightforwardly to the hotspot for shopper data. Paying clients straightforwardly for their data is one procedure. However, it is a costly one. It can influence showcasing advertisement benefit for web-based media networks like Facebook or Instagram. If advertisers need to pay clients straightforwardly for information, they will be more averse to pay interpersonal organizations. New crypto-disapproved social channels like Steem and Earn.com have sprung up, which let advertisers draw in with these stages' considerable number of clients to buy subtleties and other individual data. These organizations are an expected arrangement, yet clients may need a nontrivial cash measure for their data. The potential gain is that the clients willing to give a particular organization their data are bound to be possible clients.

Cryptographic money is part later on for online media, and computerized promoting is as yet questionable. The impact online media has on developing and estimating computerized currency might be turned over, making it ready for new crypto-disapproved informal organizations. Advanced advertisers, then again, may have to dish out more shopper research dollars to get the information they need to make publicizing progress. The returns a large part of buyers' hands' capacity, one more turn to digital currency appropriation. Be that as it may, the future could be important for everybody (*Cryptocurrency: Social Media Influence and Digital Marketing Pitfalls*, n.d.). While the rundown posts the two benefits and weaknesses to the advanced promoting industry, the most significant test to face can be gathering essential data from shoppers. Online advertisers may think it is challenging to accomplish the objectives and destinations in their advanced promoting methodology. Despite the great degrees of shopper authority over their data, cryptographic forms of money are developing selection and consistently expanding capacities in various ventures overall demonstrate that they can change the fate of instalment frameworks and computerized advertising (*8 Ways Cryptocurrency Is Changing Digital Marketing - Simpliv Blog*, n.d.).

1. Get Micropayments

Individuals by content these days are barraged they did not request or is not fit to their requirements. In any case, many would address a reasonable cost for the content they like from suppliers their trust. It is the place where micropayments come in. With micropayments, clients would now be able to make a little instalment for each piece of substance they read when paying for a membership, which is generally encouraged by digital money. It does not just push content suppliers to distribute great substance individuals will want to pay for, yet it also permits perusers to cast a ballot with their cash by going somewhere else. No perusers mean no benefits for distributors with this model. However, with promotion upheld content, site hits and novel guests are the only important thing.

2. For what Reason Aren't Micropayments More Popular?

One of the primary issues with Bitcoin and an assortment of digital currencies are expenses and scaling. If one needs to pay more in expenses for each microtransaction one make, at that point, it does not sound good as a peruser. Nonetheless, there is one approach to bypass this issue, and that is by utilizing what is known as channels. Through instalment channels, one does not need to make a progression of small instalments and pay a charge on everyone. For this situation, instalments will be recorded as an assortment, all things being equal. Attempt to consider this to be if one went to a nearby bar and requested a tab. Instalment channels work a similar way essentially. At the point when one opens a channel, it resembles when a barkeep opens a tab. They record all that one buys and charge toward the end. One channel will be shut with an instalment channel when it is finished paying for a specific substance or after the beneficiary shuts the channel. It permits saving money on expenses and permits the distributor to limit the number of exchanges being made, making the cycle less expensive and advantageous.

3. Current Content-Based Micropayment Initiatives

Numerous stages are attempting to utilize the standard of micropayments to change the idea of web-based showcasing. One model is Coinetize, a type of paywall just as an asset to the executives' framework. The framework permits the distributor to channel guests and make them pay for premium substance. Individuals can pay utilizing credits, either through their charge card or Bitcoin. The Brave internet browser is another activity that is attempting to change our relationship with content. The program permits individuals to get a quicker perusing experience and lighter advertisements. They likewise execute an instalment administration that permits individuals to pay the sites they like the most namelessly. Commitments will be then part between sites that were visited by individuals who utilized the program, in light of the time spent on every site and the number of visits. Developments like these are why one should stay refreshed and watch out for live crypto news. They may change how individuals utilize the net, and some digital currencies focused on micropayments may begin taking off out of nowhere. Monitoring late changes could permit one to contribute early and receive rewards.

THE ROLE OF CRYPTOCURRENCY IN DIGITAL MARKETING: EPILOGUE

Individuals are hesitant to give their information, making it hard for organizations to gather such data. The Personal Data Market presents a good answer for this issue, yet current contributions should defeat a few difficulties (Ha et al., 2019). Blockchain is turning into a far and wide advanced innovation that permits each exchange to be followed in a sacred manner, subsequently making it conceivable to revisit the whole history of items and item segments (Mandolla et al., 2019). One route for advanced advertisers to get client data would be by paying their clients. Since this strategy is costly, a more sensible arrangement is to utilize the Basic Attention Token. Fundamental Attention Token is a three-way network including promoters, distributors, and clients. A business opportunity for promotions, Basic Attention Token works by disposing of delegates and paying distributors and sponsors for their advertisements. Clients – while staying unknown – are additionally paid for watching these advertisements. In light of client consideration, distributers and publicists can more readily oblige their intended interest group's requirements. The Indian government doesn't consider digital forms of money legitimate delicate or coins. Thus, the public authority needs to kill the utilization of cryptographic forms of money and doesn't need such monetary standards to turn into a piece of the installment framework (*What Is the Cryptocurrency Bill & What Happens to Those Holding Bitcoins in India?*, n.d.). However, Finance serves Nirmala Sitharaman has clarified that there will not be a finished restriction on digital forms of money or, if nothing else, the innovation part of it. "From our side, we are extremely evident that we are not closing all alternatives. We will permit certain windows for individuals to do investigates blockchain, bitcoins or cryptographic money," Sitharaman had said at an India Today meeting. She said fintech relies upon such analyses, and it will have that window accessible. "We will not stop it," she said. In any case, it is the Cabinet note which will detail the sort of plan, she said, adding the note will prepare soon. "It is approaching fruition, and afterwards, it will be taken to the Cabinet. The Supreme Court had remarked on digital currency. We are certain that the Reserve Bank of India (RBI) will accept an approach to a digital authority currency," she said. She said it is a major region on blockchain innovation, and India has a lead advantage in it. "A ton of fintech organizations have gained a great deal of headway on it. We have a few introductions. Much work at the state level is occurring. What is more, we need to take it amazingly in IFSC or Gift City in Gandhinagar," the F.M. said. She said the service is wanting to have a beginning up meet basically on fintech in Gift City. "When Parliament is finished, I will presumably invest more energy executing and arranging that. On fintech and blockchain, there is a great deal of work going on in India, and we will surely empower that," the F.M. said. Prior, MoS for account Anurag Thakur had said in Parliament that there are various definitions for digital forms of money or virtual monetary standards the world over. The pastoral council (IMC), headed by previous account secretary Subhash Chandra Garg, first recommended a draft Bill to boycott cryptographic forms of money. "The public authority will take a choice on proposals of the IMC," Sitharaman had said in a composed reaction to an inquiry in Parliament. Existing laws are insufficient to manage the subject, Thakur had said. The public authority shaped the IMC, and it has outfitted its report, he said, adding there was likewise a gathering of an enabled innovation gathering, which occurred prior. Thakur said the board of trustees of secretaries, led by the Cabinet secretary, has likewise given its report, and the Bill is being finished. It will be shipped off the Cabinet soon. The SC, in March 2020, had struck down the RBI's guidelines on banks to quit offering types of assistance to crypto exchanging stages, prompting vulnerability about the situation with virtual monetary standards in India. The new enactment will clear the public authority's remain on digital forms of money (*India Will Not "shut off" All Cryptocurrency, Wants Blockchain: Sitharaman | Business Standard News*, n.d.). Governments and industry pioneers have effectively done projects to completely assess blockchain's qualities and how they should be consolidated into regular practices. A few fragments performed quicker than others. The combination of blockchain advances into regular exercises inside enormous multinationals was formally conveyed, with the cash part being the snappiest out of the squares, the advancement and the market part. Coordination of blockchain innovations can give secure, available advanced variants to all gatherings in an exchange, and brilliant agreements can be utilized to deal with the work process of endorsements and naturally move instalment upon all marks being gathered. As shown by Gartner, blockchain development has quite recently arrived at the notice cycle's stature and entered a period of decay, which is perceiving the validness of blockchain advancement. The point of view for advancement in blockchain looks wonderful, and the increments made by procuring the development are unexpected. The comprehensive agreement is that progressing the hour of expanding want was a critical development in blockchain change across the infomercial cycle. The perspective for blockchain development looks awesome, and the increments created utilizing getting the advancement will be unfathomable. How the advancement is gotten a handle on will be the best approach to how it benefits the financial business sectors and the world when everything is said in done (Yadav et al., 2020). Blockchain is a progressive innovation that can change the world with its comfort, straightforwardness, exactness and productivity in speed and cost. The development of blockchain use in money relies upon additional acquaintance and trust acquired by an expanding number of demonstrated effective utilization cases and tributes just as proper authoritative changes (Mohammad et al., 2019). Everything digital currencies can hypothetically and fill in as a trade mechanism; they are probably not going to become normal and fluid media of trade except if they can delineate utility in one of different elements of cash. Computerized monetary forms' unbendingly unyielding stockpile and fiercely fluctuating interest make them too precarious to be in any way utilized as a unit of record for years to come. Of the five, just Bitcoin can fill in as a store of significant worth because of its severe obligation to low stockpile development, soundly supported by the organization's dispersed convention and tenable exhibit of the shortfall of any power fit for modifying the inventory plan. Other digital forms of money are brought together control and use as tokens for explicit applications make them far-fetched to satisfy financial capacities (Ammous, 2018).

REFERENCES

8 Ways Cryptocurrency Is Changing Digital Marketing - Simpliv Blog. (n.d.). Retrieved March 11, 2021, from https://blog.simpliv.com/8-ways-cryptocurrency-is-changing-digital-marketing/

Ammous, S. (2018). Can cryptocurrencies fulfil the functions of money? *The Quarterly Review of Economics and Finance*, *70*, 38–51. https://doi.org/10.1016/j.qref.2018.05.010

Breidbach, C. F., & Tana, S. (2021). Betting on Bitcoin: How social collectives shape cryptocurrency markets. *Journal of Business Research*, *122*, 311–320. https://doi.org/10.1016/j.jbusres.2020.09.017

Carreira, R., Pinto, P., & Pinto, A. (2020). In J. Prieto, A. Pinto, A. K. Das, & S. Ferretti (Eds.), *A Framework for On-Demand Reporting of Cryptocurrency Ownership and Provenance B.T. - Blockchain and Applications* (pp. 131–143). Springer International Publishing.

Cryptocurrency: Social Media Influence and Digital Marketing Pitfalls. (n.d.). Retrieved January 31, 2021, from https://blog.influenceandco.com/cryptocurrency-social-media-influence-and-digital-marketing-pitfalls

Difference Between Digital Currency Vs Cryptocurrency. (n.d.). Retrieved March 13, 2021, from https://sourceessay.com/digital-currency-vs-cryptocurrency/

Giudici, G., Milne, A., Vinogradov, D., Milne, A. K. L., & Milne, A. (123 C.E.). Cryptocurrencies: market analysis and perspectives. *Journal of Industrial and Business Economics, 47*, 1–18. doi:10.100740812-019-00138-6

Guo, X., & Donev, P. (2020). Bibliometrics and Network Analysis of Cryptocurrency Research. *Journal of Systems Science and Complexity*, *33*(6), 1933–1958. https://doi.org/10.1007/s11424-020-9094-z

Ha, M., Kwon, S., Lee, Y. J., Shim, Y., & Kim, J. (2019). Where WTS meets WTB: A Blockchain-based Marketplace for Digital Me to trade users' private data. *Pervasive and Mobile Computing*, *59*, 101078. https://doi.org/10.1016/j.pmcj.2019.101078

How Cryptocurrency Will Affect Digital Marketing? (n.d.). Retrieved March 11, 2021, from https://www.qdexitechnology.com/how-cryptocurrency-will-affect-digital-marketing

How Does Cryptocurrency Work? (for Beginners) - CryptoCurrency Facts. (n.d.). Retrieved March 17, 2021, from https://cryptocurrencyfacts.com/how-does-cryptocurrency-work-for-beginners/

India will not "shut off" all Cryptocurrency, wants blockchain: Sitharaman | Business Standard News. (n.d.). Retrieved March 17, 2021, from https://www.business-standard.com/article/markets/india-will-not-shut-off-all-cryptocurrency-wants-blockchain-sitharaman-121031400754_1.html

Kumar, V., Ramachandran, D., & Kumar, B. (2021). Influence of new-age technologies on marketing: A research agenda. *Journal of Business Research*, *125*, 864–877. https://doi.org/10.1016/j.jbusres.2020.01.007

Malladi, R. K., & Dheeriya, P. L. (2021). Time series analysis of Cryptocurrency returns and volatilities. *Journal of Economics and Finance*, *45*(1), 75–94. https://doi.org/10.1007/s12197-020-09526-4

Mandolla, C., Petruzzelli, A. M., Percoco, G., & Urbinati, A. (2019). Building a digital twin for additive manufacturing through the exploitation of blockchain: A case analysis of the aircraft industry. *Computers in Industry*, *109*, 134–152. https://doi.org/10.1016/j.compind.2019.04.011

Mohammad, H. J., Yuka, N., & Krishnan, D. (2019). Cryptocurrency, a successful application of blockchain technology. *Managerial Finance*, *46*(6), 715–733. https://doi.org/10.1108/MF-09-2018-0451

onecoin-steps-to-protect-your-digital-currencies-9-638.jpg (638×479). (n.d.). Retrieved March 17, 2021, from https://image.slidesharecdn.com/tipstoprotectyourdigitalcurrencies-onecoin-171012101449/95/onecoin-steps-to-protect-your-digital-currencies-9-638.jpg?cb=1507803419

Philipp, G. J., Susanne, H.-B., & Jörg, H. (2020). Information technology and marketing: An important partnership for decades. *Industrial Management & Data Systems*, *121*(1), 123–157. https://doi.org/10.1108/IMDS-08-2020-0510

Scope of Blockchain in Digital Marketing. (n.d.). Retrieved March 11, 2021, from https://www.blockchain-council.org/blockchain/scope-of-blockchain-in-digital-marketing/

The Impact of Cryptocurrency on Digital Marketing - Digiperform. (n.d.). Retrieved March 11, 2021, from https://digiperform.com/the-impact-of-cryptocurrency-on-digital-marketing/

The Ultimate Guide to Blockchain Marketing and Cryptocurrency - Blog - Creative Bear Tech. (n.d.). Retrieved March 17, 2021, from https://cbtemailextractor.com/blog/the-ultimate-guide-to-blockchain-marketing-and-cryptocurrency/

What Cryptocurrency Means for Digital Marketers. (n.d.). Retrieved March 13, 2021, from https://www.waxmarketing.com/cryptocurrency-means-digital-marketers/

What is the Cryptocurrency Bill & What Happens to Those Holding Bitcoins in India? (n.d.). Retrieved March 17, 2021, from https://www.news18.com/news/business/what-is-the-cryptocurrency-bill-what-happens-to-those-holding-bitcoins-in-india-3432443.html

Yadav, S. P., Agrawal, K. K., Bhati, B. S., Al-Turjman, F., & Mostarda, L. (2020). Blockchain-Based Cryptocurrency Regulation: An Overview. *Computational Economics*. doi:10.100710614-020-10050-0

Yong, T., Jason, X., Rafael, B.-A., & Lakshmi, I. (2019). Ethics of blockchain: A framework of technology, applications, impacts, and research directions. *Information Technology & People*, *33*(2), 602–632. https://doi.org/10.1108/ITP-10-2018-0491

Chapter 6
Blockchain Technology in Tourism Management:
Potentialities, Challenges, and Implications

Célia M. Q. Ramos
https://orcid.org/0000-0002-3413-4897
CinTurs, ESGHT, University of the Algarve, Portugal

ABSTRACT

The tourist activity realized early on the advantages in the adoption of technology for the performance of its activities. With the emergence of the technological environment provided by Industry 4.0, blockchain technology emerges as the most disruptive and consequently more challenging technology for the tourism industry, since it has excellent potential to leverage innovation in this activity, whether in terms of products, processes, management, marketing, or institutionally. A bibliometric analysis was carried out to investigate affected studies in the tourism area, including the hotel, restaurant, marketing, and other sectors. Application of blockchain technology may be the key to boost tourism since its applicability presents several opportunities for tourism stakeholders, adds security and confidence in business transactions, can influence changes in the tourism value system, in terms of the value creation for customers, value creation for business, and in the tourism distribution chain.

DOI: 10.4018/978-1-7998-8081-3.ch006

INTRODUCTION

The practice of quality management in tourism, with employees with knowledge of the activity and quality in the provision of its service (Bontis, Janošević, & Dženopoljac, 2015), contribute to the definition of the marketing strategies and to the performance of the tourist organization, which can lead to success or failure of a company.

The critical factors of the success of the tourism industry in general, and in particular to hospitality, catering, transport and events, involves the provision of services and products that meet customer satisfaction, which must be provided with quality, properly disclosed through internet (websites and social media platforms), in order to contribute to the growth of the business, through the retention and loyalty of the customer and the raising of new customers.

In addition to loyalty, the relationship established with the customer can be measured by customer complaints, by the quality of the customer database, customer retention rate, satisfaction, customer service capacity, identification of customer needs, new strategic customers, customer sales value (Manzari, Kazemi, Nazemi, & Pooya, 2012), among others.

In this context, a new challenge has arisen since it is necessary to resort to information technologies, associated with the environment tourism 4.0, which guarantees the confidence and security of information communication through the Internet (Calvaresi, Leis, Dubovitskaya, Schegg, & Schumacher, 2019), with campaigns suited to the right customer and at the right time, wherever they are, with the aim of maintaining the reputation of tourist companies as well as the promotion of their products and services.

To overcome the challenge of security and the trust of sensitive information, associated with customers, the solution is to use blockchain technology, which will ensure (Baralla, Pinna, & Tonelli, 2019; Önder, & Treiblmaier, 2018): (i) the security of information through the use of encryption; (ii) transparency of information, because all partners can access it and verify transactions; (iii) trust between parties without the use of an intermediary, because the blockchain is decentralized and is accessed and copied by any node on the network; (iv) the immutability of the information, given the structure of the blockchain.

Blockchain technology will have a disruptive effect on tourism activity, since it will cause changes in the distribution chain, in the relationship between stakeholders, enhancing the emergence and disappearance of stakeholders, through a digital transformation that is increasingly accentuated in companies and society, as well as it will help to protect the personal data of customers used to carry out digital marketing campaigns, as well as in offering promotions according to their characteristics.

The main goal of this research is to analyze the applications of Blockchain technologies to Tourism Marketing for all the stakeholders, both on the supply side and on the demand side.

To achieve this goal, a literature review was done on the concept, and a bibliometric analysis was also done to identify studies already done on blockchain applied to Tourism.

The research question of this study is: What kind of research has been made on blockchain in Tourism? The main findings are related to the innovative applications of blockchain technology taking inconsideration the tourism distribution chain, preventing frauds, keeping the Information safe and facilitating the tourism management process.

The chapter is organized as follows: Section two summarizes the background associated to the blockchain technology applied to the tourism economic sector, Section three results presented some potentialities, challenges and solutions, Section four discusses the future research directions and present some trends. Finally, Section five concludes and presents possible future works.

BACKGROUND

Industry 4.0 is a term that represents the technological evolution of integrated information systems in a single local application, to integrated systems in a virtual (cyber-physical) world, which includes the integration of all systems, communication between equipment, the Internet of Things (IoT), integrated into a virtual space (Lee, Bagheri, & Kao, 2015; Xu, Xu & Li, 2018; Ramos & Brito, 2020).

The technological pillars of "industry 4.0" are Blockchain technology; information security; augmented reality; big data; cloud computing; IoT (Internet-of-Things); autonomous robots; and mobile Internet, among others (Saturno, Pertel, Deschamps, & Loures, 2017), will enhance the development of tourism activity contributing to the development of conditions and business models associated with "tourism 4.0", can be considered as the engine for facilitating innovation in the tourism sector.

One of the main drivers of the "tourism 4.0" or "smart tourism" (Gretzel, Sigala, Xiang, & Koo, 2015) is stimulate entrepreneurial ecosystems (Bu, 2018), these environment contributes to the development of smart destination, through digitization and vertical and horizontal integration of value chains (Stalidis, Karapistolis, & Vafeiadis, 2015); (2) smart experience, digitization of products and service offerings (Nabben, Wetzel, Oldani, Huyeng, Boel, & Fan., 2016); and (iii) smart business ecosystems, development of digital business models that include value analysis by value tourists (Gretzel et al. 2015).

One of the main tecnological pillars is Blockchain (BC) emerged in the 90s, it was considered as "an innovative technology that can be applied in various sectors of the economy… where the trust between the subjects involved can be guaranteed through an algorithm instead of a centralized organization" (Valeri & Baggio, 2020: 2), developed by Satoshi Nakamoto (Nakamoto, 2019; Tasatanattakool & Techapanupreeda, 2018), also defined as "a form of database storage that is noncentralized, reliable, and difficult to use for fraudulent purposes" (Tasatanattakool & Techapanupreeda, 2018: 473).

Overview of Blockchain Technology

To distinguish Blockchain from Bitcoin, Tasatanattakool and Techapanupreeda (2018: 473) describes Bitcoin as a form of digital currency that uses "a Blockchain public ledger to make transactions across peer-to-peer networks", generally used in financial applications, such as associated to smart contracts, that use Blockchain technology. The Bockchain Technology can be used in several applications beyond the financial, for example in healthcare systems, personal consumer needs, where it is necessary to protect the personal data.

Also, Blockchain technology (BCT) can be defined as "an online platform that chronologically records transactions and tracks assets through distributed ledger in a network" (Dogru, Mody, & Leonardi, 2018: 1). As example of the transactions in a network, can be considered sending and receiving money, payments for products and services, booking a hotel room or a flight, making a reservation, entering into a contractual agreement, transmission of personal data, and much more (Dogru et a., 2018: 1).

To Treiblmaier (2018, p. 547) blockchain can be defined as a "a digital, decentralized and distributed ledger in which transactions are logged and added in chronological order with the goal of creating permanent and tamperproof records", where the main features are: immutability, transparency, programmability, decentralization, anonymity, and consensus (Treiblmaier, 2019) as presented in table 1.

BCT functions as a chain of nodes, which hold information, where each node can only join if it receives authorization from the other nodes in the chain (Filimonau & Naumova, 2020), through a consensus protocol. Consensus is achieved by nodes that have no prior knowledge of each other, which prevents the transaction registered in the chain from being invaded and falsified later, which guarantees the trust and responsibility of the entire system (Filimonau & Naumova, 2020).

According to the Nakamoto model (2019: 3), shown in figure 1, each transaction must be verified and endorsed by the previous block, using a digital signature. In which each block is connected in chain to each other and require digital validation of the previous block that will be updated in the content of the block itself.

Table 1. Blockchain characteristics

Characteristic	Description
Immutability	Data in a blockchain is unchangeable unless a specified part of the network (e.g., most of the hashing power in Bitcoin) decides to do so. Data that has been tampered with can be easily identified.
Tranparency	Data on a blockchain is visible to a specified group of users. Most importantly, they all share the same view on the data.
Programmability	Programmable blockchains allow the specification of rules (often called smart contract) that are automatically executed in case prespecified conditions occur.
Decentralization	Blockchain technologies do not rely on a central point of control. Consensus protocols define how dispersed entities agree on what should be written onto a blockchain and the prevailing state of truth.
Anonymity	The visibility of identifying data in a blockchain ranges from full anonymity over pseudonymity to full identity.
Consensus	A consensus mechanism is applied to achieve agreement on the state of a network including the validity of transactions and how decisions can be made.
Miner	The transactions was verified.
Forks	The problem that arises when the node is used for different versions of Blockchain.
Hash	One-way function to check the integrity of a transaction or message.
Node	The ledger in the Blockchain system.
Timestamp	A data and time in the computer system used as an electronic time stamp for the transaction.

Source: Adapted from Tasatanattakool and Techapanupreeda (2018: 473) and Treiblmaier (2020: 5).

Figure 1. Blockchain model
Source: Nakamoto (2019: 3).

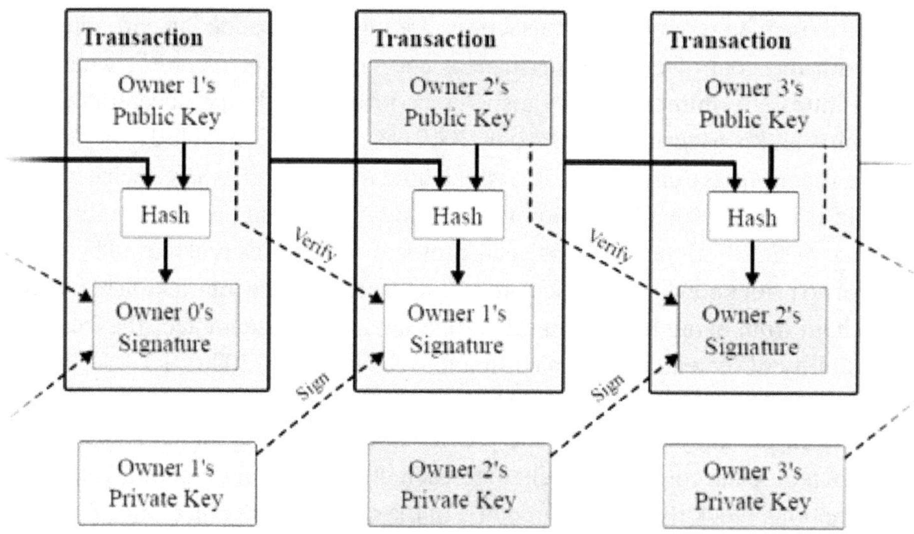

Sometimes blockchain technology is confused with bitcoin, however, it can be applied to any online digital asset transaction. In peer-to-peer bitcoin transactions are notified in the order in which they are generated, but there is no guarantee that the order of transactions is correct. This problem is solved with the use of Blockchain technology, in which there is a continuous registration of all transactions with equity and in a distributed way, that is, without a third certifier, which guarantees independence of any of the parties, as shown in the figure 2.

Figure 2. How blockchain technology works
Source: Adapted from Bitpanda (2020) and Chagas (2019).

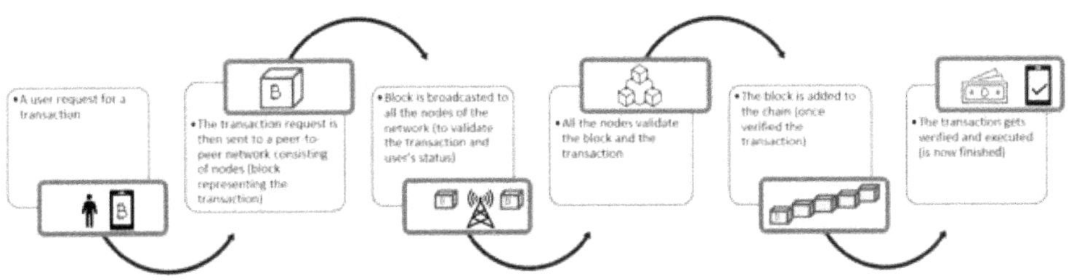

Each of the "nodes" functions as a user or server, enabling the sharing of services and information without the need for a central server. In Blockchain technology, the peer-to-peer network is composed of several computers and servers where each represents a "node" in the network. When new information enters the network, it is disseminated among all nodes in the peer-to-peer network, validated, encrypted and private. It is not possible to identify who added the information to the network, just validate it.

With blockchain technology, there is no repeated or double information, and to ensure a greater degree of security, computer programs are used that automatically execute the terms of a contract, called smart contracts. In the event, if there is a preconfigured clause in this smart contract between the participating entities, the parties involved can automatically make payments securely and according to the contract. Blockchain technology is being applied in several financial and non-financial areas.

Blockchain Technology Applications in the Tourism Industry

Blockchain technology, although recent, has been adopted by several organizations across the globe, in various sectors of the economy, including the tourism sector (Valeri & Baggio, 2020), where it can be used to manage transactions reducing the need of intermediaries (Nam et al. 2019); lower cost reduction (Rashideh, 2020), transparency (Baralla, Pinna, Tonelli, Marchesi, & Ibba, 2020); increasing revenues (Rejeb & Karim, 2019); risk reduction (Rashideh, 2020); increases the level of trust (Rashideh, 2020), creation potentiate new business opportunities (Rashidesh, 2020); focus on customer (Reagen & Singh, 2020), reduce the role of the intermediaries (Rashideh, 2020).

Including tourism, BC technology has been viewed enthusiastically by companies as it is considered secure, decentralized. Disintermediate and democratic. For Valeri and Baggio (2020: 3) BC is defined as "a growing list of records, called blocks. Which are linked using cartography" where "each block contains a cryptographic hash of the previous block, a timestamp, and transaction data". Transacted data can be financial, contracts, personal data, among others of a sensitive nature.

According to Rashideh (2020), the biggest impact that this technology can have on the tourism industry is the increase in the level of disintermediation, either through the elimination of existing ones or through the impediment of new intermediaries. With the use of cryptocurrencies as a payment method, tourists can book their accommodation and transport without resorting to intermediaries, being one of the most relevant trends for tourism (Tapscott & Tapscott, 2016).

The tourism industry is extremely competitive and diverse, where a set of relationships coexist between the different stakeholders. Technology over the years has had a disruptive effect on this activity, since the news has been quickly adopted by different participants in the tourist distribution chain, from tour operators and travel agents, airlines, hoteliers, insurance firms, payment service providers, government entities.

For the tourist consumer, BCT can support the entire process associated with the security of your financial transactions as well as the protection of your personal data (Rashied, 2020).

For organizations that carry out the governance of tourist destinations, BCT can play a relevant role since it will play a prominent role in the development of tourism activity associated with an intelligent destination, with impact in the supply chain, transportation, contracts, and payments (Kwok & Koh, 2020).

Blockchain technology presents several opportunities to reinvent tourism, even in times of economic crisis, since it can be applied through the following pillars: Digital travel identity, Digital payment, Digital financial services, Digital independency (Kwok & Koh, 2020).

- **Digital travel identity** will allow the personalization of the tourist product which contributes to improving the tourist experience and aggregates all the information as a customer so that it is possible to offer services and products according to profile.

- The digital currency or cryptocurrency (**Digital payment**) that allows payment in real time, in digital form, with quick and simple conversion to the currency of the destination, helps to promote the destination, apply special discounts, and increase the loyalty of tourists.
- It will provide a way to diversify products, as it allows the monitoring of resources, while reducing the dependence on bank entities, contributing to the development of Financial Services that may be considered by smaller companies (new Digital financial services), reducing inequalities and increasing the economy of tourist destinations, which meets the SGD (**Sustainability Developing Goals**) (SDG, 2019).
- For the destination, with the reduction of fees applied to financial services, it is possible to reduce the operating costs for the destination companies (hotels, restaurants and transport, among others), which will allow to improve the offers in terms of products and services, contributing to leverage the local economy (**Digital economic independence**).

In terms of the innovations associated to the tourism sector, can be considered four categories of innovation – product, process, managerial, and institutional (Hjalager, 2010), that conjugated with BC technology can create a powerful environment to innovate, to overcome the crisis moments and to benefiting tourist and suppliers.

The use of Blockchain technology can be used in tourism activity for several functions: (i) hospitality: revenue management, inventory control, guest history, financial management (Rashides, 2020); (ii) restaurants and gastronomy: food safety and security, customer payments, smart contracts, food recalls, product labeling (Rashides, 2020); (iii) transports: reservations and ticketing, insurance, capacity planning (Kwoh & Koh, 2020), among others.

For Kwoh and Koh (2020), application of BC technology may be the key to boost tourism, since its applicability presents several opportunities for tourism stakeholders, as shown in table 2.

Another aspect, of the nowadays society, the increase of digital consumers, the growth of artificial intelligence (AI) techniques, the increase use of Internet of Things (IoT), the heterogeneity of digital platforms that emerge all days contribute to increase the demand in the way the whole industry works, in general, and tourism, mainly with regard to security and trust in commercial transactions.

A new dimension emerges for trust and security, where it is necessary for technological innovation to emerge that is not centralized, where BCT can be considered as the main candidate for this technological revolution which could create new opportunities for the tourism industry (Calvaresi et al., 2019), however, it is necessary for tourist companies to accept and adopt.

Table 2. BCT applications and the various opportunities for the tourist industry

Reservations and Ticketing	Hotels Car rentals Flights Restaurants Events Insurance Tracking guest Tracking food
Inventory management	Capacity planning Direct distributions Supplier network
Credential management	Authenticity review Verification Rankings & Ratings
Cryptocurrency	Digital currency Cross-border remittance B2B settlement Currency exchange
Loyalty programs	Discounts Gamification Incentives/rewards
Identity management	Traveler identity Baggage tracking personalization

Source: Adapted from Dogru et al. (2018) and Kwok and Koh (2020).

The factors that lead to the acceptance and adoption of BCT by tourist companies was the target of an investigation conducted by Nuryyev et al. (2020), once IT contributes to performance and competitiveness in this economic sector, as well as to the sustainability of the business, where they concluded that payments by cryto-currency have the potential to create disruptions in the traditional way in which the tourism industry works.

The author Treiblmaier (2020: 7), based in the work of Goudarzi and Martin (2018) and Wüst and Gervis (2018), developed a decision flowchart that can help the organizations to evaluate if they need a blockchain solution, and if so, to identify which kind is most appropriate, as presented in the figure 3.

In according com Treiblmaier (2020: 8) Blockchain applications can be differentiated into public vs. private as well as permission less vs. permissioned. The latter type is the preferred option for many blockchain solutions in the supply chain.

Figure 3. Blockchain decision flowchart
Source: Treiblmaier (2020: 7).

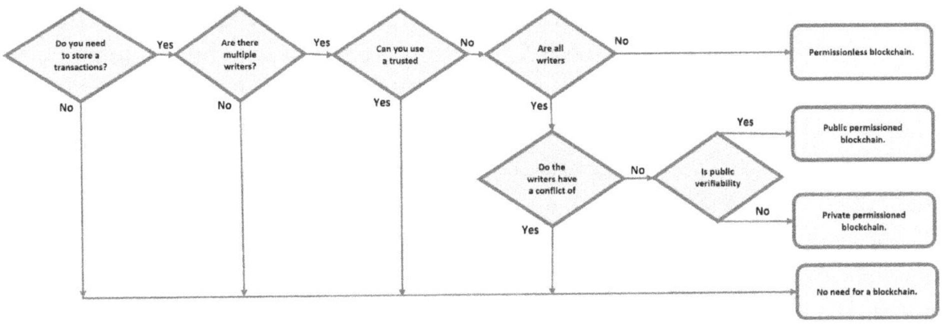

Impacts in the Tourism Industry

The Blockchain Technology will have a great impact in several industries, where the tourism is one of the principals, where they stand out as strengths: (i) are cost reductions, changes in the market structure and increased efficiency, and as weaknesses: low transaction speeds and the gap due to normalization in transactions (Treiblmaier, 2020).

In addition to the previous aspects (Treiblmaier, 2020), the BCT can have an impact on inventory management, maintenance and tracking, reservation and ticketing, payment and taxes, loyalty programs, personal data management, baggage tracking, management, and coopetition, among others.

The inventory management can use BCT to share the availability and rate of the inventory between the stakeholders (Treiblmaier, 2020), can replace the PMS (property management systems) in hospitality, and the CRS (Computer Reservation Systems) that connect channel managers and global distribution systems, changing the tourism distribution, once BCT can directly link suppliers and customers while removing the intermediaries and related expenses (HTNG 2018).

In the tourism industry, the maintenance and tracking associated to the supply chain management is one of the most important system, where the tracking food to avoid health and hygiene issues is very important to certify the origin, the track and the destiny, also in terms of the sustainability and authenticity, and in terms of the lifecycle certification to the products and to the tourism destination (Goudarzi & Martin, 2018; Nam et al., 2019).

In terms of ticketing and reservations, the BCT can be used to eliminate black markets (Larchet, 2017) and to help to manage airline tickets which involves a great number of partners (Goudarzi & Martin, 2018).

The payment and taxes also have impact once the BCT can contribute to increase the competitivity of the destination, while reduce the taxes, the intermediaries and cost associated to the currency conversions (HTNG, 2018; Kwok & Koh, 2018).

Loyalty programs can use the BCT to freely exchange with others, tourists, or industry partners, and would create a competitive market that provides additional feedback to the organizations about how they are working, and it is their reputation, this functionality will contribute to define personalized marketing campaigns (Dogru et al., 2018; Irvin & Sullivan, 2018).

The personal data management can be possible to share information between suppliers to define a global traveler identity (Bell & Holland, 2018), that can help the tourist who frequently must show their identity in flights, hotel rooms, rental cars, among others; once BCT can generate a code without reveal the personal identity; can be used to guarantee that the online reviews are valid, from the moment they are validated by the code generated by BCT.

The baggage tracking can be considered by the BCT once can facilitate the tracking location of their assets and share the current locations on their mobile devices (Ludeiro, 2018).

The management, coordination and coopetition are another organizational level that can use BCT to change the disintermediation and to help to detect the structural changes needed to increase the competitivity of the sector (Treiblmaier, 2020), while contribute to appear new forms of coordination and coopetition, to the aggregation of the travel products and services that can be distributed in a more efficient way, also contribute to appearing new stakeholders.

In a tourism complementary terms, also the BCT can be used in (Calvaresi et al., 2019):

- Tourism sharing economy: (i) resources for sale, rental or co-usage (Hawlitschek, Notheisen, & Teubner, 2018); (ii) online platforms for sharing housing (Nasarre-Aznar, 2018); (iii) online taxi-hailing platform (Zhang, Zhong, & Tian, 2017).
- Well-being/health/medical tourism: management of electronic health record (HER) (Pilkington, 2017).
- Sustainable tourism development goals: Regional tourism market (Dudin et al., 2017), tourism as a poverty decrease (Pilkington, Crudu, & Grant, 2017).
- Online Corporate Reputation: online consumers review (Önder, & Treiblmaier, 2018).
- Tourism trade: Online travel platforms (Önder, & Treiblmaier, 2018).

Despite all the potential and applications of BCT to Tourism, which highlights the elimination of intermediaries and the safe and authentic transfer of information, this technology presents challenges that must be overcome for its adoption to be more accentuated.

Potential Challenges to Overcome

In according with the authors Kwok and Koh (2018: 4), BCT can be considered "as a disruptive innovation", the pervasiveness of blockchain technology adoption in tourism industry could face several barriers, both from the tourist and business point of view, barriers exist, depend on the maturity of the markets, on the understanding of tourists, on the acceptance of local traders, and are limited in use to those with skills and technological knowledge.

The most impacting challenges that the tourism industry faces for the adoption and use of BCT are (HTNG, 2018; Kwok & Koh, 2018; Leung, & Dickinger, 2017; Polasik, Piotrowska, Wisniewski, Kotkowski, & Lightfoot, 2015; Swan, 2015):

- Miners' speed: the systems seek to quickly verify the transactions and information entered in the Blockchain, which requires costly equipment.
- Regulations: there is still a certain fear and ignorance about the regulation of this technology, as there are not yet adequate regulations for this technology.
- Energy consumption: Blockchain mining computers spend time and a lot of computing resources to validate transactions.
- Control, security, and privacy: Without the proper regulations, there is difficulty in adopting since there are no defined rules on what can be done or terms of control or security in data sharing, even with smart contracts, as contracts can be breached and as noted, justice is still at the beginning over the regulation of this technology.
- Integration: Blockchain technology is still innovative and little used and the creation of a network depends on the acceptance of companies to develop internal strategies to, finally, apply this technology on a large scale and in several partner companies.
- Cost: The price and time of transactions is reduced. On the other hand, the initial capital costs for its application are very high.
- Complex application: Its application requires the meeting of several projects, which can be a difficult task, as well as personnel with adequate training.

Despite the barriers, Blockchain is an innovative technology with characteristics to lead to the restructuring of tourist organizations and their distribution chain, as well as to add and eliminate new stakeholders (Valeri & Baggio, 2020), since this industry remains dependent of information and communication technologies, and how they affect tourist activity.

SOLUTIONS AND RECOMMENDATIONS

Solutions

Despite the potential and the challenges, there are still questions "How Blockchain Technology will dominate the travel sector? (Gjerding, 2017) "Will blockchain technology become and stay relevant for tourism?" (Thees, Erschbamer, & Pechlaner, 2020) that motivate / limit the development of the tourism industry.

For airliners and government entities, it is very important to have a travel ID, provided by BCT, which allows to integrate and innovate in terms of products and services without high costs or complex implementations (Gjerding, 2017).

New technologies are risky and BCT continues to be (HTNG, 2018), however, pioneers have advantages as they adapt more quickly and identify more quickly the improvements and adjustments that must be made as they mature in use of this technology.

Considering the characteristics of Blockchain in a summarized form (HTNG, 2018): (i) the stored data is immutable, (ii) the data is auditable, (iii) the technology maintains a history of the data as its added, (iv) the protect data integrity using cryptographic tools, (v) maintain decentralized transactions with no need for a central authority; companies must assess whether to start using BCT or wait for a later stage of maturity of this technology.

To implement BCT, companies need to investigate more about technology and realize the potential it must transform the economy and the business itself (Chagas, 2019).

The solution involves analyzing the following aspects (HTNG, 2018: 24): (i) Disintermediation of the business model, (ii) Disintermediation of partner networks may cause current supply chains to change or even see a rapid demise, (iii) Organizational impacts, and (iv) Evolving and multiple operating models.

If move ahead of time fragile decisions can be made (HTNG, 2018: 24): (i) the organizational culture may not support an approach to taking controlled and defined risk, (ii) the organization may not be armed with basic decision-making criteria or equipped to exercise external forces, and (iii) An early investment in a blockchain project needs to consider the benefits of decentralized networks versus rapid changes in technology and the possibility that blockchain technology itself is not necessarily the optimal decentralized database.

After analyzing the pros and cons of advancing or waiting for the maturity of the technology, described in the previous paragraphs, a tourist company must understand what type of BCT should be applied in a company, as described in figure 3, as it can influence the prof-of concept or the toolsets they want to use. The following identifies which BCT is a candidate for proof of concept, term used when Blockchain is being tested, and whose challenges and characteristics are aligned with your business. After identifying the challenges that the blockchain can help to overcome, make sure that its use will add value, through the application of four "acid tests" proposed by IBM (HTNG, 2018: 25): "(i) Consensus - does the use benefit the entire network company and is the entire transaction valid? (ii) Origin - is the maintenance of complete audit tracking important? (iii) Immutability - is it important that the sequence of transactions is tamper-proof? (iv) Purpose - is there a need for an agreed registration system" for all companies?"

After answering the previous questions, the step is to choose a BCT Provider or an ecosystem that is suitable for tourist activity. And finally, after choosing the platform, design develop, test, and deploy is necessary to meet the needs of the tourism business itself (HTNG, 2018: 25).

IF all the previous steps went well, you can then consider that you can switch to the BCT platform or if the initial tests did not go well, you should consider changing the BCT ecosystem (HTNG, 2018: 24).

The impacts of Blockchain on the consumer relationship with tourism organizations can be observed through changing the focus of institutions, as the disruptive potential is greater than expected in the economic, financial, and social spheres.

Recomendations

The use of BCT also should be analyzed in terms of the impact that have with the consumer relationship, associated to the tourism value system which can be defined as "a mixture of the value chain approach and the customer journey linking the services of more than two companies" (Thees, Erscghbamer & Pechlaner, 2020: 2605), where the customer journey presents the several steps of experience from a customer's point of view (Lemon & Verhoef, 2016: 69) and a journey is a result of a wide range of attractions, facilities and services of several providers (Lane, 2007; Stickdorn & Zehrer, 2009).

The use of disruptive BCT associated with the tourism value system, should be analyzed from the perspective of primary and secondary activities, where the primary ones are directly linked to the customer journey and the technological implications used and associated with the value chain (Thees et al., 2020). Secondary activities are associated with contracts, networks and financing, as shown in figure 4.

Figure 4. BCT in the tourism value chain.
Source: Adapted from Thees et al. (2020: 5-11)

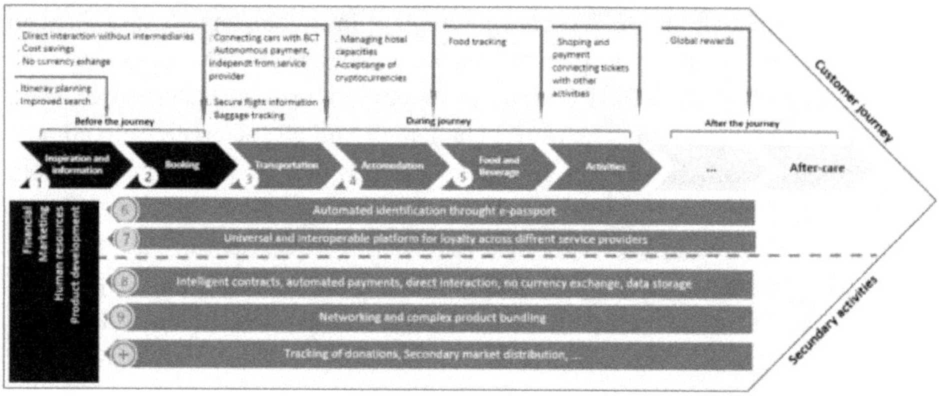

BCT can be used at each stage of the tourism value system (Thees et al., 2020): (i) Inspiration and information: BCT can contribute to do forecasts the itinerary planning, automatization and improved search algorithms, provide assistance to pan and book a trip, may increase the customer value taking in consideration the real-time availability of rooms or flights and automated booking; (ii) Booking: empower the direct communication between the tourists and the companies, permit to develop strategies to the consumer-oriented, with payments in the tourist currency which simplify the transaction process; (iii) Transportation: could be used to develop a system that manage all the flights and delays, increase the connectivity between car rentals and flights, with automated payments, increase the cooperation between stakeholders; (iv) Accommodation: contribute to a direct communication between tourist and hotelier, digital check-in and as a room keys, identity management, payment and loyalty programs; (v) Food and Beverage: as a food tracking permit to know in real-time the quality, temperature, shipments of the food which increases the customer's trust considering the traceability; (vi) Automated Identification: permit the introduction of an automated identification that contributes to the simplification of checkpoints, while storage the sensitive personal data; (vii) Loyalty programs: provide an excellent opportunity to the service providers create opportunities to the customers through the combination of several loyalty systems to provide valuable offers; (viii) Transactions, contracts and payments: permit the optimization of the transactions, decrease the number of intermediaries; and (ix) Networking and bunding: with IoT (Internet-of-things) can contribute to potentiate the cooperation between service providers and to develop universal systems, while increases the cooperation level and relations between all tourism stakeholders.

BCT can influence changes in tourism industry and in the tourism value system (Thees et al., 2020) in terms of the value creation for customers, value creation for business, the role of the intermediaries, regulations, and tourism distribution chain.

Hospitality Industry

For the hospitality, the BCT can potentiate the creation of trust, creates a direct channel between the consumer and the hotel that decrease the transactions cost while increase security and transparency through the elimination of the intermediaries, as presented in the figure 5, and contributing to the enlighten the hotel's brand (Filimonau & Naumova, 2020).

In addition to the direct channel between the hotel and the guest, BCT contributes to secure payments, more accurate demand forecasts, definition of more appropriate loyalty programs with more accurate and customer-oriented marketing campaigns, reliable comments, statistical data more precise, cooperation between service providers, among others (Filimonau & Naumova, 2020).

Figure 5. Application of the BCT in hospitality industry
Source: Filimonau and Naumova (2020: 5).

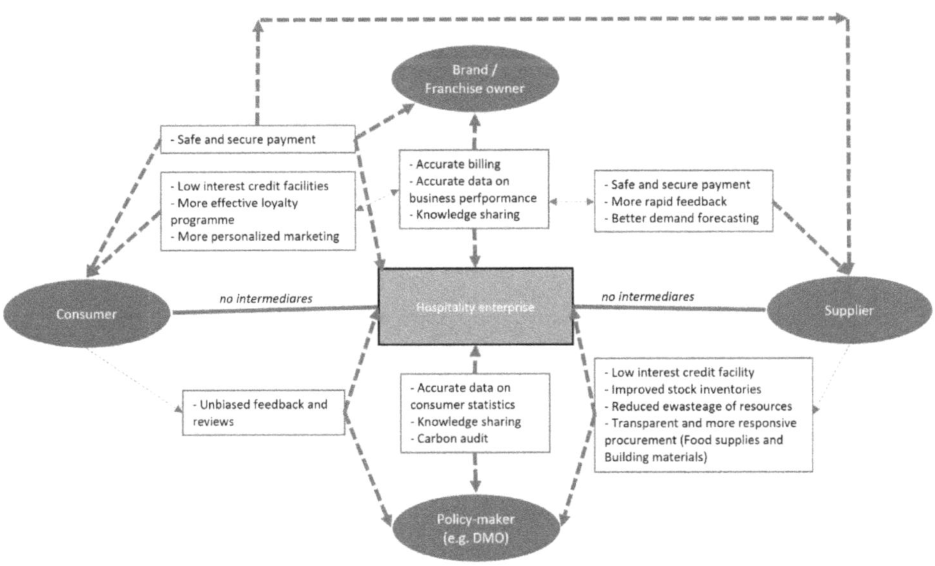

Airport Industry

For the airport industry, the BCT technology can help to track goods and passengers in real time, identifying the real position on the globe, also contributes to the management of the identity management (Vaio & Varriale, 2020), while it has a disruptive effect that increases spatial and temporal flexibility.

BCT can contribute to increase cooperation between aviation companies, air traffic controllers, airport operators with a view to increasing efficiency and coordination of operations, while reducing the fragmentation of tasks, as shown in figure 6. The combination of different maisn players on a platform allows to reduce delays, consequently, increases punctuality, decreases fuel consumption and decreases the negative effects on the environment (Vaio & Varriale, 2020).

According to Vaio and Varriale (2020), BCT also allows for the optimization of flight plans and the management of air traffic, optimizes the use of airport infrastructure and reduces congestion in landing and in traffic of transfers.

Figure 6. Application of the BCT in airport industry
Source: Adapted from Vaio and Varriale (2020: 102014).

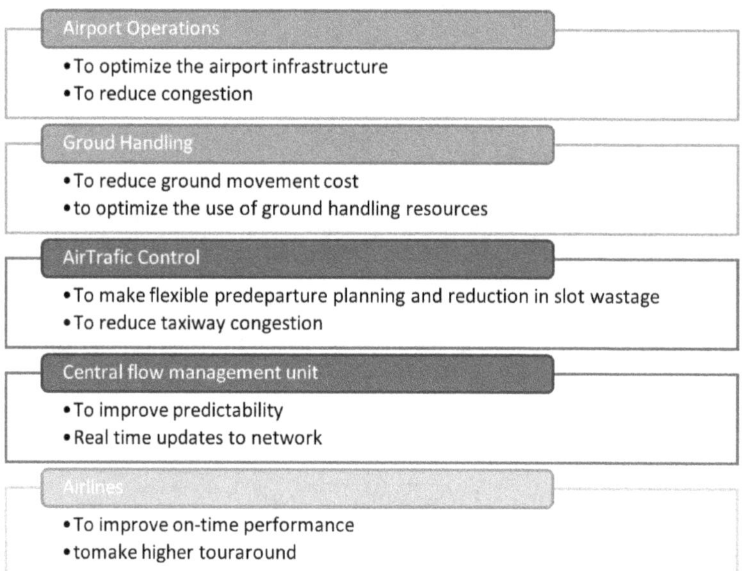

Food Industry

For Rejeb et al. (2020: 1), BCT "has emerged as a promising technology with far-reaching implications for the food industry" once the immutability, transparency and data integrity can contribute to increase trust in extend food supply chain, while reduce the risk of other forms of illicit trade.

Rejeb et al. (2020) considers four dimensions of BCT potential for the food industry, that are directly linked to the gastronomy and restaurants which are a relevant component of the tourism destination.

One of the dimensions is associated with food trading, the other three refer to the food distribution chain: traceability, collaboration, and efficiencies, which presented in the figure 7.

Figure 7. Application of the BCT in food industry
Source: Adapted from Rejeb et al. (2020: 9).

FSC Traceability	FSC Collaboration	FSC Efficiencies	Food Trading
• Ensure granular and ent-to-end traceability • Increase food safety and quality • Developed trusted food safety systems • Ensure paid authentication of food products	• Foster collaboration between FSc partners • automate information sharing process • Increase decision synchronization process • Provide high and real-time interoperability • Reduce collaboration costs • Increase trust in collaborative relationships	• Optimize and integre of FSC process • Maximize operational efficienciesand responsiveness • Provide high flexibility, faster deliveries, and customer satisfaction • Increase process transparency and visibility • Increase profitability	• Improve food trading processes and relationships • Remove trade restrictions and frictions • Streamline borderless transactions

Tourism and Blockchain have the possibility to become a strong combination once this technology can bring safety and transparency to several critical touchpoints in the travel consumer journey, which increase the level of trust between all the tourism distribution chain. The principal benefits of the combination between tourism and BCT are easy, safe and traceable payments, even in different currencies; hotel and transportation coordination and management, with reduced intermediaries and costs;

business ratings, which defines the reputation of organizations and helps tourists at the time of decision making; baggage management, allows you to know in real time where they are; reward systems to the traveler, that add value to the tourist experience.

In summary, the BCT has benefits: accurate tracking, cost reduction, guarantee of authenticity, increased transparency and permanent ledger, as presented in the figure 8, which can be applied in several economic activities, with predominance for application in financial services, where a faster and cheaper payment could save a lots of money and permit cross-border payments without transaction costs while increase transparency; health care provision, patient's encrypted health records could be shared between several stakeholders: medicals, insurance company, clinical researchers and financial companies without the risk of data fissures; property management, with more accurate and efficiency; and distribution chains, where the costumers can trust in the product authenticity and manufacturers with a complete tracking between the origin and the destination.

Figure 8. BCT benefits, applications and impacts to the travel industry.
Source: Author's elaboration

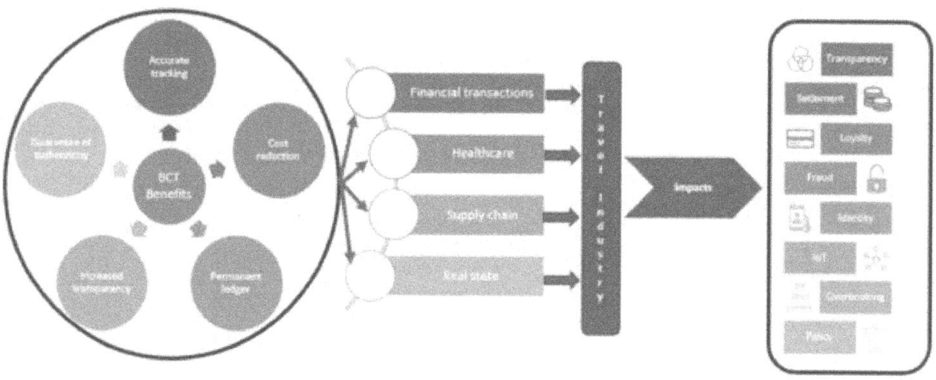

All these four application areas are relevant to the tourism industry, not including others that also coexist, commercial transactions for payment of tourist products: hotel, restaurant, transport, and events; for the protection of your personal data, such as health, for the management of apartments, hotel rooms and resorts, and about the distribution chain, it mainly affects the food that is sold in restaurants and associated with gastronomic events. For example, some applications relevant to the travel industry: smart contracts, sharing economy, supply chain audits, intellectual property management and identity management.

Consequently, have impacts in travel industry: transparency in the commercial relationships between all the stakeholders in the tourism distribution chain, settlement in the definition of commercial relationship, increase the loyalty of the consumers as a consequence the potentiality of the rewards, creation of a digital identity that facilitate the travel and check-ins, IoT to establish the communication more ease and quick between all the parties, previous detection of overbooking and allow the management to avoid the situation of excessive travelers, policy which control all the materials status while increases the balance of justice and costs in commercial transactions between those involved.

FUTURE RESEARCH DIRECTIONS

BCT introduces various benefits in the tourism industry (Thees et al., 2020), mainly value creation to the customer, increase the service quality, development of new business models, potentiate cooperation between all the parties in this economic sector.

With this technology can be created distributed and autonomous marketplaces, such as a virtual shopping mall, which brings together several brands and stores in one place, where Blockchain guarantees the transfer of assets in a safe, private, self-regulating, and fast manner, allowing flexibility to the cashier and asset management (Chagas, 2019).

In addition to the other disruptive effects that this technology will cause, BCT will change business models and the way of communicating with consumers, through the use of new technological features and the definition of new strategies supported by digital marketing, mainly motivated by to empower people through the protection and security of their personal data, through authentication and transparency that will condition the disappearance of confusing advertising and the verification of genuine products (Newman, 2019).

The combination of BCT with data analysis tools will allow to increase the quality of data considered relevant for decision making in tourism, since BCT has a mechanism for decentralized trust across a network of participants using data encrypted. Although BCT presents two challenges for the data analytical processes: (i) the high number of assets and transactions and (ii) transparency for all participants in the tourist distribution chain, which will imply the need to define a consortium between organizations operating in this activity.

On the other hand, data and analytics leaders have an opportunity to use smart contracts for trusted data sharing and can emerge as new business partners associated with tourism.

BCT will provide confidence to all companies that participate in a transaction network whose participants are unreliable, where all transactions and changes of state are publicly documented, unalterable and continuously verified.

Currently, the combination of BCT and data analysis is still taking its first steps in any economic activity, however, the tourism sector has been one of the first to adopt new technologies, which may also be a factor that will lead to the rapid adoption of this technology for the tourism industry.

The adoption of BCT is still at an early stage as the technology's maturity and interoperability phase has not yet been reached, which will take several years until BCT technologies become dominant on the market, including the integration of existing data in organizations. and analytical tools, which can lead to very high costs whose benefits do not outweigh.

For the adoption of BCT, tourism organizations need to rethink their mode of operation as well as reformulate their business models, equated with a technological architecture of distributed computing and an environment characterized by industry 4.0, that is, combined with other technologies that are considered in this evolution: IoT, cybersecurity, cloud computing, advanced robotics, big data analytics, among others (Ramos & Brito, 2020).

With BCT, a verified and trust data will growing massively and the huge amount of customer data (big data) at the disposal of tourism industry actors is allowing a more pervasive analysis and more efficient predictions based on behavioral information which will contribute to define marketing strategies with focus on the a personalized customer, once it will be possible to develop mass strategies which achieve a specific client if the organizations consider the combination with marketing intelligence automation tools.

CONCLUSION

BCT due to its characteristics of transparency, trust and security has aroused the interest of several economic sectors, with an emphasis on the area of banking, health and distribution chains and property management. The tourist activity develops in these areas so the potential of BCT is evident, since it will help in financial transactions, in the protection of personal data related to health, in the distribution chain of tourist products, including food, and in the management of properties among tourists.

The main benefits, among others that are also relevant, are economic transactions with secure information, cost reduction due to the decrease in intermediaries, decentralized and always functioning operation, increased transparency leading to increased trust and authenticity. For the tourism area, and as a benefit to highlight for tourists, it is also worth mentioning the secure payment even in different currencies, reduction of distribution costs paid to OTA (Online Travel Agencies), creation of universal rewards programs, protection of tourist data, prior detection of overbooking.

ACKNOWLEDGMENT

This paper is financed by National Funds provided by FCT - Foundation for Science and Technology through project CinTurs (UID/SOC/04020/2020).

REFERENCES

Baralla, G., Ibba, S., Marchesi, M., Tonelli, R., & Missineo, S. (2018, August). A blockchain based system to ensure transparency and reliability in food supply chain. In *European conference on parallel processing* (pp. 379-391). Springer.

Baralla, G., Pinna, A., Tonelli, R., Marchesi, M., & Ibba, S. (2020). Ensuring transparency and traceability of food local products: A blockchain application to a Smart Tourism Region. *Concurrency and Computation*, *33*(1), e5857. doi:10.1002/cpe.5857

Bell, A., & Hollander, D. (2018). *Blockchain and distributed ledger technology at travelport*, 1–12. Retrieved from https://www.travelport.com/sites/default/files/travelport-blockchain-whitepaper.pdf

Bitpanda. (2020). *How does a blockchain work?* Bitpanda Academy. https://www.bitpanda.com/academy/en/lessons/how-does-a-blockchain-work/ blockchain-in-aviation-white-paper.pdf

Bontis, N., Janošević, S., & Dženopoljac, V. (2015). Intellectual capital in Serbia's hotel industry. *International Journal of Contemporary Hospitality Management*, *27*(6), 1365–1384. doi:10.1108/IJCHM-12-2013-0541

Bu, N. (2018). The 22nd Session of the UNWTO General Assembly–Special Session on Smart Tourism: Chengdu, China, 14–15 September 2017. *Anatolia*, *29*(1), 143-145.

Calvaresi, D., Leis, M., Dubovitskaya, A., Schegg, R., & Schumacher, M. (2019). Trust in tourism via blockchain technology: results from a systematic review. In *Information and communication technologies in tourism* (pp. 304–317). Springer. (Original work published 2019)

Chagas, E. (2019). *Blockchain: A Revolução Tecnológica e Impactos para a Economia*. Núcleo do Conhecimento. https://www.nucleodoconhecimento.com.br/tecnologia/blockchain

Di Vaio, A., & Varriale, L. (2020). Blockchain technology in supply chain management for sustainable performance: Evidence from the airport industry. *International Journal of Information Management*, *52*, 102014. doi:10.1016/j.ijinfomgt.2019.09.010

Dogru, T., Mody, M., & Leonardi, C. (2018). *Blockchain technology & its implications for the Hospitality Industry*. Boston University.

Dudin, M. N., Burkaltseva, D. D., Tsohla, S. Y., Voronin, I. N., Yanovskaya, A. A., & Guk, O. A. (2017). Peculiarities of sustainable tourism development in the Russian Federation. *Journal of Environmental Management & Tourism*, *8*(24), 1559–1566.

Filimonau, V., & Naumova, E. (2020). The blockchain technology and the scope of its application in hospitality operations. *International Journal of Hospitality Management*, *87*, 102383. doi:10.1016/j.ijhm.2019.102383

Gjerding, K. (2017, March 28). *How blockchain technology will dominate the travel sector*. Retrieved from https://www.forbes.com/sites/forbesfinancecouncil/2017/03/28/how-blockchain-technology-will-dominate-the-travel-sector/#3b9dae4d9de5

Goudarzi, H., & Martin, J. I. (2018). *Blockchain in aviation*. Retrieved from International Air Transport Association. https://www.iata.org/contentassets/2d997082f3c84c7cba001f506edd2c2e/

Gretzel, U., Sigala, M., Xiang, Z., & Koo, C. (2015). Smart tourism: Foundations and developments. *Electronic Markets*, *25*(3), 179–188. doi:10.100712525-015-0196-8

Hawlitschek, F., Notheisen, B., & Teubner, T. (2018). The limits of trust-free systems: A literature review on blockchain technology and trust in the sharing economy. *Electronic Commerce Research and Applications*, *29*, 50–63. doi:10.1016/j.elerap.2018.03.005

Hjalager, A. M. (2010). A review of innovation research in tourism. *Tourism Management*, *31*(1), 1–12. doi:10.1016/j.tourman.2009.08.012

HTNG. (2018). *Blockchain for hospitality*. Retrieved from Hospitality Technology Next Generation. https://www.hospitalitynet.org/file/152008497.pdf

Irvin, C., & Sullivan, J. (2018). *Using blockchain to streamline airline finance*. Retrieved from Deloitte Development LLC website: https://www2.deloitte.com/us/en/pages/consulting/articles/airlines-blockchain-finance.html

Kwok, A. O., & Koh, S. G. (2019). Is blockchain technology a watershed for tourism development? *Current Issues in Tourism*, *22*(20), 2447–2452. doi:10.1080/13683500.2018.1513460

Lane, M. (2007). The Visitor Journey: The new road to success. *International Journal of Contemporary Hospitality Management*, *19*(3), 248–254. doi:10.1108/09596110710739949

Larchet, V. (2017). *Blockchain: solution for the black market threat to the tourism industry*. Retrieved from SecuTix website: https://www.secutix.com/wp-content/uploads/2017/

Lee, J., Bagheri, B., & Kao, H. A. (2015). A cyber-physical systems architecture for industry 4.0-based manufacturing systems. *Manufacturing Letters*, *3*, 18–23. doi:10.1016/j.mfglet.2014.12.001

Lemon, K. N., & Verhoef, P. C. (2016). Understanding customer experience throughout the customer journey. *Journal of Marketing*, *80*(6), 69–96. doi:10.1509/jm.15.0420

Leung, D., & Dickinger, A. (2017). Use of Bitcoin in online travel product shopping: The European perspective. In *Information and communication technologies in tourism* (pp. 741–754). Springer. (Original work published 2017)

Ludeiro, A. R. (2018, June). Blockchain technology for luggage tracking. In *International Symposium on Distributed Computing and Artificial Intelligence* (pp. 451-456). Springer, Cham.

Manzari, M., Kazemi, M., Nazemi, S., & Pooya, A. (2012). Intellectual capital: Concepts, components and indicators: A literature review. *Management Science Letters*, *2*(7), 2255–2270. doi:10.5267/j.msl.2012.07.018

Nabben, A., Wetzel, E., Oldani, E., Huyeng, J., Boel, M., & Fan, Z. (2016). Smart technologies in tourism: Case study on the influence of iBeacons on customer experience during the 2015 SAIL Amsterdam event. *International Tourism Student Conference*, 1-32.

Nakamoto, S. (2019). *Bitcoin: A peer-to-peer electronic cash system*. Manubot. https://git.dhimmel.com/bitcoin-whitepaper/

Nam, K., Dutt, C. S., Chathoth, P., & Khan, M. S. (2019). Blockchain technology for smart city and smart tourism: Latest trends and challenges. *Asia Pacific Journal of Tourism Research*, *24*(5), 71–87. doi:10.1080/10941665.2019.1585376

Nasarre-Aznar, S. (2018). Collaborative housing and blockchain. *Administration*, *66*(2), 59–82. doi:10.2478/admin-2018-0018

Newman, D. (2019). How Blockchain Is Changing Digital Marketing. *Forbes*. https://www.forbes.com/sites/danielnewman/2019/09/18/how-blockchain-is-changing-digital-marketing/?sh=5ed0b1d416eb

Nuryyev, G., Wang, Y. P., Achyldurdyyeva, J., Jaw, B. S., Yeh, Y. S., Lin, H. T., & Wu, L. F. (2020). Blockchain Technology Adoption Behavior and Sustainability of the Business in Tourism and Hospitality SMEs: An Empirical Study. *Sustainability*, *12*(3), 1256. doi:10.3390u12031256

Önder, I., & Treiblmaier, H. (2018). Blockchain and tourism: Three research propositions. *Annals of Tourism Research*, *72*(C), 180–182. doi:10.1016/j.annals.2018.03.005

Pilkington, M. (2017). *Can blockchain technology help promote new tourism destinations? The example of medical tourism in Moldova*. Academic Press.

Pilkington, M., Crudu, R., & Grant, L. G. (2017). Blockchain and bitcoin as a way to lift a country out of poverty-tourism 2.0 and e-governance in the Republic of Moldova. *International Journal of Internet Technology and Secured Transactions*, *7*(2), 115–143. doi:10.1504/IJITST.2017.087132

Polasik, M., Piotrowska, A. I., Wisniewski, T. P., Kotkowski, R., & Lightfoot, G. (2015). Price fluctuations and the use of Bitcoin: An empirical inquiry. *International Journal of Electronic Commerce*, *20*(1), 9–49. doi:10.1080/10864415.2016.1061413

Ramos, C. M. Q., & Brito, I. S. (2020). The Effects of Industry 4.0 in Tourism and Hospitality and Future Trends in Portugal. In A. Hassan & A. Sharma (Eds.), *The Emerald Handbook of ICT in Tourism and Hospitality* (pp. 367–378). Emerald Publishing Limited. doi:10.1108/978-1-83982-688-720201023

Rashideh, W. (2020). Blockchain technology framework: Current and future perspectives for the tourism industry. *Tourism Management*, *80*, 104125. doi:10.1016/j.tourman.2020.104125

Reagan, J. R., & Singh, M. (2020). Transportation, Travel, and Tourism Evolution. In *Management 4.0. Blockchain Technologies*. Springer.

Rejeb, A., & Karim, R. (2019). Blockchain technology in tourism: Applications and possibilities. *World Scientific News*, *137*, 119–144.

Saturno, M., Pertel, V. M., Deschamps, F., & Loures, E. D. F. (2017). Proposal of an automation solutions architecture for industry 4.0. In *Proceedings of the 24th International Conference on Production Research*. Poznan: ICPR.

SDG. (2019). *Sustainable Development Goals (SDG)*. Retrieved from: https://sustainabledevelopment.un.org/

Stalidis, G., Karapistolis, D., & Vafeiadis, A. (2015). Marketing decision support using Artificial Intelligence and Knowledge Modeling: Application to tourist destination management. *Procedia: Social and Behavioral Sciences*, *175*, 106–113. doi:10.1016/j.sbspro.2015.01.1180

Stickdorn, M., & Zehrer, A. (2009, November). Service design in tourism: Customer experience driven destination management. In *First Nordic conference on service design and service innovation* (pp. 1-16). Oslo: Academic Press.

Swan, M. (2015). *Blockchain: Blueprint for a new economy*. O'Reilly Media, Inc.

Tapscott, D., & Tapscott, A. (2016). Blockchain revolution: how the technology behind bitcoin is changing money; business; and the world. New York: Academic Press.

Tasatanattakool, P., & Techapanupreeda, C. (2018, January). Blockchain: Challenges and applications. In *2018 International Conference on Information Networking (ICOIN)* (pp. 473-475). IEEE. 10.1109/ICOIN.2018.8343163

Thees, H., Erschbamer, G., & Pechlaner, H. (2020). The application of blockchain in tourism: Use cases in the tourism value system. *European Journal of Tourism Research*, *26*, 2602–2602.

Treiblmaier, H. (2018). The impact of the blockchain on the supply chain: A theory-based research framework and a call for action. *Supply Chain Management*, *23*(6), 545–559. doi:10.1108/SCM-01-2018-0029

Treiblmaier, H. (2019). Toward more rigorous blockchain research: Recommendations for writing blockchain case studies. *Front Blockchain*, *2*(3), 1–15. doi:10.3389/fbloc.2019.00003

Treiblmaier, H. (2020). Blockchain and Tourism. Handbook of e-Tourism, 1-21. doi:10.1007/978-3-030-05324-6_28-1

Valeri, M., & Baggio, R. (2020). A critical reflection on the adoption of blockchain in tourism. *Information Technology & Tourism*, 1–12. doi:10.100740558-020-00183-1

Wüst, K., & Gervais, A. (2018). *Do you need a blockchain? In: 2018 Crypto valley conference on blockchain technology*. CVCBT. doi:10.1109/CVCBT.2018.00011

Xu, L. D., Xu, E. L., & Li, L. (2018). Industry 4.0: State of the art and future trends. *International Journal of Production Research*, *56*(8), 2941–2962. doi:10.1080/00207543.2018.1444806

Zhang, N., Zhong, S., & Tian, L. (2017). Using blockchain to protect personal privacy in the scenario of online taxi-hailing. *International Journal of Computers, Communications & Control*, *12*(6), 886–902. doi:10.15837/ijccc.2017.6.2886

Chapter 7
Developing a Model to Highlight the Relation of Digital Trust With Privacy and Security for the Blockchain Technology

Subhodeep Mukherjee
GITAM University, India

Venkataiah Chittipaka
https://orcid.org/0000-0002-7804-0796
GITAM University, India

Manish Mohan Baral
Birla Institute of Technology, India

ABSTRACT

Digitalization uses digital technology to change a business model and provide new revenue models and value-producing opportunities. Blockchain is a type of database that stores various kinds of information in blocks that form a chain of information. It is one of the secured ways of transferring and storage of data. Blockchain is helping in creating trust for digitalization among its users. This research aims to study the impact of trust in blockchain by analyzing the privacy and security concerns that can impact the user attitude and its intention to the adoption process. For this structure, literature review is performed. Five variables are used, and they are attitude, privacy, trust, security, and intention. A questionnaire is developed for survey-based research in the software firms, banking sector, and digital marketing companies. For analysis, exploratory factor analysis and structural equation modeling are used. A model is developed that shows a good fit, and the parameters are satisfied.

DOI: 10.4018/978-1-7998-8081-3.ch007

INTRODUCTION

Over the last few years, blockchains (BC) have undergone exponential growth (Kshetri, 2018). BC applications range from healthcare, banking, transport, risk management, and media to public and social services, as BC goes beyond being just another buzzword (Grover et al., 2019). Addressing the security risks affecting BC seems to be the key to further development (D. H. Shin, 2017). The success of BC has been a critical problem in maintaining privacy and protection in BC (Du et al., 2019). There is an absence of exploration on security in BC, notwithstanding the expanding weakness issue, prompting a restricted comprehension of what security issues and trust mean for the BC experience. How many clients trust the administrations, cooperation's, and associations behind them becomes progressively critical as BC develops (Bancroft and Scott Reid, 2017). As clients collaborate with BC, they expect the merchandise they have paid to acquire, and their information won't be controlled (D. Shin & Ibahrine, 2020). Even though unmistakably trust matters in computerized settings, there has been an absence of explanation concerning what trust is, how it works/can be set up, and what advanced trust comprises. Various research has inspected client protection issues and firm assurance rehearses in a complex mechanical setting. It has stayed obscure how parts of protection/security influence an individual's psychological acknowledgment measure in the advancing BC setting (Casino et al., 2019). BC innovation is crucial for security and protection since it can work without an affirmed outsider. BC security issues are firmly associated with protection worries in BC (Kshetri, 2018). It isn't put away in an isolated area, while dispersed record innovation is scrambled. Firms don't have complete oversight over the subtleties. User data could be diverted via several servers when stored in BC due to this decentralized structure (Coita et al., 2019). In a BC, data is vulnerable, and other entities in the chain may access it. When information is deliberately or erroneously encrypted before being sent to a chain, no one can access it unless decoded (Fortuna & Risso, 2019). BC transactions are vulnerable to hacking through chain nodes, despite privacy-enhancing technologies. For this study, five variables are being used and they are attitude (AT), privacy (PR), trust (TR), security (SEC), and intention (IN).

The research questions that will be addressed are:

RQ1: Is BC addressing the trust issues of the users.
RQ2: How much secured is the usage of BC?
RQ3: Whether BC is providing privacy to its users?

The further chapter is arranged as follows section two describes the literature review, followed by section three research hypotheses, followed by section four research methodology, followed by section five results, followed by section six.

LITERATURE REVIEW

Overview of Blockchain Technology

BC is a technology for Decentralized Transaction and Data Management. This includes a ledger that maintains an ongoing collection of data records. BC can be viewed as a decentralized registration database and an accounting system, with many use cases, including registration, inventory, and any asset exchange (Longo et al., 2019). With remarkable and disruptive potential to redefine vast sections of our financial system and modify specific basic frameworks of how the economy is treated, BC has been prescribed. BC is often compared to the advent of the internet and its extensive effect on almost every industry to highlight the potential of this (Agbo & Mahmoud, 2020). What distinguishes technology is that it allows trust to emerge from intelligent code that has never been effective in history before (Tapscott & Kaplan, 2019). The evidence mechanism of all transactions on the network that removes the need for any third-party broker is a critical element of innovation in the BC, as users put confidence in the consensus algorithm instead (Beck et al., 2017). They have significant value through a greater degree of objectivity and proven faith (Dai et al., 2019). BC technology threatens an established business model with these elements, which depend on third parties to verify and trust (Macrinici et al., 2018).

Transaction data for a given period are registered into a block and added in a linear sequential order to the BC starting from the genesis block (the block containing the very first transaction). To guarantee that all blocks remain legitimate and are not tampered with, hashing algorithms are in place (Melkić & Čavlek, 2020). Essentially, the BC consists of blocks linked to the previous one, each containing a transaction list. Deciding the block is added and what BC current state is selected via the consensus process, which is also determined based on a BC network in which one works, something discussed in the next portion. Each block on the BC is in chronological order, so the BC contains a complete history of all transactions (Pournader et al., 2020).

Blockchain for Digital Trust

BC technology's social effects are enormous. It has also allowed people in vulnerable socio-economic circumstances to access micropayments and microloans (D. D. H.

Shin, 2019). The technology of BC provides a meaningful opportunity to identify a way through the problems of fraud. The BC and smart contracts' decentralized features mean that no separate party is required for an agreement based on its platform (Fernández-Caramés & Fraga-Lamas, 2018). In innovative agreements, it is feasible to add clauses that state that commitments are fulfilled if such outcomes are achieved (Willie, 2019). It is also possible to use innovative agreements to control the circulation of currency. Organizations are expanding their BC ventures to change the products and enterprises that are dispersed, acquire new experiences to gain the upper hand, and lift their monetary and operational proficiency (Marsal-Llacuna, 2018). The assurance of buyer information and business and exchange records is reinforced because BC record records are encoded, consecutive, and changeless. The trust-based framework is the weakest point for BC (Kshetri, 2018). BC data and assets are available to abuse by programmers or unfamiliar specialists, and individual information isn't characteristically private. Security-related issues are essential factors in assessing the BC economy's practicality as the BC fills in different fields of various spaces (Sadhya & Sadhya, 2018). The eventual fate of computerized exchanges in the advanced information economy will keep on moving BC and change the quintessence of advanced trust (D. Shin & Bianco, 2020). Digital BC trust can be described as allowing user heuristics that reflect their level of trust between security and privacy (Park et al., 2018).

We find some consequences for companies in our attempt to conceptualize the BC. BC makes major transformations possible (Kaur et al., 2018). Cash is becoming digital. The company is going to become collaborative. Agreements would be immutable between parties. Smart contracts and self-executing software are the laws of business operations (Prause, 2019). The companies are distributed across the network. The contractors become shareholders. The properties and the goods will become companies. The need for any requirements or even institutions of current companies would be removed by BC (Rohmah et al., 2020).

RESEARCH HYPOTHESIS

Since BC-based platforms provide numerous revolutionary features, it is essential to understand users' preferences, how they are generated, and how the understood affirmation of users impacts satisfaction, affecting intentions (J. S. Kim & Shin, 2019). The theory explains how human behaviors and subjective norms establish or trigger behavioral intent (S., 2017).

Security (SEC): Given the rising concerns regarding BC protection (Kamble et al., 2019), this study discusses the effect of users' recognized SEC on the plan to adopt BC. Perceived safety is the degree to which users feel safe and secure to do stuff in such circumstances. It is possible to regard subjective protection as the reflective picture of risk affinity. A mediated online network's SEC might not be based on technological security aspects alone. The most profound reason for a failure to implement technical services may be low subjective protection (Mou et al., 2017). Continuous research has been undertaken to conceptualize and theorize a set of variables that explain the position of subjective safety (Vidan & Lehdonvirta, 2019).

H1. SEC positively impacts the TR of its users in the adoption of blockchain.
H2. SEC positively impacts users' AT for blockchain adoption.

Privacy of the users (PR): PR is essential in BC, similar to perceived security. PR is seen in this study as the extent to which a consumer assumes that their data is secure and will not be misused. PR is sometimes used interchangeably with the security issue (D. Kim et al., 2019). One of the most critical challenges in diverse technical environments is information protection. The definition of privacy was conceived as a user's ability to handle and control the circumstances under which their personal information is collected and processed (Rios et al., 2018). Distributed ledger features, BC services influence expectations of the privacy guarantee of service (J. S. Kim & Shin, 2019). Exchanging procedures for obtaining knowledge increases the feelings of protection and confidence of users (Klinger et al., 2018).

H3. PR positively impacts the TR of the users in the adoption of blockchain.
H4. PR positively impacts users' AT for blockchain adoption.

Trust (TR): Trust is a core aspect of BC applications (D. D. H. Shin, 2019). TR is suggested as a critical element in this regard. Trust is viewed as a guaranteed reliance on the character or expertise of a client's eagerness to be defenseless against another client's activities dependent on the understanding that a specific movement would be done by the other. Trust has been reliably discovered to be a primary factor in trades, including danger in online settings. Internet business and computerized innovation research has reliably discovered that trust is emphatically connected to customer acknowledgment (Mou & Shin, 2018). The more astounding clients' trust in the online help, the less exertion it will take for clients to check such administrations to determine their existence and authenticity. Since confidence in advanced media and innovation has as of late been viewed as a crucial issue (D. Shin & Biocca, 2018), it is fundamental to research whether trust influences a BC administration.

H5. TR positively impacts users' AT for blockchain adoption.

Attitude for blockchain adoption (AT): Their social expectation impacts individuals' activity to lead the conduct, and the conduct aim is influenced by the mentalities of an individual (D.-H. Shin, 2013). As the immediate predecessor of conduct, the social object is the intellectual sign of human availability to play out given behavior (Glaser, 2017). Per TRA, the disposition towards conduct is communicated as a person's trust in the objective conduct's exhibition. Their convictions and evaluations direct the mentality of an individual towards the activity. Since the TRA has been broadly applied to different innovative settings, especially arising advances, the TRA's principal premises likewise apply to a BC setting.

H6. AT has a positive impact on the IN.

RESEARCH METHODOLOGY

Responses were collected through a structured questionnaire from the employees of the software companies, banking sector, and digital marketing firms operating in India. The sample was selected from each strata through the Random Sampling method as it allows population harmony from the subpopulation (Hair et al. 2010). The questionnaires were sent to 559 respondents, but only 315 respondents returned usable questionnaires, valid for analysis. To avoid a common method, bias the research team has taken few fundamental precautions during the pre-data collection stage. At the beginning of the questionnaire, a note indicated the survey is intended for academic research, and data confidentiality will be maintained.

In the gathered dataset, the first cleansing was finished by case screening, trailed by factor screening so clarification can be given to the variety in the information. It is a need to follow this cycle so that there were no missing qualities in the dataset. From the information cleaning measure, it was reasoned that the disappeared qualities were extraordinarily sparse, and in this way, they were not viewed as a principal supporter of any predisposition. No cases were therefore removed. However, after the data is collected, the research team applied Harman's single factor test. Exploratory factor analysis was performed, and the results show that the first factor explains maximum variance (37.083%) below the recommended value of 50% (Podsakoff et al., 2003).

Table 1 below shows the demographics of the respondents. A questionnaire method was used. Respondent's characteristics for gender 57% were male respondents followed by 43% female respondents. Respondents' working firms were 43% from software firms, followed by 30% digital marketing companies, followed by 27% banking firms.

Table 1. Demographics of the respondents

Sl. No.	Characteristics	Percentage
I	**Gender**	
A	Male	57
B	Female	43
II	**Respondents Working Firms**	
A	Software Firms	43
B	Banking Firms	27
C	Digital Marketing Companies	30

RESULTS

Reliability and Validity

The reliability test was performed for each factor based on Cronbach's alpha (α) value introduces Cronbach's alpha for the constructs. The importance of all indicators or dimensional scales should be above the recommended value of 0.70 (Nunnally and Bernstein, 1994). Utilization of 7 points Likert scale was done in preparing the structured questionnaire. For analyzing the information collected, SPSS 20.0 and Amos 22.0 was used. The variable SEC has four indicators SEC1, SEC2, SEC3, and SEC4, and its α value is 0.823; TR has three indicators TR1, TR2, and TR3, and its α value is 0.839; PR has three indicators PR1, PR2, and PR3, and its α value is 0.840; AT has four indicators AT1, AT2, AT3, and AT4, and its α value is 0.850. Hence, all the values are within the threshold. Composite reliability (C.R.) was also measured for the entire component. The variable SEC has CR value 0.882; TR has CR value 0.898; PR has CR value 0.903; AT has CR value 0.893. The five constructs' C.R. values are > 0.7, indicating that the composite reliability measures are reliable (Hair et al. 2010).

Exploratory Factor Analysis (EFA)

Principal axis factoring was performed to identify meaningful bias and express the same qualities. The KMO value for this research is 0.851. The minimum level set for this statistic is 0.60 (Tabachnick & Fidell, 2007). The significance value is 0.000, which is less than 0.05, i.e., the probability value level acceptable. The extraction method used was principal axis factoring. Only the eigenvalues which have values greater than one are extracted as it explains maximum variance. For the components, the percentage of total variance explained by component 1 (40.181%), component

2 (12.291%), component 3 (10.266%), and component 4 (8.805%). The cumulative percentage of total variance explained by all four components is 71.544%. The Rotated Component Matrix is important for interpreting the results of the analysis. Rotation helps group the items, and each group contains more than one item at-least, which simplifies the structure. Hence, this is the aim of the goal of rotation. In this research, we have achieved this aim. This helps to identify the cross-loadings on more than one group, and then it can be corrected by removing those items which are cross-loaded. In this research, the loadings having less than |.40| are suppressed because loadings more than |.40| are typically considered high. So, in the end, we achieve a simple structure. Fourteen total variables were grouped under four various components. The rotation method used was varimax rotation. All the 14 variables listed were grouped under four multiple components. AT1, AT2, AT3, and AT4 are grouped under the first component with values of 0.816, 0.853, 0.854, and 0.761. SEC1, SEC2, SEC3, and SEC4 are grouped under the second component with values of 0.835, 0.787, 0.759, and 0.845. TR1, TR2, and TR3 are grouped under the third component with values of 0.811, 0.922, and 0.855. PR1, PR2, and PR3 are grouped under the fourth component with values of 0.839, 0.956, and 0.809.

Confirmatory factor analysis (CFA) was performed in the next stage, which constructs identified from the literature survey can be tested and how well the variables represent the constructs. Structural equation modeling (SEM) was used for testing the model fit of the proposed research model (Byrne, 2010). An extra thorough trial of build legitimacy is the purported factorial legitimacy, which depends on the factor investigation's aftereffects. Its primary role is to characterize their basic structures among its factors remembered for the examination. When their instrument shows the normal structures inside, this could have been demonstrative to construct validity (CV) (Moerdyk, 2009) and, explicitly, factorial validity.

Construct Validity

A significant logical idea to assess the validity of a measure to develop a CV. CV is the degree to which a test quantifies the concept or development expected to quantify. CV is generally tried by estimating the relationship in appraisals got from a few scales. No cut-off characterizes CV (DeVellis et al., 2003).

This research's primary goal was to analyze the structural components, a CV that includes investigating the interior connections among things or subscales speaking to a specific measure, utilizing such factual examinations as correlation, exploratory and confirmatory factor analysis, and reliability analysis.

To evaluate this validity, Fornell and Larcker (1981) suggested that the construct's average variance extracted (AVE) should be more than the square of the correlation between that construct and the other constructs. Table 2 represents the values for construct correlation and AVE. The variance extracted and squared correlation for AT and SEC is 0.662 and 0.243; AT and TR are 0.709 and 0.177; AT and PR are 0.714 and 0.169; SEC and TR are 0.697 and 0.193; SEC and PR are 0.702 and 0.088; TR and PR are 0.749 and 0.169. Hence, the value of variance extracted is more than the squared correlation value. As a result, divergent or discriminant validity is satisfied.

Table 2. Construct correlation and AVE

	AVE	Variance Extracted Between Factors			
		AT	SEC	TR	PR
AT	0.821	1			
SEC	0.807	0.662	1		
TR	0.863	0.709	0.697	1	
PR	0.868	0.714	0.702	0.749	1

Structural Equation Modeling

To test the hypothesis, SEM was used (Byrne, 2010). AMOS 22.0 was utilized for this research because of its powerful graphic representations and user-friendly interfaces. The results of the significant paths of the model are shown here. Figure 1 represent the final and latent variables and their indicators, mediating, and dependent variables. There are four latent variables. The latent variables along with its indicators are AT: Attitude has four indicators AT1, AT2, AT3, and AT4; PR: Privacy has three indicators PR1, PR2, and PR3; TR: Trust has three indicators TR1, TR2, and TR3; SEC: Security has four indicators SEC1, SEC2, SEC3, and SEC4. One dependent variable is IN: Intention, four indicators IN1, IN2, IN3, and IN4.

The value of chi-square is 422.435, and the degree of freedom is 129. The estimations of absolute fit indices are: CMIN/Df 3.275, CMIN represents the chi-square value, and Df represents the degree of freedom, and the value is less than 5, which is the accepted threshold value. The comparative fit index (CFI) is 0.901; Tucker-Lewis's coefficient (TLI) is 0.883; goodness of fit index (GFI) is 0.872; adjusted goodness of fit indices (AGFI) is 0.830; normed fit index (NFI) is 0.865, and incremental fit index (IFI) is 0.902 are having values in the threshold level and is acceptable (Byrne 2010).

Table 3 shows the path estimate analysis results. The result demonstrates the six hypotheses are supported by P-value (Hair et al. 2010). The multiple square correlations (R^2) measure how well a regression line estimates the real data points between 0 and 1, which states how well one variable predicts another (Hair et al.

2010). More the value closer to 1 better is the model's ability to predict technology (Kline, 2015).

Figure 1. Model showing relation of digital trust

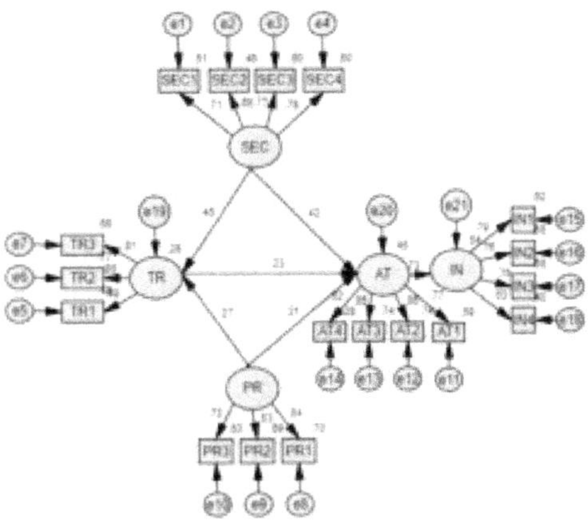

Table 3. Structural model results

	Estimate	S.E.	C.R.	P	Hypothesis
TR<---PR	0.216	0.049	4.385	0.000	Supported
TR<---SEC	0.554	0.087	6.372	0.000	Supported
AT<---TR	0.325	0.096	3.398	0.000	Supported
AT<---SEC	0.721	0.122	5.927	0.000	Supported
AT<---PR	0.347	0.066	5.232	0.000	Supported
IN<---AT	0.518	0.049	10.67	0.000	Supported

DISCUSSION

Firms operating in a digital mode need to provide digital trust for their users. Users will get digital trust if the technology is secured, reliable, and privacy for the information being shared (Agbo & Mahmoud, 2020). This research aims to find out the impact of digital trust in BC adoption on users. BC technology is one of the latest innovative technology which provides proper security and transparency to the systems (Kshetri, 2017). BC technology is being used in many industries like finance, supply chain, manufacturing, etc. (Grover et al., 2019). BC in digital marketing provides transparency, security, and accessibility of monetary and data flows. It is forming a direct data exchange between consumers and brands.

The four components' Cronbach's alpha and composite reliability values were above 0.7, which is the recommended level (Nunnally 1978; Hair et al. 2010) for the four factors. The construct's KMO value is 0.851, which is also above the recommended level of 0.6 (Hair et al. 2010), which allows the data for factor analysis. The total variance explained was 71.544%, and in the rotated component matrix, the variables were grouped under four groups. Only the loadings which are above |.40| are considered in this research because those are considered to be typically high and hence are more significant (Hair et al. 2010). For further analysis in this research, four components were utilized. The component AT stands for Attitude. AT states the point of view for adopting BC by considering three aspects privacy, trust, and security. It comprises four sub-components AT1, AT2, AT3, and AT4 with values of 0.816, 0.853, 0.854, and 0.761, which shows that it has very high loadings (>|.40|). The component PR stands for Privacy. PR refers that how much secured is th information is that will be shared. Users need to have privacy in their systems (D. D. H. Shin, 2019). It comprises three sub-components PR1, PR2, and PR3, with values of 0.839, 0.956, and 0.809, which show very high loadings (>|.40|). The component TR stands Trust. This plays a significant role in any technological innovation action as users cannot accept anything without trust. The technical providers need to make the systems trust it (Antoniadis et al., 2019). It comprises three sub-components TR1, TR2, and TR3, with values of 0.811, 0.922, and 0.855, which show very high loadings (>|.40|). The component SEC stands for Security. This has to be provided by the service providers to have their data in a secured platform (Coita et al., 2019). The acceptance rate will be low if the platform is not much secured. It comprises four indicators: SEC1, SEC2, SEC3, and SEC4 with values of 0.835, 0.787, 0.759, and 0.845, which shows very high loadings (>|.40|). Based on EFA, the SEM was performed in AMOS 22.0. The value of chi-square is 422.435, and the degree of freedom is 129. The estimations of absolute fit indices are: CMIN/Df 3.275, CMIN represents the chi-square value, and Df represents the degree of freedom, and the value is less than 5, which is the accepted threshold value. The comparative fit index (CFI) is 0.901; Tucker-Lewis's coefficient (TLI) is 0.883; goodness of fit index (GFI) is 0.872; adjusted goodness of fit indices (AGFI) is 0.830; normed fit index (NFI) is 0.865, and incremental fit index (IFI) is 0.902 are having values in the threshold level and is acceptable (Byrne 2010). Also, in the final structural model, the TR and PR was supported ($\beta = .216$, $p = .000$); the TR and SEC was supported ($\beta = .554$, $p = .000$); the AT and TR was supported ($\beta = .325$, $p = .000$); the AT and SEC was supported ($\beta = .721$, $p = .000$); the AT and PR was supported ($\beta = .347$, $p = .000$); the IN and AT was supported ($\beta = .518$, $p = .000$) in the current study. The current research will also serve as a base for conducting future research using the SEM approach in several other segments and other nations' perspectives.

CONCLUSION

This research aims to study the impact of trust in BC by analyzing the privacy and security concerns that can impact user attitude and intention to adopt. A structured literature review is being performed using various databases. SEC, PR, TR are identified as the main drivers for AT. A questionnaire was developed for survey-based research in various sectors. The target population was mainly the employees working in these firms. Firms taken for a survey are software companies, the banking sector, and digital marketing firms operating in India. We performed exploratory factor analysis from the data collected, which helped group the variables, and then structural equation modeling was performed. A model was developed which satisfied all the parameters. The proposed hypothesis for the study was accepted.

REFERENCES

Agbo, C. C., & Mahmoud, Q. H. (2020). Blockchain in Healthcare. *International Journal of Healthcare Information Systems and Informatics, 15*(3), 82–97. doi:10.4018/IJHISI.2020070105

Antoniadis, Kontsas, & Spinthiropoulos. (2019). Blockchain Applications in Marketing. *7th International Conference on Contemporary Marketing,* 1–7. https://www.researchgate.net/publication/337439697_Blockchain_Applications_in_Marketing

Beck, R., Avital, M., Rossi, M., & Thatcher, J. B. (2017). Blockchain Technology in Business and Information Systems Research. *Business & Information Systems Engineering*, *59*(6), 381–384. doi:10.100712599-017-0505-1

Casino, F., Dasaklis, T. K., & Patsakis, C. (2019). A systematic literature review of blockchain-based applications: Current status, classification and open issues. In *Telematics and Informatics* (Vol. 36, pp. 55–81). Elsevier Ltd., doi:10.1016/j.tele.2018.11.006

Coita, D. C., Abrudan, M. M., & Matei, M. C. (2019). *Effects of the Blockchain Technology on Human Resources and Marketing: An Exploratory Study*. doi:10.1007/978-3-030-12453-3_79

Dai, H. N., Zheng, Z., & Zhang, Y. (2019). Blockchain for Internet of Things: A Survey. *IEEE Internet of Things Journal, 6*(5), 8076–8094. doi:10.1109/JIOT.2019.2920987

Du, W., Pan, S. L., Leidner, D. E., & Ying, W. (2019). Affordances, experimentation and actualization of FinTech: A blockchain implementation study. *The Journal of Strategic Information Systems, 28*(1), 50–65. doi:10.1016/j.jsis.2018.10.002

Fernández-Caramés, T. M., & Fraga-Lamas, P. (2018). A Review on the Use of Blockchain for the Internet of Things. *IEEE Access: Practical Innovations, Open Solutions, 6*, 32979–33001. doi:10.1109/ACCESS.2018.2842685

Fortuna, F., & Risso, M. (2019). Blockchain Technology in the Food Industry. *Symphonya. Emerging Issues in Management, 2*(2), 151. doi:10.4468/2019.2.13fortuna.risso

Glaser, F. (n.d.). *Pervasive Decentralisation of Digital Infrastructures: A Framework for Blockchain enabled System and Use Case Analysis*. Retrieved February 16, 2021, from https://github.com/ethereum/wiki

Grover, P., Kar, A. K., Janssen, M., & Ilavarasan, P. V. (2019). Perceived usefulness, ease of use and user acceptance of blockchain technology for digital transactions–insights from user-generated content on Twitter. *Enterprise Information Systems, 13*(6), 771–800. doi:10.1080/17517575.2019.1599446

Kamble, S., Gunasekaran, A., & Arha, H. (2019). Understanding the Blockchain technology adoption in supply chains-Indian context. *International Journal of Production Research, 57*(7), 2009–2033. doi:10.1080/00207543.2018.1518610

Kaur, P., Sharma, M., & Mittal, M. (2018). Big Data and Machine Learning Based Secure Healthcare Framework. *Procedia Computer Science, 132*, 1049–1059. doi:10.1016/j.procs.2018.05.020

Kim, D., Park, K., Park, Y., & Ahn, J. H. (2019). Willingness to provide personal information: Perspective of privacy calculus in IoT services. *Computers in Human Behavior, 92*, 273–281. doi:10.1016/j.chb.2018.11.022

Kim, J. S., & Shin, N. (2019). The impact of blockchain technology application on supply chain partnership and performance. *Sustainability (Switzerland), 11*(21), 6181. Advance online publication. doi:10.3390u11216181

Klinger, U., & Svensson, J. (2018). The End of Media Logics? On Algorithms and Agency. *Journals.Sagepub. Com, 20*(12), 4653–4670. doi:10.1177/1461444818779750

Kshetri, N. (2017). Blockchain's roles in strengthening cybersecurity and protecting privacy. *Telecommunications Policy*, *41*(10), 1027–1038. doi:10.1016/j.telpol.2017.09.003

Kshetri, N. (2018). 1 Blockchain's roles in meeting key supply chain management objectives. *International Journal of Information Management*, *39*, 80–89. doi:10.1016/j.ijinfomgt.2017.12.005

Longo, F., Nicoletti, L., Padovano, A., d'Atri, G., & Forte, M. (2019). Blockchain-enabled supply chain: An experimental study. *Computers & Industrial Engineering*, *136*(July), 57–69. doi:10.1016/j.cie.2019.07.026

Macrinici, D., Cartofeanu, C., & Gao, S. (2018). Smart contract applications within blockchain technology: A systematic mapping study. In Telematics and Informatics (Vol. 35, Issue 8, pp. 2337–2354). Elsevier Ltd. doi:10.1016/j.tele.2018.10.004

Marsal-Llacuna, M. L. (2018). Future living framework: Is blockchain the next enabling network? *Technological Forecasting and Social Change*, *128*, 226–234. doi:10.1016/j.techfore.2017.12.005

Melkić, S., & Čavlek, N. (2020). The impact of blockchain technology on tourism intermediation. *Tourism (Zagreb)*, *68*(2), 130–143. doi:10.37741/t.68.2.2

Mou, J., & Shin, D. (2018). Effects of social popularity and time scarcity on online consumer behaviour regarding smart healthcare products: An eye-tracking approach. *Computers in Human Behavior*, *78*, 74–89. doi:10.1016/j.chb.2017.08.049

Mou, J., Shin, D.-H., & Cohen, J. F. (2017). Trust and risk in consumer acceptance of e-services. *Electronic Commerce Research*, *17*(2), 255–288. doi:10.100710660-015-9205-4

Park, Y. J., Chung, J. E., & Shin, D. H. (2018). The Structuration of Digital Ecosystem, Privacy, and Big Data Intelligence. *The American Behavioral Scientist*, *62*(10), 1319–1337. doi:10.1177/0002764218787863

Pournader, M., Shi, Y., Seuring, S., & Koh, S. C. L. (2020). Blockchain applications in supply chains, transport and logistics: A systematic review of the literature. *International Journal of Production Research*, *58*(7), 2063–2081. doi:10.1080/00207543.2019.1650976

Prause, G. (2019). Smart contracts for smart supply chains. *IFAC-PapersOnLine*, *52*(13), 2501–2506. doi:10.1016/j.ifacol.2019.11.582

Rios, R., Fernandez-Gago, C., & Lopez, J. (2018). Modelling privacy-aware trust negotiations. *Computers & Security*, *77*, 773–789. doi:10.1016/j.cose.2017.09.015

Rohmah, D., Maharani, S., Kholis, M., Taqwa, S., & Setyaningrum, H. (2020).. . *Traceability and Tracking Systems of Halal Food Using Blockchain Technology to Improve Food Industry Competitiveness., c*. Advance online publication. doi:10.4108/eai.13-2-2019.2286199

S., S. (2017). Factors Influencing the Adoption of Cloud Computing by Saudi University Hospitals. *International Journal of Advanced Computer Science and Applications, 8*(1), 41–48. doi:10.14569/IJACSA.2017.080107

Sadhya, V., & Sadhya, H. (2018). Barriers to Adoption of Blockchain Technology. *Proceedings of the 24th Americas Conference on Information Systems*, 1–10.

Shin, D., & Bianco, W. T. (2020). In Blockchain We Trust: Does Blockchain Itself Generate Trust? *Social Science Quarterly, 101*(7), 2522–2538. doi:10.1111squ.12917

Shin, D., & Biocca, F. (2018). Exploring immersive experience in journalism. *New Media & Society, 20*(8), 2800–2823. doi:10.1177/1461444817733133

Shin, D., & Ibahrine, M. (2020). The socio-technical assemblages of blockchain system: How blockchains are framed and how the framing reflects societal contexts. *Digital Policy. Regulation & Governance, 22*(3), 245–263. doi:10.1108/DPRG-11-2019-0095

Shin, D. D. H. (2019). Blockchain: The emerging technology of digital trust. *Telematics and Informatics, 45*(September), 101278. Advance online publication. doi:10.1016/j.tele.2019.101278

Shin, D.-H. (2013). User experience in social commerce: In friends we trust. *Behaviour & Information Technology, 32*(1), 52–67. doi:10.1080/0144929X.2012.692167

Shin, D. H. (2017). Conceptualizing and measuring quality of experience of the internet of things: Exploring how quality is perceived by users. *Information & Management, 54*(8), 998–1011. doi:10.1016/j.im.2017.02.006

Tapscott, D., & Kaplan, A. (2019). *Blockchain Revolution in Education and LifeLong Learning: Preparing for Disruption, Leading the Transformation*. www.blockchainresearchinstitute.org/contact-us

Vidan, G., & Lehdonvirta, V. (2019). Mine the gap: Bitcoin and the maintenance of trustlessness. *Journals.Sagepub.Com, 21*(1), 42–59. doi:10.1177/1461444818786220

Willie, P. (2019). Can all sectors of the hospitality and tourism industry be influenced by the innovation of Blockchain technology? *Worldwide Hospitality and Tourism Themes, 11*(2), 112–120. doi:10.1108/WHATT-11-2018-0077

APPENDIX

Table 4. Measurement item details

Constructs	Indicators	Measurement Items	Source
Security	SEC1	I believe that blockchains are processed with the relevant data I provide.	(Grover et al., 2019)
	SEC2	I am confident that I will secure my private information.	
	SEC3	I believe that the information I provide with blockchains can be viewed only by legitimate parties.	(Grover et al., 2019)
	SEC4	Blockchain is one of the most secured platforms to share data	
Privacy of the users	PR1	I'm sure that I know everyone who gathers the information I provide when using blockchains.	(D. Kim et al., 2019)
	PR2	I know the exact nature of the information gathered during blockchain use.	(D. Kim et al., 2019)
	PR3	I am not concerned about the possibility of misuse of the information that I provided on the blockchains.	(D. Kim et al., 2019)
Trust	TR1	Blockchain is a reliable service	(D. D. H. Shin, 2019)
	TR2	To protect my privacy, I can depend on blockchains.	(D. D. H. Shin, 2019)
	TR3	User can rely on Blockchain to fulfil its promises.	
Attitude for blockchain adoption	AT1	I would generally have positive feelings for blockchains.	(D. D. H. Shin, 2019)
	AT2	I am appealing to the idea of using blockchains.	(D. H. Shin, 2017)
	AT3	Using blockchains would be a good idea.	(D. H. Shin, 2017)
	AT4	Top management has a positive attitude in the usage of blockchain	
Intention	IN1	In the future, I plan to use blockchains.	(D. H. Shin, 2017)
	IN2	I plan as far as possible to visit blockchains websites.	(D. H. Shin, 2017)
	IN3	In the future, I intend to use blockchains.	(D. H. Shin, 2017)
	IN4	At present we are using some of the applications of blockchain	

Chapter 8
Design Family Health Management System Based on Ethereum Blockchain Interaction With MyEtherWallet Using Solidity

Devi Parameswari C.
Kalasalingam Academy of Research and Education, India

Ilayaraja M.
Kalasalingam Academy of Research and Education, India

ABSTRACT

A family health management system deals with a safe and secure way of managing family member health details such as illness diagnosis, treatment, medical prescriptions, medical reports, and life insurance policies. All health records are encrypted and stored in chronological order utilizing blockchain technology so that authenticity, integrity, security, and privacy of the records are safeguarded. All stages of medical treatment are documented and stored for ease of future reference by the family. This becomes very handy if a person changes doctors and/or relocates to some other place/country for varied reasons. All the necessary health reports are shared with the life insurance company so that insurance claims become hassle free, if applicable. Medicine details are cross-verified with the manufactures to avoid fake drugs. This chapter explores the compatibility of using ethereum with the interactive MyEtherWallet to implement the proposed model.

DOI: 10.4018/978-1-7998-8081-3.ch008

INTRODUCTION

Emerging technologies, as described by Industry 4.0, include emerging business and financial possibilities for healthcare networks. As per the Computing Technology Industry Association (CompTIA), the world's top 10 emerging innovations in 2019 were the Internet of Things (IoT), artificial intelligence, 5/6g Networks, server-less Computing, Blockchain, Robots, Biometry, 3D Printing, Augmented Reality/Virtual Reality, and Drones

Blockchain technology is a peer network for transferring digital assets and data without any hassle intermediate technologies and supports the popular crypto currency bitcoin. Bitcoin was first announced in 2008 and implemented by Nakamoto in 2009 (Rayome, 2019). The chain will continue to grow when new blocks are added. All transactions occur in a decentralized manner, eliminating the need for any intermediaries to verify transactions (Tsai et al., 2016). Blockchain has some key features, such as decentralization, transparency, variability and adaptability. Blockchain operates in a decentralized environment and employs digital signatures, cryptographic hash and distributed core technologies, consensus mechanisms.

Figure 1. Blockchain architecture

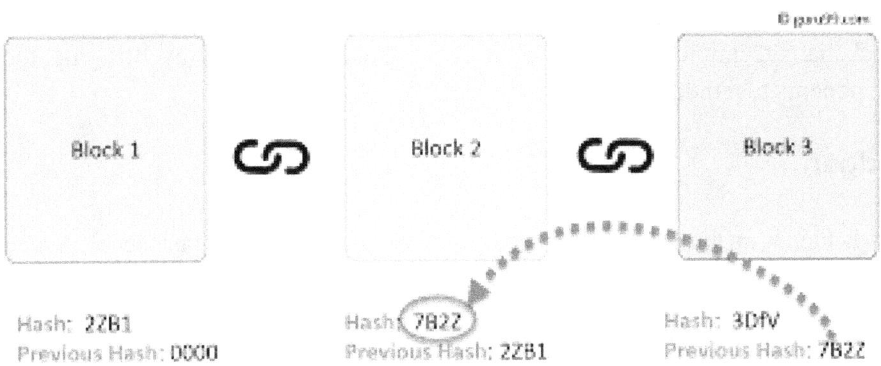

The blockchain network has a decentralized information system (Meng et al., 2018; Gipp et al., 2016) contain information about past transactions. It specifies the method for performing and checking transactions, as well as the overall functioning of the network and its participants (Mehdi et al., 2017). The term "distributed registry data" is often used to describe this network. Each node that works on a specific network is saved (Suveen et al., 2017; Ahram et al., 2017). The previous block hash record is used to connect transaction information to the chain on blockchain networks (Ovais, 2017).

Taxonomy of Blockchain Systems

Current blockchain networks are classified into four forms of blockchains: private, public and hybrid.

Public Blockchains: The public blockchains have a completely decentralized network, where all participants can access and participate in the consensus process blockchain material (e.g. Bitcoin and Ethereum.)

Private Blockchains: private block chains are used to track data transfers between various departments and individuals, who are devoted to single enterprise solutions. Each participant requires permission to be a member of the network as soon as it is a known member.

Consortium Blockchains: A blockchain consortium is a network approved and publicly accessible to a privileged community only. It can be used to track participant data exchanges as an auditable and securely synchronized distributed database.

Hybrid Blockchains: hybrid blockchains merge privately and publicly. A public blockchain is then used to make the headline fully visible, with a private blockchain running behind the header which can control access to the changes in the header.

Blockchain Components

The technology of Blockchain consists of many components that work together. Blockchain technology will make its users such guarantees by bringing these components together.

Ledger

Blockchain is an immutable record or digital record at the most basic level. A record keeping infrastructure that enables the guides of the blockchain to say a story is the heart of the blockchain. This story typically focuses on asset ownership and history, although leads can be used to record almost any conceivable data.

Cryptography

Another important aspect of blockchain technology is cryptography, or the idea of transferring information in a secure or authenticated style in blockchain technology, encryption can be used to ensure secrecy, provide immutability to ledgers, and validate claims made towards resources monitored and stored on the blockchain. Now, every information in a block is joined together using a feature called a "cryptographic hash."

Peer to Peer Network

Blockchain makes extensive use of current network systems technology, especially peer-to-peer security mechanisms. Blockchain is developed on the same emerging technologies that support our modern internet. By removing single points of failure found in conventional client/server networking models peer-to-peer (P2P) system architecture increases consistency and load balancing.

Assets

Assets are something that needs a record of ownership to exist. Health records, event passes, a car title, or a patent are examples of tangible, non-monetary, or informational assets. Blockchain began as a way to track the movement of digital "tokens" or "coins" like Bitcoin and other crypto currencies.

Merkle Tree

For quick and efficient data validation, blockchain uses Merkle trees. Merkle trees create a root hash of all of the data in a block to summarize it.

Consensus Algorithms

Consensus ensures that all network nodes verify transfers and accept on their sequence and existence on the ledger. The way consensus structures assign and reward transaction verification is the most significant difference between them. The most often used are proof-of-work (PoW) and proof-of-stake (PoS).

LITERATURE REVIEW

The multichannel data sharing, which requires medical data to be readily accessible to other organizations, such as a physician, accessed by a health care provider or research institute, is among the most serious issues. Data analysis and management are being redefined by blockchain technology across a variety of medical processes. It enables the exchange of health data due to the advancements in electronic health data, cloud data storage, and medical records access (Weber et al., 2016). To ensure data protection, (Wu et al., 2018) suggested a health management framework. Those who have proposed that regulations for health data management and data be developed using a distributed approach.

Since it is flexible, widely accessible, and has a stable cost scheme cloud computing can be defined an essential approach for medical storing data delivery (Yang et al., 2018).In (Walker-Roberts et al., 2018), a study was conduct to address data security and privacy issues. In (Wang, 2018) search techniques were presented for encrypted health records in public cloud. In (Yao et al., 2018) identity based approach is proposed for authentication in cloud-based healthcare applications. In the past, only patients and health professionals may see a patient's medical treatment and make this data private. The entire medical facilities and stakeholders will use blockchain technology to provide patient data, which will gain greatly in future medical operations. To provide patient data, both medical facilities and stakeholders can use blockchain technology, which will significantly benefit major health activities. Estonia and Guard time, a blockchain health service organization, have shown that a free medical facility can be placed on the blockchain and that it benefits greatly through the use of blockchain and IoT technologies.

There are several startups which use blockchain to manage patients' identities, support patients-focused healthcare, record and monitor individual medicine, create policies in which patients can securely share their perspective with different stakeholders on their health records and information etc. It is incredibly useful to store stored information and patient data on health. The development of wearable devices, including intelligent reloading clocks, exercise bands, monitoring devices and integrated body chips that control patient data, was the result of technological advances in the healthcare sector. These smart gadgets have aided in the betterment of patient data flow. Blockchain technology offers solutions to health data issues. (Wang, 2018; Yao et al., 2018)

Ethereum and Smart Contracts

Ethereum has been proposed by Vitalik Buterin which gives platform for developers to build programs on the blockchain. Ethereum helps create smart contracts and decentralized applications without any middleman.

A Smart contract or crypto contract is computer program automatically control by the digital transaction between the two parties based on some conditions. Smart contract is a program which is built to blockchain applications by using Solidity, Serpent, Viper and LLL languages. The Blockchain database contains information details. One cannot change stored records and reduces attacks from hackers. There is no middle man and cost effective. Smart contract is self-verifiable and executable.

MyEtherWallet (MEW)

- Taylor Monahan launched MyEtherWallet.com (MEW) in 2015with Kosala Kvhnuke Hemachandra, declared another organization and wallet service called MyCrypto.com.
- MyEtherWallet, otherwise called the MEW wallet, is one of the most well known Ethereum wallets.
- MEW Wallet is a site that allows one to create an Ethereum wallet.
- We can utilize this wallet to store, send and secure ether.

Family Health Management System Model

In this paper, we show how Blockchain technology can be used to handle medical data. We developed the framework for data processing and exchange focus on clinical requirements. Figure 2 illustrates a family medical management system of four key components: a doctor, a patient, a pharmacy, a drug production business, and possibly a health insurance company. The block stores all of the health record data, and the components will communicate with one another. Login is used to verify each component. Each part can carry out more tasks after effective authentication.

Figure 3 below shows how the components interact with other components and the overall process flow of this system. A family member with an ailment sends messages to Doctors for Consultation. First, the member (patient) visits the Doctor who responds immediately or charges a low fee or travel time from the member's place to the doctor's clinic is less. The member with ailment undergoes medical diagnosis/clinical tests. Next, the member with ailment gets medical prescription from the Doctor. Medical Prescription is sent to all registered (with the system) pharmacists and Druggists. Medicines are purchased from the pharmacy store who supplies the medicines immediately and / or at low price. The Purchased medicines/ product details are sent to medicine manufacturers to authenticate the origin of the medicines; thereby avoiding duplicate medicines. The member's medical reports are digitized. The member's digitized medical reports are encrypted in Ethereum platform. The member's encrypted reports are linked using block chain technology. The member's earlier health reports (in the encrypted form) are accessed by the member/Doctor from the local server. All health reports of the family member linked using block chain technology are communicated to the Life Insurance Company as and when they become available, in the chronological order.

Figure 2. Main components of family health management system

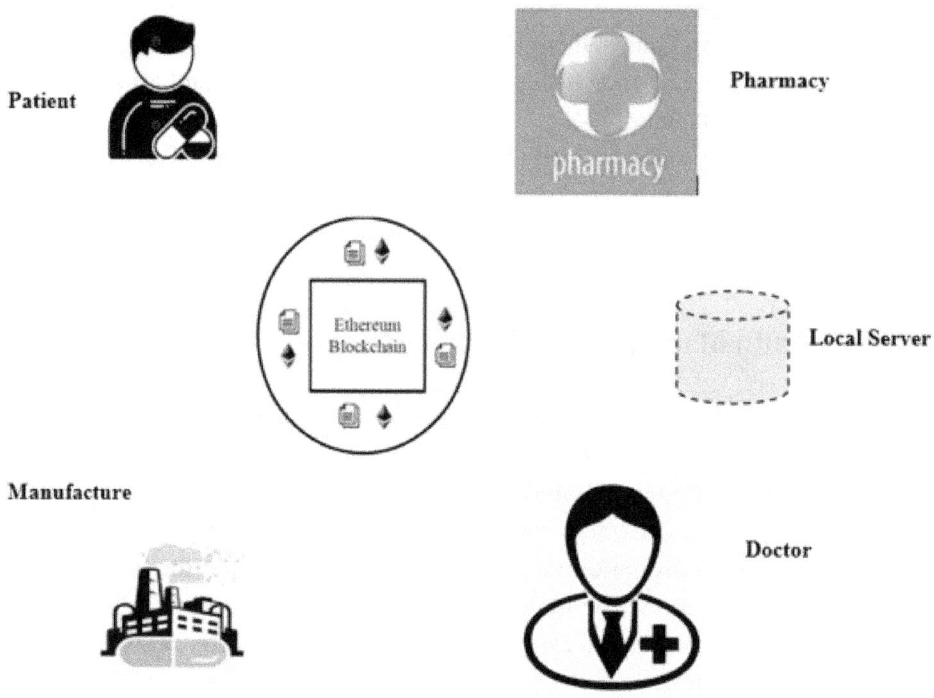

Figure 3. Work flow for family health management system

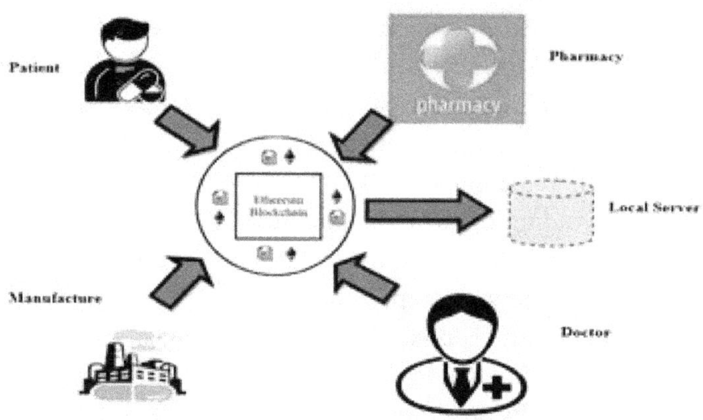

RESULTS

We present below implementation details of the family health management system. We can use various tools such as ganache-cli, Remix IDE and MytherWallet v3.40.0. Remix is a browser-based compiler and IDE that enables users to create Ethereum deals with Solidarity language and debug transactions. ganache-cli is a fast and customizable blockchain prototype. MyEtherWallet act as client interface. The implementation is done on the Intel®Pentium®3558U @1.70 GHz processor with 4GB RAM.

The sample code for this framework is shown in Figure 4, and this section shows a compiler, solidity language, and EVM edition. When we press the compile button, the compilation process begins.

Figure 4. Solidity compiler

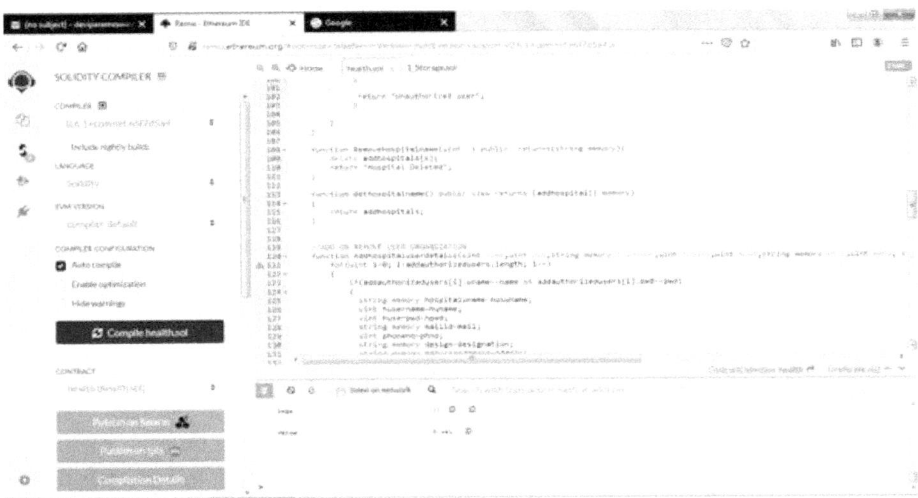

ganache-cli used Node.js package through npm and written using javascript. We used the command npm install -g ganache-cli. After installation, put the ganache-cli command and press Enter button. There are 10 default accounts with their private keys

Deploy Smart Contract and Test It

After successful compilation, we will deploy a code to MyEtherWallet. We can download it from https://github.com/kvhnuke/etherwallet/releases and run the local host.

Figure 5. Ganache-cli

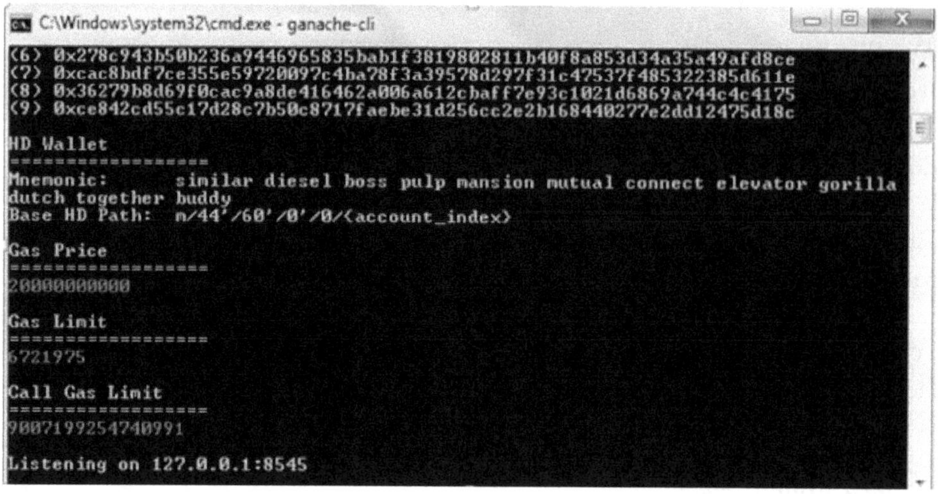

We select the particular contract of byte code, copy it, and paste it into the byte code in ordering the contract in MyEtherWallet. After pasting the byte code, the gas limit appears. To access the wallet, MyEtherWallet needs a private key. Open the command prompt, copy a key from one of the wallets, and then select Unblock button.

Figure 6. Deploy contract

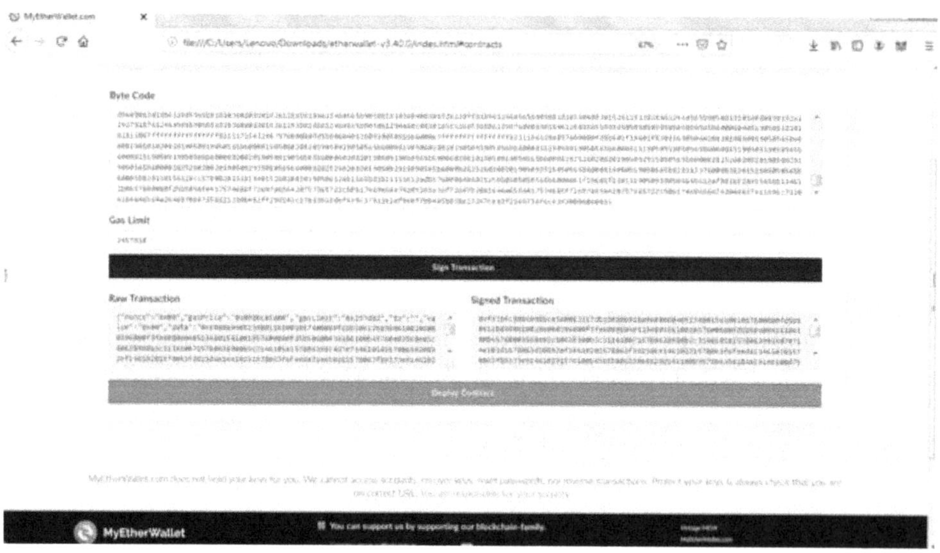

After entering the byte code and accessing the wallet, press the Signature Transaction button, which will make the transaction verifiable. Now we click on deploy contract button, and click confirm the transaction button to send the smart contract to the blockchain network.

Figure 7. Contract created

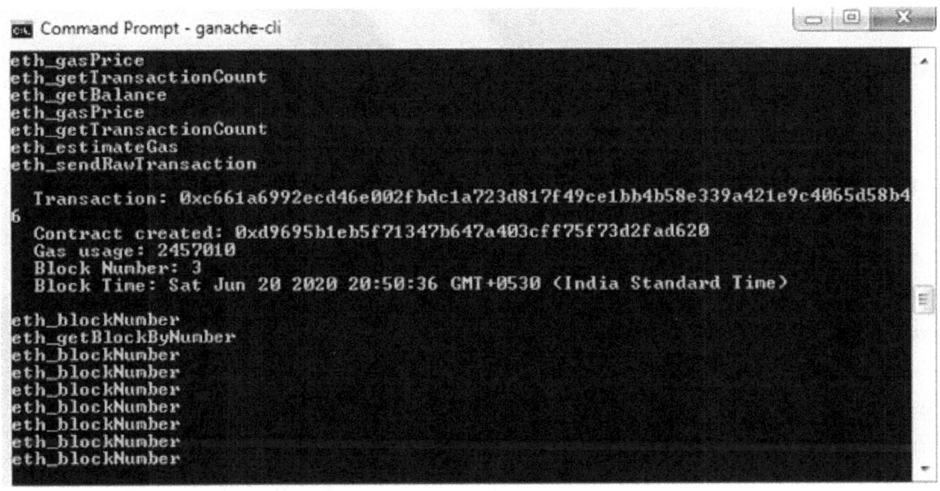

Figure 8. Interact with contract

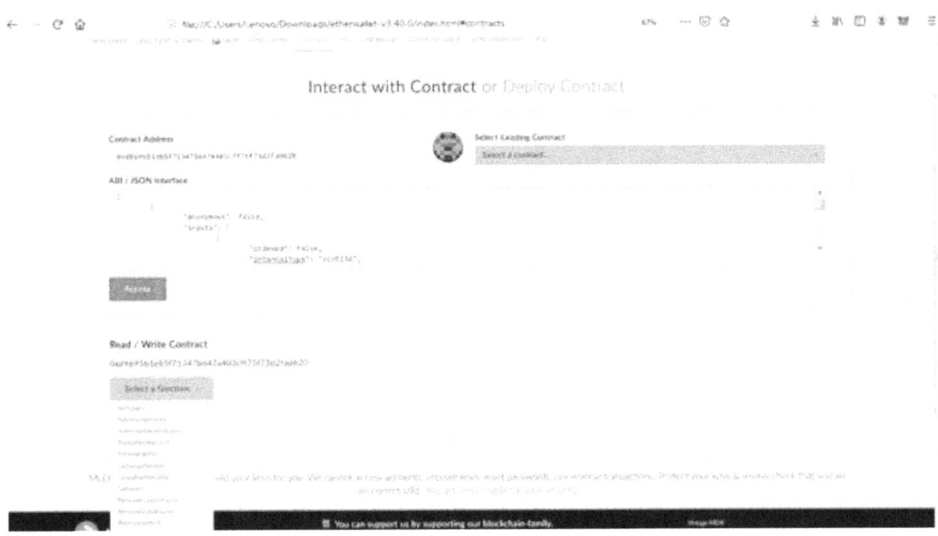

We can check in ganache-cli whether it has been used successfully. Open the command window and here we can see that a contract creation transaction is being created in a block.

Now to test it, open the command prompt and copy the created contract address. Then Goto MyEtherWallet and paste the contract address. Next go to the Remix IDE afterwards, copy the ABI (Application Binary Interface) and paste it. The ABI interface holds details on the methods available in the specific contract. After selecting Access button, we can get all the functionality.

Family Healthcare Management System: Algorithm

Admin Module

The admin module starts with the user's login authentication. They can add or delete hospital data, as well as appoint or de-assign approved users, after effective authentication.

Sample code:

Algorithm 1. Assign/De-assign of users

```
function  AddUsers(string memory name,string memory mail,uint
uname,uint paswd,uint level) public {
        addauthorizedusers.push(addauthorizeduser(name,mail,una
me,paswd,level));
        emit authouser(name,mail,uname,paswd,level);}
function Getusers() public view returns (addauthorizeduser[]
memory) {
        return addauthorizedusers;}
```

Algorithm 2. Add/remove hospital details

```
function Addhospitalname(uint name,uint pwd,string memory
hosname,string memory addres) public  returns(string memory) {
  for(uint i=0; i<addauthorizedusers.length; i++){
            if(addauthorizedusers[i].uname==name &&
addauthorizedusers[i].pwd==pwd) {
              string memory hospitalname=hosname;
              string memory hosaddress=addres;
              addhospitals.push(addhospital(name,hospitalname,h
```

```
osaddress));
              emit add_hospital(name,hospitalname,hosaddress);
              return "Authorized user";}
             else{
              return "Unauthorized user";} } }
   function Removehospitalname(uint x) public  returns(string
memory){
        delete addhospitals[x];
        return "Hospital Deleted";}
```

Algorithm 3. Events in healthcare management system

```
event authouser(string name,string mail,uint uname,uint
paswd,uint level);
event add_hospital(uint name,string hosname,string addr);
event add_hospitaluser(string name,uint uname,uint pwd,string
mail,uint phno,string designation,string addr);
event add_patient(string name,uint uname,uint pwd,uint
phno,string designation,string addr);
event add_patientrecord(uint name,string hospname,string
hospaddr,string dname,string diseasename,string
prescriptiondetails,uint date,uint numofdays);
```

Algorithm 4. Add/Remove doctor details

```
function Addhospitaluserdetails (uint name,uint pwd,string
memory hosuname,uint huname,uint hpwd,string memory mail,uint
phno, string memory designation,string memory addres) public
returns(string memory) {
 for(uint i=0; i<addauthorizedusers.length; i++) {
          if(addauthorizedusers[i].uname==name
&&addauthorizedusers[i].pwd==pwd){
              string memory hospitaluname=hosuname; uint
husername=huname;
              uint huserpwd=hpwd;  string memory mailid=mail;
              uint phoneno=phno; string memory
design=designation;
              string memory hosuseraddress=addres;
```

```
addhospitalusers.push(addhospitaluser(hospitaluname,husername,h
userpwd,mailid,phoneno,design,hosuseraddress));
 emit add_hospitaluser(hospitaluname,husername,huserpwd,mailid,
phoneno,design,hosuseraddress);
             return "Authorized user,Details added"; }else
{return "Unauthorized user"; }  } }
function Removehospitaluser(uint x) public  returns(string
memory){
        delete addhospitalusers[x];
        return "User Deleted"; }
function Gethospitalusers() public view returns
(addhospitaluser[] memory {
        return addhospitalusers;}
```

Algorithm 5. Get the particular patient records

```
function Getpatientrecords(uint pname,uint pwd) public
returns(getpatientrecord[] memory{
        for(uint i=0; i<addpatients.length; i++){
            if(addpatients[i].patientusername==pname &&
addpatients[i].patientpasswd==pwd){
              string memory hospiname=addpatientrecords[i].
hospitname;
              string memory hospiadd=addpatientrecords[i].
hospitaddr;
              string memory doctname=addpatientrecords[i].
doctorname;
              string memory diseases=addpatientrecords[i].
dises;
              string memory tablets=addpatientrecords[i].
prescription;
              uint da=addpatientrecords[i].date;
              getpatientrecords.push(getpatientrecord(hospiname
,hospiadd,doctname,diseases,tablets,da));

              return(getpatientrecords);    }    }    }
```

The patient module begins at requires the user to authenticate themselves through the login. After successful authentication, they are able to add/remove a medical record for themselves, and view the medical records.

Algorithm 6. Add/ remove medical records

```
function Addpatientrecords(uint name,uint pwd,string memory
hospname,string memory hospadd,string memory docname,string
memory disease,string memory tabname,uint noofdays) public
returns(string memory) {
for(uint i=0; i<addpatients.length; i++) {
            if(addpatients[i].patientusername==name &&
addpatients[i].patientpasswd==pwd) {
              uint pname=name;
              string memory hospiname=hospname;
              string memory hospiadd=hospadd;
              string memory doctname=docname;
              string memory diseases=disease;
              string memory tablets=tabname;
              uint da=block.timestamp;
              uint noday=noofdays;
addpatientrecords.push(addpatientrecord(pname,hospiname,hospiad
d,doctname,diseases,tablets,da,noday));
 emit add_patientrecord(pname,hospiname,hospiadd,doctname,disea
ses,tablets,da,noday);
              return "Authorized user,Patient Records added";}
    else{ return "Unauthorized user"; }  }   }
 function Removepatientrecords(uint x) public  returns(string
memory){
        delete addpatientrecords[x];
        return "Patient Deleted";}
```

Estimated Costs

When it comes to incorporating blockchain into healthcare, it's important to estimate the cost of implementing smart healthcare services. The main goal is to implement a scheme that will provide a viable clinical healthcare sector with all of blockchain's advantages. To avoid network abuse and to solve other computer-related problems, all programmable transactions in the Ethereum blockchain pay some charges. As a result, all activities, simulations, message calls, smart contract development, and storing on EVM need gas in order to complete all of these tasks.

The cost of deploying smart contracts for the healthcare management framework has been compiled. There is an expense known as gas to run an application on the Ethereum blockchain. As the basic requirement to operate the company, all the transactions need 21,000 gas. If a consumer interacts with a smart contract with Ethereum, 21,000 gas is needed with additional gas associated with the running of that particular smart contract. The gas for medical smart contracts was compiled for contract deployment to communicate with the various contracts. The functions/ operations involved in smart contracts consume more gas, resulting in more fees, which are more complicated. The results show that the cost of implementing smart contracts for the healthcare management system is very low. In terms of the medical system, this expense is very reasonable, and everyone will be willing to pay this small amount in order to maintain control over their EHR and protect their medical data for the rest of their lives.

The resource consumption of Ethereum is measured in gas, which is a unit. Gas consumption is proportional to transaction information, as shown in Figure 9. Since the user's chosen Gas Price for the transaction will differ. The higher the price of gas, the higher the transaction cost and the sooner the transaction can be checked.

Figure 9. Transaction count vs. gas usage

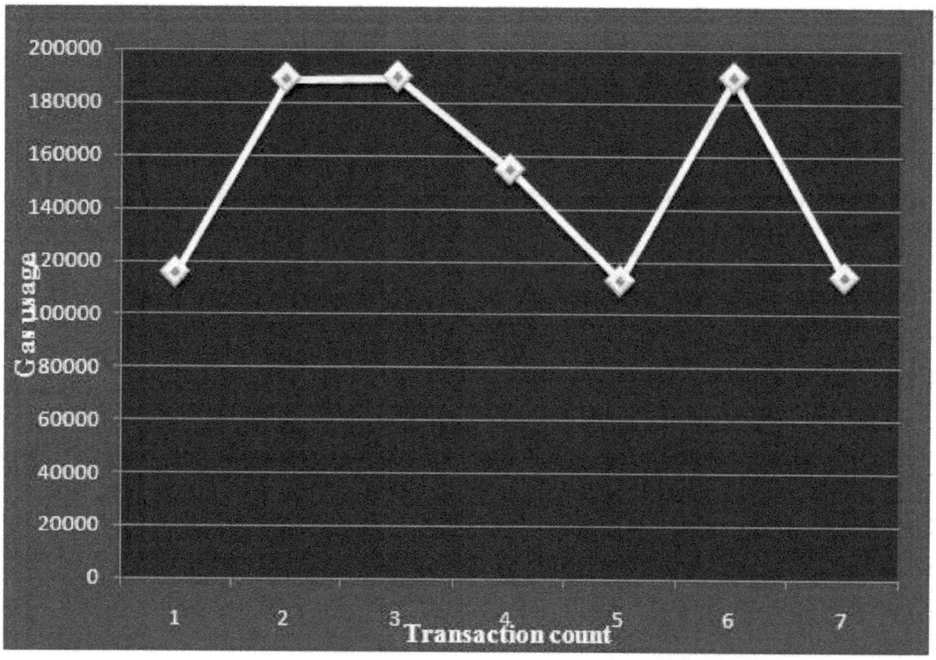

CONCLUSION

The use of blockchain in healthcare systems is critical in today's healthcare industry. It can help with efficient collection of data and verification, corrective, collated, static, tamper-resistant data from various sources, and stable data with a lower risk of cyber-crime. For access control policies, we have a machine architecture and algorithm. We have developed blockchain technology based health management system using a smart contract on ethereum framework. It shows how diffusion policies can be useful in managing and organizing huge amounts of medical data. We presented a smart contract based approach to provide access, audit and sharing of medical records. The system ensures EHR data confidentiality, protection, and usability, as well as better control over access. The system allows patients to securely exchange their medical records with physicians, pharmacies, manufacturers, and insurance companies while retaining full control of their medical records' privacy. More features and modules will be added to the system in the future.

ACKNOWLEDGMENT

The first author thanks the management of Kalasalingam Academy of Research and Education for providing scholarship to carry out the research.

REFERENCES

Ahram, T., Sargolzaei, A., Sargolzaei, S., Daniels, J., & Amaba, B. (2017). Blockchain technology innovations. *Proceedings of the 2017 IEEE Technology and Engineering Management Conference (TEMSCON)*, 8–10.

Gipp, B., Kosti, J., & Breitinger, C. (2016). Securing Video Integrity Using Decentralized Trusted Time stamping on the Bitcoin Blockchain. *Proceedings of the Mediterranean Conference on Information Systems (MCIS)*.

Mehdi, B., & Ravaud, P. (2017). Blockchain technology for improving clinical research quality. *Trials*, *18*, 335.

Meng, W., Tischhauser, E. W., Wang, Q., Wang, Y., & Han, J. (2018). When intrusion detection meets blockchaintechnology: A review. *IEEE Access: Practical Innovations, Open Solutions*, *6*, 10179–10188. doi:10.1109/ACCESS.2018.2799854

Ovais, A. (2017). Block Chain Technology: Concept of Digital Economic. University Library of Munich.

Rayome, A. D. (2019). *Top 10 Emerging Technologies of 2019*. TechRepublic.

Suveen, A., Krumholz, H. M., & Schulz, W. L. (2017). Blockchain technology: Applications in health care. *Circulation: Cardiovascular Quality and Outcomes*, *10*, e003800.

Tsai, W. T., Blower, R., Zhu, Y., & Yu, L. (2016). A system view of financial blockchains. *IEEE Symposium on Service-Oriented System Engineering (SOSE)*, 450–457. 10.1109/SOSE.2016.66

Walker-Roberts, S., Hammoudeh, M., & Dehghantanha, A. (2018). A Systematic Review of the Availability and Efficacy of Countermeasures to Internal Threats in Healthcare Critical Infrastructure. *IEEE Access: Practical Innovations, Open Solutions*, *6*, 25167–25177.

Wang, H. (2018). Anonymous Data Sharing Scheme in Public Cloud and Its Application in E-health Record. *IEEE Access: Practical Innovations, Open Solutions*, *6*, 27818–27826.

Weber, I., Xu, X., Riveret, R., Governatori, G., Ponomarev, A., & Mendling, J. (2016.) Untrusted business process monitoring and execution using blockchain. In *International Conference on Business Process Management*. Springer.

Wu, H. T., & Tsai, C. W. (2018). Toward blockchains for health-care systems: Applying the bilinear pairing technology to ensure privacy protection and accuracy in data sharing. *IEEE Consum. Electron. Mag*, *7*, 65–71.

Yang, Y., Li, X., Qamar, N., Liu, P., Ke, W., Shen, B., & Liu, Z. (2018). MedShare: A Novel Hybrid Cloud for Medical Resource Sharing among Autonomous Healthcare Providers. *IEEE Access: Practical Innovations, Open Solutions*, *6*, 46949–46961.

Yao, X., Lin, Y., Liu, Q., & Zhang, J. (2018). Privacy-preserving search over encrypted personal health record in multi-source cloud. *IEEE Access: Practical Innovations, Open Solutions*, *6*, 3809–3823.

Chapter 9
Investigation on Industry Applications of Blockchain Technology

Dhaya R.
https://orcid.org/0000-0002-3599-7272
King Khalid University, Saudi Arabia

Kanthavel R.
King Khalid University, Saudi Arabia

ABSTRACT

Blockchain (BC) is a collective, indisputable ledger that makes easy the course of action of recording dealings and footpath possessions in an industry system. On the other hand, BC is significant in business that sprints on information. A BC network can follow instructions, expenditure, financial records, manufacture, and many more. Yet, the difficulties of BC in industry like mindfulness and getting, association, culture, cost and proficiency, regulation and administration, and security and protection must be properly dealt with to gain the advantages fully. Hence, the objectives of this chapter are to investigate various applications of industries that involve BC technology, the challenges, evolution of BC in industry applications, and its need, types of BC, and networks for industries and comparison. Further, the chapter discusses how to manage the hyperconnected supply chain in terms of industrial applications in terms of scalability, integrity, and legacy.

DOI: 10.4018/978-1-7998-8081-3.ch009

INTRODUCTION

Blockchain is an organized information dependent on chains of information blocks and the construction is reliant on specific guidelines set somewhere around its makers. The distinction between BC and the remaining information bases is the finished by means of absence of a self-contained place. For this situation, the information base is accessible all the while to all clients and in the event that somebody changes something, at that point, all information from different clients is immediately synchronized (Alladi et al., 2019).

The upside of the innovation is that the information added to the data set cannot be erased or changed by one client without showing the progressions to the wide range of various proprietors. These properties make BC the main instrument accessible for trading information and securing data. The advantages of BC are appealing to organizations. BC in the energy area permits clients to screen exchanges, control yield, and check the source of authentication. Most tasks are right now being worked on, however, their pertinence and significance have for quite some time been perceived by delegates of the business. There is no uncertainty that over the long run, the number of BC arrangements in different areas of the economy will be incremented altogether, and the advantages of their usage will turn out to be very evident.

BC in the auto business is viewed as an apparatus for the capacity and transmission of information by savvy vehicles. Likewise, the innovation can be utilized to store information about explicit vehicles in different libraries. Blockchain won't yield into account the tarnishing of information about a vehicle. For instance, after a vehicle is put available, all information about it, including data about help and fixes, will be put away utilizing BC. Subsequently, the proprietor of a vehicle will be capable, whenever, to check the number of solutions it has gone through, mishap information, and other data (Puthal et al., 2018).

BC innovation makes it conceivable to follow the whole way of made merchandise, from the transportation offices at a manufacturing plant to clients in stores. Because of the way that BC is totally straightforward; it makes it conceivable to facilitate exchange subtleties among all members in the creation chain. The level of inferior quality extra parts among all post-retail parts is very high, and a significant number of them rapidly come up short, which harms the standing of vendors and vehicle makers the same. Utilizing BC, an identifier can be made for each part that allows the following of the whole way of the extra part from the maker to the customer.

Blockchain innovation has developed extraordinarily since the presentation of Bitcoin. First decentralized distributed electronic money framework has been started. With its decentralized and trustless nature, Blockchain innovation can prompt new freedoms and advantage organizations through more noteworthy straightforwardness, upgraded security, and simpler detectability. BC arrangements are not just restricted to the trading of cryptographic forms of money. The various advantages that this innovation can present to organizations in a wide range of ventures, through its conveyed and decentralized nature are Greater Transparency; increased Efficiency because of its decentralized nature, Blockchain eliminates the requirement for brokers in numerous cycles for fields, Better Security than other record-keeping frameworks in light of the fact that each new exchange is scrambled and connected to the past exchange, improved Traceability as with the BC record, each time trade of products is recorded on a Blockchain, a review trail is available to follow where the merchandise came from and Blockchain as a service for simpler Integration as Blockchain innovation into their organizations effectively, without interruption to their everyday measures. Blockchain has the potential for some, utilization cases, appropriate to a large number of ventures(Salman et al., 2018)

This chapter is organized in to four main parts namely, the need of BC for industrial purpose and its strength, key elements and benefits of BC in industry, supply chain management and advanced block chain expertise, technology and eco- system to rewire industry.

DEVELOPMENT OF BLACKCHAIN IN INDUSTRY PURPOSES AND ITS NEEDS

Industrial rationale shave started to arise to get better income or ready execution by dividing changeless information between organizations, government substances, and exchange associations. Blockchain innovation has been demonstrated feasible and practical as a community and permission less stage with the one-decade record of Bitcoin. The Figure 1 shows the need of BC in industrial applications.

Figure 1. Need of BC in industrial applications

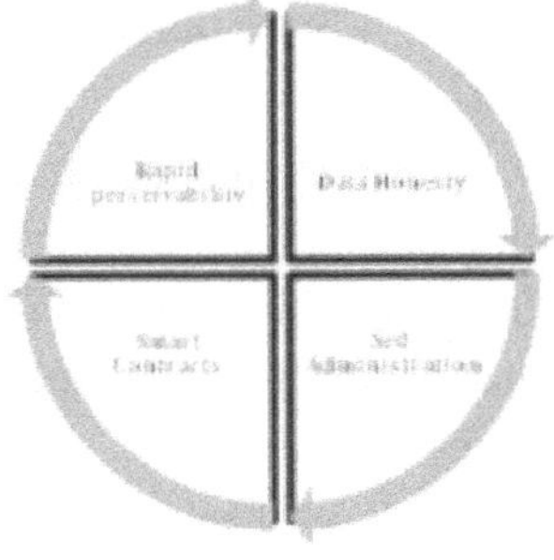

Need of Blockchain in Industrial Applications

Blockchain gives a few key highlights that build it a significant innovation for industrial organizations. These comprise:

- Rapid perceivability amid members with secure ongoing account of exchanges and information sharing
- Data honesty among accomplices and now and again contenders who ordinarily would not be confided in sources. Likewise, numerous layers of cryptography and mechanized principles forestall hacking.
- Self-administration utilizing a disseminated data set and installed foundation for information sharing and exchanges i.e., no focal power.
- Smart contracts implanted in a BC give business measure computerization. A BC exchange can start predefined rationale and business steps to execute business exchanges and installments.(Christidis & Devetsikiotis, 2016)

Blockchain Strengths in Industrial Domains

BC is a safe appropriated record giving detectable quality, a survey trail, and speedier trades at diminished cost. BC uses a mix of various layers of encryption, a scattered data base, and execution reasoning for data decency and secure trades. Trust is decentralized and rests with the BC show without a central force or agent, for instance, an organization or bank. BC maintains trust in complex cycles, motorizes existing business measures, dispenses with specialists, hinders coercion, and gives straight forwardness (Fernández-Caramés & Fraga-Lamas, 2018).

- **Blockchain Assures Immutable, Trusted Data**: BC is a decentralized information base that stores a record of exchanges on various hubs across an organization. For foreordained process duration, exchange information related by each progression in a production network or other business measures are aggregated into a scrambled "block." Bitcoin, for instance, enters all coin trades worldwide into another square like clockwork. At regular intervals, another square is added to the current series of squares to make a "chain"(Nakamoto, 2008).
- **Immutable Data:** Each square gives a "solitary form of reality" about exchanges and exercises happening across a biological system of a perplexing business measure. While members in a BC may get to, assess, and add to the information; numerous layers of encryption keep them from adjusting or erasing existing information. The first data "waits," leaving a lasting and public data trail of exchanges.

- **Visibility with No Central Authority:** The decentralized administration in BC eliminates the requirement for a focal position or outsider delegate like a specialist. These sorts of substances normally storehouse the information with restricted admittance by others and require manual strategies for sharing. BC furnishes prompt electronic access with high perceivability among the members. The various layers of encryption, justification, and an appropriated data set guarantee approval and information uprightness so shared data can be trusted, regardless of whether a portion of the members may not be dependable (Ferrag et al., 2018) .
- **Managing Ownership with Blockchain**: BC gives the foundation to programming applications to oversee proprietorship. This regular business measure incorporates:
    - Identify the resource
    - Identify the proprietor
    - Secure move of the resource starting with one proprietor then onto the next
    - Visibility by all members

Table 1 shows the strengths, weakness, opportunities and threats of BC in Industry domain

Table 1. BC -strengths, weakness, opportunities and threats in industry domain

potency	restriction	prospect	intimidation
• Cost proficiency • Speedy access information • Information sharing	• Less number of programming's • Less number of framework merchants • Lack of capacity	- Lower hazard - Information control - Far off access	- Non norm - Interoperability - novelty variation

BLOCKCHAIN IN INDUSTRY 4.0

Blockchain and its incentive in Industry 4.0 are yet to be completely characterized. Nonetheless, there are a few zones where BC gives planned advantages. A large number of us have just caught wind of consumption in monetary exchanges where trust can be gotten from the utilization of BC. Unfamiliar monetary standards and fiat money issues are killed and there can be an observed continuum in stockpile exchange where numerous levels in the inventory base are included(Fernández-Caramés & Fraga-Lamas, 2019).

These are generally extraordinary methods of overseeing exchanges. There are a couple of different regions where blockchain may add an incentive in Industry 4.0. One of the zones could be the place where the BC incorporates item, gathering, or segment recognizing data. This could help in evaluating and overseeing quality issues with a more significant level of particularity. The figure 2 shows the history revolutions in industry(Shen & Pena-Mora, 2018) .

Figure 2. Industry revolution

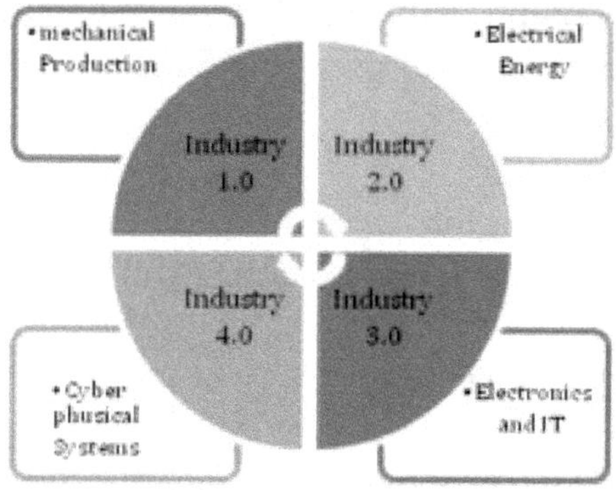

An ideal illustration of this is with respect to reviews. Ordinarily, reviews are all over in light of the fact that the issue could make hurt and the capacity explicitly distinguish items displaying the deformity can't be promptly recognized. With BC, the entirety of the data about an item, its sub-congregations, parts, and its dissemination way to market would all be able to be remembered for the BC. Clearly, you would prefer not to trouble the BC with superfluous information, yet there is a bunch of information at each progression in the production network that can enormously lessen the expense and disturbance identified with reviews in the current climate(Zhou et al., 2015).

There are three different territories that are significantly more explicit to Industry 4.0 for BC applications and advantages. The first identifies with the above circumstances though inserts the likelihood to all the more promptly track essential administration and item data for market that require much greater detectability, for example, medical services or military items. BC can be developed with the new data gathered by cameras and sensors, more data than might actually be gathered by a human in a short measure of time.

Another potential application is in utilizing the inalienable encryption of a BC . This might actually secure a portion of the information sent over a public organization from unapproved review or control. Albeit potential assurances might be given, these may not kill the chance of your information communicated over a public organization being summoned, and subsequently uncovered in that way(Fraga-Lamas & Fernández-Caramés, 2019).

Advanced plans, for example, those utilized in AM – 3 Dimensional making craft an entire issue around licensed innovation the board and control. From various perspectives, a portion of the plans out there on the public organization are accessible for programmers to take and use voluntarily. Blockchain could help ensure the IP of creators of computerized plans. A BC can be utilized to oversee monetary exchanges yet additionally control the utilization of the advanced property. The figure 2 shows the core worth driver of Industry 4.0(Davies, 2015).

Figure 3. Core worth driver of industry 4.0

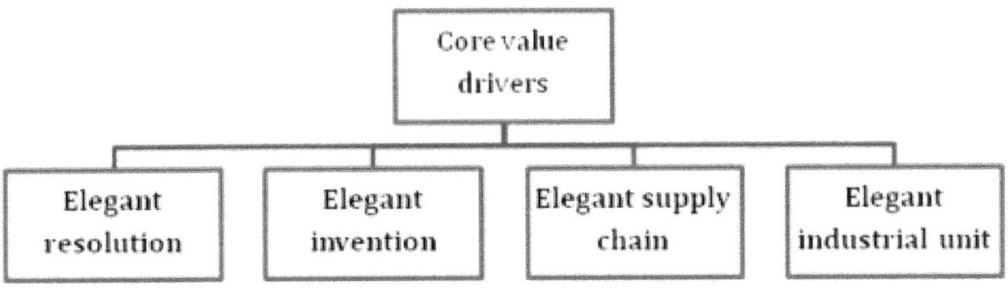

KEY ELEMENTS AND BENEFITS OF BLACKCHAIN IN INDUSTRY

The main bit of leeway of BC conveyed record is diminished operational expenses. "Cost can be removed from existing cycles by eliminating mediators or the authoritative exertion of documentation keeping and exchange compromise. Industries are considering these business advantages and embracing BC innovation for its wide-arriving at potential outcomes. From assembling to medical care to stock up network and past, BC has a lot to bring to the table. National Aeronautics and Space Administration is thinking about utilizing a BC to guarantee believed, secure airplane flight information. Other conceivable use cases incorporate installment handling, copyright security, solid information reinforcement, data storing, title moves, and even assessment guideline and consistence (Yang et al., 2019).

Focal Points of Block Chain Innovation for Business

- Delegation, safety, and truthfulness.

- Account authorization deprived of holding to be contingent on third party authentication.
- Data configuration can't be accustomed or removed.
- Certified cryptography preserve the information records in a secured manner.

Industry Application Domains of Blackchain Technology

The industry application domains of blockchain technology are as in figure 4.

- **Automotive:** Drive inventive versatility administrations, inventory network discernibility and safer monetary exchanges.
- **Banking and monetary administrations:** Bring trust, straightforwardness and improved client experience to monetary administrations.
- **Government:** Ensure information stewardship to secure resident data, keep up trust and guarantee the precision of freely available reports.
- **Healthcare**: Streamline clinical information across associations and empower patients to control their clinical information to build the nature of care.
- **Insurance:** Revolutionize the trust that powers protection with a permanent establishment of straightforwardness and mutual perspective.

Figure 4. Industry application domains

- **Media and diversion:** Build an environment of trust around advanced substance use — music, motion pictures, TV, publicizing, dependability focuses and the sky is the limit from there.
- **Retail and shopper merchandise**: Harness BC to rethink the item legitimacy, operational greatness and purchaser experience.
- **Telecommunications:** Reshape ways to deal with information protection, improve operational proficiency, pull in new clients, and improve their experience(Shrouf et al., 2014).
- **Travel and transportation:** Speed exchanges, diminish extortion and smooth out tasks to move travelers, faculty and packages all the more effectively.

BLOCKCHAIN AND SUPPLY CHAIN MANAGEMENT

BC expertise can be making use of to determine numerous difficulties of the Supply Chain manufacturing, for example, multifaceted documentation maintenance and following of items. By BC expertise, a superior robotized choice to regulate the concentrated information bases is advertised. Aside from the proof maintenance and following, there are a few alternate manners by which the BC knowledge helps the working of a production network.

1. **Beginning stage Tracking**: Because of an uncommonly high volume of trades and various parts in the stock shackles, still the associations with incredibly highly developed personnel misplace the track to trades. This disappointment draws extra transparency costs and on occasion failure of client information expenses loathsome client connection and product label debilitating. BC-based creation network the heads gives provenance following and record keeping which makes the information getting straightforward with introduced sensors and RFID marks. The thing history can be followed straightforwardly from the reason to the current situation whenever. Similarly, such precision in provenance following can be utilized to distinguish and hinder fakes even in complex reserve chains(Weyer et al., 2015).
2. **Cost Reduction:** An outline coordinated by APQC and the Digital Supply Chain Institute of stock organization workers uncovers that more than half percentage of people accept that lessening of costs is the most elevated bit of leeway of BC in Supply Chain Management. This is an aftereffect of the consistent thing following promoted. With BC extra cost can be diminished while keeping up the security of the trades. Also, the go betweens and go-betweens in the stock organization are cleared out. This declines the risks of

cheats and cleverness of things and overhauls exact record keeping and save reserves

3. **Building Confidence**: With various individuals in the baffling stock organization, building trust in the structure is central for smooth exercises. For instance, the trustworthiness of the records should be with the ultimate objective that when a part in the reserve passes the information to the accompanying level part, the gatherer should have the alternative to rely upon the information certainly. Also, the managerial trained professionals, being accomplices should have the alternative to rely upon the information and records.

Advantages of Utilizing Block Chain in Supply Chain Management

- **Interoperability:** The BC innovation permits information to be interoperable which facilitates the information dividing measure between the producers, retailers, merchants, and project workers. The straightforwardness in information sharing aides diminishing postponements and clashes. Additionally, it keeps merchandise from stalling out in the store network cycle in light of the fact that every item can be followed increasingly which makes the odds of removals uncommon.
- **Adaptability:** Surplus limit is accessible quiet with this innovation. It offers adaptability with which huge information bases can be gotten from numerous areas around the globe. While keeping up exclusive expectations of security the clients can redo as per the information feed. The most rewarding component of this is 'specific approvals' which implies the member will have the option to see the information for which he has the authorization. The consent to permit the information to be gotten to can be allowed unequivocally to the members. Aside from these, there are other advantages of receiving BC innovation in supply system the executives(Fernández-Caramés et al., 2018):
    - Lessen or dispense with misrepresentation and mistakes
    - Advance stock administration
    - Reduce dispatch costs
    - Minimize delays in administrative work
    - Identify any issue more rapidly
    - Build customer and member trust

BC can possibly turn the inventory network industry for good. BC has the best use of the inventory network the board and is required to develop at a high speed in the coming future. The way to appropriately execute and work a production network is to keep straightforward and start to finish availability. To receive the rewards of applying BC in the store network industry, corporate should start to insert the more up to date framework today. For higher rewards and improved execution, the massive desk work and complex information bases need a substitution and there is no preferable substitute over BC.

ADVANCED BLOCK CHAIN EXPERTISE, TECHNOLOGY AND ECO- SYSTEM TO REWIRE INDUSTRY

Everybody's fixated on BC and all things considered. Blockchain is an innovation that can tackle probably the most vexing mechanical, expert and individual issues we face. Be that as it may, notwithstanding the style, multifaceted nature and security of the innovation, the interactions BC will empower, and the forceful BC selection bend, there's not almost enough conversation about how BC will affect exchange handling across different vertical businesses. Indeed, BC will overhaul entire businesses. The application scope of BC innovation is more extensive than suspected. There are as of now convincing markers of extensibility. One is the model stages and applications previously conveyed. Another is the proceeding with speculations by Virtual centers.

Blachchain Networks for Industries

Despite the fact that BC is getting less complex to send in the processing plant, it's anything but a panacea for challenges in industrial tasks. A valid example is continuous information. For applications that require almost quick information trade, for example, the on-line directing of creation hardware, the inactivity time involved in utilizing BC is inordinate. The five use cases for BC in the manufacturing plant of things have been explained to come to show the numerous accessible chances as follows:**Improving Track and Trace:** Organizations can utilize BC to trade information effectively, precisely, and safely inside complex stock chains. BC can give an unchanging, perpetual advanced record of materials, parts, and items, in this manner elevating start to finish perceivability and giving a solitary wellspring of truth to all members. These advantages are important if the inventory network incorporates different members with the free IT frameworks, or if there is an absence of trust among members or a continuous need to locally available new members.

Securing and Monetizing Critical Intellectual Property: Organizations across assembling businesses face a basic to secure IP. Alongside cost, IP security is a basic thought in choices about whether to make parts in-house or to get them from a provider(Onik et al., 2018).

One chance is for an organization to utilize BC innovation to help demonstrate that it possesses IP in case of a patent debate. BC is additionally one of a few arrangements accessible to assist an organization with ensuring and keep up control of IP while adapting advanced resources. For example, machines associated with a BC can create parts by utilizing computerized configuration records remembered for the data set. The organization that claims the IP utilizes an authorizing model to make the restrictive data accessible through the BC to the organization that creates the part(Jay et al., 2019).

Disentangling and Safeguarding Quality Checks: By utilizing BC to help quality control, an organization can improve an incentive for clients, another essential goal of the plant of things to come. Today, without BC, offering full straightforwardness and complete documentation to clients as to the nature of cycles and items needs exorbitant help from focal gatherings that work IT stages. Notwithstanding assisting clients with following and follow inbound parts the length of an inventory network, BC makes permanent documentation of value checks and creation measure information. The data set exceptionally labels every item and naturally engraves each exchange, adjustment, or quality mind the BC . To empower this application, the creation arrangement should incorporate computerized quality watches that produce and compose inference straightforwardly to the BC. This utilization case upholds combined admittance to information and can dispose of the requirement for inbound quality control to confirm watches that the provider performs. It might likewise decrease the requirement for reviews by unique hardware producers or focal specialists to check quality controls. Gatherings will have the option to utilize the innovation's declaration the decision-making abilities to acquire full straightforwardness into every significant archive, in this way guaranteeing legitimacy(Mohamed & Al-Jaroodi, 2019).

DIFFICULTIES OF BLACKCHAIN INNOVATION FOR INDUSTRY APPLICATIONS ASPECTS

The BC is promoted as the main mechanical advancements that have just charmed a decent piece of significant enterprises presently the time has come to comprehend the huge difficulties of BC industry.(Mondragon et al., 2018)

Versatility: The capacity to deal with countless clients at a solitary time is as yet a test for the BC business. BC innovation includes a few complex calculations to deal with a solitary exchange. As an ever increasing number of individuals are becoming accustomed to it, the normal exchanges have likewise expanded significantly. It seriously hit the preparing velocity of the exchanges as a higher number of individuals infer more PCs composing and getting to the organization making an in common unwieldy framework.

Programmers and Shadow Managing: The one thing that theBC business needs is a bunch of administrative omission making it an unstable climate and an obvious objective for market control. For example, the scandalous one coin trick where a great deal of speculators lost cash believing it to be the following progressive advanced money was uncovered to be a plot trick. Regardless of how great you are with your digital currency understanding, there is consistently an opportunity that the online wallet you are utilizing may get hacked or be hindered by the public authority because of some shadowy practices (Mohamed et al., 2019).

Complex to Comprehend and Embrace: Blockchain innovation and the complexities it includes makes it difficult for a layman to comprehend a lot its advantages. Prior to jumping into this progressive application, one necessities to peruse it and comprehend the standards of encryption and circulated record. Another point that makes BC difficult to receive is that monetary foundations are sufficient to give secure installment entryways and different administrations at moderate costs contrasted with the expenses caused with BC.

Security: Blockchain is an open record which is noticeable for everybody to see. It is a fundamental perspective by and large; however it turns into a risk whenever utilized in a touchy climate. BC innovation actually needs to go far to be received on a wide scale. The record should be redesigned in a manner that permits confined admittance and is available just to individuals who are approved to see it(Zhong et al., 2017).

Expenses: Block chain is actualized generally for killing the costs identified with outsiders and go-betweens engaged with the way toward moving qualities. However, the BC innovation is very helpful, it is as yet in the early phases of development making it extreme to incorporate into the inheritance frameworks. It makes it a costly issue generally forestalling its appropriation by the public authority just as private firms.

The BC is an imaginative innovation however needs a great deal of mechanical headways. In any case, innovation has an inborn property of developing and can generally discover a route through any difficulties. Along these lines, we cannot say that blockchain is going anyplace at any point in the near future yet will set aside effort to upset the innovation area totally.

CONCLUSION

This chapter presented an investigation of various applications of industries that involve the chief role and contributions with BC technology. In addition to that challenges, Evolution of Blackchain in industry applications have also been analyzed, In the later section of this chapter dealt in describing and interpreting the classifications of BC for Industries with the comparative analysis. Further, the proposed chapter talked over managerial aspects of the hyper connected supply chain in terms of industrial applications in terms of scalability, integrity and legacy. From the studies it has been inferred that by means of distributed technology of blackchain, which can be effectively used to roadway and authenticate records connecting to the attribution of anitem for consumption for usage by the consumers. Moreover, it is concluded that through the efficient utilization of blockchain, the physical manufactured goods as well as things movement and digital in the form of information flow supply chain can be had a better connection with the commercial side of a business.

REFERENCES

Alladi, Chamola, Parizi, Kwang, & Choo. (2019). Blockchain Applications for Industry 4.0 and Industrial IoT: A Review. *IEEE Access*. doi:10.1109/ACCESS.2019.2956748

Christidis, K., & Devetsikiotis, M. (2016). Blockchains and smart contracts for the internet of things. *IEEE Access: Practical Innovations, Open Solutions*, *4*, 2292–2303. doi:10.1109/ACCESS.2016.2566339

Davies, R. (2015). *Industry 4.0 digitalisation for productivity and growth* (Vol. 1). European Parliamentary Research Service.

Fernández-Caramés & Fraga-Lamas. (2018). A review on the use of blockchain for the internet of things. *IEEE Access, 6.*

Fernández-Caramés & Fraga-Lamas. (2019). A review on the application of blockchain to the next generation of cybersecure industry 4.0 smart factories. *IEEE Access, 7.*

Fernández-Caramés, T. M., Blanco-Novoa, O., Suárez-Albela, M., & Fraga-Lamas, P. (2018). A uav and blockchain-based system for industry 4.0 inventory and traceability applications. Multidisciplinary Digital Publishing Institute Proceedings, 4(1), 26. doi:10.3390/ecsa-5-05758

Ferrag, M. A., Derdour, M., Mukherjee, M., Derhab, A., Maglaras, L., & Janicke, H. (2018). Blockchain technologies for the internet of things: Research issues and challenges. *IEEE Internet of Things Journal.*

Fraga-Lamas & Fernández-Caramés. (2019). A review on blockchain technologies for an advanced and cyber-resilient automotive industry. *IEEE Access, 7.*

Jay, L., Moslem, A., & Jaskaran, S. (2019). A blockchain enabled cyberphysical system architecture for industry 4.0 manufacturing systems. *Manufacturing Letters*, *20*, 34–39. doi:10.1016/j.mfglet.2019.05.003

Mohamed, N., & Al-Jaroodi, J. (2019). Applying blockchain in industry 4.0 applications. *2019 IEEE 9th Annual Computing and Communication Workshop and Conference (CCWC)*, 852–858. 10.1109/CCWC.2019.8666558

Mohamed, N., Al-Jaroodi, J., & Lazarova-Molnar, S. (2019). Leveraging the capabilities of industry 4.0 for improving energy efficiency in smart factories. *IEEE Access: Practical Innovations, Open Solutions*, *7*, 18008–18020. doi:10.1109/ACCESS.2019.2897045

Mondragon, A. E. C., Mondragon, C. E. C., & Coronado, E. S. (2018). Exploring the applicability of blockchain technology to enhance manufacturing supply chains in the composite materials industry. *2018 IEEE International Conference on Applied System Invention (ICASI)*, 1300–1303. 10.1109/ICASI.2018.8394531

Nakamoto. (2008). *Bitcoin: A peer-to-peer electronic cash system*. Academic Press.

Onik, M. M. H., Miraz, M. H., & Kim, C. (2018). A recruitment and human resource management technique using blockchain technology for industry 4.0. *Smart Cities Symposium 2018*, 1–6. 10.1049/cp.2018.1371

Puthal, D., Malik, N., Mohanty, S. P., Kougianos, E., & Das, G. (2018). Everything you wanted to know about the blockchain: Its promise, components, processes, and problems. *IEEE Consumer Electronics Magazine*, *7*(4), 6–14. doi:10.1109/MCE.2018.2816299

Salman, T., Zolanvari, M., Erbad, A., Jain, R., & Samaka, M. (2018). Security services using blockchains: A state of the art survey. *IEEE Communications Surveys and Tutorials*, *21*(1), 858–880. doi:10.1109/COMST.2018.2863956

Shen & Pena-Mora. (2018). Blockchain for cities—a systematic literature review. *IEEE Access, 6*.

Shrouf, F., Ordieres, J., & Miragliotta, G. (2014). *Smart factories in industry 4.0: A review of the concept and of energy management approached in production based on the internet of things paradigm. In 2014 IEEE international conference on industrial engineering and engineering management*. IEEE.

Weyer, S., Schmitt, M., Ohmer, M., & Gorecky, D. (2015). Towards industry 4.0-standardization as the crucial challenge for highly modular, multivendor production systems. *IFAC-PapersOnLine*, *48*(3), 579–584. doi:10.1016/j.ifacol.2015.06.143

Yang, R., Yu, F. R., Si, P., Yang, Z., & Zhang, Y. (2019). Integrated blockchain and edge computing systems: A survey, some research issues and challenges. *IEEE Communications Surveys and Tutorials*, *21*(2), 1508–1532. doi:10.1109/COMST.2019.2894727

Zhong, R. Y., Xu, X., Klotz, E., & Newman, S. T. (2017). Intelligent manufacturing in the context of industry 4.0: A review. *Engineering*, *3*(5), 616–630. doi:10.1016/J.ENG.2017.05.015

Zhou, K., Liu, T., & Zhou, L. (2015). Industry 4.0: Towards future industrial opportunities and challenges. *2015 12th International conference on fuzzy systems and knowledge discovery (FSKD),* 2147–2152. doi:10.1109/FSKD.2015.7382284

Chapter 10
Risk-Resilient Supply Chain Using Blockchain Technology

Bhoomi Gupta
Maharaja Agrasen Institute of Technology, India

Harsh Yadav
Maharaja Agrasen Institute of Technology, India

ABSTRACT

Recently, blockchain technology has been recognized for other industries than finance, proving it's potential other than cryptocurrencies and bitcoin. Supply chain is one of the exponentially growing industries which needs to undergo through changes in order to survive in tomorrow's economy. There are many risks involved in current supply chains that can be potentially eliminated with the implementation of blockchain. This chapter analyses the various aspects of blockchain technology and how other technologies can be integrated with it to deliver exceptional solutions. Various risks present in the current system are discussed along with how those risks can be handled using blockchain, contributing towards building a risk resilient supply chain.

INTRODUCTION

With an exponential rise in the number of products and services, and the rising number of risks and threats to the Supply Chains of these products, there is an immediate need to move ahead from traditional supply chains and make a more robust, transparent and scalable system to manage them and protect them from these treats.

DOI: 10.4018/978-1-7998-8081-3.ch010

Supply Chain

Supply chain consists of an out-sized number of steps between the origin of the merchandise to the consumer. Because there are numerous transactions between parties like the supplier, logistics, wholesale, retail and at the top the customer, and since the varied parties maintain independent views of their transaction history there are many issues requiring resolution of disputes. A supply chain can be often very fragmented, which makes it difficult to track the origin and the location or the position of the product within the chain. There also are problems with fraud and theft of fabric during a supply chain. The participants can share the information securely in a Blockchain powered supply chain network which reduces the risk of tampering and hence able to score rewards in terms of more precise and efficient process of transaction (Corporate Finance Institute, n.d.).

Traditional Supply Chains

Traditionally, Supply Chain has consistently been upheld the "four Vs": volatility, volume, velocity and visibility and experts had the objective of improving prompts in terms of complete cost, administration quality and backing for development. These needs aren't probably going to fluctuate, yet with the new difficulties of the present relentless world, new advanced advances should build the degree of execution.

These chains were developed decades ago, and the supply chains present today are turning out hard to manage and are not capable of supporting the chains which distinguish the globalized digital economy. The outdated supply chains are built upon centralized systems which do not provide the traceability, transparency, accountability and efficiency which is required in today's economy.

While few leading companies have started to realize that traceability, transparency and accountability gives a very crucial competitive advantage in global trade, and when it comes to conscious capitalism, changes should be made towards achieving that goal. In order to secure their place in the changing economy, the supply chains should be developed using technologies like Blockchain in order to evolve them for tomorrow's world.

Challenges in Traditional Supply Chains

In these supply chains, there isn't any presence of a Universal Database. Even though everything is connected in today's world, many organizations still prefer to keep their databases restricted to themselves. All the parties are keeping their individual records and are shared only upon the other party's request. Due to this, there are many communication gaps between these parties which make room for the exploiters.

Inability of tracing the assets is also one of the obstacles found in supply chain management. Once the products come out of production and proceed on their journey to the consumer, there are a number of steps in between and the product can't be traced throughout the life cycle efficiently. This makes it easy for exploiters to tamper with the product in between these steps (Bhardwaj, 2019).

Since all the parties maintain their individual databases, their capital and efforts are often invested into collecting the same information again and again which causes an extreme rise in the associated cost.

Due to the discontinuity in the present Supply chain management systems, it is a very tedious and high-cost task to figure out at which point in the chain the quality has been compromised, or the product has been tampered or replaced. And due to the centralized structure, there are multiple risks like code of conduct violations and frauds in a company's process which shows us the dire need to improve the risk management process in supply chain systems.

How Does Blockchain Solve the Problem

Blockchain provides a number of advantages over traditional supply chains which can be helped to drastically improve the existing systems. Particularly when Blockchain is combined with other disruptive technologies like big data, machine learning and Internet of Things (IoT).

Blockchain carries on the communication of data and information to the entities on a real-time basis in a supply chain network. When in a blockchain based supply chain, any new change takes place all the entities in the chain can be informed about this in real-time making it an overall smoother process throughout the life cycle of the product. And by replacing the traditional documents needed for the transaction by smart contracts, the process can be made a lot more faster and efficient.

It also provides enhanced security and secure transmission which makes sure that correct information is transmitted in the supply chain network. Blockchain's fundamental use of cryptographic hashing in order to facilitate every update in the chain ensures us authenticity and security. And it provides transparency in the supply chain to all the parties like manufacturers, consumers as well as third parties like regulators which are associated with the product. With this, those with the specified access to the chain can trace and track the products or services throughout the chain. In case of a product moving in the chain, the producers can easily track the source of any faulty or impure components, consumers or retailers can verify the origin and authenticity of the product, and the regulators can easily verify if the products or services are following the specified regulations and standards (Chang et al., 2017).

LITERATURE SURVEY

The traditional supply chain is pretty outdated at this point and has many flaws which need to be addressed in order to face tomorrow's economy. Technological advancements and globalization are leading supply chain implementations with new technologies dealing with the risks throughout the process, new ways to reduce their costs, increase the efficiency and increase their profits. Supply chains are a very essential part of many industries, evolving the supply chains enables the company to grow their business. The major factors on which the supply chains are going through changes throughout the industry are reduction of costs, automation, expansion and data analytics.

Visibility in Supply Chains

One of the main factors involved in SCM systems are visibility. The organizations should be aware of what is going on in their chains to make sure they are functioning like the way they should but many of them don't have the complete visibility access of their own supply chains. According to a survey, 62% companies reported that they have restricted or limited visibility of their supply chain, 15% have only visibility on production, 17% have extended visibility of supply chains and only 6% businesses have full visibility access throughout the chain (Forbes Insights, 2018).

Logistics

Logistics is another crucial part of supply chains. Shipping and transportation are very important steps as they are involved from receiving raw materials, to transporting the finished product to intermediaries and finally the consumers. The factors involved in logistics contribute in determining the overall cost of the operations. Statistics say that the costs involved in logistics are predicted to grow in the coming years. Logistics activities currently contribute towards 12% of the global GDP (Partida, n.d.). Blockchain can be implemented to track the commodity throughout its journey and with its help it can become easier to determine the location of the product at any instant and in case of any faults and failures in the chain, it can be identified instantly as compared to traditional supply chains where it takes days, and in cases weeks to determine the point of fault.

Use Cases of Blockchain

Reduction of Costs

In a blockchain based supply chain the products can be tracked in real-time which helps in reducing the overall cost incurred in logistic operations. A survey conducted by Digital Supply Chain Institute (DSCI) and APQC about supply chain workers, states that more than a third of people stated reductions in costs as the biggest advantage of using Blockchain is supply chains (Black, 2017).

On successful application of blockchain in supply chains in order to speed up the administrative processes, the overall costs are reduced due to the removal of extra steps. And even after this reduction, the security of all the transactions and steps is intact. Implementing this system eliminates intermediaries and middlemen in the supply chain which brings down the costs and saves from the risks such as duplicacy and frauds (Gupta, 2020). This improves the efficiency in the system and due to accurate maintenance of records, the risk of losing commodities is also minimized.

Provenance Tracking

Supply chains in large organizations and companies involve a large number of components and step. Therefore, it becomes extremely difficult to keep track for all the records, even when it comes to big corporations. Due to the lack of transparency and trust, customer relations and costs suffer which brings down the organizations' image.

When a supply chain management system is made using Blockchain technology, maintaining records and tracking the sources becomes smooth and easy as the commodities can be tracked and their information can be made accessible by integrating embedded sensors, QR Codes, and RFID tags. The commodity can be tracked throughout its life cycle from its origin to the consumer. This precision in tracking makes it easy to detect risks and frauds in the supply chain (Walmart, 2019).

Establishment of Trust

In a complex, segmented and branched supply chain, having trust between the parties is very crucial for a smooth flow in the chain. The manufacturers should be able to trust the sources of raw materials, and later on the logistics team to safely transfer the commodity, the retailers should be able to trust the producer for the quality and constituents of the product. Even when it comes to regulatory boards, trust is a very important factor. A blockchain based system, due to its immutable nature, makes it tamper proof and helps in establishing trust (Kamath, 2018).

Case Studies

Walmart

Whenever a food-borne disease outbreak takes place, it takes effort and several days to determine its source. Walmart implemented a system with IBM considering blockchain technology might be suitable for a decentralized food supply chain. This food traceability system was developed on Hyperledger Fabric.

In order to test this system, Walmart followed two approaches, or two Proof of Concepts. One of them was to track mangoes which were sold in the US stores of Walmart, and the other one was based in Walmart's China stores to track pork. The two products worked successfully. The time taken to track the provenance of mangoes in Walmart, US came down from 7 days to 2.2 seconds due to this system. In case of Walmart's China stores the system was capable of uploading certificates to ensure authenticity improving the trust factor in the system.

Walmart is expanding their blockchain based systems and at the moment they use this Hyperledger Fabric based system to track more than 25 products. These products include various fruits, dairy products, meat products, and also some packaged products. They are aiming to expand their network and implement more solutions using blockchain technology (Scott, 2017).

wBext360

Bext360 is a company which provides high-quality agricultural products, straight from the source. One of their primary products is coffee. They have developed the world's first system for blockchain traceable coffee. Coffee comes on the second spot in the list of most traded commodities of the world. However, a major proportion of the coffee in the world is manufactured by small farmers who depend on various factors promising them very unstable and less income. Bext360 has partnered up with various organizations such as Moyee Coffee, Great Lakes Coffee, and Coda Coffee to develop a more transparent system which promises more equity to the coffee farmers (Chowdhury, 2019).

They have utilized various Artificial Intelligence, Machine Learning and IoT solutions to implement this system. One of their chains aims to source coffee from Eastern Uganda in Africa to Denver, US. Their machine known as Bextmachine is used to determine the grades and quality of coffee beans using ML and IoT. This machine is also based on blockchain technology which helps to track the coffee's origin and also to pay the farmers digitally with mobile application. The path from the origin to the destination is tracked down using blockchain. By the use of this platform, all the stakeholders i.e. retailers, consumers, roaster and farmers have access to the data throughout the supply chain. This allows to determine any faults in logistics and also to provide better return to the farmers producing higher quality products.

Also the payments to the farmers, parties involved in logistics, roasters, and all other stakeholders are carried using blockchain technology if possible. After implementing this system the overall efficiency of the system is drastically improved, tracking the product has become easier, the costs are decreased, the farmers are paid well, and the consumers are promised high quality products.

TECHNICAL APPROACH

Blockchain

A blockchain fundamentally is a distributed ledger which is on a peer-to-peer network. A blockchain is a series of blocks which contains the data stored in every node, each node signifying the participants of the chain. In the chain every block represents a record which is timestamped and is verified by the protocols of the blockchain network and is secured via hashing, or public-key cryptography. Because of this there is no requirement for a trusted central entity. Therefore blockchain is a decentralized database without any single central entity. A number of participating nodes are present in this database, which follow a set of protocols, according to which they behave in the network and store the information in a specified structure. The contents of a blockchain are immutable. Therefore the ledger is accessible as an immutable source of data.

Figure 1. Connection of blocks in blockchain

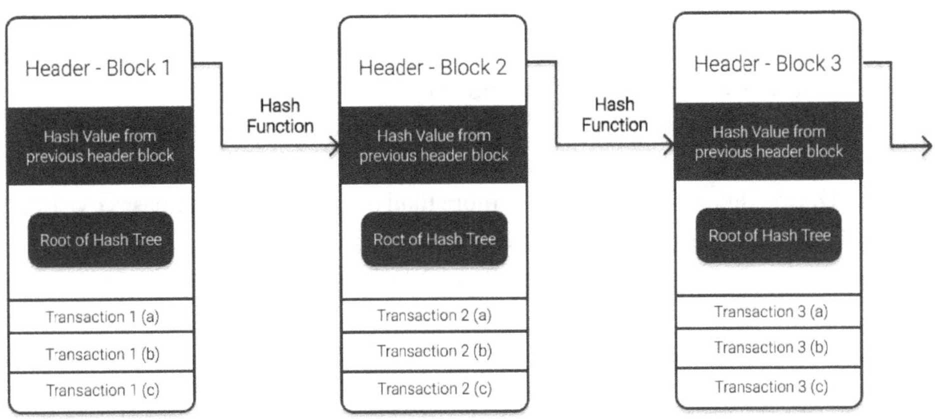

Proof of Work

In a Blockchain network, Proof of Work(PoW) is the original consensus algorithm. This algorithm is responsible for providing conformation of the transaction and creation of a new block to the chain. In case of every transaction a group of people called miners compete in order to complete the transaction in the network. This process is known as mining. When the miners successfully validate the transaction by creating a valid block, they are rewarded. Bitcoin and Etherium are some popular applications of Proof of Work. In the case of Bitcoin, the miner who is the first to validate the transaction is awarded with some Bitcoins.

The principle on which PoW works is a mathematical puzzle which requires intense computational power and energy to solve in order to successfully validate the transaction and it becomes complex as we move further in the chain. Generally, the miner with high computational power wins. In Proof of Work, the validity of block is verified by the other nodes present in the system by making sure that the hash corresponding to the data is less than a present number.

Proof of Stake

In case of Proof of Stake (PoS), the computational power and energy constraints of PoW are taken out of the picture and are replaced by stake. Stake represents an amount of currency that can be locked up for some period of time which results in their increased chances to be the next miner during addition of a new block. Cryptocurrencies like Blackcoin and Nxt use PoS.

Protocol of Consensus

Along with the creation of digital currency Bitcoin by Nakamoto, a protocol of consensus was also developed which provided confidence and trust on a peer-to-peer network without a central intermediary. The three pillars on which this protocol stands is: consensus, decentralization and cryptography.

Here decentralization states that the participants are distributed over the database and everyone in the system has the potential of accessing the data. Because of decentralization there is a possibility of more than one version of databases existing. Now, the consensus comes into play, the entities in the system agree upon the source of truth which is feasible due to the Proof of Work and computational power.

The miners which are present in some specific nodes constantly work and solve mathematical problems which consume energy and computational power, once that problem is solved another block can be added to the chain or in the database. The source of truth is the longest chain within the blockchain system. The last pillar and the most crucial one is cryptography. Cryptographic technology is crucial for data integrity and digital signatures. In Bitcoin blockchain, SHA-256 cryptography is applied in order to generate hash values which, when combined with the other 2 pillars, make this protocol unique. Due to one-way creation of hash value, data integrity is ensured by SHA-256 which means that the hash value is always derived by input data but the original data input can't be received using the hash value.

Figure 2. A simple transaction in blockchain

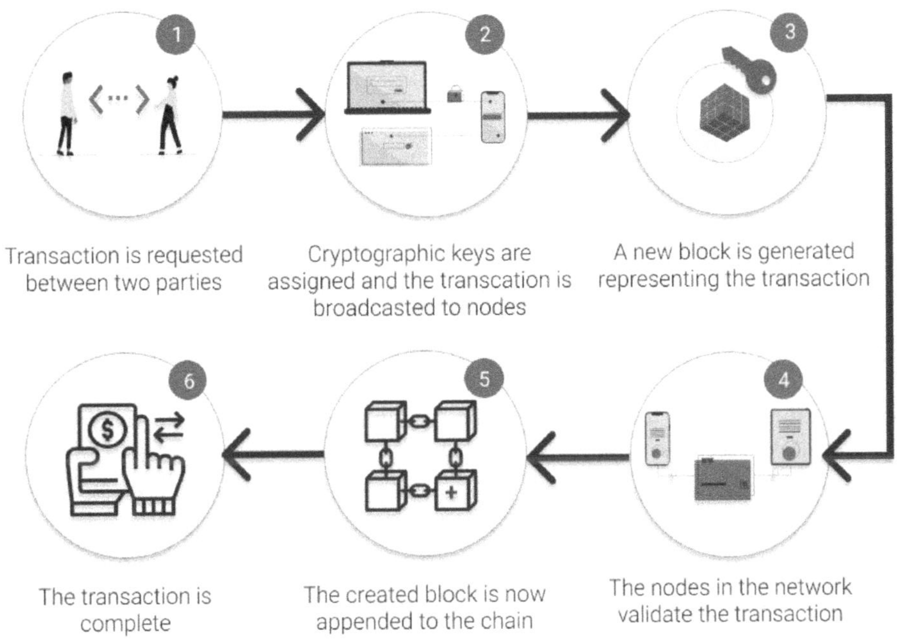

Smart Contracts

Smart contracts are pieces of code which are implemented with blockchain and this is a self executing code which is specified with the conditions required for a transaction. This contract consists of the terms of agreement between the parties of the transaction. They are used to enforce an agreement without any involvement of an intermediary. The transactions done by smart contracts are irreversible. Using smart contracts, transactions can be made between parties irrespective of their identity, without any presence of a legal system or a central authority. Smart contracts are used to manage the access rights between the parties and their tokenized assets efficiently. The access rights are stored and implemented on a blockchain where they can't be modified, tampered and deleted. Therefore, smart contracts give us a public and verifiable method in order to implement rules, regulations, and business logic with a piece of code, audited and implemented by a majority of nodes in a peer-to-peer network.

Smart contracts can be implemented for many use cases. They can be implemented for simple transactions of money transfer between two parties. But, they can be used for maintaining and updating ownership and legal rights for parties, such as intellectual property and property registries. They have the potential to be implemented in a number of use cases in different industries.

TECHNICAL APPROACH

The stakeholders involved in a big supply chain can be very high, with very wide ranges which means that association between the parties can be very complex. Implementing a blockchain solution can be very helpful in helping and boosting the modern supply chains, especially in the case of improving the trust factor between the stakeholders. In traditional supply chains there are frequent cases of failures, frauds and human errors, hence the proposed system should be robust, effective, efficient and should be able to handle these risks from traditional systems. This system should be able to handle data effectively, maintain the records and create a smooth flow of data throughout the network. A blockchain based system aims to track the entire system from the extraction of raw materials, the production in factories all the way to the consumer, which is a very complex task in the traditional systems (Saini and Gupta, 2019).

The proposed system aims to connect all the stakeholders in the system through a decentralized network which is transparent and immutable. Various stakeholders should have access to the information they need in order to establish trust between the parties maintaining the authenticity of the product. Smart contracts will help to implement the tracing process and to achieve secure data provenance.

In a generalized supply chains the stakeholders present are:

1. **Provider of raw materials**: The source from which the raw materials are brought to the factory or processing unit which can be different depending on the industry. Different materials used in the production can range from metals for producing machines such as automobiles, plastic and wires for producing electronics and seeds, chemicals in cases of agricultural supply chains. Implementing blockchain helps building trust for authenticity of the raw materials and to keep track of raw material and how it is integrated with the product till reaching the end customer.

2. **Producer:** These are the entities which take the raw materials and build components which will be then put together in order to make the product. This can also vary depending on the type of industry and can be referred using different names depending on the type of commodity produced. In the case of agricultural chains, the farmers are producers who take the raw materials and produce the grains and provide them to industries. Use of blockchain enables the producer to trust the raw material source enabling the production of quality products.
3. **Manufacturer/Processor:** These are the stakeholders which take the components produced by the previous entities and combine them together. They can be classified in many categories as well, but in most cases they bind the smaller components into final products. In case of agricultural chains these are the ones responsible for any processing of crops, grains and packaging them. In traditional systems, they have limited capabilities of verifying the quality of raw materials and also tracking their product to the next stage, but having a digital supply chain means a good connected network of suppliers and distributors.

Figure 3. Architecture of a generalized supply chain

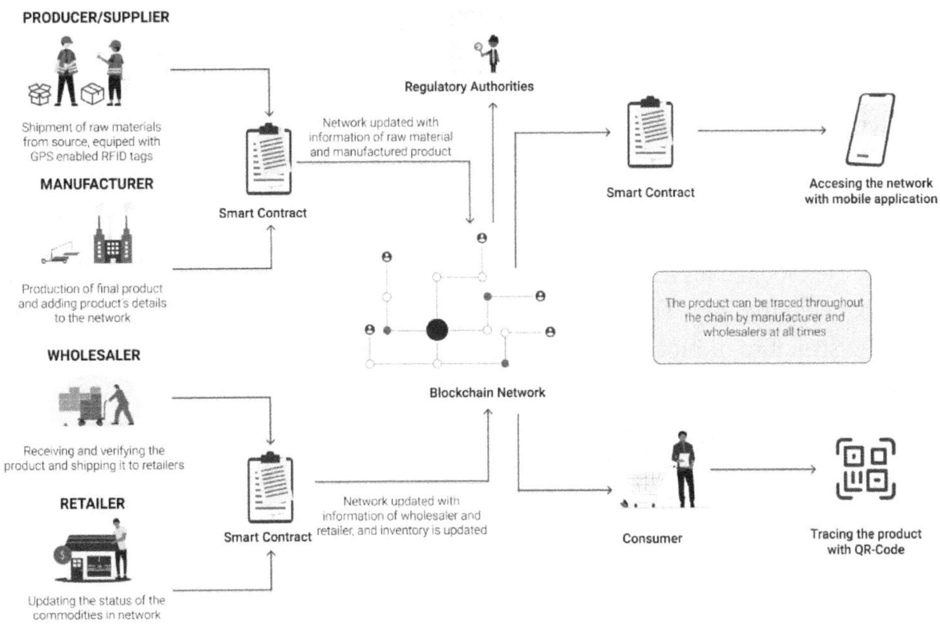

4. **Wholesaler/Retailer:** These entities receive the final products in bulk from the manufacturer and they are responsible for selling and transporting the products to small retailers or the stores from where the people can buy them. Using a blockchain based system makes it convenient for them to check the provenance and the logistics conditions.
5. **Consumer:** They are the final entity in the chain who buy the products and use them. In a blockchain network they have a full transparent view of the whole journey of the product.

During this whole process there is heavy involvement of logistics between and among each step. Different stakeholders also have to comply with different rules and regulations specified by the authorities. And the information related to logistics should be made available to the concerned parties in the network and the information related to different stakeholders can be made accessible to the authorities and the regulatory boards easily through this platform.

Blockchain Layer

This is the most important component of the architecture which is implemented using smart contracts describing the core functionalities of blockchain networks. This layer is responsible for verifying and registering the transactions in the ledger by establishing consensus among the nodes of the network. The complexity of this module will change depending on the type of technology used to implement blockchain. The overall blockchain data structure is built in this layer. The consensus algorithms and protocols used for the system depending on the use case, determines the speed of efficiency of processing the transactions.

Blockchain layer consists of modules to handle the transactions in order to save them in the blockchain ledger. The consensus module and the transaction modules are connected directly. They function together along with the middleware used to form the structure of blockchain. The data stored after each transaction consists of the addresses of sender and receiver, hash, timestamp, amount of the transaction and some other important specified information.

Middleware

These are the layers and modules acting as an interface between the blockchain layer and the end layer. The functionalities provided by this layer include storing the e-invoices of the transaction efficiently in the database. The functionality of uploading these documents such as receipts and e-invoices is implemented here.

This module interacts with the application layer with the help of APIs for integrating the upload of certificates facility in the software.

In order to maintain authenticity in the system, the verified users of the platform are provided with accreditation certificates which are necessary for transacting in the network. These certificates are also stored in a blockchain which are verified before every transaction.

Smart Contracts

A module is designed as a part of middleware in order to manage the smart contracts. It takes care of the operations related to Smart contracts such as creating them, their deployment and triggering them according to the specified conditions. It consists of all the necessary information that is required to authenticate a transaction. Whenever an e-invoice is uploaded to the portal, this module takes those inputs with all the fields available in the document and a new smart contract is created. This smart contract is then deployed in the blockchain network and is triggered according to the conditions and performs the task it's supposed to do.

Figure 4. Smart contract implementation in blockchain

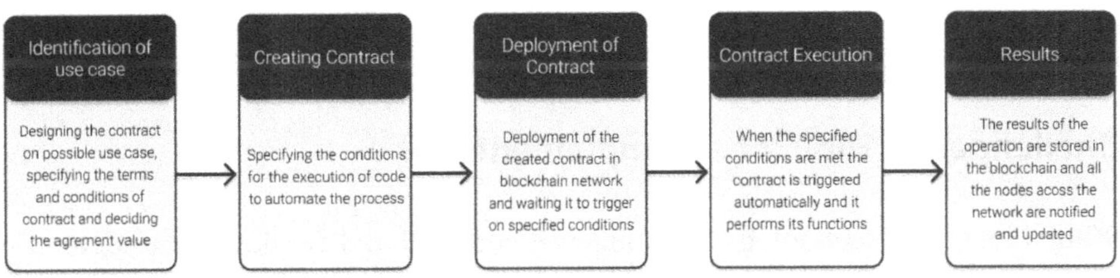

They can be coupled with some IoT devices for tracking the location of commodities, and can be used to track the product throughout the chain. Tracking the provenance of goods can be made easier by using them. The products should be fitted with devices like RFID tags with GPS, which can be scanned at every stage of production and logistics which makes it convenient for all the stakeholders to track the product and provenance at every step.

These contracts also enable the users to make efficient and secure transactions directly on the network. At the time of the order, the customer must have sufficient currency present in their wallet which is being used in the blockchain, which can be moved to the other party once the goods are moved and the transaction can be concluded safely.

Blockchain with IoT

In order to develop a risk resilient chain, Blockchain should be coupled with other disruptive technologies in order to make a robust system. One of these technologies is Internet of Things (IoT). IoT with blockchain can provide exceptional traceability solutions and can make provenance tracking easier than ever. Devices such as GPS enabled RFID tags can be integrated with raw materials, components and finished products which can enable the stakeholders to track the product throughout the chain. Using these devices and blockchain's network, the participants can have real time access to data at each step. Thanks to the immutable nature of blockchain, these details can not be altered or deleted preventing frauds and this can drastically improve the efficiency and security in transactions and movement of goods across borders. With the help of IoT devices which can keep a track of the actual status of logistics, and have the ability to execute the payment terms on the completion of shipment, banks can be given access to the contract, the invoice and the status of delivery. This can make it easy for them to check the authenticity of the product, validate the transaction, and speed up the payment process. There can be many other use cases of IoT in supply chains such as smart-thermometers can be integrated with products in food supply chains which can give a live temperature feed making it easier to monitor it throughout the chain. Blockchain and IoT can be combined to solve many problems encountered by supply chains today and contribute towards making them risk resilient.

Challenges in Blockchain Implementation

While blockchain technology has immense potential and is widely considered as an effective solution for the issue with traditional supply chains, there are several challenges in their implementation. The application of blockchain needs drastic changes in the currently existing system. There are many platforms using which blockchain can be implemented, and thorough research should be conducted while implementing these solutions and opting the most appropriate technologies suitable for each use case prioritizing the chain's needs.

Scalability and Performance

A blockchain's performance is judged on the basis of the time it takes to validate a single transaction and to store it on the chain. The transaction to be stored needs to be validated by a majority nodes in the network. Whereas scalability specifies the blockchain's capability to handle more transactions with increasing needs and also to handle addition of more nodes in the network. The type of consensus mechanism used for implementing the chain is a key factor in determining the performance. As the number of nodes increases in the system, the transaction takes more time to process due to the increase in the number of nodes required for validation. The complexity of smart contract is another key factor in determining the processing time of transaction.

Privacy

The blockchain being transparent and immutable also acts as a data privacy concern. The decentralized architecture of blockchain poses a threat as the data can be accessible to everyone in the network, and it can be used to provide inside information to the competitors. Even though the access rights to the information in the network can be specified but maintaining a user's right to privacy is very difficult in an open blockchain. There is a need of a governance mechanism in the system which determines who can join the network, what data is accessible to them, how smart contracts and IoT devices are implemented and the encryption mechanism.

CONCLUSION AND FUTURE SCOPE

There are many obstacles and challenges in tomorrow's evolving supply chains which need to be handled with evolving technologies. Blockchain technology along with other disruptive technologies have immense potential and capacity to benefit present supply chains. It aims to provide a transparent, efficient, decentralized and immutable network to manage supply chains. Although there are many challenges in the implementation and there is a need to research and analyze the type of blockchain and specific technology for different use cases, nonetheless a blockchain based solution can be implemented for improved traceability, efficient provenance tracking, fast transactions and building trust, contributing towards making the supply chain truly risk resilient.

REFERENCES

Bhardwaj. (2019). *How is blockchain disrupting supply chain management*. https:// appinventiv.com/ blog/blockchain-in-supply-chain/#2,of

Black, A. (2017). *Using Blockchain for Supply Chain Transparency and Traceability*. https://medium. com/ blockchain-review/the-visible-supply-chain-ab73a80863fd

Chang, Y., Iakovou, E., & Shi, W. (2017). Blockchain in global supply chains and cross border trade: a critical synthesis of the state-of-the-art, challenges and opportunities. *International Journal Geodis*. https://geodis.com/sites/default/files/2019-03/170509_GEODIS_WHITE-PAPER.PDF

Chowdhury, N. (2019). *Consensus Mechanisms of Blockchain. In Inside Blockchain, Bitcoin, and Cryptocurrencies*. Auerbach Publications. doi:10.1201/9780429325533

Corporate Finance Institute. (n.d.). *What is a supply chain?* CFI. https://corporatefinanceinstitute.com/ resources/knowledge/strategy/supply-chain/

Forbes Insights. (2018). *Logistics, Supply Chain and Transportation 2023 – Change at Breakneck, Speed*. http://info.forbes.com/rs/790-SNV-353/images/Penske_report-final- digital.pdf

S. Gupta and B. Gupta, "Securing Honey Supply Chain through Blockchain," in IoT Security Paradigms and Applications, CRC Press, 2020

Kamath, R. (2018). Food Traceability on Blockchain: Walmart's Pork and Mango Pilots with IBM. *The Journal of the British Blockchain Association*, *1*(1), 1–12. doi:10.31585/jbba-1-1-(10)2018

Konstantopoulos, G. (2017). *Understanding Blockchain Fundamentals: Proof of Work & Proof of Stake*. https://medium.com/loom-network/understanding-blockchain-fundamentals-part-2-proof-of-work-proof-of-stake-b6ae907c7edb9

Partida, B. (n.d.). *APQC, Blockchain and its potential for supply chain innovation*. https://www.apqc.org/ System/files/K08553_APQC_Blockchain%20in%20Supply%20Chain%2,0Operations.pdf

Saini, V., & Gupta, S. (2019). Blockchain in Supply Chain: Journey from Disruptive to Sustainable. *J. Mech. Contin. Math. Sci.*, *14*(2). Advance online publication. doi:10.26782/jmcms.2019.04.00036

Scott, M. (2017). *Bext360 and the World of Blockchain Traceable Coffee*. https://medium.com/@ Theurbane journalist/bext360-and-the-world-of-blockchain-traceable-coffee-4ee1d9bba560

Walmart. (2019). How Walmart brought unprecedented transparency to the food supply Chain with Hyperledger Fabric. *International Journal of Production Research*.

Chapter 11
Role of Cryptocurrency in Digital Marketing

Sonal Trivedi
Chitkara Business School, Chitkara University, India

Reena Malik
Chitkara Business School, Chitkara University, India

ABSTRACT

Today, the world has become a digital platform where technology has become an important part of day-to-day life. The world is growing at a rapid pace where there is a new innovation every other day. As days are passing, every aspect of life has become online. Companies have also identified the scope and opportunity of digital marketing. This chapter discusses how cryptocurrency is a challenge for digital marketing. This study is an exploratory study that involves secondary data collection. The objective of the research is to identify the influence of cryptocurrency on digital marketing. The findings of the study suggest that digital marketing is a data-driven marketing technique, and cryptocurrency is a payment mode that hides data; thus, the popularity of cryptocurrency as a mode of payment is a challenge for digital marketing.

INTRODUCTION

Cryptocurrency

Cryptocurrency has brought complete change in the way individuals make payments. It has totally replaced the other payment mechanism such as bank transfer, payment

DOI: 10.4018/978-1-7998-8081-3.ch011

via credit card and others. In these modes of payment, the information of customer was apparent. For instance, if a customer makes payment via debit card, the information of customer such as name of bank, name of card holder, type of card and frequency of payment is visible. On the other hand, if payment is made via cryptocurrency, all such information is hidden. In case of cryptocurrency, the amount is digitally transferred leaving behind no track.

Digital Marketing

Digital marketing is the method of promotion and sales of goods and services by using marketing techniques of online platforms which are in trend. Online marketing techniques includes SEO (Search Engine Optimization, SMM (Social Media Marketing), e-newsletters, etc.

Role of Cryptocurrency on Digital Marketing

From the above explanation of digital marketing, it is clear that companies require a lot of information of customer which are majorly extracted from their records of payment. For example, if a customer is regular buyer of bread and is making payment using debit cards, then a lot of companies providing related services such as jam, butter, brown bread, etc will pitch that customer by provides discounts and sales messages to him personally via SMS or e-mail. But if the customer is making payment via cryptocurrency, it will become harder for companies to extract the data of customer. The reason behind this is that cryptocurrency has no record of payment history. Thus, cryptocurrency payment is a challenge for digital marketing.

PROBLEM STATEMENT

The evolution of digital technology and availability of internet has changed the way marketing is practiced today. Digital technology has enabled marketers to collect a lot of data about customers and with the use of big data, marketers analyses the customer loyalty, retention and engagement to maximize their performance. Blockchain technology is based on the concept of distributed ledger and stores data securely. It uses a technology named cryptography which ensures that the information is accurate and secure. There are various studies on the significance of blockchain in supply chain management and financial sector. However, there is a lack of study in the field of impact of blockchain technology in the field of digital marketing. The present paper focuses on the role of cryptocurrency in digital marketing.

PURPOSE OF STUDY

The main purpose of present study is to understand the potential benefits and challenges of blockchain technology on the future of digital marketing. The study in beneficial for marketers, managers, academicians and individual in general.

OBJECTIVE OF STUDY

Thus, the objective of present study can be summarized as-

- How cryptocurrency impacts the application of big data in digital marketing?

LITERATURE REVIEW

This chapter covers the systematic study of previous theories of the bigdata, cryptocurrency, blockchain and digital marketing. Literature review further clears the research objective of the study.

Digital Marketing

The concept of digital marketing started in year 1990. Digital marketing is a concept which helps marketers to connect with customers and their need (Brosnan, 2012). Digital marketing is a broad term which covers topic such as customer data mining, e-commerce, mobile marketing, social media marketing, Search Engine Optimization, etc (Langan et al. 2019). Digital marketing applies technology such as databases, e-mail, mobile, Web, digital TV etc. to connect with customers with the objective to improve customer acquisition and retention (Chaffey, 2010). Businesses opted digital marketing as a competitive advantage, to increase customer interaction and brand building (Tiago & Verissimo, 2014). Thus, Digital marketing is the method of promotion and sales of goods and services by using marketing techniques of online platforms which are in trend. Online marketing techniques includes SEO (Search Engine Optimization, SMM (Social Media Marketing), e-newsletters, etc.

Big Data

Data is fact or information about an individual which in its raw form may not be important but its interpretations can be veery significant for marketer (Alshura et al., 2018). Big data is referred to has huge data sets. Thus, analyzing a huge data set becomes a challenge for marketers. Big data analytics is a methodology to analyze huge data sets and improve the operations of companies (Gruschka et al. 2018).

Application of Big Data in Digital Marketing

In this era of digitalization, a lot of customer data is available such as number of clicks, likes, shares, comments, retweets, tags, blogs, customer review, etc. Such data can be used by marketers for better understanding of competitor and customers (Langan et al. 2019). These data can be used by marketers to frame and evaluate their marketing strategy (Kannan & Li, 2017). Marketers also face challenges in using big data in digital marketing such as vast data, irrelevant and unimportant data, extracting relevant information, advertising budget, etc (Joshi & Marthandan, 2019). Additionally, consumers are day-by-day becoming conscious about privacy of their data (Pingitore et al. 2013).

Blockchain

It is a technology which is derived from distributed ledger technology (Saberi et al. 2019). Blockchain are of two types- public and private (Underwood, 2016). A pubic blockchain permits everyone to access it thus it is open on the other hand, private blockchain permits only known users, thus it is closed (Underwood, 2016).

Cryptocurrency

Cryptocurrency is digital currency which is launched with the purpose that it will act as an exchange medium using solid cryptography for safely creating and monitoring currency units and substantiating fund transfer. Various encryption algorithms are used in it and cryptographic techniques such as hashing functions, public private key pairs, elliptical curve encryption, etc. This reduces the chances of fraud in transactions. Cryptocurrency is decentralized as there is no government intervention. It depends on block chain technology which is a distributed ledger technology. Blockchain works on the network of computers which has same database and keep on updating records through consensus on pure mathematics basis (Hong, Park & Yu, 2018).

It is difficult to trace cryptocurrency as no one has any idea regarding the location and amount in your wallet. While, Fiat currency is traceable because the data is maintained in the bank. Hence, government authorities have total information regarding your transactions.

Regulations related to cryptocurrency

Cryptocurrency is totally opposite of traditional system of financing. It does not rely on government control over exchanges and transactions. Thus, regulatory authorities are facing challenges from virtual currency which surpasses regulated financial institutions such as banks, exchanges and clearing houses. Few believe that sooner or later, cryptocurrency will also come under rigid regulatory system. Others say that too rigid system slower the rate of innovation and growth (Urquhart, 2017).

European Securities and Market Authorities believes that monitoring and controlling of block chain is necessary as it is growing popular. They believe that this technology has changed the way securities are traded. ESMA is also evaluating the function of cryptocurrency from the point of view of virtual currency, as ICO and as distributed ledger technology (Antonopoulos, 2017).

Institute such as Financial Regulatory Industry Authority and National Futures Association have set an example of self-regulations. The success of BitCoin goes to immense use of internet by users and less rigid system. The case would not be same if there was licensing for setting up a website or application.

Blockchain in Relation to Marketing

Blockchain is expected to carry both challenges and opportunities in relation to marketing (Ertemel, 2018). This technology will bring the security of personal data of consumer and will disrupt the present marketing environment (Kshetri and Voas, 2019). Parssinen et al. 2018 discussed in his paper that blockchain technology will bring transparency and trust in field of advertising and marketing. The present environment of digital marketing has brought various intermediaries on which marketers depend for data of customer (Parssinen et al. 2018). Implementation of blockchain technology will bring transparency in digital marketing (Ertemel 2018). Blockchain technology will allow marketers to empower over fradulant activities such as pay-per-click frauds (Kshetri & Voas, 2019). Due to Blockchain technology, data will be owned by customers and companies will directly contact customers to take their feedback instead of intermediaries (Ertemel, 2018). Thus, blockchain will dissolve this practice of collecting large customer data and selling it to corporates (Ertemel, 2018). Hence, this technology may solve the issue of frauds and lack of transparency for marketers but will increase the challenge for present online advertising practices (Parssinen et al. 2018).

Figure 1 shows the opportunity offered by implementation of Blockchain technology. Thus, it can be said that there is a great impact of a digital currency on digital marketing.

Figure 1. Opportunities offered by blockchain
Source – Stratablue.com

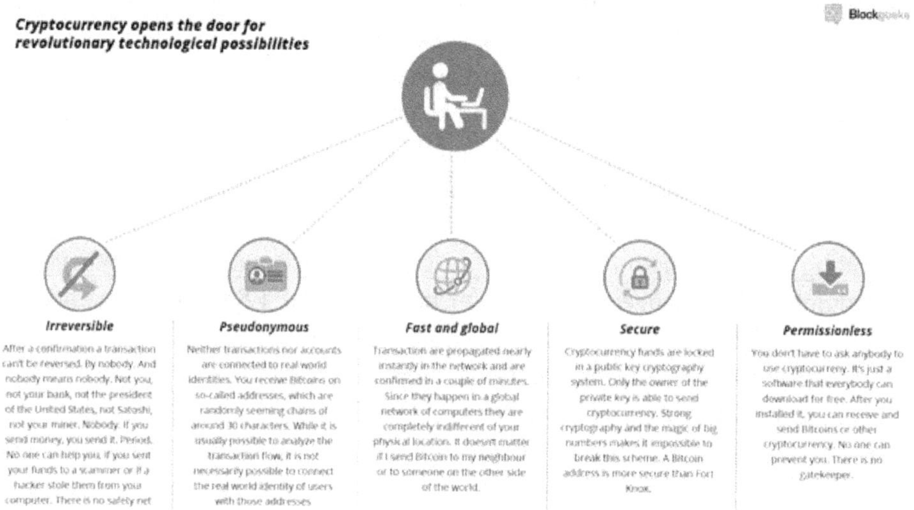

SWOT ANALYSIS OF CRYPTOCURRENCY

STRENGTH

- Bitcoin (one of the popular cryptocurrencies) has limited supply and hence it will never be overvalued with increase in demand like other valued objects (Er-Rajy, 2017).
- It provides an opportunity of safe investment for investors to keep their surplus wealth and will not come under the strict regulations of government.
- The demand for BitCoin has increased over the period of time because of its price variability, safety and increasing growth rate (Mirzayi & Mehrzad, 2017).
- Bitcoin out cast the competition as it is the only currency which can be exchanged, purchased and sold quickly.

WEAKNESS

- visibility of ledger transaction to all
- susceptibility to cyber attack
- cannot handle overload of transactions

- user will hesitate to use because of the risk of system going down due to overload of transaction (DeVries, 2016)
- Case of Silk road (website dealing in drugs, criminal activities and other illegal activities) has raised a question mark on digital currency.
- It is difficult for government to track down such illegal sources because of BitCoin (Vassiliadis et al. 2017)
- It will become mode of payment for criminals
- There are various cases of cyber security and hacking which has caused huge loss of money such as Mt. Gox resulting into drop in the use of BitCoin as it lacks security

OPPORTUNITIES

- BitCoin is an opportunity as it provides scope of improvement for future research in technology (Billah & Atbani, 2019)
- there are chances of cryptocoin technology to become legal
- It has filled the gap which was there in traditional banking system
- Two users of BitCoin can easily connect with each other with the help of QR Code
- there is a scope of better application and website for cryptocurrency (Eyal et al. 2016)
- It may be traded on stock market like any other commodity such as gold
- It is growing day by day and gaining popularity in international market

FINDINGS

The impact of cryptocurrency on digital marketing can be summarized as below-

1. Customer will be owner of his data

As discussed in this paper, digital marketing is based on data/information of customer. Companies use customer data to plan their marketing strategies to pitch the prospective customer. These data help companies to extract the prospective customer on the basis of his purchase history. If the use of cryptocurrency as mode of payment will increase, the customer will become the owner of his data and it will not be revealed to others. Thus, companies will face challenge in collecting data related to purchase history and purchase pattern of customer.

2. Impact on online advertisement

One of strategies of digital marketing is online advertisement. Customer today make their purchase decision on the basis of online advertisements they see and which matches to their current need. Earlier companies use to gather information regarding need of customer on the basis of his purchase pattern and then used to pitch customer through online advertising. Since, cryptocurrency will hide the data of customer, companies can not pitch customer through online advertising.

3. Reduced interference of intermediaries

When a customer makes regular payments through same mode, the intermediary saves those details and suggests and directs customer to complete the transaction. For example, when a customer use Amazon as platform for purchase of good and uses his debit card for regular payments, Amazon saves the payment detail of customer and directs customer for payment during his future purchases. If customer will use cryptocurrency as mode of payment, his details will not be available with intermediaries like amazon.

4. Increased customer privacy

In this era of internet, the information of individual is available everywhere such as Google, Facebook, etc. This information of customer is sold to companies for digital marketing. The companies strategize their digital marketing on the basis of details of customer. The use of cryptocurrency will increase the privacy of customer and players such as Google, Facebook will not have access to customer information.

5. Purchase of customer Data

Digital marketing depends on the data of customer and companies purchase customer data from popular platforms of interaction such as Google, Facebook etc. If usage of cryptocurrency is increased then these platforms will not be able to access customer data. In such cases, companies may require to contact customer directly for gaining information. Thus, increase use of cryptocurrency is a threat to social media marketing also.

6. Positive impact of cryptocurrency on digital marketing

Companies are presently spending a lot on social media marketing and purchase of customer data. This expenditure is made by companies to provide customized advertising to target audience. Thus, cryptocurrency will hide this data and save companies from spending a lot of money in collecting this data. Thus, companies can use digital platforms to directly reach to the customer rather than depending on these intermediaries and spending a lot of money in purchasing data.

CONCLUSION

The impact of cryptocurrency is that it provides customer the complete control of his data. Thus, companies cannot influence them to purchase a good or service they are not in need or have interest. It will become difficult for marketers to frame digital marketing strategies to reach to their target as marketers will lack information related to purchase pattern of customer. BitCoin can be used in any country as it does not require currency conversion and hence it is liked by many people as a means of transaction in spite of its various disadvantages. It uses block chain technology to maintain the ledger of all transactions. There are no charges on transactions through BitCoin. Its increase awareness will attract more users. It is going to change the face of digital marketing.

REFERENCES

Alshura, M. S., Zabadi, A., & Abughazaleh, M. (2018). Big Data in Marketing Arena. Big Opportunity, Big Challenge, and Research Trends: An Integrated View. *Management and Economics Review, 3*(1), 75-84.

Amsyar, I., Christopher, E., Dithi, A., Khan, A. N., & Maulana, S. (2020). The Challenge of Cryptocurrency in the Era of the Digital Revolution: A Review of Systematic Literature. *Aptisi Transactions on Technopreneurship*, *2*(2), 153–159. doi:10.34306/att.v2i2.96

Antoniadis, I., Kontsas, S., & Spinthiropoulos, K. (2019). Blockchain Applications in Marketing. *Proceedings of 7th ICCMI.*

Antoniadis, I., Spinthiropoulos, K., & Kontsas, S. (2020). Blockchain Applications in Tourism and Tourism Marketing: A Short Review. In *Strategic Innovative Marketing and Tourism* (pp. 375–384). Springer. doi:10.1007/978-3-030-36126-6_41

Antonopoulos, A. M. (2017). *Mastering bitcoin: Programming the open blockchain.* O'Reilly Media, Inc.

Billah, M. M. S., & Atbani, F. M. (2019). SWOT Analysis of Cryptocurrency an Ethical Thought. *Journal of Islamic Banking & Finance, 36*(1).

Brosan, F. (2012). What works where in B2B digital marketing. *Journal of Direct, Data and Digital Marketing Practice, 14*(2), 154–159. doi:10.1057/dddmp.2012.29

Chaffey, D. (2010). Applying organisational capability models to assess the maturity of digital-marketing governance. *Journal of Marketing Management, 26*(3-4), 187–196. doi:10.1080/02672571003612192

DeVries, P. D. (2016). An analysis of cryptocurrency, bitcoin, and the future. *International Journal of Business Management and Commerce, 1*(2), 1–9.

Dey, P. P. (2019). Cryptocurrency: Its Implications and. Evincepub Publishing.

Er-Rajy, L., El Kiram My, A., El Ghazouani, M., & Achbarou, O. (2017). Blockchain: Bitcoin wallet cryptography security, challenges and countermeasures. *Journal of Internet Banking and Commerce, 22*(3), 1–29.

Ertemel, A. V. (2018). Implications of blockchain technology on marketing. *Journal of International Trade, Logistics and law, 4*(2), 35-44.

Eyal, I., Gencer, A. E., Sirer, E. G., & Van Renesse, R. (2016). Bitcoin-ng: A scalable blockchain protocol. In 13th USENIX symposium on networked systems design and implementation (NSDI 16) (pp. 45-59). USENIX.

Gruschka, N., Mavroeidis, V., Vishi, K., & Jensen, M. (2018, December). Privacy issues and data protection in big data: a case study analysis under GDPR. In *2018 IEEE International Conference on Big Data (Big Data)* (pp. 5027-5033). IEEE. 10.1109/BigData.2018.8622621

Herhausen, D., Miočević, D., Morgan, R. E., & Kleijnen, M. H. (2020). The digital marketing capabilities gap. *Industrial Marketing Management, 90*, 276–290. doi:10.1016/j.indmarman.2020.07.022

Hong, K., Park, K., & Yu, J. (2018). Crowding out in a dual currency regime? Digital versus fiat currency. *Emerging Markets Finance & Trade, 54*(11), 2495–2515. doi:10.1080/1540496X.2018.1452732

Joshi, P. L., & Marthandan, G. (2018). The hype of big data analytics and auditors. *EMAJ: Emerging Markets Journal, 8*(2), 1–4. doi:10.5195/emaj.2018.153

Kannan, P. K., & Li, H. A. (2017). Digital marketing: A framework, review and research agenda. *International Journal of Research in Marketing, 34*(1), 22–45. doi:10.1016/j.ijresmar.2016.11.006

Kshetri, N., & Voas, J. (2019). Online advertising fraud. *Computer, 52*(1), 58–61. doi:10.1109/MC.2018.2887322

Langan, R., Cowley, S., & Nguyen, C. (2019). The state of digital marketing in academia: An examination of marketing curriculum's response to digital disruption. *Journal of Marketing Education, 41*(1), 32–46. doi:10.1177/0273475318823849

Mirzayi, S., & Mehrzad, M. (2017, October). Bitcoin, an SWOT analysis. In *2017 7th International Conference on Computer and Knowledge Engineering (ICCKE)* (pp. 205-210). IEEE. 10.1109/ICCKE.2017.8167876

Penny, T. L. (2018). *Basic Attention Token & Brave: Digital Marketing on the Blockchain.* Academic Press.

Pingitore, G., Meyers, J., Clancy, M., & Cavallaro, K. (2013). *Consumer concerns about data privacy rising: What can business do.* Academic Press.

Saberi, S., Kouhizadeh, M., Sarkis, J., & Shen, L. (2019). Blockchain technology and its relationships to sustainable supply chain management. *International Journal of Production Research, 57*(7), 2117–2135. doi:10.1080/00207543.2018.1533261

Saberi, S., Kouhizadeh, M., Sarkis, J., & Shen, L. (2019). Blockchain technology and its relationships to sustainable supply chain management. *International Journal of Production Research, 57*(7), 2117–2135. doi:10.1080/00207543.2018.1533261

Tiago, M. T. P. M. B., & Veríssimo, J. M. C. (2014). Digital marketing and social media: Why bother? *Business Horizons, 57*(6), 703–708. doi:10.1016/j.bushor.2014.07.002

Underwood, S. (2016). Blockchain beyond bitcoin. *Communications of the ACM, 59*(11), 15–17. doi:10.1145/2994581

Urquhart, A. (2016). The inefficiency of Bitcoin. *Economics Letters, 148*, 80–82. doi:10.1016/j.econlet.2016.09.019

Urquhart, A. (2017). Price clustering in Bitcoin. *Economics Letters, 159*, 145–148. doi:10.1016/j.econlet.2017.07.035

Vassiliadis, S., Papadopoulos, P., Rangoussi, M., Konieczny, T., & Gralewski, J. (2017). Bitcoin value analysis based on cross-correlations. *Journal of Internet Banking and Commerce, 22*(S7), 1.

Chapter 12
The Integration of the Blockchain Technology Into Wine Tourism

Çiğdem Unurlu
https://orcid.org/0000-0001-5653-6013
Trakya University, Turkey

ABSTRACT

The aim of this study is to offer some suggestions to both the tourism industry and the practitioners in terms of making wine tourism and wine supply chain more transparent and traceable. From this point of view, in the current study, in which the blockchain technology in wine supply chain is examined, first the technology of block chain has comprehensively been assessed, and later the operational principles of blockchain technology are discussed. Afterwards, the blockchain technology was attempted to be integrated into wine tourism and wine supply chain. Hence, a new model was proposed. In this respect, the outputs that can be obtained via the use of blockchain technology in wine tourism and wine supply chain are revealed in this study.

INTRODUCTION

Globalization and the companies' search for a new market have complicated all of the processes about product management. For instance, there may be several suppliers from many different countries in the production and supply chain process of a product. The processes such as customs clearance, invoicing and transportation have to be carried out together at the same time. Thus, this chaos in supply chain

DOI: 10.4018/978-1-7998-8081-3.ch012

affects the performance of supply chain in a negative way and increases the risk perception of the consumer about the product. This chaos, this disorganization and these delays in the supply chain cause the consumers to experience some problems such as loss of confidence in product (Christopher 2011). On the other hand, block chain technology ensures confidence to consumers in both food safety and the sustainability of safe shopping (İrak&Topçu, 2020). When the wine tourist is able to track the whole journey of the wine purchased from the vineyard to the retailer and have the specific information about the product, it is possible for him/her to make stronger decisions (Montecchi, Plangger & Etter, 20 19). As a matter of fact, Industry 4.0 has transformed lifestyles, emotions and ideas of wine tourists and it has also led to the emergence of new consumption patterns and new paradigms. In 21st century, the winds of change have inevitably strengthened due to both the effects of technological improvements and the pandemic. These winds of change have also affected the wine tourism and changed the behaviour patterns of the wine tourists. It is considered that all these changes are going to improve the quality of wine (Apelasyon, 2020).

Blockchain technology, which is the most popular technology of Industry 4.0, offers radical solutions to the problems seen in production processes. Blockchain technology promises a high level of trust to stakeholders for several reasons such as enabling production processes to be more transparent, increasing the traceability of transactions during the production and preventing fraud. This technology reduces costs and accelerates transactions by eliminating intermediaries (Akben & Çinar, 2018). Blockchain technology, which has been in use since 2008, is being used more commonly day by day. Even though it has not been matured enough yet, the blockchain technology is estimated to be used more intensively in several different sectors to share information in the future. The applications that can be built in wine tourism and wine supply chain thanks to this technology are extremely exciting. Thanks to the blockchain applications, wine supply chain and wine tourism have been obtaining significant gains in some important aspects such as cost, trust, speed, transparency and quality. With the help of blockchain technology, the data flow in wine supply chain has been gaining acceleration and auditing has become easier due to the autonomous nature of this technology. On the one hand, the data obtained via blockchain technology, can be used as a data mine in wine tourism and wine supply chain. In this point of view, this technology ensures food safety in a sustainable way in wine tourism and wine supply chain and increases productivity in wine tourism and wine supply chain as the need for workforce is decreased. On the other hand, it is considered that wine tourism and wine supply chain are going to obtain a more autonomous structure owing to this technology. In conclusion, it is considerably crucial for companies to use new generation technologies like blockchain to improve their efficiency (İrak & Topçu, 2020).

With the implementation of blockchain technology in the supply chain, it is possible to increase the awareness of the wine tourists about the product. Hence, wine tourists can access plenty of information about the product via this technology. Information such as the origin of the product, the processes applied to the product and the storage information will facilitate the purchasing decision process of the wine tourist. Furthermore, information such as the originality of the product and storage data of the product affects the risk perception of wine tourists. As a result, this technology enables the wine tourist to be in a stronger position in the market. In this respect, the main purpose of this study is (1) to assess the use of blockchain technology in wine tourism and wine supply chain; (2) to examine the gains of the stakeholders in wine supply chain and wine tourism with the use of blockchain technology and (3) to guide the stakeholders in tourism sector in terms of the use of blockchain technology. Thus, first of all, a comprehensive literature review on blockchain technology was conducted. Afterwards, the operation and principles of blockchain technology were assessed. Subsequently, the elements in wine tourism and wine supply chain were discussed and the practicality of blockchain technology in wine supply chain and wine tourism was evaluated. In the following parts of the study, other blockchain applications in wine tourism and wine supply chain were assessed. The most significant motivation of this current study, which explains and offers the promising blockchain technology as a solution to the chronic problems in wine tourism and wine supply chain, is to shed light and make suggestions to stakeholders in wine tourism and wine supply chain.

THE CONCEPT OF BLOCKCHAIN AND ITS OPERATION

Even though there is no definite definition of blockchain, this concept was first introduced with the concept of bitcoin in 2008 by Satashi Nakamoto. Blockchain technology is described as blocks of data linked together thorough encryption (Jacobovitz, 2016). Blockchain technology is described as a technical diagram and there are many nodes in this diagram. This diagram consists of blocks formed by the encryption of these several nodes. These blocks are connected to each other linearly in a chronological order. On the other hand, these blocks are regarded as digital fingerprints and verify records and transactions in the system (Tian, 2016). Blockchain is a digital ledger which enables encrypted transactions to be recorded over a decentralized distributed structure and operates through a consensus. Transactions can be carried out without the need for an intermediary institution thanks to blockchain technology. The structures, where all sorts of precious data are recorded, are called "blocks". Briefly, it is possible to consider blockchain structure as the distribution of trust without a central authority (Yener, 2020). All over the world, blockchain technology has been the focus of attention of different sectors in terms of verifying each other in a secure way. Moreover, the advantage of competition can be accomplished in several processes from the manufacturer to the supply chain and the costs can be minimized due to the basic features of blockchain technology. With the help of this technology, all functions and all business processes can be controlled effectively in a distributed structure.

Blockchain technology is defined as a unique crypto currency system (Jiang et. al, 2017). It consists of chronologically ordered and encrypted chained blocks that store data and can be synchronized and verified over the network of the participants (Erbaş, 2019). The main reason of the interest in blockchain technology is that it allows transactions to be carried out on a quite secure basis without the need for any intermediary. Records in this technology are saved in a ledger and these records can be traced by all participants in the system. The participants, who enter the system, are directed to a network and all transactions are recorded in an irreversible way.

There are lots of advantages of blockchain technology. These will be stated in the following lines. The first one is the fact that this technology verifies data of multiple nodes. The second one is that it does not allow to change the records. Lastly, the consensus of all participants is assured. Hence, security is quite high in blockchain technology thanks to these three advantages. It is highly easy and quick to access the system for all participants in the network. Owing to its distributed ledger structure, malicious transactions can be detected immediately and these transactions can be intervened. Human errors are quite few in this technology due to the setup of the system. Also, there is no need for a centre in blockchain technology as it possesses a distributed ledger setup. Therefore, transaction costs are not high in blockchain technology. It is possible for the participants to see all transactions taking place in the chain simultaneously. Thanks to the verification protocols, data accuracy and data quality are high in blockchain technology (Durğay & Karaarslan, 2018, Bakan & Şekkeli, 2019).

Blocks are added one after another like a chain ring and form the structure of blockchain. Since each block involves the summary of the previous block, this technology is compared to a chain. For this reason, if a change occurs in one block, all subsequent blocks must be changed, too. However, this situation does not allow the data and the transactions in the blocks to be altered (Durbilmez, 2018). The first block in blockchain is called "Genesis Block". If you start looking back from any block, you finally reach Genesis block (Consumer, 2016). Basically, a block consists of two structures. These are the header of the block and the data in the block. The data in the block can be any structure which contains a value. On the other hand, data, which do not belong to the block, are demonstrated in the header of the block (Durbilmez, 2018). Information such as the time stamp and the hash value of the previous block takes place in the header of the block (Durbilmez &

Türkmen, 2019). One block in the chain chronologically points to the preceding block. This happens since each block contains the hash value of the previous block (Foroglou & Tsilidou, 2015).

Merkle Tree

Every block involves the hash value of the previous block in blockchain, too and this hash value is obtained via the use of Merkle tree algorithm. The Merkle tree is used to maintain the relationships of several data sets, the data immutability and the integrity of the data (Görmez, 2017). Merkle tree is an effective labelling method that provides secure and efficient verification of data structures (Merkle, 1998). A block consists of two parts, the header of the block and the data root which contains transaction records. The hash function is used in Merkle tree in order to ensure the integrity of the data. Participants can be sure that the original data and its summary have not been altered thanks to hash function. The basic aims of hash function are to control the integrity of the data, to ensure that the data have not been altered and to reduce large sizes of the data to smaller sizes (Bilim Çağı, 2020). Transactions, which have been added into the block in Merkle tree, are summarized in binary groups. This process continues in binary groups until a summary is obtained (Çarkacıoğlu, 2016). Hence, a tree-like figure is formed from the binary group summaries and this structure is called "Merkle tree" (Akkaya, 2020).

The block header involves the title of the block, timestamp, hash value of the previous block and the value of nonce (Number Only Used Once). On the other hand, hash function is used in the data root. With the use of hash function, large data can be transformed into smaller data of a fixed length. It can also be understood that the original data have not been altered due to hash function, which can be evaluated as a hash function, too. For instance, after a trade has been summarized with the hash function, these summaries are organized as hash trees in Merkle tree. Hashes are summarized in pairs (p2p) and these transactions continue until the apex of the tree. Thus, the second part of the tree, which is the data root, is formed as well (Yener, 2020).

Decentralization

Decentralization is one of the most fundamental principles of blockchain technology. As it has a distributed ledger structure, responsibility is distributed to whole network in this technology. This feature of blockchain technology is its most critical structural feature. The most significant reason why this feature is so critical is because the system has the ability to continuously verify itself with its distributed structure without the need for an intermediary or authority. Due to this setup of this technology, data cannot be kept under the monopoly of any authority or intermediary institution. Consequently, the risks such as changing the data or controlling the data are not in question (Güven & Şahinöz, 2018; Kırbaç, 2020). Blockchain technology owes its decentralization setup to qualifications such as (1) distributed ledger, (2) digital Id, (3) accountability, and (4) peer to peer/P2P network.

Figure 1. Merkle tree (Blockchain, 2019).

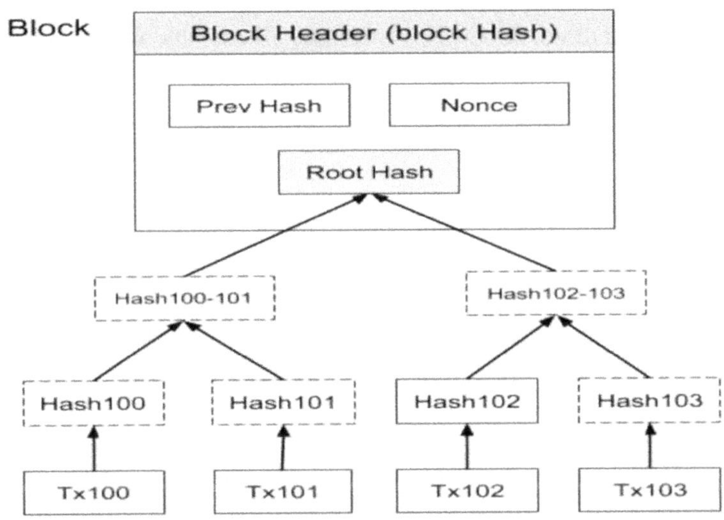

Distributed Ledger: The setup of blockchain technology is in the form of a distributed ledger. The data appear in a node and in a complicated form. In this setup, all nodes in the system can access the database. However, none of the nodes has the ability to control the data in the database. Each new node in the blockchain can be verified by all of the nodes without the help of an intermediary institution or an authority (Iansiti & Lakhani, 2017; Kırbaç, 2020).

Digital Id: The protection of personal data is of great importance in our era. In blockchain-based identity systems, which can also be referred to as global open ledgers, personal data is not shared explicitly or directly. Instead of sharing personal data in an explicit way, digital data, hash functions, digital signatures and cryptographic techniques are used. On the other hand, these data are set up by the system (Kırbaç, 2020).

Accountability: Another feature of blockchain is accountability. Owing to the distributed ledger structure and decentralized setup of blockchain, transactions can be carried out in a more secure and transparent way. This feature of the system points at the accountability of the blockchain. The participants in the network can perform data operations without the need for an authority (Kırbaç, 2020).

Network Peer to Peer: Peer to Peer/P2P, Network P2P is another feature of blockchain. In the blockchain database, the parties communicate from one end to another through nodes without the need for any authority to communicate with each other. Every participant (node) in the network has equal power and accomplishes in the same tasks. In financial technologies, the term "peer-to-peer" is used for the exchange of crypto currencies with the help of a distributed network. Thus, it is possible to trade between peers (between buyers and sellers) without any intermediaries (Nakamoto, 2008). Nevertheless, all data and records in blockchain system are stored by the nodes (Iansiti & Lakhani, 2008; Kırbaç, 2020)

Smart Contracts

Although the use of currency is not mandatory in blockchain technologies, every value, which can be expressed numerically, can be transferred via this technology. The smart contracts feature of this technology eliminates the need for intermediaries. By the use of smart contracts, all stakeholders learn the terms and conditions of the contract and can fulfil them automatically. Smart contracts are partially or fully self-regulating and self-executing. Due to these features, smart contracts are separated from traditional contracts and provide savings in transaction costs with high security (Kırbaş, 2018).

Smart Contracts are formed when the contracts whose conditions have been confirmed by using the data in block chain are filled automatically. There is a wide range of smart contracts usage. They can perform the exchange of any value such as property or money between the parties without the need for an intermediary and they do not allow any trust problems. The code in smart contracts consists of the terms and conditions that were agreed on between parties. When the conditions are met automatically, the contracts are filled automatically (Rodrigue, 2018; Kırbaç, 2020). It is possible to face risks related to payment processes while performing any commercial transactions in the supply chain structure. Thanks to the smart contracts feature of blockchain technology, these kinds of risks can be eliminated and payments can be controlled before the commercial transaction. Commercial transactions and payments take place simultaneously in this technology (Lefroy, 2017).

Transparency and Traceability

There is a constant bidirectional data transfer between the participants in the process of supply chain management. In this process, problems may occur due to insecure data such as incorrect information and delays. Furthermore, these problems affect the production management in a negative way and cause organizational inefficiency. It is possible to eliminate such inefficiency and risks with the help of the distributed database of blockchain technology. Each node in blockchain technology is able to monitor data in the database. This situation points at the transparency of blockchain technology. With its distributed ledger setup, blockchain technology is more transparent and traceable compared to systems, which are managed from one centre. On the other hand, the data and the transactions recorded in this technology, in which algorithms are used cannot be changed in any way (Iansiti & Lakhani, 2017). In terms of the security and the sustainability of the product, blockchain technology contributes significantly to the supply chain and increases the transparency, traceability and security of the system (Villalmanzo, 2018; Kırbaç, 2020). The most comprehensive innovation proposed by blockchain technology is the confidence in the accuracy of the data stored in blocks. The blockchain has been designed to lose its integrity in case of altering the data in blockchain technology. For this reason, the system verifies itself in a sustainable way and does not allow third parties to intervene (Kırbaç, 2020). Thus, the immutability of records is one of the most significant advantages of the blockchain network.

Blockchain Consensus Mechanisms

Transactions, which are carried out in blockchain technology, have to be verified so as to be included in the system. Consensus is used for this. Consensus protocols determine the nodes which are going to make changes in blockchain technology (Karaarslan & Akbaş). Consensus protocols are used for security reasons (Akkaya, 2020). All data in blockchain system are recorded on a distributed ledger. All of the participants in the network must agree on the data in the distributed ledger. In the databases, which are not distributed and centralized, consensus is provided by the central authority while there are consensus protocols in the databases with a distributed ledger system (Medium, 2020). In blockchain technology, in order to get involved in a system with a number of participants, the transaction in question has to be approved by all parties in the system. When all of the participants in the system agree with each other, it is called "consensus". The validity of every transaction recorded on the blockchain is accepted by all participants thanks to consensus. The most used consensus mechanisms are Proof of Work (PoW) and Proof of Share (PoS) (Usta & Dağtekin, 2017; Kırbaç, 2020).

Proof of Work (PoW): Highly powerful processors are required in order to add a new block to the blockchain in this protocol. The computer, which accomplishes this operation is called "miner" and this process is called "mining" (Altunbaşak, 2018). At the end of this process, the first miner who decodes the hash function is rewarded and its transactions are approved (İslam, 2019). Hence, a consensus is provided in the system (Akkaya, 2020). In proof of work (PoW), the participants have to accomplish a work in order to get involved in the system. This protocol proves that the participant has made an effort for the product or the service. In this system, the participant has to keep some devices which are powerful enough to analyze and verify all block in this system. The process of generating the proof of work may be considered as a quite low probability random process. This system is frequently used in crypto currencies (Bentov et. al., 2016; Kırbaç, 2020).

Proof of Share (PoS): The confidence based on the energy expended is at stake in proof of work. However, in proof of share, a consensus is achieved according to the amount of share (crypto money) the participants possess. In other words, the more shares a node has in the system, the more s/he has the right to publish the subsequent block (Kardaş, 2019).

BLOCKCHAIN-BASED PRACTICES IN WINE TOURISM

Wine tourism, which is special interest tourism, is a type of integrative alternative tourism that occasionally exhibits eco-tourism and agro tourism features. As a niche marketing, wine tourism, which aims at developing the target destination by using the attractions of the wine houses and wine regions, is special interest tourism. Wine tourism is an alternative tourism type and in wine tourism, the tourists are provided with the opportunity of experiencing the traditional lifestyle of the destination thanks to the wine houses and wine regions (Getz, 2020). Wine products, wine production systems, wine producers, vineyards, landscape destination features and cultural values are among the most significant attractions of wine tourism. It is possible to activate wine tourism by making use of these attractions. Furthermore, social attractions can be used as an element of attraction in wine tourism, which is carried out for recreational purposes such as wine tasting, enjoying nature, eating and drinking (Williams, 2001). The main attraction element in wine tourism is the wine and the culture related to wine. In wine tourism, which can be defined as agro tourism, rural tourism and occasionally eco-tourism, it is possible for wine producers to meet the needs of wine tourists thanks to direct selling and marketing opportunities (Yıldız, 2009). Emphasis is laid on the sense of place in wine tourism. Tourists are provided with the chance of gaining experience and acquiring knowledge about wine in wine tourism where the sustainable development of the destination is preserved by creating a sense of place.

Thanks to the distributed ledger structure and invariable structure of the blockchain technology, it is possible to question originality of all food and beverage products used in touristic consumption with wine in wine tourism. Thus, it is possible to ensure the transparency of the information about the quality of wine. Moreover, an ideal atmosphere can be created for the effective promotion of all food products used in wine tourism (Galvez et. al., 2018). Therefore, tourists can obtain in-depth information about all the food and beverage products in the menu due to the blockchain technology and they can also carry out research on these products in detail in wine tourism. By the use of this technology, it is possible to provide information about the origin of the wine along with the images of the wine, which is served in wine houses or wine regions. Hence, wine tourists can see all the information about when and how all food and beverage products, including wine, went through from the field to the plate placed in front of them. On the other hand, in practice, wine tourists will be able to reach all these processes by scanning the barcodes or the QR codes on their smartphones and thus they will be able to learn all features of the wine served to them. In a far-reaching context, the widespread use of this technology in special interest tourism such as agro tourism, gastronomy tourism and wine tourism, where food and tourism are served together, the destinations will be provided with a competitive advantage. Blockchain technology is a considerably effective technology in terms of determining the quality of wines, particularly in wine tourism in which wine is the main attraction. Owing to this technology, it is possible to record a great deal of information such as the place, where the grapes are grown, the structure of the soil in the same region, the level of exposure to sunlight, the entire journey in the distribution channel and the storage conditions. As a matter of fact, the education and income level of the wine tourists is remarkably high although wine tourism is a niche market. This tourist group, whose social-economical qualities are extremely high, will want to access plenty of information about the quality of wine in order to be able to have a unique wine experience. This expectation of the wine tourist can be met in an effective way as this technology has collaborative characteristics. For instance, cultural food products are preserved and controlled with this technology in gastronomy tourism in Italy. For this purpose, blockchain technology was used in a project called "Penfold Platform" and the journey of food products in the supply chain was controlled in a meticulous way (Rejep & Karim, 2019). From this point of view, tourism businesses will be able to obtain a greater share from the market with the integration of this technology into the wine supply chain. Thus, they will be able to gain a competitive advantage. On the other hand, this technology can be used in all food products such as cheese served with wine, hence providing the tourist with a unique wine experience.

The need for intermediary institutions is eliminated thanks to the distributed ledger structure and smart contracts feature of block chain technology. It is thought that the need for tourism agencies and tour operators in wine tourism will be completely eliminated owing to this technology in the future. On the other hand, tourism is a sector which requires international money transfers. With the crypto currency feature of this technology, the need for intermediaries such as banks in the tourism sector and therefore in wine tourism will also disappear. As a matter of fact, all values, which can be expressed numerically, can be transferred without intermediaries by the use of this technology. Nevertheless, Onder & Treiblmaier (2018) stated that blockchain technology will create a different form of consumer-to-consumer (C2C) markets. Markets in this form also do not need intermediary institutions. If markets in these forms are integrated into wine tourism, wine companies and wine tourists, who have a share in the market, will be provided with significant savings. In fact, intermediaries such as travel agencies, tour operators and banks increase the cost of touristic product. It is probable to obtain noteworthy savings in wine tourism thanks to this technology, which eliminates the need for intermediaries. To sum up, blockchain technology brings transparency to the wine supply chain as well as increasing the traceability of the process in wine tourism. This situation helps the wine tourist experience high-quality wine and thus increases the satisfaction of the tourists significantly. However, Goudarzi and Martin (2018), Irvin and Sullivan (2018), Kwok and Koh (2018) and Willie (2019) stated that blockchain technology is an effective technology in personal marketing practices and creating consumer loyalty. Hence, it is considered that this technology can be used for personalized marketing practices in wine tourism in the future. In wine tourism, it is considered that this technology will create significant opportunities for tourism companies in terms of increasing the loyalty attitudes of tourists.

Böen Company uses caps with blockchain technology on its wine bottles so as to provide protection against fraud and to inform wine tourists about the brand. The originality of the wine can be checked by means of high-tech caps, developed by the Italian packaging master Guala Closures and a London-based technology company, Sharpened. It is also possible to check whether the bottle has been opened or not by this way. Due to these high-tech caps, wine tourists can instantly access the data about the wine bottle by touching their smart phones to the cap of the bottle (Blockchain, 2019). The Shanghai Wine and Liquor Blockchain Alliance stated that as the consumption of wine increases, wine fraud also increases. Hence, they have claimed that the most effective way to prevent this problem is to use blockchain technology. By developing a public blockchain project, Shanghai Waigaoqiao Direct Imported Goods Company has enabled wine tourists to see the certificate of the wine by means of their smart phones as well as enabling them to see the stages the wine has gone through during its production. Thus, Shanghai Waigaoqiao Direct Imported Goods Company has achieved a 10% increase in the sales by the use of this tracking system. Wine tourists can be sure of the originality of the wine they have purchased and shop in a more secure way thanks to this tracking system. The transparent and secure nature of blockchain technology has improved the effectiveness and the productivity of wine supply chain and wine tourism (Blockchain, 2019). With blockchain technology, wine tourists can access more information about the production of wine and can easily learn whether the wine is supplied in an ethical and sustainable way. All of these information communication technologies strengthen the consumer. A number of sectors are obtaining great productivity and developing new business models by the use of blockchain technology. A transparent and secure asset management is possible with blockchain technology, which is especially used in logistics, particularly in the supply chain. Therefore, blockchain technology is considered to shape logistics sector significantly in the near future (Danyal, 2020).

By integrating IoT (Internet of Things) technology into blockchain technology, many problems in food industry and tourism industry are solved and noteworthy savings are made in the sector. With these technologies, it is possible to eliminate losses in the wine supply chain and track the entire journey of the product from the producer to the consumer. This technology requires the use of chips, in which every stage of the product's journey between the producer and the consumer is recorded in an unchangeable way. Everyone, who is involved in this process, can access and observe the data whenever they want to. This technology is considered to be a secure and transparent ecosystem, which is effective against cases or incidents such as fraud and theft. According to the report of VeChain, it is estimated that in the forthcoming seven years, approximately 300 billion dollars of food products can be monitored per year through this technology. According to this report, it is estimated that 20% of the incomes from global wine sales is obtained via fake wine sales (Okan, 2020). It is possible to eliminate these loses in the wine tourism by making use of blockchain technology. For that reason, industry leaders such as IBM, Walmart, Carrefour and California Giant Berry Farms show an immense interest in this technology. Blockchain and IoT technologies, which can be integrated with each other, can be more effective when they are used together. For instance, by means of IoT sensors, information about the product like temperature is directed to the blockchain network and the companies can be provided with information throughout the wine supply chain. This information obtained from the blockchain provides the participants with the information about the originality and the general quality of the product. The combination of these two technologies is predicted to bring noteworthy savings to the industry. Briefly, blockchain technology, in which the traceability of products is in question, has the ability to be articulated to many business models (Okan, 2020). Tian (2016) used blockchain and RFID (Radio Frequency Identification) technologies for food safety in his study. In this study, products can be tracked from the harvest field to the market shelves and the data related to transportation can be recorded in the blockchain by the use of RFID technology. Tian (2016) has stated that food safety can be ensured by this way. Thanks to the integration of RFID technology into blockchain technology, wine tourists can question the quality and the security of the product. With the integration of blockchain technology into QR code technology, consumers can monitor the whole production journey of grapes by scanning the QR code. It is required for the consumer to download the necessary application to his/her smart phone in order to scan the QR code. For instance, consumers can question the originality of the coffee beans thanks to the "thank my farmer" application of Farmer Connect Company. By the help of blockchain technology, which can be integrated with technologies such as QR code, RFID and IoT, consumers are able to question the security of the products. Thus, it is possible to ease the concerns of consumers about the health of their products (Blockchain, 2020).

In this century, in which the consumer is more conscious due to the information communication systems, food safety is a crucial problem. Particularly in food industry and wine tourism, where the originality and the naturalness of the product are considerably important, the consumer wants to access a great deal of information about the product and therefore ask for the traceability of the product s/he has purchased. For this reason, the transparency and the traceability of the supply chain in food industry is a frequent problem, which is discussed as an up-to-date issue. Several companies in the food industry can effectively control their products, monitor and track every stage from the production of the product to its consumption by the use of blockchain technology. Hence, companies can identify the source of defective products and prevent the problem easily. BIM Blockchain General Manager Marie Wieck states that blockchain is a new generation transaction solution and it provides the companies, which operate together in the supply chain, with the necessary opportunities to be able to use a common language. With the help of this technology, a great deal of scattered and asynchronous information about the product can be collected and a consensus can be achieved by this way. On the other hand, blockchain technology plays a key role in terms of meeting the demand of transparency of the consumer and providing the sustainability of the food safety (Okan, 2020). Nowadays while some of the wine consumers have self-confidence in their choices of wine, other consumers prefer to get suggestions. Therefore, the most effective way to be successful in wine marketing is to follow the socio-demographic characteristics of wine consumers. Monitoring the changes of behaviour patterns and the profile of wine consumers are two key elements of the success in wine marketing. Popular culture symbols such as smart phones, Ipod and Mp3 player take a greater part in the lives of today's wine consumers. Digital communication plays a significant role in the lives of this generation, which is known as the "millennium generation" or "the Y generation" (Apelasyon, 2020).

The Integration of Blockchain Technology into Wine Supply Chain

In this part of the study, firstly, the elements of wine supply chain had been evaluated, and then, blockchain technology was tried to be integrated into wine supply chain. A modelling was invented for the adaptation of blockchain technology to wine supply chain and it was also assessed how blockchain technology works in this modelling (Muthukkumarasamy & Tan, 2017). The actors of wine supply chain are:

Vine Growers (Vignerons): The cultivation of grapes is called "viticulture" (winegrowing), the land cultivated to grow grapes is called "vineyard" and a person who grows grapes to make wine is called "vigneron". The vineyard is not planted on every soil, even if it is planted, it does not produce fruit. Therefore, the soil must have suitable conditions so that the grapevine can be cultivated when the vineyard is planted. Sandy soils or sandy-clay soils are the most ideal types of soil for viticulture (Talas, 2020). Vine growers are the first actors of wine supply chain and they are also one of the most important stakeholders in the chain. Wine supply chain begins in the vineyards. Vine growers are grape cultivators, who grow grapes, harvest grapes and prepare the best conditions for grapes. In the cultivation of grapes, parameters such as temperature, soil moisture and fertility are highly important for the quality of grapes. Vine growers try to control these conditions in order to grow high quality grapes. Besides being responsible for growing high quality grapes, vine growers also sell these grapes to wineries. Furthermore, vine growers have to save the data about the altitude of the land and the structure of the soil where grapes are cultivated, climatic factors, the sort and the origin of grapes, their relative humidity, the rainfall, sunshine hours, planting distance, the type of the soil, fertilization-irrigation, vine treatments, grape pruning and similar factors in the blockchain database (Biswas et. al., 2017).

Wine Producer: Wine producers apply a series of physical and chemical processes in order to obtain wine from the grapes they have purchased. The wine producer must record the purchasing date of grapes, the information about the supplier, the sort, the origin and the production details of grapes (fermentation, separating sediment, filtration, aging, bottling and storing) and the chemical content of the wine on the blocks so as to facilitate the traceability of the wines and to make this process transparent (Biswas et. al., 2017).

Bulk Wine Distributor: Bulk wine distributors are responsible for purchasing bulk wine from the wine grower and for blending and transferring this wine to their cellars. Instead of sending the wine bottles to the cellar, bulk wine distributors can arrange also for the transfer of the wine bottles for packaging. At this stage, all information such as the date of the purchase of bulk wine, its storage data, the transactions applied, the sample taken from the bulk wine, the results received from the analysis of these samples and the shipping data must be recorded on the blocks (Biswas et. al., 2017).

Transit Cellars: Cellars are places where barrelled or bottled wines are stored and matured in a dark place at a specific and steady temperature. Transit cellars are also responsible for wine storage, wine shipping, wine sampling and the analysis of the samples like bulk wine distributors. At this stage, the purchasing date, storage information, the shipping date, the procedures applied to the bulk wine, samples taken from the bulk wine and the results of the analysis of these samples etc. must be recorded on the blocks in the blockchain database (Biswas et. al., 2017).

Filler/Packer: Fillers or packers buy the bulk wine from distributors or transit cellars. Wines are packaged in various ways such as bottles, butts and barrels. The labelling of the bottles is fulfilled at this stage. It is also highly crucial to ensure the consistency of the product information recorded in the blockchain database and the label information at this stage. Finally, wine filling, wine packaging and shipment information must be recorded on the blocks along with the purchasing date, storage data, the procedures applied, sampling and analysis data of the bulk wine at this stage (Biswas et. al., 2017).

Finished Goods Distributor: At this stage, finished goods distributor buys boxes or pallets for the shipment of the wines, which are ready for sale. The most significant responsibility of finished goods distributor is to inform the wholesaler or retailer about the purchasing date and the shipment of the goods at this stage. Moreover, if there has been a re-labelling process at this stage, it must definitely be recorded in the blockchain database (Biswas et. al., 2017).

Wholesaler: Wholesalers buy wine boxes or wine pallets from "finished good distributor" and sell the purchased wine to retail stores. The wholesalers are in charge of storing, invoicing and distributing wines. The wholesalers also ensure the consistency of the data saved in the blockchain database and take the label information on the products into consideration for this purpose (Biswas et. al., 2017).

Retailer: Retailers buy the bottled, canned or boxed wine, whose production processes have been completed from wholesalers. On the other hand, they are responsible for selling the products purchased from wholesalers to consumers. When the retailer sells a box or bottle of wine, s/he has to record the transaction in the blockchain database in order to prevent the reuse of the same label. Retailers are expected to save their storage and sales data of wines in the blockchain database. When this data is recorded in the blockchain database, it is possible for the consumer to access all data saved in the blockchain database by using the identification number of the product s/he has purchased (Biswas et. al., 2017).

In fact, wine supply chain starts in vineyards. Grape grower is the first block in blockchain. In other words, the wine producer can also be considered as "genesis block". The block, which is going to be added to the system, is controlled by all other miners in the system before a new block is created in the chain. All participants in the chain receive a batch number along with an identity code. Batch number shows the amount and the producer of the supplied wine. Afterwards, the wine producer adds the saved data to the next block in the same way and shares this data with other participants in the network. The added block and the saved data are shared with all of the participants in the network. Thus, the block is controlled and added in the chain. This process is repeated for all blocks added to the network. In some situations, the shared data may be critical. For this reason, this data can be encrypted with the help of cryptography keys. Hence, the confidentiality of this data is ensured. It is possible to trace each wine bottle in this network. The consumer can track all data related to the wine s/he has bought by scanning the label of the wine bottle or reading the QR code (Cuel & Cangelosi, 2020).

In Figure 3, there is an example of supply chain for small and medium sized enterprises that produce wine. In wine supply chain, services such as chemical purchases, equipment purchases, bottling-packaging services, shipment and marketing take place in the required goods and services group apart from the distributor.

In Figure 4, the journey of wine bottles within blockchain technology in wine supply chain is illustrated. As it can be seen, the wine producer provides every bottle with a digital ID and these bottles are registered in blockchain technology with these IDs. When the wine producer sells these wine bottles to the distributor, s/he transfers the digital ID data of the wine bottles as well. This transaction is repeated for all intermediaries in the distribution channel. The seller in the distribution channel also verifies the data in the blockchain network with these digital IDs. Hence, the originality of the wine is confirmed. Briefly, thanks to blockchain technology, the wine producer can save the production data and the journey of wine bottles, which s/he has produced through the distribution channel chronologically. All participants within the network can trace the journey of the wine bottles and learn about the production of wines with the help of this technology.

Figure 2. Data flow in wine supply chain (Cuel & Cangelosi, 2020).

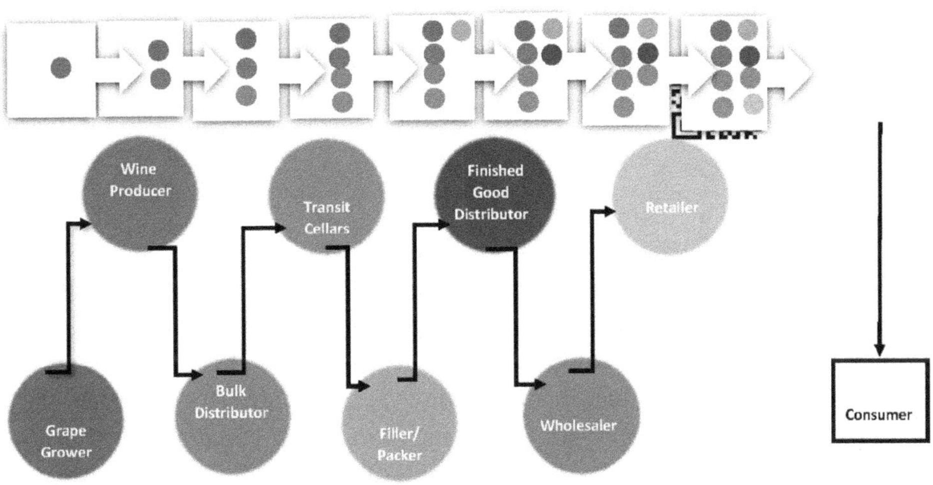

Figure 3. Supply chain for SME producers (Westlund & Engström, 2019).

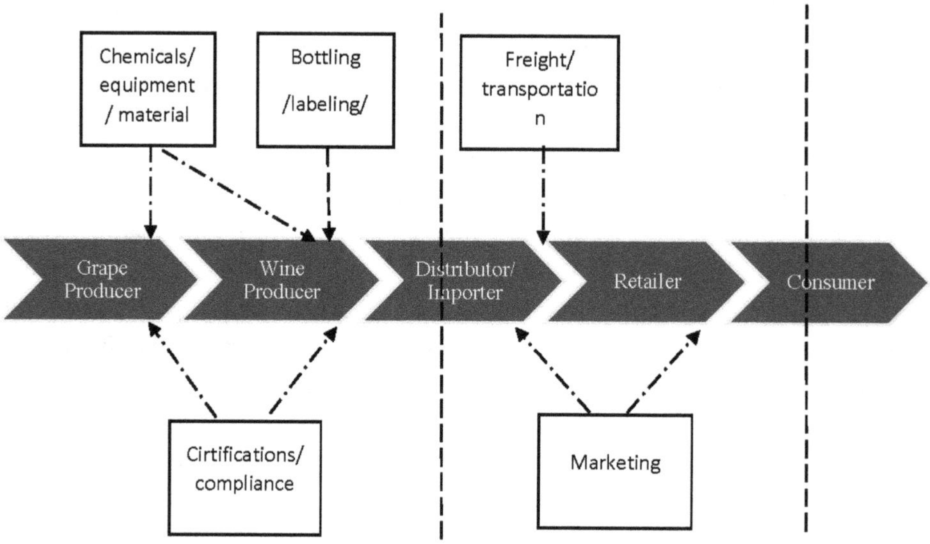

Figure 4. The blockchain journey of wine bottles (Vinfolio, 2020).

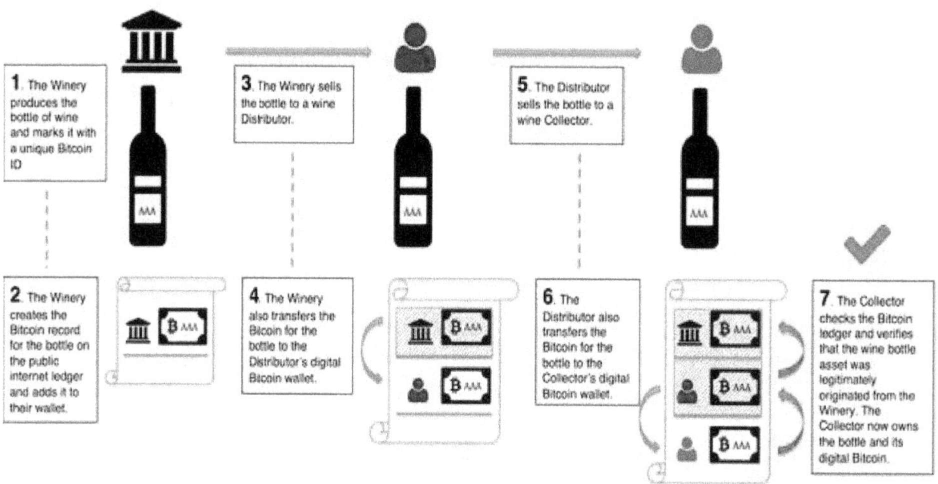

When blockchain technology is adapted to wine supply chain, it is possible to trace the bottle through the distribution channel. Thus, every participant in the supply chain can make precise predictions about the supply of wine bottles. By means of smart contracts feature of blockchain technology, each company, which takes place in wine supply chain, can perform purchasing processes automatically and by this way, it might be possible to save both time and money. Thanks to smart contracts feature of blockchain technology, transactions will be accelerated and the security of transaction will increase. Wine producers, who use blockchain technology, will be able to save the data about the originality of their own products, the places where the products are stored, product details, certificates of the products and the records of the products in one place. The fact that all data are collected in one place will make these data more accessible. This fact is going to make transactions more transparent and prevent fraud. Wine consumers will be able to see the information such as the origin of the product, its producer, its production date and storage conditions instantly due to this technology (Decons, 2020).

CONCLUSION

Blockchain technology, which has become more widespread day by day and has already started to occupy our lives and minds more and more since 2008, is a new generation technology where values such as money, products and information can be exchanged. This technology is considered to be a transparent and trustworthy setup which can be traced by technology users. Every transaction added to the network is recorded and signed digitally against forgery. The algorithm of the system checks every record added to the network and adds it to the chain if the algorithm approves it. None of the records, which has not been approved by the algorithm, is added to the chain. This situation increases the reliability of the system and it protects the system against fraud. It is possible to track and monitor all records simultaneously when it is used with technologies such as RFID, IoT and QR. Even though chains are not standard in blockchain technology, each network has a unique chain structure. Nevertheless, this technology is not widely used yet for several reasons such as breaking the traditional structure in production, having a unique setup and requiring high technology costs. However, as a consequence of the widespread use of this technology in future, it is estimated that the costs will decrease and this technology will be used by more enterprises. As this technology is still quite new, more methodological and applied academic studies should be carried out so as to provide the adaptation of it to different industries (Bakan and Şekkeli, 2019).

Most of the processes from the harvest of grapes to the production of the wine including the pricing of the wine, the distribution of the wine and the publicity of the wine can be monitored via this technology. By the use of blockchain technology, the whole journey of the wine bottles in the supply chain can be tracked by all stakeholders and thus the food safety, which is demanded by the wine industry, is ensured. On the other hand, wine consumers and wine tourists can be certain of the originality of the product and access the data necessary in making a decision in the purchasing process rapidly. The certificates of the wines, which have been produced, are recorded and saved in the blockchain in an unchangeable way. All of the stakeholders in wine supply chain and wine tourism join a common interface in the blockchain and their digital data are saved in the blockchain. Owing to the blockchain technology, it is possible to access a great deal of different and asynchronous data related to wine supply chain and wine tourism simultaneously. This data saved in the network can be used as a data mine in the wine tourism and reliable statistical information about the wine tourism can be obtained with the help of this data. The comprehensibility of the shared data to all participants in the network is another significant problem in the blockchain-based wine supply chain and wine tourism. Therefore, a common language is required to be used in the usage of this technology. In brief, when it is taken into consideration that the participants in the network will be using a different technical language related to wine, developing a common technical language is going to contribute into the comprehensibility of the data. It is probable to access information about the originality of the product thanks to this technology, which improves food safety and enables the sustainability of safe shopping. Since all processes in the wine industry get rid of centralized structure, the industry becomes more transparent and all processes become more organic with the help of this technology. Therefore, new strategies can be developed in wine tourism and wine supply chain by means of this technology, worthwhile cost saving can be accomplished and the satisfaction of the customer/wine tourist can be improved. This immature, but promising technology must be adapted to other various sectors (Gerdan, 2019). This technology should be considered as a digital trust in wine tourism in order to reduce uncertainties between the producer and the consumer in supply chain. Moreover, this technology, which provides the transfer of information through a peer-to-peer transaction network, contributes to financial efficiency in wine supply chain and wine tourism with the use of smart contracts. It is estimated that this technology, which contributes to sustainable food security, will also make a contribution to rural development in the future (Gerdan, Koç & Vatandaş, 2020). A monitoring system for supplying wine can be established with the help of blockchain technology, and a long-term stability in prices can be achieved by determining the origin of the increases in price (Armutlu, 2019). In summary, this technology decreases the costs in wine supply chain and wine tourism while it increases productivity, transparency and trust.

REFERENCES

Akben, İ., & Çinar, S. (2018). Lojistik ve tedarik zinciri yönetiminde Block- chain: Vaatler, uygulamalar ve engeller. Anadolu I. Uluslararasi Multidisipliner Çalişmalar kongresi, 2018, Diyarbakır.

Akkaya, G. C. (2020). *An Overview about Blockchain Technology Based Crowdfunding* (Unpublished Master's Thesis). Dokuz Eklül University, İzmir.

Altunbaşak, T. A. (2018). Taxation with Blockchain Technology. *The Journal of Finance, 174*, 360–371.

Apelasyon. (2020). *Şarap Sektörü Değişen Tüketici Profilinin Farkında mı?* http://apelasyon.com/Yazi/267-sarap-sektoru-degisen-tuketici-profilinin-farkinda-mi

Armutlu, B. (2019). *Application of Blockchain in Apple Supply and Currency Exchange Offices Sector* (Unpublished Master's Thesis). Hacettepe University, Ankara.

Bakan, İ., & Şekkeli, Z. H. (2019). Blockchain Technology and Its Applications in Supply Chain Managements. *International Journal of Society Researches, 11*(18), 2848–2877.

Bentov, I., Gabizon, A., & Mizrahi, A. (2016). Cryptocurrencies Without Proof of Work. *International Conference on Financial Cryptography and Data Security,* 142-157.

Biswas, K., Muthukkumarasamy, V., & Tan, W. L. (2017). Blockchain based wine supply chain traceability system. *Future Technologies Conference.*

Blockchain. (2019a). *Blockchain, Çin şarap ticaretine şeffaflık getirdi.* https://bctr.org/blockchain-cin-sarap-ticaretine-seffaflik-getirdi-10284/

Blockchain. (2019b). *Merkle Tree.* https://tech-story.net/blockchain-merkle-tree/

Blockchain. (2019c). *Şarap Şişelerinde Blockchain Teknolojisi Kullanılacak.* https://bctr.org/sarap-siselerinde-blockchain-teknolojisi-kullanilacak-10273/

Blockchain. (2020). *Çiftçiden tüketiciye kahve takibi blokzinciri ile sağlanıyor.* https://bctr.org/ciftciden-tuketiciye-kahve-takibi-blokzinciri-ile-saglaniyor-17362/

Çağı, B. (2020). *Hash Fonksiyonu Nedir?* https://www.bilimcag.com/nedir/hash-fonksiyonu-ozetleme-fonksiyonu-nedir/

Çarkacıoğlu, A. (2016). *Crypto-Currency Bitcoin.* Capital Markets Board of Turkey. https://www.spk.gov.tr/SiteApps/Yayin/YayinGoster/1130

Cuel, R., & Cangelosi, G. M. (2020). In Vino Veritas? Blockchain Preliminary Effects on Italian Wine SMEs. In R. Agrifoglio, R. Lamboglia, D. Mancini, & F. Ricciardi (Eds.), *Digital Business Transformation. Lecture Notes in Information Systems and Organisation* (Vol. 38). Springer. doi:10.1007/978-3-030-47355-6_20

Danyal, D. (2020). *Farklı Sektörler İçin Blockchain Çözümleri*. https://medium.com/@devrimdanyal/farkl%C4%B1-sekt%C3%B6rler-i%CC%87%C3%A7in-blockchain-%C3%A7%C3%B6z%C3%BCmleri-c02815b609d9

Decons. (2020). *Tedarik Zinciri ve Lojistik'te Blockchain*. https://medium.com/@decons/tedarik-zinciri-ve-lojistikte-blockchain-1bd9e7b67669

Dummies, C. (2016). *Bitcoin for Dummies*. John Wiley and Sons.

Durbilmez, S. E. (2018). *The Role and Applications of Blockchain Technology in Financial Services Sector* (Unpublished Master's Thesis). Marmara University, Istanbul.

Erbaş, S. (2019). New generation technology in marketing and advertising: Blockchain. *Journal of Gumushane University*, *7*(2), 712–729.

Galvez, J. F., Mejuto, J., & Gandara, S. J. (2018). Future challenges on the use of blockchain for food traceability analysis. *Trends in Analytical Chemistry*, *107*, 222–232. Advance online publication. doi:10.1016/j.trac.2018.08.011

Gerdan, D., Koç, C., & Vatandaş, M. (2020). Use of Blockchain Technology in Traceability of Food Products. *Journal of Agricultural Machinery Science*, *16*(2), 8–14.

Gerdan, G. (2019). *Blockchain, Food Safety, Food Traceability, Supply Chain, Egg Production, User Interface Design* (Unpublished Master' Thesis). Marmara University, Istanbul.

Getz, D. (2000). *Explore Wine Tourism: Management, Development & Destinations*. Cognisant Communication Corporation.

Görmez, B. (2017). *Finansal Sektörde Yıkıcı Yenilik: Dağıtılmış Defter Teknolojisi ve Türkiye Sermaye Piyasalarının Durumu (Distributed Ledged Technologies/ Blokchain)*. Capital Markets Board of Turkey. https://www.spk.gov.tr/SiteApps/Yayin/YayinGoster/1136

Goudarzi, H., & Martin, J. I. (2018). *Blockchain in aviation*. Retrieved from International Air Transport Association website: https://www.iata.org/contentassets/2d997082f3c84c7cba001f506edd2c2e/blockchain-in-aviation-white-paper.pdf

Güven, D. V., & Şahinöz, E. (2018). *Blokzincir- Kripto Paralar- Bitcoin / Satoshi Dünyayı Değiştiriyor*. Kronik Publishing, Istanbul.

Iansiti, M., & Lakhani, K. R. (2017). The truth about blockchain. *Harvard Business Review*, *95*, 118–127.

İrak, G., & Topçu, Y. E. (2020). The effect of the implementation of blockchain technology in the supply chain cost. *International Journal of Management Economics and Business*, *16*(1), 171–185. doi:10.17130/ijmeb.700862

Irvin, C., & Sullivan, J. (2018). *Using blockchain to streamline airline finance*. Retrieved from Deloitte Development LLC website: https://www2.deloitte.com/us/en/pages/consulting/articles/airlines-blockchain-finance.html

İslam, A. (2019). *Blockchain technology and crypto currencies: Current situation, potantial and risk analysis* (Unpublished Master's Thesis). Marmara University, Istanbul.

Jacobovitz, O. (2016). Blockchain for identity management. Technical Report, The Lynne and William Frankel Center for Computer Science Department of Computer Science, Ben-Gurion University, Beer Sheva, Israel.

Jiang, P., Guo, F., Liang, K., Lai, J., & Wen, Q. (2017). Searchain: Blockchain-based private keyword search in decentralized storage. *Future Generation Computer Systems*, (12), 1–12.

Karaarslan, E., & Akbaş, M. F. (2017). Blockchain based Cyber Security Systems. Blokzinciri Tabanlı Siber Güvenlik Sistemleri. *Uluslararası Bilgi Güvenliği Mühendisliği Dergisi.*, *3*(2), 16–21.

Kardaş, S. (2019). Blokzincir Teknolojisi: Uzlaşma protokolleri. *Journal of Dicle University Egineering*, *10*(2), 481–496.

King, S., & Nadal, S. (2012) *Ppcoin: Peer-to-Peer Crypto-Currency with Proof-of-Stake*, Self-Published Paper.

Kırbaç, G. (2020). *The evaluation of the Blockchain in supply chain at 3PL Companies with quality function deployment* (Unpublished Doctoral Thesis). İzmir Katip Çelebi University, İzmir.

Kırbaş, İ. (2018). Blockchain Technology and Its Application Areas in Near Future. *The Journal of Graduate School of Natural and Applied Sciences of Mehmet Akif Ersoy University*, *9*(1), 75–82.

Kwok, A. O. J., & Koh, S. G. M. (2018). Is blockchain technology a watershed for tourism development? *Current Issues in Tourism*. Retrieved from https://www.tandfonline.com/doi/abs/ 10.1080/13683500.2018.1513460

Lefroy, W. (2017, 9 November). *Blockchain: Changing Interaction in the F&A Supply Chain*. Rabobank: https://www.rabobank.com/en/raboworld/articles/blockchainchanging-interaction-in-the-fand-

Medium. (2020). *Consensus mekanizmaları*. https://medium.com/@BlockchainIST/consensus-mekanízmalari-951c9c8d2a3e

Merkle, R. C. (1988). *Protocols For Public Key Cryptosystems*. www.merkle.com: http://www.merkle.com/papers/Protocols.pdf

Montecchi, M., Plangger, K., & Etter, M. (2019). It's real, trust me! Establishing supply chain provenance using blockchain. *Business Horizons*, *62*(3), 283–293. doi:10.1016/j.bushor.2019.01.008

Nakamoto, S. (2008). Bitcoin: A Peer-to-Peer Electronic Cash System. *Consulted*, 1–9.

Okan, Ş. (2018). *Nesnelerin İnterneti Blockchain Teknolojisiyle Buluşuyor*. https://magg4.com/nesnelerin-interneti-blockchain-teknolojisiyle-bulusuyor/

Onder, I., & Treiblmaier, H. (2018). Blockchain and tourism: Three research propositions. *Annals of Tourism Research*, *72*, 180–182. Advance online publication. doi:10.1016/j.annals.2018.03.005

Reinkrul. (2020). *Implementing a Merkle Tree in Go*. Academic Press.

Rejeb, A., & Karim, R. (2019). Blockchain Technology in Tourism: Applications and Possibilities. *Sustainable Technology eJournal*.

Rodrigue, J. P. (2018). *Efficiency and sustainability in multimodal supply chains*. International Transport Forum Discussion Paper, No. 2018-17, Organisation form Economic Co-operation and Development (OECD), International Transport Forum.

Sullivan, J. (2018). *Using blockchain to streamline airline finance*. Retrieved from Deloitte Development LLC website: https://www2.deloitte.com/us/en/pages/consulting/ articles/airlines- blockchain- finance.html

Talas, D. (2020). *Bağcılık Nedir?* https://www.bilgiustam.com/bagcilik-nedir/

Tian, F. (2016). An agri-food supply chain traceability system for China based on RFID & blockchain technology. *13th International Conference on Service Systems and Service Management (ICSSSM)*, 1-6.

Tian, F. (2016). An agri-food supply chain traceability system for china based on RFID & Blockchain technology. In *Service Systems and Service Management (ICSSSM), 13th International Conference on*. IEEE.

Usta, A., & Doğantekin, S. (2017). *Blockchain 101*. MediaCat Publishing.

Villalmanzo, I. V. (2018). *Blockchain: Applications, Effects and Challenges in Supply Chains* (Unpublished Master's Thesis). Tampere Technology University.

Vinfolio. (2020). *Digital Provenance: How Wine Bottles Will Be Tracked Using Bitcoin.* https://blog.vinfolio.com/2014/10/06/the-future-of-wine-provenance-is-bitcoin/

Westlund, S., & Engström, R. P. (2019). *Increasing transparency in the supply chain with blockchain technology A case study of small and medium sized South African wine producers* (Unpublished Master's Thesis). Karlstad University, Sweden.

Williams, P. (2001). The Evolving Images of Wine Tourism Destinations. *Tourism Recreation Research, 26*(2), 3–10. doi:10.1080/02508281.2001.11081338

Willie, P. (2019). Can all sectors of the hospitality and tourism industry be influenced by the innovation of blockchain technology? *Worldwide Hospitality and Tourism Themes, 11*(2), 112–120. Advance online publication. doi:10.1108/WHATT-11-2018-0077

Yener, E. (2020). *The role of blockchain Technologies in digital business and a model proposal: Blockchain based second hand vehicle trade platform* (Unpublished Master's Thesis). Istanbul Medipol University, Istanbul.

Yıldız, Ö. E. (2009). *Wine Tourism in Turkey – An Exemplary Product Development Model in Çeşme* (Unpublished Master's Thesis). Dokuz Eylül University, İzmir.

Chapter 13
Adoption of Blockchain Technology:
A Case Study of Walmart

Minky Sharma
https://orcid.org/0000-0002-9956-6754
Chandigarh University, India

Pawan Kumar
Chandigarh University, India

ABSTRACT

In today's world, society has become totally digitalized where technology is playing a very important role in everyone's life. Blockchain is a method that is useful in recording information and makes its difficult to change, hack, or fraud system. A blockchain is fundamentally a digital ledger of volume of transactions that is distributed across the overall network of IT system on the blockchain. This technology acts as a reliable layer in the evolution of e-commerce. Walmart has been working with IBM on a food safety blockchain solution to add transparency to the decentralized food supply ecosystem by digitizing the food supply chain process. This chapter will cover the concept and origin/emergence of blockchain technology and implications of blockchain technology in supply chain (Walmart), the significance and role of blockchain technology for the users and the stakeholders, the implications for the users, challenges faced by Walmart during the adoption of blockchain technology, and the approachability of Walmart to IBM for the implication of blockchain to their organization.

DOI: 10.4018/978-1-7998-8081-3.ch013

INTRODUCTION: EMERGENCE OF BLOCK CHAIN IN MODERN ECONOMIES

A block chain is fundamentally a digital ledger of volume of transactions that is distributed across the overall network of IT system on the block chain. This technology act as a reliable layer in the evolution of E-commerce. Block chain working like a machine of recording of transactions in such a manner that it will secure the device or computer from any kind of fraud and manipulation. Block chain is an innovation in the digital world and it has become famous among the innovators, technocrats at present.

This technology is revolutionary in nature in terms of information and computation technology (ICT), the Block chain technology is based on Cryptography which is used as a software protocol by the public. A public choice/modern structural approach to block chain economics will help shed light on how this new technology can influence the economy. Backfeed is an Ethereum-based network (Ethereum is a decentralised generalised block chain that serves as the basis for a cryptographically safe transaction-based state machine). We can discuss this in detail from the beginning, which was only eight year ago (Nakamoto 2008). The block chain technology that underpins Bitcoin is probably the most well-known (Swan 2015). It is a decentralised distributed Ledger scheme (Evans 2014). The blockchain, is considered as a specific technology in relation to digital currencies, Block chain is a solution which is technological in terms of double-spending problem, which had previously won all efforts to establish not decentralised Peer to peer electronic cash system. The block chain, according to Nakamoto2, give solution to this issue by integrating the shared file information system (or ledger) with network established processes that update the database using a proof-of-work consensus mechanism.

As per (Buterin 2015), the value and prospects of Bitcoin, on the other hand, have no impact on the worth and importance of Blockchain Bitcoin is a blockchain-based application in which the bitcoin ledger entries recorded are generated by the protocol. Block chain should be regarded in terms of modern form of "general purpose technology". In the form of a distributed public ledger that is highly transparent, robust, and effective (i.e. decentralised database). Any centralised system that coordinates important information can be broken using such a distributed ledger. One example of a centralised ledger is government money; another is government property titles or identities registration. This technology is not trust worthy, which means it doesn't rely on third-party verification (i.e. trust), however rather on a consensus with powerful mechanism based on crypto economic rewards to be checked by the validity of a transaction in the information management system. This keeps them secure even though there are strong or malicious third party seeking to discourage users from participating.

In the 15th century the Venetian Republic established double entry bookkeeping where Ledgers are traditional technology that hasn't replaced much after all this. They were digitised since 20th century, but they remained centralised until the blockchain was invented in 2008. As per (Nussbaum 1933, Allen 2011) The ledger is an accounting technology that keeps track of owners who own what and is vital to modern capitalism.

Block Chain Consists of Three Important Concepts: Blocks, Nodes and Miners (bulletin.com)

Blocks

Every chain is made up of several blocks, each of which has three basic elements:

- The details contained in the block.
- A nonce is a 32-bit whole number. When a block is formed, a nonce is generated at random, which then generates a block header hash.
- The hash is a 256-bit number that is associated with the nonce. It has to begin with a large number of zeros (i.e., be extremely small).

A nonce generates the cryptographic hash when the first block of a chain is generated. Unless it is mined, the data in the block is considered signed and forever linked to the nonce and hash.

Miners

Mining is the mechanism by which miners add new blocks to the chain. When a block is successfully mined, all nodes on the network approve the update, and the miner is compensated financially.

Nodes

Decentralization is one of the most significant principles of blockchain technology. The chain cannot be owned by a single machine or entity. Instead, the nodes attached to the chain form a distributed ledger. Any type of electronic device that holds copies of the blockchain and keeps the network going is referred to as a node.

According to McDermott (2017), "Block chain solves problems of the business where confidence is a factor" by offering what conventional databases can't: data immutability, speed, and security of dissemination. Walmart worked with IBM to develop and implement its food provenance pilots using blockchain technology

(Tiwari, 2016). Walmart's block chain pilot's progress hinged on cooperation with government departments. Blockchain technology and its potential piqued regulators' attention because it coincided with their work (McDermott, 2017). Walmart was able to introduce blockchain technology to pork protection and supply chain management after forming a team and obtaining regulatory approval. Blockchain outperformed other innovations [supply chain with restricted infrastructure, social media, radio frequency identification (RFID), enterprise resource planning (ERP), and IoT combined with RFID] in a report on the Indian organic food industry using analytic hierarchy method research. A network based on blockchain technologies ensures fair trade and a circular economy, and blockchain will help farmers increase the quality of their products in the supply chain.

Albertsons Companies (Eugene, Oregon, USA) is one of the leading food and drug stores in the United States, with approximately 2300 outlets throughout the world. In Albertsons, food safety is a crucial step. The opportunity to trace any move from the field to the customer's cart, due to product provenance, can be very empowering for their consumers. Albertsons aims to test IBM Food Trust to help solve the problems that have historically arisen when tracing high-risk foods like romaine lettuce. The world's largest grocery retailer will begin by tracing bulk romaine lettuce from one of its delivery centres, then extend to other food categories through its distribution network. The need for more reliable methods of tracing items and easily finding possible causes of pollution. As a result, retailers are experimenting with emerging technology in order to strengthen the system that serves the global food supply chain. Furthermore, Albertsons would support both customers and market players in achieving food traceability. Furthermore, a system of record can be developed for food items and can be used to monitor and authenticate artefacts as they pass through the supply chain, as well as a digital record of any purchase or contact. From the date of packaging to the temperature at which an item was delivered to its appearance on a grocery store shelf, all is registered. For major retailers and customers, improved openness will resolve a wide variety of food safety concerns.

According to the Website 101Blockchains[1], The Block chain technology was first introduce in 1991-2008 by "Stuart Haber and Scott Stornetta" who worked first time on this technology. In year 2009-2013 the various coins were introduced in the line of block chain technology which includes Bitcoin, Ethereum & NOE. In year 2009 Satoshi Nakamoto Publish Bitcoin White Paper and in year 2010 the First Bitcoin of 10,000BTC was purchased .In year 2013 Bitcoin Marketplace Surpasses $1 Billion and "Vitalik Butetin" released Ethereum White Paper. EOS.IO is a new blockchain protocol for the implementation of decentralised applications that was announced by block one in year 2017. In fig 1 the step by step view is explained to show how Blockchain works as it starts from the 1st step i.e A user requests for a transaction than in 2nd step A block representing the transaction is created than in 3rd step The block is broadcasted to all the nodes of the network than in 4th step All the nodes validate the block and the transaction after that in 5th step The block is added to the chain and at last step 6th step is The transaction gets verified and executed till transactions get verified and executed is being presented in a flow as a process. In year 2015-2018 The Evolution of Blockchain Technology Increased use of cryptocurrency, as well as companies using technology to improve efficiency, demonstrate this trend.

Figure 1. Process of blockchain technology
Note- The step by step process of Blockchain has been shown in above Fig: 1 *https://101blockchains.com/wp-content/uploads/2018/07/How_Does_a_Blockchain_work.jpg*

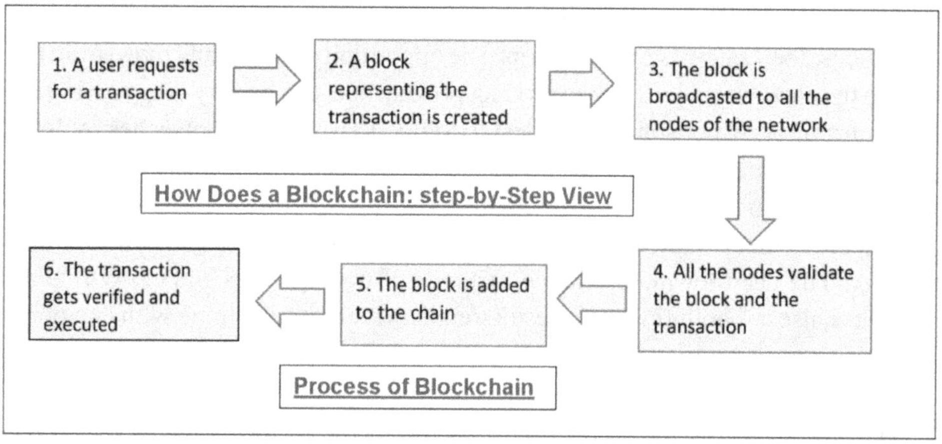

IMPLICATION AND APPLICATION OF BLOCK CHAIN TECHNOLOGY IN SUPPLY CHAIN (WALMART)

Block chain when connected with the supply chain than it will be considered as a part of Marketing. Saberi et al. (2019, p. 2120) discuss many aspects of the blockchain that can be used in the sense of supply chain management. When it comes to the flow of knowledge in supply chains, attributes like reliability, traceability, and authenticity become important. These characteristics, combined with the help of smart contracts, have the potential to allow supply chains to be built without relying on the trust layer as a foundation (Saberi et al., 2019, p. 2120). Unlike the many implementations of blockchain in financial contexts, however, all of the technology's usable roles in the supply chain setting have yet to be decided. As a result, there are still opportunities to interpret and apply the data.

Blockchain facilitates monitoring through the entire supply chain by encouraging all users of the blockchain network to see the same data. The risk of cheating other participants is excluded when all members have access to the same material (Tribis et al., 2018, p. 5). Furthermore, the advantages of blockchain in supply chain management are built on the technology's ability to minimize costs by, for example, replacing intermediaries such as auditors. As a result, the technology allows the supply chain manager to reduce the cost per unit. Inside supply chains, block chain technologies have the power to make additional improvements to society's sustainability. The traceability feature allows you to ensure that the whole process, from sourcing to customer execution, is carried out correctly (Saberi et al., 2019, p. 2122) Important considerations like civil rights and labor practices can be reflected on the blockchain, assisting consumers in making well-informed purchasing choices. Furthermore, environmental claims could be another domain where blockchain could be useful (Saberi et al., 2019, p. 2123). Aspects such as greenhouse gas emissions and used goods could both be viewed and handled using blockchain (Saberi et al., 2019, p. 2123), effectively assisting in the development of transparency in these areas. This, though, necessitates a degree of clarity that enables consumers to see this data. This must be decided early on in the process of developing the blockchain solution, since this is where the extent of privacy and network users must be determined (Saberi et al., 2019, p. 2120).

The food Supply Chain, in particular, started to recognize the value of strategic Supply Chain collaboration, with the aim of bolstering customer trust in the global food system . After the E.coli outbreak at Chipotle Mexican Grill, which resulted in 55 cases of contamination, the relevance of openness and accountability across supply networks was highlighted. As a result, a number of the world's leading supermarkets and food firms, including Dole, Unilever, and Walmart, began collaborating with IBM on Blockchain technology accessibility for providing food traceability information.

1. https://101blockchains.com/ultimate-blockchain-technology-guide/

About the fact that Block chain technology has yet to be established as a proven technological medium for optimum Supply chain results, engineers have already begun combining block chain and the Internet of Things to include "resilient, genuinely peer-to-peer distributed networks, providing the freedom to communicate with peers in a "trustless" (Firms can do business without having trust on one another), auditable manner," rather than as another IT or database solution ([17], p. 2301). They believe it will not only enhance trust among system participants (who are involved in a transactional relationship such as buyers, suppliers, and distributors), but also allow a trustless system that ensures the protection of transactions. Its advantages include improved product protection and security, quality control, reduced unlawful counterfeiting, Supply chain longevity, inventory management and replenishment expansion, new product design and production, and reduced SC transaction costs. The block chain, a relatively new IT network, has mostly been used in electronic money markets. Because of Block chain technology features like information transparency, software immutability, and smart contracts, its implementation to Supply chain cooperation is supposed to be beneficial.

ADOPTION OF BLOCKCHAIN BY E-COMMERCE COMPANIES

Customer, inventory, and sale details are all abundant in the E-commerce store. For accurate performance, these data must be properly stored and managed. This problem is addressed by block chain technology, which combines transactions into blocks and connects each block into a chain. Since each block is saved on its own disk, it is stable, scalable, and durable. If you run a Magento 2 e-commerce store, you can consider integrating it with Blockchain technology to get the best results. Despite the positive effect that the e-commerce market has had on the global economy, things have not been looking well for e-commerce retailers, who have faced several obstacles since the industry's birth. It has been searching for a stable technical infrastructure that can sustain it and solve the many problems it faces for years. Fortunately, Blockchain technology is now capable of doing the same[2] .

When Blockchain approaches major economic markets, a growing array of e-Commerce software development companies are discussing the potential use of Blockchain in a variety of fields other than banking, such as E-commerce. The e-commerce industry has changed the way people buy all over the world. Now, Blockchain is poised to revolutionize the way the E-commerce industry works. E-commerce using Blockchain would help to create a revolutionized economy. Although both Blockchain and E-commerce allow for transfers, Blockchain allows them both faster and more safe.

Block chains are specialized networks that are linked to the outside world using cutting-edge technologies.

However, not every Blockchain is the same. There are four kinds of Block chains which are widely used in E-commerce. For E-commerce retailers, all four of these options are readily available.

1. Bitcoin
2. Ethereum
3. IBM
4. Custom

Bitcoin: Bitcoin is a cryptocurrency that is the driving force behind the development of Blockchain technology. Several well-known companies have embraced Bitcoin, including Tesla, Microsoft, Google, and Shopify. Following that, a slew of other companies began to consider Bitcoin as a payment option. Accepting Bitcoin for payment processing is a convenient way to use Blockchain, as well as a way to tap into the vast cryptocurrency market.

Ethereum: It is also a cryptocurrency like Bitcoin. However, as opposed to its competitor, it has its own combination of advantages and disadvantages. While it has not gained the same level of popularity as Bitcoin, the network is capable of hosting a variety of other cryptocurrencies. Hosting smart contracts is one of Ethereum's most common applications. The fact that Ethereum provides merchants with a place to operate their full-fledged Block chains makes it perfect for E-commerce vendors.

IBM: IBM does not have a block chain of its own. The Blockchain technology that it offers, on the other hand, is incredibly useful for large, diverse online retailers.

Custom: This is the most straightforward and adaptable Blockchain solution for E-commerce merchants. Companies would be able to customize Blockchain to suit their unique needs with the help of a Blockchain development company. It is therefore very cost-effective in the long run for increasing gross margins[3].

The E-Commerce companies which are following Block chain technology:

There are different categories of E-commerce which are adopting the Block chain technology or are in the process of doing so are mentioned as:

1. **Banking and Finance:** includes HSBC, VISA etc[4].
2. **Supply Chain:** includes Unilever, Walmart etc.
3. **Healthcare:** includes DHL, Pfizer etc.
4. **Insurance:** includes MET life, AIG etc.
5. **Energy:** includes Shell, Siemen etc.
6. **Trade:** includes Scotiabank, SEB etc.
7. **Internet of things:** includes Common wealth bank, Van dorp etc.
8. **Travel**: includes Lufthansa, British Airways etc.
9. **Real Estate:** includes Westfield, JLL etc.

1. **Banking & Finance:** the various Organisation of Banking & finance are also working on the adoption of block chain industry some of them are discussed below:
    a. **A.1. HSBC:** By the end of March 2020, HSBC intends to launch a blockchain-based network. More importantly, they would migrate from paper-based records to a completely digital, decentralised Vault platform.

As a result, their investors can now monitor their funds in real time. It will also have some private functions.

b. **A.2. VISA:** Visa is one of the Blockchain technology firms that has progressed significantly in the industry. They had previously launched a Blockchain network for business-to-business payment services in 2016. However, putting the project online took some time. By the end of 2019, they hoped to have covered 90 markets in which companies could make payments.

2. **B. Supply Chain:** The block chain technology has been adopted by different organisation Supply chain few of which are explained below:
   a. **B.1. Unilever:** Unilever is another company that uses block chain in its supply chain. In fact, Unilever is using technology to manage its tea business. They can monitor all of their supply chain transactions with the aid of technology. Furthermore, they can monitor suppliers to ensure that quality is maintained at all times.
   b. **B.2. Walmart:** Walmart has long been a supporter of block chain technology. In fact, IBM's supply chain technology – the hyper ledger Fabric platform – is being used to support the company's supply chain operation. They also plan to monitor their foods all the way back to their farmers and allow consumers to verify the provenance before purchasing an item.
3. C. **Healthcare:** In the health care industry they are also moving ahead for the adoption of Block chain technology some of the organisations are mentioned below:
   a. **C.1. DHL:** DHL is another major corporation that has adopted block chain technology. They're working on a proof of concept with Accenture to monitor pharmaceuticals from the point of origin to the end user. As a result, businesses will be able to finally eliminate any tampering or counterfeit drug problems that they face on a daily basis.
   b. **C.2. Pfizer:** Pfizer is another major corporation that has adopted block chain technology. Clinical Supply Block chain Working Group (CSBWG), led by Biogen and Pfizer, recently completed proof of concept for monitoring records and maintaining the digital inventory of pharmaceutical products.

In fact, the group includes GlaxoSmithKline, Merck, AstraZeneca, and Deloitte, among others.

4. **D. Insurance:** There are different Insurance companies which are accepting Block chain technology and some are going to adopted:

a. **D.1. MetLife:** MetLife is another major corporation that has adopted block chain technology. In reality, Lumen Lab is MetLife's Singapore-based incubator business, and they're working on Life chain with NTUC Income and Singapore Press Holdings (SPH). You can use this website to assist your loved ones in determining whether the deceased had insurance or not, and it will automatically file an insurance claim if needed.

b. **D.2. AIG:** AIG, or American International Group, is a publicly traded corporation that uses Blockchain technology. They are currently collaborating with International Business Machines Corp on the creation of a smart insurance platform. They will eventually cover all of the complicated foreign insurance issues with the help of the web.

5. **E. Energy:** Organisations related to Energy are as following which have adopted Block chain industry and those who are going to adopt this in coming future.

a. **E.1. Shell:** Shell is one of the energy firms that has adopted block chain technology. Shell plans to use block chain for crude oil trading alongside Sinochem Energy Technology Co Ltd and Macquarie. Furthermore, they have previously investigated the technology for use in the oil industry. In either case, the platform makes it simple to monitor goods while still encouraging openness and preventing fraternisation.

b. **E.2. Siemen:** Another corporation that is investing in block chain for energy is Siemens. Furthermore, the firm recently stated that it intends to bring creativity to the energy sector. In any case, they plan to extend the solution to include Power Generation Services as well. They hope to create more sustainable energy systems as a result of this.

6. **F. Trade:** on the basis of trade there are different organisations adopting the block chain technology

a. **F.1. Scotiabank:** For the trade market, Scotiabank is using Alpha point's network. They do, however, send out trial trading documents to test the platform's functionality. They're still going strong, so it's fair to say the project was a success. The project will assist you in digitising your money, managing trading paperwork, and a variety of other tasks.

b. **F.2. SEB:** With block chain, SEB is also in the trading niche. They are now using CGI's Trade360 platform to manage all of their regulatory and transactional needs. The best part is that the platform is entirely capable of managing financial aspects of trading while still providing a solid architecture.

7. **G. Internet of things:** the block chain technology adopted by various organisations on the basis internet of things such as:

a. **G.1. Common wealth bank:** The Commonwealth Bank is another interesting example in the IoT block chain market. They're using the distributed ledger to solve two big problems: global trading and wealth sharing. In any case, incorporating IoT into the block chain framework allows them to monitor all global trading processes in real time.

b. **G.2. Van dorp:** Van Dorp is also using the technology in the IoT room. In fact, they're working with Time series on a smart home project that will connect any smart home device to the block chain platform. Since block chain is encrypted, smart home devices will be completely safe when communicating with one another.

8. **H. Travel:** In the Travel industry there are different organisations which adopted and working with Block chain technology in present or coming future.

   a. **H.1. Lufthansa:** One of the big players in the travel sector is Lufthansa Industry Solutions. And, in order to fully realise the value of block chain, they launched the Block chain for Aviation project (BC4A). Participants are expected to include aircraft manufacturers, logistics companies, MRO service providers, software developers, and others.

   b. **H.2. British Airways:** British Airways is collaborating with the start up VChain to improve the efficiency of their security checkpoints. In fact, security audits consume a significant amount of time and resources. It can also cause flight delays, which is inconvenient for both the airlines and the passengers. As a result of the technology, they can ensure a faster performance.

9. **Real Estate:** block chain technology has been adopted by various Real estate organisation are as follows:

   a. **I.1. Westfield:** For real estate bank guarantees, Westfield is using block chain. It is primarily intended for leaseholders in retail markets. In either case, Westfield's live project will last eight weeks, during which time they will decide if the technology is suitable for them. They are, however, certain that it would make it easier for them to grant commercial leases.

   b. **I.2. JLL:** JLL is another large corporation that has adopted block chain technology. It is currently being used in the valuation of commercial real estate in Spain. They say that they can use this method in the development and financing of real estate, as well as in the sale and rental of land. JLL Japan was the driving force behind the initiative.

GROWTH STORY OF BLOCK CHAIN ADOPTION BY WALMART AND ITS IMPACT ON ITS BUSINESS:

The case study on Walmart is being conducted on the bases of their market shares as we have taken the market share value of different companies such as Walmart, Hindustan Unilever, UPS, VISA, Ford and FedEx as shown in **Table 1**

Table: 1 presents the companies' percentage who had adopted the Blockchain technology for their organisational work from which it is justified that the market share holding of Walmart is the highest (66%) among other stated organisations with 38.90%, 35%, 16%, 5.94%, 5.50% so that why the case study has been conducted on Walmart in this chapter. The detail growth history of Walmart has been explained with the basic introduction of the Walmart and the hyperledger.

Table 1. Market share percentage of companies

Companies adopted Blockchain technology	Market share in 2019
Walmart	66%
Hindustan Unilever	38.90%
UPS	35%
VISA	16%
Ford	5.94%
FedEx	5.50%

Note: on the bases of the market share as shown in above table: 1 the case study of this chapter has been done.

Walmart Inc. (NYSE: WMT) helps consumers save money and live better in grocery stores, online, and on their mobile devices all over the world. Every week, nearly 265 million customers and members visit our more than 11,200 stores and e-commerce websites through 55 banners in 27 countries. Walmart hires over 2.2 million associates worldwide and produced $500.3 billion in sales in fiscal year 2018.

Hyperledger is an open source community project aimed at advancing block chain technology through industries. It's a multinational partnership involving leaders in banking, finance, IoT, manufacturing, supply chain, and technology. The Hyperledger Project is hosted by the Linux Foundation.

"Creating a (traceability) mechanism for the entire food supply ecosystem has been a problem for years, and no one had found it out," says Karl Bedwell, Senior Director of Walmart Technology. Because of its emphasis on confidence, immutability, and transparency, we thought block chain technology could be a good fit for this problem." With its open, shared ledger, block chain seemed tailor-made for the food system!" Walmart began working on two proof of concept (POC) projects with IBM after the company's interest in block chain technology was verified.

In October 2016, Walmart and its technology partner IBM revealed two projects: one to track the origin of mangos sold in Walmart stores in the United States, and the other to trace pork sold in Walmart stores in China. "Yiannas" began by establishing a benchmark for the mango POC. He purchased a bag of sliced mangoes from a nearby Walmart and asked his team to figure out where they came from as quickly as possible. After calling and emailing distributors and suppliers, the team received a response about seven days later. By market standards, this was not bad, but Walmart needed to do a lot better[5].

As a result, they collaborated with IBM to develop a block chain-based food traceability framework. Archana Sristy, Director of Engineering at Walmart she explained the core design and the main setup of the applicability and integration of enterprise system with IBM. She explained the concept of GS1 (the standards authority in barcodes and labelling) to define the data attributes for block chain upload the chain code was written by IBM.

Suppliers used new labels and used a web-based interface to upload their results. For the two products, the Hyperledger Fabric block chain-based food traceability framework worked. It allowed for the uploading of certificates of authenticity to the block chain for pork in China, adding more trust to a system where trust was previously a major problem. And the time it took to trace the provenance of mangoes in the United States went from 7 days to... 2.2 seconds!

Working with Hyperledger was a good experience for the Walmart team. "It seemed that the Hyperledger group had already been working on answering every question we had," **Bedwell** says. The Walmart team, for example, was concerned with interoperability with other block chain-based traceability systems when designing a fully open system. Hyperledger recently revealed its partnership with Ethereum, as if in response to their concern. "It seems that the Hyperledger group is solving all that companies are concerned about," he adds. As shown in Fig 2 the working of Walmart year wise has been explained as in October 2016 Walmart announces two POCs for Blockchain based food tracking after that in August 2017 After the Successful POCs, Walmart works with IBM, Nestle, and Unilever to Launch IBM Food Trust Likewise in year September 2018 Walmart traces over 20 products with the system powered by Hyperledger and after that in same duration Walmart announces that all supplies of the fresh leafy greens will be required to start using the Blockchain-based system in 2019.

Walmart also uses IBM Block chain, which is based on Hyperledger Fabric, to monitor over 25 items from five different suppliers. Produce like mangoes, bananas, and leafy greens; meat and poultry like chicken and pork; dairy like yoghurt and almond milk; and even multi-ingredient goods like packaged salads and baby foods are among the items on the list. "This solution allows us to see the entire chain in seconds!" Yiannas says of the effect. We can take a jar of baby food and look at where it was made, as well as track all of the ingredients back to the farms!"

Figure 2. Year wise working of Walmart
Note: In different years various announcements were made by Walmart has been shown in above fig: 2 hyperledger.org/wpcontent/uploads/2019/02/Hyperledger_CaseStudy_Walmart_Graphics_Timeline2.png5-https://www.hyperledger.org/learn/publications/walmart-case-study

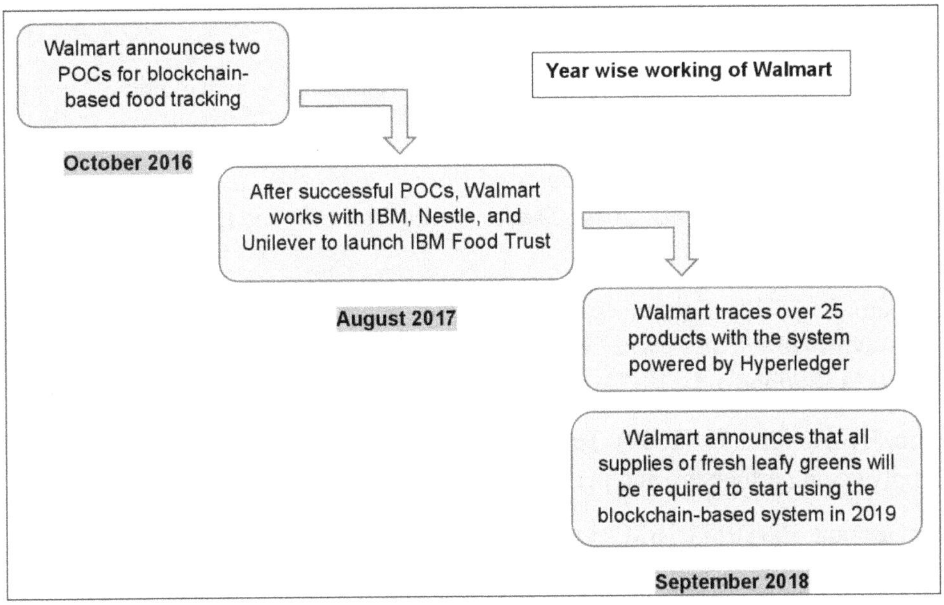

In collaboration with IBM Food Trust, Walmart expects to expand the system to more goods and categories in the near future. In reality, the company recently announced that it would begin requiring all of its fresh leafy greens (such as salad and spinach) suppliers to use the system to monitor their products.

In a letter to suppliers, Walmart wrote, "We have shown that using the IBM Food Trust network, which relies on block chain technology, we can reduce the amount of time it takes to monitor a food item from a Walmart Store back to source in seconds, as opposed to days or sometimes weeks."

The company may start tracking other data, such as sustainability, in addition to the products' journey.

REFERENCES

Brauer, J., & Linnala Eriksson, B. (2020). *Blockchain's influence on digital marketing: An exploratory study examining blockchain in relation to big data and digital marketing*. Academic Press.

Buterin, V. (2015). *Visions part I: The value of blockchain technology*. https://blog.ethereum.org/2015/04/13/visions-part-1-the-value-of-blockchain-technology

Davidson, S., De Filippi, P., & Potts, J. (2016). *Economics of Block chain*. Academic Press.

Ertemel, A. V. (2018). Implications of blockchain technology on marketing. *Journal of International Trade, Logistics and Law*, *4*(2), 35-44.

Evans, D. (2014). *Economic aspects of Bitcoin and other decentralised public-ledger currency platforms*. Coase-Sandor Institute for Law and Economics working paper #685.

Kamath, R. (2018). Food traceability on block chain: Walmart's pork and mango pilots with IBM. *The Journal of the British Blockchain Association*, *1*(1), 3712. doi:10.31585/jbba-1-1-(10)2018

Kim, J. S., & Shin, N. (2019). The impact of blockchain technology application on supply chain partnership and performance. *Sustainability*, *11*(21), 6181.

McDermott, B. (2017). IBM's vice president of blockchain business development, interviewed by R. Kamath, June 23, 2017. Academic Press.

Nakamoto, S. (2008). *Bitcoin: A peer-to-peer electronic cash system*. https://bitcoin.org/bitcoin.pdf

Nussbaum, F. (1933). *A History of the Economic Institutions of Modern Europe: An Introduction of 'Der Moderne Kapitalismus' of Werner Sombart*. Crofts.

Pärssinen, M., Kotila, M., Rumin, R. C., Phansalkar, A., & Manner, J. (2018). Is blockchain ready to revolutionize online advertising? *IEEE Access: Practical Innovations, Open Solutions*, *6*, 54884–54899. doi:10.1109/ACCESS.2018.2872694

Rejeb, A., Keogh, J., & Treiblmaier, H. (2020). How Blockchain Technology Can Benefit Marketing: Six Pending Research Areas. *Frontiers in Blockchain*, *3*, 3. Advance online publication. doi:10.3389/fbloc.2020.00003

Saberi, S., Kouhizadeh, M., Sarkis, J., & Shen, L. (2019). Blockchain technology and its relationships to sustainable supply chain management. *International Journal of Production Research*, *57*(7), 2117–2135. doi:10.1080/00207543.2018.1533261

Shih, D. H., Lu, K. C., Shih, Y. T., & Shih, P. Y. (2019). A simulated organic vegetable production and marketing environment by using Ethereum. *Electronics (Basel), 8*(11), 1341.

Swan, M. (2015). *Block chain: Blueprint for a New Economy*. O'Reilly Media.

Tan, B., Yan, J., Chen, S., & Liu, X. (2018). The Impact of Blockchain on Food Supply Chain: The Case of Walmart. In M. Qiu (Ed.), Lecture Notes in Computer Science: Vol. 11373. *Smart Blockchain. SmartBlock 2018*. Springer. doi:10.1007/978-3-030-05764-0_18

Tan, B., Yan, J., Chen, S., & Liu, X. (2018, December). The impact of blockchain on food supply chain: The case of walmart. In *International Conference on Smart Blockchain* (pp. 167-177). Springer.

Tiwari, T. (2016). *Profit alert: Walmart is adopting the blockchain right now*. Palm Beach Research Group. palmbeachgroup.com/content/palm-beach-daily/profit-alert-Walmart-is-adopting-the-blockchain-right-now/32499

Tribis, Y., Bouayad, H., & El Bouchti, A. (2018). Supply chain management based on blockchain: A systematic mapping study. *MATEC Web of Conferences, 200*, 1-8. doi:10.1051/matecconf/201820000020

van Hilten, M., Ongena, G., & Ravesteijn, P. (2020). Blockchain for Organic Food Traceability: Case Studies on Drivers and Challenges. *Frontiers in Blockchain, 3*, 43.

Chapter 14
Impact of Blockchain on E-Commerce:
A SCOT Analysis

Palvinder Kaur
https://orcid.org/0000-0002-4436-2842
University of Delhi, India

Manminder Kaur
Guru Nanak Khalsa Institute of Technology and Management, Technical Campus, India

ABSTRACT

The current disruption has created many challenges for all businesses in the short run, but it has created many opportunities in the long time. By helping in crisis and recovery, blockchain can play a prominent role in accelerating post-crisis digital transformation initiatives. Trade has become more efficient, more inclusive, and less costly through blockchain. These innovative technologies in the fourth industrial revolution are transforming the world by making the processes more inclusive and efficient.

INTRODUCTION

The COVID-19 global Pandemic emphasizes the reticulation of the world, which requires rapid, coordinated action and collaboration; massive amounts of critical information continue to be trapped in hardened data silos and legacy processes. For sustainable growth ahead in a changing world can be possible through the trusted

DOI: 10.4018/978-1-7998-8081-3.ch014

platform to automate outdated ways of working by rapidly joining the scattered data and unlock actionable imminent to navigate through this crisis. Establishing trust between all participants is another problem. That trusted platform can be Blockchain, and Blockchain-based solutions are helping us tackle today's most overwhelming challenges. Digitization is related to efficiency, and the transparency issue is now at the forefront. This particular situation has highlighted the lack of preparedness for this sort of disaster.

Technological Innovations have changed the world so fast that they alter the way we think, behave and do business. Technological progress constantly changes the history of the world and helps to make it a modern world. The ex-cogitation of the steam engine and the discovery of electricity leads to mass production, and the use of the computer network helps manage different production stages, directive to a division of production rise to global value chains. The steam power revolution connected the world like never before. The invention of ships laid the foundation for globalization. More recently, technologies such as Optical Character Recognition to read container numbers, Radio Frequency Identification and QR codes to identify and trace shipments, and essential digitization of trade documents have improved international trade reliability and efficiency. Trade has become more efficient, more inclusive, and less costly through BlockChain. These innovative technologies in the Fourth Industrial Revolution are transforming the world by making the processes more inclusive and efficient. Block-chain is, as The Economist (2015) calls it, a "Trust Machine".

Thus, the current disruption has created many challenges for all businesses in the short run, but it has created many opportunities for a long time. By helping in crisis and recovery, Blockchain can play a prominent role in accelerating post-crisis digital transformation initiatives.

There is a rapid growth in e-commerce with the fast growth of globalization and the Internet. New techniques are germinating to store the data, its management of consumers, goods and Seller. Lots of benefits can be taken by collecting this data. The colossal data needs a very streamlined cognition model in the Blockchain from the point of security. Counterfeit product affliction is a tremendous challenge for e-commerce companies. Henceforth, the Network encryption algorithm is required to study the impact of Blockchain on e-commerce here, particularly in the case of counterfeit products. This paper also studies the Strength, Challenges, Opportunities and Threat (SCOT analysis) of Block-chain on e-commerce.

DEVELOPMENT OF BLOCK-CHAIN

Block-chain can work like a game-changer, a revolution and have untapped potential. Block-Chain is an endlessly thriving database conglomerate in 'blocks' and then 'chained' using secret writing and cryptography. It is a digital record of a written account or transaction, a ledger distributed with all parties, and here data is highly secured, permanent by using cryptography technology. Block-chain is a trusted ledger with all participants who can access and assess at any time without the need of central authority because information once added is time-stamped. Hence Block-Chains are called highly Resilient.

According to Jeremy Wilson from Barclays Corporate Banking, block-chains technology is a leapfrog technology and will become the new operating system on the planet. Block-chain is a cloud-based global spreadsheet or *Distributed Ledger of Transactions* known as Blockchain-based DLT. Initially, this technology was used for digital currencies or Crypto-currency, Bitcoins in 2008 by unidentified individuals.

Blockchains and Bitcoins are linked, but they are different things. Block-chain works as virtual infrastructure for Bitcoins. The roots of Bitcoin were linked with 'Cypherpunks', where members were advocating cryptography for secure transactions as an itinerary for social and political changes. The Cypherpunks is a peer-to-peer system without any central authority, which is found in the banking system. The 2008 financial crisis provided a fertile ground for the operationalization, uptake and expansion of cryptocurrencies, and Bitcoin in particular (Bustillos, 2013).

Ethereum's quantum is another juncture in the development of Block-chain and where difference is due to the intelligent contracts made by computer programming that self-execute after meeting the specific conditions. Creative contract exercises without imposer and third-party inferences or delay. Thus Automating transactions is a revolutionary characteristic of Blockchain for trade. Smart contracts are not competent and like the contracts in a legal sense (Deloitte, 2018). Smart contracts are not a type of Blockchain actually, but rather a function of blockchain technology. The automated existence of smart contracts makes them an exciting tool to use in trade to automate transactions. This technology is used by the bank of China while using its digital currency to give more transparency and efficiency to the financial sector. Block-chain is cost-effective, suitable for banking products and financial literacy, and increases financial inclusion with geographical access (Schuetz & Venkatesh, 2019).

SCOT ANALYSIS OF THE IMPACT OF BLOCK-CHAIN TECHNOLOGY ON E-COMMERCE COMPANIES

It predicts the E-commerce business of India would achieve its business at $99 billion by 2024 (Goldman Sach, 2020). These e-commerce companies have increased during the Pandemic when people do not want to go outside and fulfil their demand through these e-commerce companies. Many new companies emerge, and already existing companies start investing in this business model according to the market's size and style. Facebook had started to enter into e-commerce companies by purchasing 9.9 per cent ($5.7 Billion) of Jio Retail. Many other e-commerce companies are now going to start online grocery stores.

One significant thing is that now producers want to sell their product directly to the consumer. They get feedback on their product instantly, and it helps them improve their products without any inter-mediators. The pace of e-commerce companies is too fast that the target can achieve in 2025. It is like a revolutionary change in the retail sector of India. Thus, different firms have more interest in Blockchains due to their transparent, secure and unaltered nature. Almost all sectors from finance to e-commerce, food safety and supply chain management are using this technique. Many new venture and startups are growing and working on it since 2017 (CB Insights, 2018).

Strength

1. **Digital Records**: In this model, all papers are digitized, which decreases the transaction cost. It gives the authenticity of the transactions.
2. **Data on IoT**: IoT facilitates getting product traceability and information related to production, ordering, and delivery.
3. **Distribution Management**: Impact of Technological development on retail distribution is new business models and consequently play an essential role in the growth of robust online shopping, e-commerce platforms like Amazon and Alibaba. Block-Chain technology provides possibilities in the Logistic industry to start any venture with its adoption and deployment (Dobrovnik and Kummaer, 2018).
4. **Transparent**: Conventional e-commerce companies have lack opacity. It is now effortless to have the history of all transactions, and digital transactions make automatic payment transfer convenient through intelligent contracts. Block-chain with the Internet of things gives pace to consumers' demand to deliver more clarity, adaptability, and fewer risks. Smart contracts store data in blocks to Seller and consumer with complete information of the transaction and can be used as a solution in case of a dispute.

5. **Un-Tampered**: Blockchain technology is a decentralized distributed ledger, and every transaction record and the un-tampered feature of this technology forbid the risk of fraud by tracking fictitious goods and fraudulent actions. The transparent nature expedited giant Alibaba to invest to a great extent in blockchain technology.
6. **Trace-Ability Mark**: Traceability Tags are pretty different from Bar codes. It does not require additional infrastructure and hardware to attach unique mark and record in blocks logically connected.

Thus, trusted and tamper-free *trade product, transaction and logistic* information through blockchain model propose here. An ordered chain based on the Hash index is created, and information transports to another text block.

Figure 1. Model on trade product trace tags

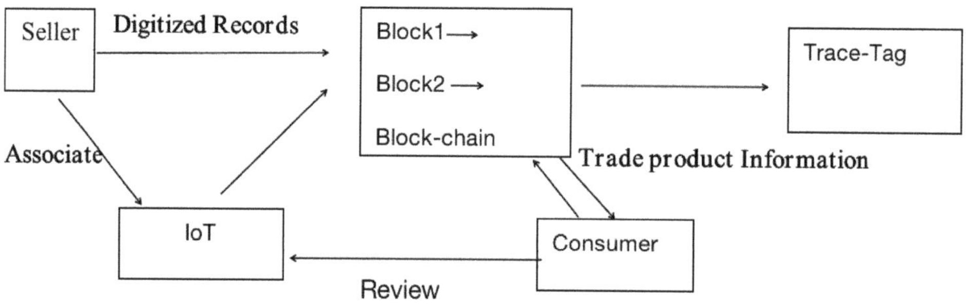

Seller transfers information regarding the source of product, raw material used to produce it and its manufacturing date through IoT. Model is providing reliable and tamper-free information of Trade product Trace tags.

Challenges

1. The use of this technology in the e-commerce field is at its infant stage. It may not overturn all at once; however, assurance of security clarity will facilitate the transactions in future.
2. Privacy of consumer's data and its commercial use is also a big challenge.
3. Most of the counterfeit products sale on e-commerce sites, and it is tough to distinguish them from an authentic product. At the same time, counterfeit product producing firms pay to increase the reviews of the product. This technology can not detect it.

Figure 2. Logistic information model

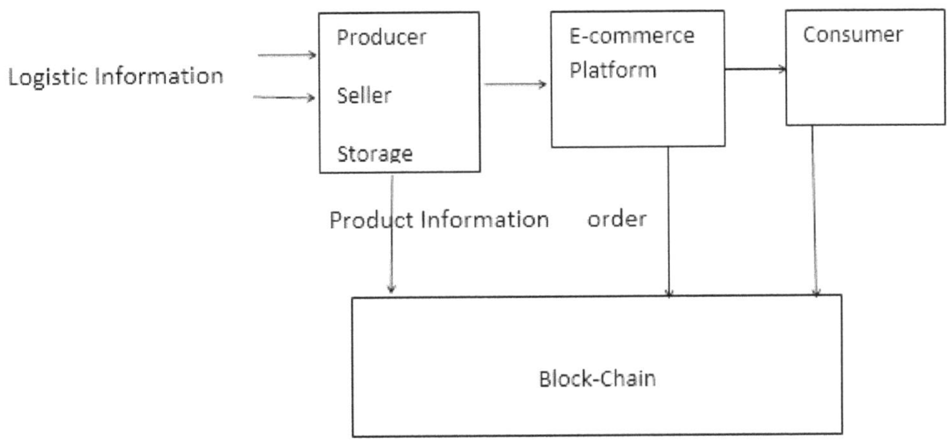

4. The technology has to scale up in an efficient enough way to meet the challenge.
5. It still has a long way to go before it can prove itself in the world of trade. Awareness among the Seller and buyer is essential for the use of Blockchain.

Opportunities

1. The Blockchain can affect the sales and revenue of these online companies.
2. The consumer gets quick and trusted solutions by Block-chain Technology, which increases the number of new consumers and hike the revenue.
3. Block-chain is used in online shopping to utilize a peer-to-peer marketplace without a central authority. Thus, new competitors can enter very quickly, and consumer can directly contact them through this platform like Amazon do.
4. An intelligent contract final when the transaction completes, and the consumer receives and verifies the good. Automating and revolutionary transaction method through intelligent contracts will be an attractive tool for e-commerce companies by cutting costs and streamline processes.
5. To decrease the role of counterfeit firms, e-commerce companies agree with the Seller about the authenticity of the product with the consent of the product owner. Then buyer receives only the original product. It is possible through the bar code of that product.
6. Infrastructure for the future: It provides e-commerce companies with a further boost, and a new technology-based business model will help increase the market and gross revenue. Block-chain could well become *the infrastructure* for the future.

Threat

1. In times where many physical products are digitized, and almost every physical process replicates on the digital layer that has largely taken control over the tangible world, security has become vital for e-commerce companies.
2. Management of the security of the consumer is a significant threat for the government.
3. These technologies show complex governance challenges in both domestic and cross-border trade. From the lack of governance framework to incompatible licensing and taxation requirements, outdated trade agreements and an increase in counterfeit good, these technologies will not help to take root and bear fruits automatically.
4. The consequences of missing standards will hamper the desired smooth exchange of data, which can otherwise ease collaboration, allows instant and better responses to disruptions, and drives optimization and security.

Figure 3. Anti-counterfeit product tag

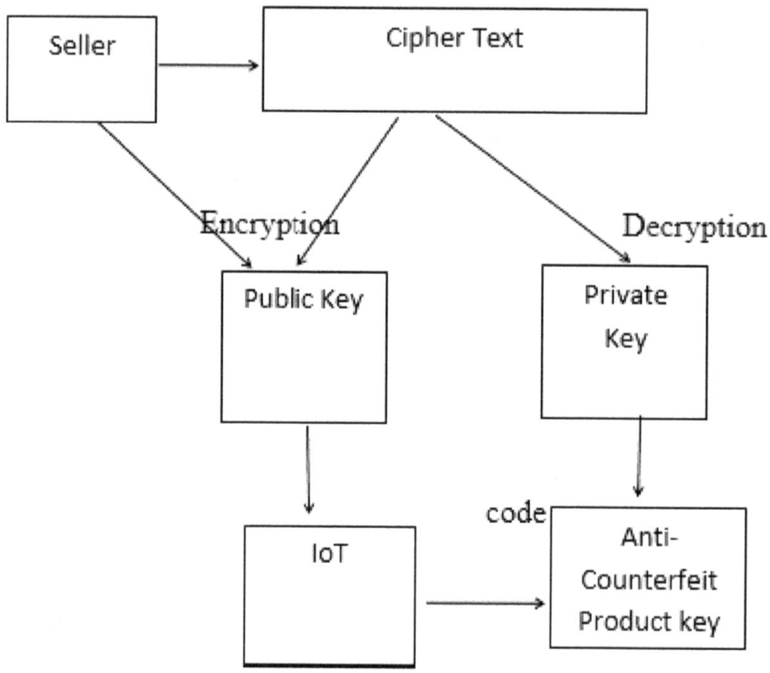

MATHEMATICAL ALGORITHM BLOCK-CHAIN MODEL FOR ANTI-COUNTERFEIT GOOD

A mathematical algorithm model is used to create a good trace mark based on elliptic curve cryptography (ECC), a public, secure essential encryption technique. It is a faster, smaller crypt-analysis that provide a secure and convenient transaction of product. RSA algorithm will create keys in this process, and only private, the authorized user will be able to use the given information. Hence the product authorization will be occurred by these marks and will also handle the threats and challenges of Block-chain.

RSA is an asymmetrical cryptography algorithm. There are two mathematical linked keys, the Public and Private key. The public key is known to all, and the Private key must not be shared with anyone and should keep it as a secret.

Key Generation

1. Select two Large Prime number, p and q.
2. Calculate n=p*q (Larger the value of p and q, more secure will be the key)
3. Choose $\Phi(n)= (p-11)* (q-1)$ with the use of Euler's function
4. Choose value of e randomly $1<e<\Phi(n)$ and $g<d \{\Phi(n),e\}=1$
5. Calculate $d^{o}e^{-1} \bmod \Phi(n)$ and $e^{-1o} \bmod \Phi(n)$, then $de \bmod \Phi(n)=1$
6. Public Key= {e,n} & Private Key = {d,n}
7. Encryption (e,n) where M<n thus Cipher Text $C= M^{e} \bmod n$
8. Decryption when $M= c^{d} \bmod n$

The public key used in encryption, and (d,n) is the private key used for decryption. The public key can calculate through the ECC algorithm, and a unique product code will generate based on area, batch, number and time. So the mathematical algorithm through RSS and ECC is used to encrypt the data and information. RSA decides the security based on the larger number of n. these two methods provide the security based upon the statement of distinct pairs; it makes anti-counterfeit product mark very nonhazardous.

CONCLUSION

Today, customers and buyers have limited visibility and ability to validate the actual value of products and services they wish to purchase. The main concerns will be regarding the price, which might be an inaccurate reflection of the valid and actual value of the product. Limited transparency also causes risks for manufacturers and brands resulting from illicit practices and the environmental impact of certain forms of production. DLT and Blockchain can help to reassure consumers, mitigating and eliminating risks around food security, conflict minerals, counterfeit goods, forced and child labour, corruption. Then there will be more benefits than its challenges with the progress of this e-commerce.

REFERENCES

Accenture. (2017), *Banking on Block-chain – "A Value Analysis for Investment Banks"*. New York: Accenture. www.accenture.com

Aluhairi. (2020). *Why COVID-19 makes a Compelling case for the Wider Integration of Blockchain*. World Economic Forum.

Asian Development Bank (ADB). (2017). *Trade Finance Gaps, Growth, and Jobs Survey*. ADB Brief N. 83.

Barclays. (2016). *The Blockchain Revolution in Trade Finance*. Author.

Bell. (2019). Applications of blockchain in International Trade: An Overview. *The Romanian Economic Journal*.

BitFury Group. (2015). *Public vs Private Blockchains*. White Paper.

Boston Consulting Group. (2017). *Digital Innovation in Trade Finance: Have We Reached a Tipping Point?* Author.

Boucher, P. (2017). How blockchain technology could change our lives, European Parliament Research Service. Academic Press.

Buterin, V. (2013). *Ethereum: The Ultimate Smart Contract and Decentralized Application Platform*. Ethereum's White Paper.

Chang. (2019). Exploring Blockchain Technology in International Trade: Business Process Re-engineering for Letter of credit. *Industrial Management and Data System, 119*(8).

Del Castillo. (n.d.). Blockchain toolkit to Fix broken Food Supply Chains. *Forbes*.

Deloitte. (2016). *Blockchain in Insurance*. Author.

Deloitte. (2017). *Blockchain & Cybersecurity*. Author.

Deloitte. (2018). *Blockchain, legal implications, questions, opportunities and risks*. Deloitte Legal.

Framingham. (2019). *Worldwide BlockChain Spending forecasts to Reach $2.9 Billion in 2019*. International Data Centre.

CB Insights. (2017). *The March Of Financial Services Giants Into Bitcoin And Blockchain Startups In One Chart*. Author.

Insights. (2018). *Blockchain startups absorbed 5X more capital via ICOs than equity financings in 2017*. Author.

Jensen. (2020). How Global Trade Digitization could Support COVID-19's Economic Rebound. *The Economic Times*.

Liao & Fan. (2020). *Supply Chain Have been Upended: how to make them more resilient?* World Economic Forum.

Norbug. (2019). *Unblocking the Bottlenecks and making the Global Supply Chain Transparent: How Blockchain Technology Can update Global Trade*. The School of Public Policy Publication.

The Economist. (2015). *The Trust Machine – The Promise of the Blockchain*. Author.

Chapter 15
Analytical Impact of Technology on the COVID-19 Pandemic

Devesh Bathla
Chitkara Business School, Chitkara University, Punjab, India

Shraddha Awasthi
Chitkara Business School, Chitkara University, Punjab, India

ABSTRACT

COVID-19 has totally changed the way that we live, and it also changed the way we work. It changed the way all the businesses run. Many of the businesses today either shut down due to lack of technological performance or the others moved towards the online mode to sustain the market. During the time of this pandemic, the businesses had no choice other than to shift to online mode. Some of the businesses operate offline, and it was not possible for them to shift online in a very short time due to lack of technology, lack of knowledge, etc. They faced much difficulty to operate their business smoothly. So, the impact of technology during the COVID-19 pandemic played a very important role throughout the world. When this pandemic was at its peak, technology became a lifeline of the human beings. This chapter shows the trend of digital technology during the COVID-19 pandemic and some innovations during this pandemic.

DOI: 10.4018/978-1-7998-8081-3.ch015

PURPOSE

The main purpose of this research paper is to analyse the trend of technology in Covid-19 pandemic. And also to analyse the impact of technology during the time of this pandemic and what happen if these modern technologies is not such advanced, then how Covid-19 affects our life. And what are some of the negative impact of these technologies in our daily life during the pandemic and after the pandemic.

FINDINGS

Today all the countries around the globe are working on the technology and innovations to find the treatment of this novel corona virus. And technology plays a very vital role in finding the antidotes of the virus. Whenever the antidotes of the virus are not come into the market all the work is done from the home especially job persons. All the little things which are essential are managed through homes. And all thinks to the technology which makes our life easier in this pandemic.

METHODOLOGY ADOPTED

This work is done by the secondary data collection as well as primary data collection from the many different sources and from the survey to many different people of different age groups and from the professional research papers. This research paper is basically based on analysis of the impact of technology in Covid-19. Some graphs and chat also make this research paper more effective and make a clear picture of this research paper.

RESEARCH IMPLICATIONS

This research paper gives a clear cut picture of the role of technology in the modern world. It also helps the analyst to understand the importance of technology in the 21th century. By some of the analytical data this research paper shows the impact of modern technology and what are the causes arise if it is not there. This paper offers bit of knowledge in the importance of technology in Covid-19 and how these technologies help us to change the way of thinking, working, creativity etc. in the upcoming future. This research also shows some of the negativity that we need to face because of increasing the demand of modern technology and how it affects on the life of people. Does this technology helps people to create more employment or it increases the unemployment rate? Does it affect the daily life of the people and how people react when they are completely surrounded by these technologies? The reason for this research paper is to start answering this kind of some big questions which is somewhere in the every human beings. And another reason for this research is to distinguish some new areas.

EVOLUTION

Everything was running fine in the beginning of 2020. It was like every previous year for ourselves until we get to know the unexpected future. We all are not aware about our coming future in the next 2 to 3 months. A virus named as Corona virus began in the city of Wuhan in China on the end of 2019. This virus rapidly spread throughout the world very quickly. Many people affected by this virus and can't survive. Some of the symptoms of this deadly virus are fever, cold and cough, headache etc. This virus wildly spread throughout the world and forced us to sit in our home. All the countries that are either super power or small developing countries faced a heavy economic loss in the beginning of this virus. All the work was completely closed and government make very strict rules and regulations regarding this pandemic. All the peoples were suggested to sit on their homes and do their work from home. Almost all the different sectors are stick to come online rather than continue with the offline work. Education, Industries, Multinational companies, Entertainment and many more they all became dependable on online platforms.

INTRODUCTION

When the pandemic was not there we are already do our some works through mobiles, laptops, digital media but from when the pandemic was announced and we are forced to sit in our home then we are now more addicted towards the technology. It becomes more important for us as compared to pre-covid situation. Now this pandemic makes people totally dependable on the technology. In the pre-covid situation people get up in the morning and be ready to going for their work but today they start their working day as sitting in front of laptops, mobiles etc to attend meetings, to attend lectures etc. Now people use webcam and mike to see their teams and communicate with each other regarding their future plans and projects. Every sector is totally dependable on online platforms. Now we can say that digital technology plays a very vital situation on current scenario and brought new innovations in the time of this pandemic (Bogoch, I.I et al, 2020).During the time of lockdown everyone was in fear of rapidly decrease in the economic growth and they want to work to handle the situation, and technology made the work easier and more effective. Many countries faced a heavy economic lose but it may go to the worst condition without these new age modern technology. Today most of the companies are working on online portals to work effectively on Zoom, Google Meet, and WebEx etc. These online portals became the lifeline for the companies and for the other sectors. Because of these online portals the education system is also running well and the students attend their classes from home and learning in an effective manner without any delay. By the help of this modern technology it is easier for the teachers to teach the students and involve them in curricular activities. Now the education pattern is completely changed and many online certifications courses also introduced for the students to learn new things in the different area they wish to learn and get the certificates which is useful for them in the future. By the help of this modern technology government also launched many online portals sites to fight with corona virus like ArogyaSetu app to examine the users and inform them the number of infected person on their locality. These digital technologies can facilitate pandemic strategy in a way that was really very difficult to achieve manually. E-commerce companies are also doing very well in this pandemic because of such advance technologies like Amazon, Flip kart, big basket etc because it becomes the first choice of the customers as a safety measures. These days many people want to purchase the product from online platforms because of safety measures and also because these platforms also provide quality schemes for their valuable customers. As people rely on technology it becomes more profitable for online business and online market places. At the time of this pandemic gaming sector is also doing very well as it introduced many quality games for the engagement and entertainment of the people and mainly they focuses on the youth. It also helps people to engage somewhere and think less which cause depression in this pandemic about the future and it also helps to reduce the stress of the people (Thomas Liji 2020).

If we talk about the health sector then again technology play a very important role. In the Covid-19 situation digital technology can help in a very effective manner and that are very much difficult to achieve manually without such new age technology. It was very challenging for the government to manage such large population without the help of technology and modern equipments which shows the results in seconds. Today many develop countries focused on the usage of these advance technology to detect virus and began the treatments of the infected persons as soon as possible. Every sector are now more focus in advancing there tools and techniques as compared to the pre-covid situation. In this pandemic the people realise the actual use of modern technology is how much important and how it can help us to protect from the deadly virus. In this pandemic everything we can do is very fast and more appropriate because of the technology. We just have to click a single button in our laptops and mobiles and various kinds of work are done at a same time. This technology not only created value to our professional life but also to our personal life too. When all the things were closed and most of the people just stay on their home with no work in hand then these technology helps to engage them in some activities. So that people faced that lockdown easily and they don't feel bored. If this new age technology was not there at the time of lockdown then I think most of the people are suffered from depression and stressed. And these all cause another health issue which was more dangerous. So in this research paper we are examining the major impact of the corona virus disease on the digital technology and we are also examining the possible scenario of pre-Covid situation.

INNOVATION TOWARDS DIGITAL TECHNOLOGY IN COVID-19

When all the world are facing the challenges to fight with the navel corona virus then digital technology comes in our life as a blessings and due to this we are able to fight with this virus in a very effective manner. This technology doesn't help to vanish the virus completely but it help to stop the spreading of the virus to the worst condition. These digital technologies play a very important role to empowering the people and warning the people. When the pandemic was on their peak and all the people are in rush to purchase the masks and hand sanitizers to protect themselves and their family, the stock of these items were vanish from the market very soon then digital technology play a very important role with providing these essential items from where it was available. And during the time of shortage of these essential items technology helps the scientists to make Automatic Mask Machines to produce masks more quickly and it is also very cheaper than the other one. The masks which are produced by this Automatic mask Machines are nearly 35% more cheaply than the other masks (Xiao and Fan, 2020). During the time of pandemic many organisations comes with some great innovative ideas to protect themselves from the virus and it also push the digital world one step towards the modern digital world where all the things done in seconds. Like wireless thermometer that play a very important role to check the temperature of the people from some distance so that many others are not being affected by this virus. Like some low cost ventilator were innovated by the scientists and there teams for the people who are not in a position to spend very much in medical treatments.

Some PPE kits were also innovated by the team of scientists to protect the doctors who are in the hospital to treat the patients who are positive with the corona virus. These advance PPE kits helps to protect the doctor from the spreading of virus from the patients. Today robotic technology is very trending in this pandemic and in many places it is already using like Airports, Malls, Hospitals etc like Automatic shoes cleaner to clean the shoes from spreading the virus and automatic doors to avoid touching the things. Digital transaction is now also very trending in this pandemic and all the people more prefer to make payment with online payment sites like Paytm, PayPal, Google pay etc to avoid touching the currency and contribute in the spreading the virus. Now most of the stores are using online transaction rather than the cash payments. Even now many vegetable vendors who sit on the corner of the road and sell their vegetables are using this online payment system. So by this we can easily interpretate that what is the role of digital technology in the modern world and especially during the time of Covid-19.

There are also many innovations which we can see in upcoming future who contribute in pushing the technology very much towards the complete technological world. Now when the Covid-19 pandemic is nearly about the end and now scientists and engineers are planning to change the scenario of working completely and we will also see the change of transportation in the upcoming future like Hyper loop train who ran in the vacuum tube with the speed of more than 1000kms per hour. Like electric cars that ran on the road in upcoming future which is completely pollution free so by this all we can say that now the world is moving towards technological world even more fast after the Covid-19 pandemic comes into existence. To avoid workers gathering many online portals were introduced by the different organisations to work from home and be safe. Today online portals like Zoom, Google Meet, and WebEx etc become the first choice of the workers who want to work from home and they work even more effectively. So this all things are just done due to the modern technology and innovation of new age technologies.

ROLE OF TECHNOLOGY AND RESEARCH METHODOLOGY

So this research paper gives the clear cut picture of the trending role of technology in the Covid-19 situation and how it helps to change our behaviour, our daily routine and our working system. It also shows the importance of technology in the current world and how much we are dependable on that. So this research is based on primary data as well as secondary data from many different sources (Bhawana PN,2020). The primary data is conducted among more than 100 participants. All the participants are from different age group, different occupations and genders. So the chart on the analysis part is mix responses of all the participants which show us that how much technology impact our life in Covid-19 pandemic. The purpose of this survey is to analyse how much changes comes in the people before Covid-19 and during this pandemic. This analysis also show us how much people moves towards digital technology as a primary source of living in the pandemic. Many people are now dependent on OTT platforms and E-learning platforms to pass their time without getting bored. Online entertainment channels like Netflix, Amazon

Prime, and Hotstar etc are become the first choice of the people and they spend a lot of money to watch these channels by making monthly and yearly payments. This research paper is also a combination from the different research paper which is written by some famous researchers. So the mixture of primary and secondary data makes a great research (Riva et al., 2020).

During the time of pandemic technology comes with some great innovations and role of that innovation play a very important role to saves our life and stop the situation to going into the worst. Role of technology is very helpful for workers especially for the white collar workers who are comfortably work from home and also spend their lot of time with their family members because before Covid-19 all were complaining that they don't get enough time to spend with their family members. So for this all thanks goes to the new technological world which makes our life easier in Covid-19 pandemic. And we have to thanks our great scientists and engineers for such great innovations which helps us to stay in our home comfortably and calmly and these technology doesn't get us realised how worst is the condition outside.

Analysis of Data and Their Interpretation

So this analysis is done through the primary data which is collected from the peoples of different age groups and different occupations from survey. There are lists of some questions by which it is easy for us to interpretate how technology impact in Covid-19 in your life and what are their major role during the time of pandemic.

It was seen that almost 50% of the respondents agree that they are more addicted towards the digital technology during the time of Covid-19. Almost 20% people say that no they are not addicted towards the modern technology in this pandemic they are concentration to their work and spent their time with their family members. And almost 30% respondents don't know the exact answer they are agree with both the statement.

It is observed that almost 31.1% of the respondents agree that they are addicted to the digital technology and they use electronic gadgets for more than 8 hours in a day during lockdown in Covid-19. Almost 26.2% respondents say that they use modern technology for 4-6 hours. Almost 19.7% people agree that they use technology for 2-4 hours and only 11.5% of the people agree that they use this modern technology for less than 2 hours because they utilize their time to learn some new skills.

70.5% of the respondents agree that our life become more dependable on the digital and social media platforms after the outbreak of Covid-19. They think as technology became more advanced it controls our life and we all become totally dependable to the new age technology in the upcoming future. Almost 13.1% of the respondents are not agreeing with this statement that we became dependable of technology; they believe the situation will go as usual as it can today. There will nothing change in our life due to modern technology. And almost 16.4% of the respondents doesn't actually know that we became dependable on technology or not in the future.

Respondents have chosen which online portals sites they prefer more during their meetings and conferences. Almost 31.1% respondents choose Google meet as their most preferred online portal sites because it is very easy to handle and it is very simple to understand their features. Especially the students who are studying in school and colleges more prefer to attend their classes on Google meet. Almost 24.6% of the respondents choose Microsoft Teams for meetings. Mostly white collar jobs people choose this site because of security reasons and it is paid site so small age group people especially students avoid this site. Almost 19.7% of the respondents choose Zoom because it is easy to use and it works on either poor connectivity network areas. Only 9.8% of the respondents choose WebEx because it is very heavy site and it also create problem when the network strength is poor. And many people avoid to use WebEx because of that reason.

24.6% of the respondents agree that they spent their time during the lockdown just by engaging themselves on social media. They agreed they use social media to make new friends and try to pass the time. Almost 16.4% of the respondents agreed that they play a lot of video games to spend their time during lockdown. These peoples are mostly youth between the age group of 15-30 years who play a lot of games on PC, Mobile, play station and Tablets. Almost 16.4% of the respondents say that they utilize there most of the time in E-learning platforms to learn online certification courses which is helpful for them in the coming future courses. 36.1% of the respondents say they were utilize their time somewhere else rather than these online sites. And only 6.6% of the people utilize their most of the time in Live streaming sites like Netflix, Amazon Prime etc.

In this almost 54.1% of the respondents agreed that they watched motivational videos because during the time of lockdown they start thinking negatively so that motivational videos and some meditation helps them to stay calmly and always think on the positive direction. Almost 29.5% of the respondents say that they don't watch these videos rather then this they spend their time with their family members and learn new skills to engage themselves. And almost 16.4% of the respondents say they occasionally watch these kind of videos when they feel alone and when try to spend their time somewhere.

FINDINGS

The modern technology has totally evolved in fighting with the novel corona virus. The entire globe is totally depending on these technologies to protect their peoples from this virus. It helps the mankind in the entire difficult situation which arises during the period of lockdown. The government also took many big steps to secure their citizens from this virus. During the period of this pandemic when everyone was on fear to go outside and purchase the daily need items then this modern technology help us a lot. By these technologies we can purchase anything that we want for our daily need just by click a single button from home. All for this all thanks to the technology which supports us during the time of pandemic and protect us from the novel corona virus disease. If this corona virus come 20 to 30 years back then I think the situation gone to be the worst because the technologies was not very much advanced at that time and the treatment was not very much effected as compared to today. So by the change of time the advancement in the technology can save our life in this pandemic and it will also saves our life in the coming future from many another these kind of viruses.

By the help of Scientists and engineers today I think we are blessed with this kind of innovation by which we are able to fight with the corona virus. In this pandemic some great innovation and upgraded technologies not only helpful for us in this pandemic but it also play a very important role in the future. As the things become more advance the innovation of such things and the use of these things also upgraded day by day.

DIGITAL TRANSACTION IN COVID-19

Digital technology in the today's world is very important in all the sectors. Today all the things we do is done by digital technology from a small transaction to a big deal of the companies. Now we all are merging to the cashless economy and in this digital technology comes first because of this cashless economy is not possible. All the things are done digitally it also helps the people to cure themselves from frauds. The cases of cheating and frauds are increasing in this pandemic because many people are unemployed so they do it to earn money from somewhere. But this advanced digital technology is very much secured and many companies also give some cash back and vouchers to their valuable customers (Kaur, Navleen et al 2020). Now the government also give some benefits to those customers who prefer digital transaction to promote cashless economy. In the times of Covid-19 when all of us avoid to touch the things at public places and especially the currency notes then only digital transaction was the only mode of payment so it helps us to do contactless payment and contactless receiving of money. After the demonetization in India now we all the moving toward the cashless economy very fast and in the coming future the whole economy will be cashless economy and the problem of black money will also be minimized to the great end. And it allows us to do transaction without any delay because digital payments are done at any time 24/7.

HEALTHCARE TECHNOLOGY

Now if we talk about the health care technology then we can say that today healthcare technologies are very much advance and because of it we are able to fight with the novel corona virus and secure ourselves and our family from this virus. When the corona virus was on their peak and the cases of this virus increased day by day and everybody was rushing through the hospitals just because of these technologies the doctors are able to treat the patients effectively. Many people who were positive with this virus are alive today just because of modern technology of treatment because it is very fast and effective way of treating the patients. When all the hospitals were full with the patients and it was the major challenge to the government to do something to treat other patients then again technology play a very important role. Government and some other private companies make some self assessment online app by which people get to know they are in safe zone or not. And if someone finds that they are in red zone they have to quarantine themselves for some period of time. By these helpful apps people get to know they are safe or not. Many apps also introduced for the people to concern the doctors from that apps virtually and take proper medication to stay fit and healthy.

In the times of Covid-19 this sector was the most effected sector, so it was very important at that time to complete focus on this sector. The scope of this sector is very much wider in this pandemic and after the pre-Covid situation. During the time of Covid-19 when it was on their peak telemedicine was on booming because of rapid growth in the demand of medicine from online. Many people shifted to the telephonic consultation rather than physical consultation in this pandemic.

In this pandemic situation the first thing comes to every people minds is vaccines. Now it almost one year from when this pandemic starts spreads throughout the globe. All the teams of scientists in every corner of the world start searching on vaccines. It's almost one year and now some countries claim that they make the vaccines but none of them are 100% effective. Some countries claim that their vaccine is 70% effective some claim that their vaccine is 90% effective. But according to this percentage we say that it's just because of technology and spirits of scientist who make this possible otherwise the situation gone to be the worst. And it is almost impossible to defeat corona virus without vaccines. So the technology in the healthcare comes as a blessing in this pandemic and it also play very important role in the future.

E-LEARNING PLATFORMS

When the government announced the lockdown in the mid of March the big problem arises with the students. This corona virus affects the education of students, because of complete lockdown and rapidly increases in the cases everyday all the students were forced to sit in home. All the educational institution was closed and the time of the students were completely wasted for few months. All the parents were worried about their children's future. And they also don't want that government allow school and colleges to reopen in this pandemic because they also wanted to protect their children's from this virus. It becomes a major issue for the government and educational institution to find a way to teach students in this pandemic in an effective manner so that they cope up with their syllabus. So in this situation again technology plays a very important role in educational sector. Many companies and educational institution came up with some online learning portals which helps them not just to teach the students but also do digital conferencing through that portals (Manjunath, B. S, 2020). Many companies introduced these online portals to learn digitally in an effective manner through cloud computing like Zoom, Google Meet, Microsoft teams etc. Through these online portals students attend their classes from their homes and they easily interact with their teacher's digital conferencing. Through these online portals teachers not only teach their students but they also assigned some assignment to the students and they have to show their work by share their screen to the teachers. The benefits of these online portals are that the students don't make proxy and they learn on screen which is more practical then theory from different books.

Many companies and educational institution also introduced some e-learning platforms which helps the students to learn what they want from that platforms. And the students also do some certifications courses from that platforms in this pandemic from their home and these certification courses helps them in future. There are many such sites like Coursera, Byju's, Udemy, and E&Y etc. which offer great learning in very small amount of money. Many big companies and universities are collaborated with these online e-learning sites like Google, Microsoft, Oxford, Harvard etc and they offer some of their courses and specializations to study online and get certificates from that company or universities.

SOME NEGATIVE EFFECTS

As we all know every coins have two figures, same is with the technology in this Covid-19. In the above of this research paper we talk about all the positive things related to technology that how it helps to improve our life style and how technology helps us to fight with the novel corona virus. And how this modern technologies help us to do our work from home and save ourselves from this virus in this pandemic.

But it is also very important to discuss the negative side of these technologies by which we think it comes in our life as a blessings. No doubt. This technology helps us a lot in the time of corona virus to save the life of people and monitor the daily report of the patients who suffered from this virus. But in many areas it destroys our life and the life of children. If we talk about this pandemic when all the things gets online and everyone in this world are working from their home. Government and educational institution allow the students to attend the classes online. Some of the students take it very seriously to focus on the studies but for some students it comes as an opportunity to make proxy and show their teacher and patents that they studied. Most of the time they engaged themselves on social media and OTT platforms by which the future of those students are in danger because of lack of proper knowledge about what teacher taught in the class. And they will face many difficulties during their final examinations and placements opportunities. By this technology many people today are in depression, anxiety etc. These days many news comes related to social media about cheating and frauds but still people are curious to make friends online which are not known.

During the lockdown period when all of the people work from home to till now many cases came related to mental, aggressiveness and eyes problems. All the day people engage to complete their work on mobile and laptop and this cause mental depressions and eyes problem. These gadgets hold the attention of the people for long period of time and it cause eyestrain. By which many people depend on glasses and some other problem also arises due to long sitting in front of laptops and mobile phones like neck, head, and shoulder pains.

Due to these common problems many people also face difficulty in sleeping. Many of us use these gadgets during our sleeping time and we continuously focus on the screen which creates many problems in our eyes and our health. During this pandemic many people especially youth were engaged on OTT platforms to watch movies and web series whole night and this creates an unbalance between working time and sleeping time. Due to continuous busy with these technologies most of the people reduced their physical activities by which they gain extra fat which creates a negative effects on health like diabetes, obesity, and premature death etc.

Due to take more interest on this technology especially during this pandemic children face many issues like lack of creativity, lack of attention, low performance, aggressive behaviour, addicted towards these technologies and poor quality of sleep etc. and it leads to create a big problem in the future. I cannot say that use of technology is bad but there is must be a limit because current boom in the technology in this pandemic change our daily lifestyle. There are lot of positivity we see of technology in this pandemic but there are also some possible risks due to this technology. So it is important to find the right way to use these technology if want to take full advantage of this.

CONCLUSION

So, in this research paper we get to know more about the technology and how it offers the solution to overcome in this pandemic. In this research paper we get to know what the different roles of technology in the lockdown when all of us were stuck in our houses and not able to go anywhere. Many people who are in some jobs were faced many difficulties to work properly from home but somewhat they were able to do their work was just because of some modern technologies. This technology helps the people to complete their work in an effective manner and it also provide a high quality work experience. By the help of some online portals people attend their meetings, online classes and conferences. Apart from the work these technologies also helps in keeping connected with our family and friends during the period of lockdown.

This modern technology also contributes their important role in the health sector. In Covid-19 situation daily thousands of people admitted into the hospitals and was a very challenging job to take care of such large population at a same time from monitoring to testing and treatments of the patients by the doctors. So in this situation government and many big companies launch online health checkups apps to know the situation in locality and self examination sites (Mattiuzzi and Lippi, 2020). These apps also show the number of cases in a day and it also aware the people which come under a red zone area. In the entertainment sector many OTT platforms gain huge profit because of people suddenly moving to online entertainment channels due to Covid-19. Many people start investing their lot of time in such platforms and some invest their time in gaming, social media etc. Due to these platforms many people engage themselves in this and it also saved many people from depression and anxiety.

But all the coins have to side figure and same is with the technology. In much research paper you only find just the merits of the technology in Covid-19. But in this research paper you find the complete analysis of merits and demerits of the technology during Covid-19 pandemic. In the above paragraph we see how technology become so important for us in this pandemic but now we also focus on some disadvantage of this technology. These technologies create a bad impact on many students because of some OTT platforms and lot of gaming sites it distract the mindset of the students from study. Now a day's most of the students spend their time on gaming and OTT platforms so that they perform very poor in their final examination. And many people who work from home they may face some major issues related to their eyes. Many people also observe that they become aggressive and they violent on a small things. Due to continuous engagement on these such technologies like mobile phone, laptops, tablets etc many people feel very less energetic and these such problems creates a big impact on the people in the future. So the people need to understand how to use technology and how much to use it so it can't affects our health and we take full advantage of technology.

REFERENCES

Bogoch, I.I., Watts, A., Thomas-Bachli, A., Huber, C., Kraemer, M.U., & Khan, K. (2020). Potential for global spread of a novel coronavirus from China. *Journal of Travel Medicine, 27*(2).

Kaur, N., & Sahdev, S. (2020). Fighting COVID-19 with technology and innovation, evolving and advancing with technological possibilities. *International Journal Of Advanced Research In Engineering & Technology., 11*, 395–405. doi:10.34218/IJARET.11.7.2020.039

Liji, T. (2020), *Analysis of India's Battle with Covid-19.* https://www.news-medical.net/news/20200504/Analysis-of-Indias-battle-with-COVID-19.aspx

Manjunath, B. S. (2020, April 14). *Covid-19: 8 ways in which technology helps pandemic management.* Https://Cio.Economictimes.Indiatimes.Com/

Mattiuzzi, C., & Lippi, G. (2020). Which lessons shall we learn from the 2019 novel coronavirus outbreak? *Annals of Translational Medicine*, *8*(3).

PN. (2020, August 5). *Role of Technology in the Era of COVID-19 Pandemic.* https://news.cleartax.in/role-of-technology-in-the-era-of-covid-19-pandemic/

Riva, G., Mantovani, F., & Wiederhold, B. K. (2020). Positive Technology and COVID-19. *Cyberpsychology, Behavior, and Social Networking*, *23*(9), 581–587.

Xiao, Y., & Fan, Z. (2020, April 27). *10 technology trends to watch in the COVID-19 pandemic.* https://www.weforum.org/agenda/2020/04/10-technology-trends-coronavirus-covid19-pandemic-robotics-telehealth/

Chapter 16
Blockchain and the Future of Digital Marketing

Hameed Khan
Guru Ramdas Khalsa Institute of Science and Technology, Jabalpur, India

Kamal Kumar Kushwah
Jabalpur Engineering College, India

ABSTRACT

Blockchain is a unique new technology affecting the way facts are stored and shared electronically. Blockchain in digital advertising reflects clarity, security, and access to waft revenue and streamflow. It can promote digital advertising to consumers, which is profitable in spending big money on digital advertising campaigns. As per new technology, consumers can share and improve their statistics simultaneously with advertisers and advertisers. Blockchain technology can be considered to restore data control to statistical owners focused on digital advertising. Today's society has grown into a very digital one where local technology plays a significant role in everyone's lives. Moreover, society is advancing rapidly at an alarming rate with innovation in every corner and other business made online. The authors of the concept chose to find out how blockchain works could affect significant facts in digital advertising. The idea is to select challenging issues and beneficial opportunities when applying blockchain to digital marketing content.

BLOCKCHAIN INTRODUCTION

A blockchain is a medium-sized database that can no longer be managed by a single central system but by numerous users such as locations. The facts contained in the

DOI: 10.4018/978-1-7998-8081-3.ch016

device are exceedingly impervious and encrypted with security algorithms. It cannot be modified or updated by way of the user. Any file or information can be saved in chain blocks under blockchain theory (Atlam et al. 2020). Technology is gaining traction in many domains. In a blockchain trading system, economic statistics and health information continue to be permanent and unchanged. Therefore, Blockchain (technology) is a new, transparent, and secure tool for industries such as advertising (Alt R, 2020). You can look at our blockchain tutorials online earlier than studying Blockchain (technology) in marketing and advertising.

HOW DOES BLOCKCHAIN TECHNOLOGY WORK?

Blockchain technology is a network of blocks that eliminates the need for third-party or middle-class people. It puts data in one place by distributing it in blocks to all participants in the network. The blockchain website is not owned by anyone but is available to all participants. A safe and secure way to store data, Blockchain creates direct communication between buyer and seller (Digital examiner, 2019). Blockchain tech is a significant driving force in financial technologies, digital and cryptocurrencies that are proof of that. It helps to make transactions wholly secure and undeniable. Market eliminates fraudulent authorization via the encrypted network. It has made the processes more precise and more cohesive.

BLOCKCHAIN IN DIGITAL MARKETING

Blockchain is a relatively new technology and is the way information is stored and distributed electronically. Blockchain in digital advertising provides clarity, security, and access to cash flow and data flow (MartechAdvisor, 2019). It can improve digital marketing to consumers, benefit businesses from spending more on digital advertising campaigns. With this new technology, consumers can share and sell their information directly to advertisers and advertisers. Data is driving the market these days. Blockchain technology has the potential to restore data control to data owners targeted at digital advertising. Creates direct data exchange between consumers and products (Debika Sihi, 2020). User recruitment is of high quality, leading to reliability and the use of customer data. Let's take a look at some critical points on how Blockchain can prove profitable in digital advertising.

- Blockchain, a distributed ledger technology (DLT) technology that allows data to be stored globally on thousands of servers - while allowing anyone on the network to see everyone's entries in real-time rather than the best marketing apps (Kollmann et al. 2020). But before we delve deeper into its influence on digital marketing, let's take a look at the challenges in digital advertising that hurt retailers and consumers.

- Blockchain technology is best known for the explosion of Bitcoin, but it has now spread to many different sectors. One of the areas where it hits hard is digital marketing. So now is a good time to write digital marketing and blockchain guidelines. These emerging technologies have shaped the way we do business by tracking records so that we see money like Bitcoin being distributed (Rejeb A et al. 2020). It is all based on a system that has widely distributed. Some users on the network may view the Blockchain but cannot make changes to existing records. Instead, it is renewed with a guaranteed transaction and added to the block. Let's start by looking at some of the ways this benefits digital marketing.
- Digital marketing is a data-driven marketing strategy that relies heavily on information about consumer patterns and styles. However, Blockchain offers requesting data directly to customers instead of aggregators and sources like Google or Facebook. Blockchain has a wide range of digital marketing, although research work is ongoing and cases are used in various contexts. This technology has the potential to transform e-commerce and website design through collaboration (Sihi D. 2020). Apart from that, Blockchain is an excellent tool for checking the authenticity and authenticity of the content. One can test cheating, duplicate content, which is why thoroughly verifying 'content' using Blockchain.
- In social media, users can choose which ads to watch and which Blockchain they can verify once they have seen the video—restoring power and power to the end-user and ending the domination of unwanted online users that eliminates data days' free for all. In digital marketing, the Blockchain offers three key elements, accuracy, reliability, and transparency.

MODIFY COLLECTED WAY DATA

All digital marketing strategies are based on data collection, so companies that want to use blockchain technology will need to change their policy. Let's look at traditional data collection. The user will visit their favorite product online and sign up to use a secure server. The gatekeepers were then assured that they would do the right thing in detail - grey state-like nightfall. On the other hand, if a product uses blockchain technology, there is no gatekeeper. When a user registers, they create a transaction. The activity is stored in a block where it is authenticated on multiple devices before authorization. Users retain their original data while the Blockchain is created in a ledger, using verified signatures. Think of it as a key that locks their data behind a door. Only someone with keys can open their data door (Weking et al. 2020).

It removes the average person currently needed in digital advertising. Others presently control this existing space between user and business. For example, Google serves as a link between customers and companies. Using blockchain technology will remove them because the Blockchain itself will work for users, so there will be no need for Google to choose which ads to display on a website. Another significant issue is that blockchain data is transparent, so it tends to create a high level of consumer confidence. For example, people can look at their favorite products to see where all the ingredients come from or find that their interests are at stake.

A Few Notable Features of Blockchain Technology:

- More open and democratic advertising: No more unnecessary costs for advertising campaigns, clever ads to target the right people. Collect data directly from the user and pay them a token or cryptocurrency (Three 2 Five Marketing 2021).
- Reliable Marketing Strategies: It is easy to research and track product purchases and product performance. Accuracy in product design. The actual model of the world.
- Cheap Ad: Reduced ad costs and limited ad metrics make it easy to measure ROI. It helps to filter bot clicks, false views, etc.
- Globe Download: Blockchain is a symbol of cryptocurrency events that are money that crosses borders and does not require any exchange.

Blockchain is the future, ready to transform several sectors and change the way we look at the Internet (BDA News, 2020). It is the key to sharing information and empowering people. Blockchain is a technology that will make the Internet a democracy.

USING BLOCKCHAIN BUILDING CONNECTION WITH USERS

Blockchain and digital currency such as digital currency exchanges are available to exchange the way manufacturers and consumers conduct business.

Building blocks we consider how the Blockchain will affect how manufacturers and customers connect; it is essential to keep the built-in benefits in mind.

- **Blockchain is Still being Distributed:** Everyone participates in an equal play category.

- **Anonymous Blockchain:** Participants no longer rely on their ownership of power in discussions or activities.
- **Blockchain is a Democracy:** Everyone has a reason to support the integrity of every exchange.

These combined benefits provide a framework to help the progressive growth of this currency exchange and power building style, building trust with retailers and customers to share with others (Peters et al., 2015). With the automation that promises AI and IoT, the demand for transparent, secure, and open exchange like a blockchain will transform the trading, security, and customer experience deeper.

Today, cryptocurrencies are becoming increasingly popular as a way to save money - like gold deposits. Blockchain helps to transform customer attention and acceptance among publishers, advertisers, and consumers. Basic Attention Token is the first technology to use the Blockchain in these advertising ideas and medium marketing.

Customer

One of the most significant blockchain advantages of advertisers and buyers is the arrival of non-consumer goods and their owners on the Blockchain. Blockchain ensures a world where people use their records and can reduce the type and amount of information shared.

When developing a blockchain strategy, products should integrate customer management and see what it will mean for their customer relationships. For consumers to have their own identity, who may choose to remain anonymous in companies, merchants must develop new ways to build relationships, provide customized experiences and make new loyalty programs. An institutional question that needs to be answered is creating a functional customer experience for customers and consumers whose details you may not be familiar with.

Attention

Advertisers can also benefit more by considering customer attention like cash within them. Blockchain-based exchange trading can allow advertising networks and publishers to adjust their business fashion to reflect something consumers rely on - that social care units retain real value (Bons et al. 2020). This type of foreign currency can be converted into points in loyalty programs. Customer interest is no longer taken lightly and has a high value would be the most important trade in the retail industry. With products, they can be assured that they only pay for a high level of understanding of the first level and involvement. For publishers, they get excellent ads that build deeper connections with their readers and viewers. While all these lucrative exchanges occur, customer numbers have never been the product of a company or a publisher of all the people to win.

Security and Privacy

With the growing issue of privacy, there will also be an increase in blockchain management frameworks that empower consumers to give free access to privacy and charge facts and interests. To achieve this, stores will need to adopt BAT-compliant technology that demonstrates a commitment to transparent and equitable cost-sharing.

Adopting and enabling blockchain structures within product integrity and organic transactions further reduces record debt and product potential surrounding data security. This will be even more important to keep product recognition in check as consumers become more and more obsessed with forgetting their preferences and make transactions more effective in the entire developing IoT applications community.

Remembering the essential foundations of anonymity, transparency and democracy will help entrepreneurs keep pace and succeed with new sales that empower consumers. Over and over again, marketers will benefit from improved engagement, appropriate credentials, and more significant growth and efficiency opportunities.

BLOCKCHAIN TECHNOLOGY IN DIGITAL MARKETING

Improving Advertising and Digital Campaigns

Blockchain makes it possible to connect vendors and advertisers who provide data transparency, clicks, and connections, prevent fraud and eliminate content. Information from digital advertising campaigns can sometimes be inaccurate, so that development can be complex. Monitoring real-time advertising campaigns is possible with Blockchain to get reliable metrics (Blockchain Council, 2020). Top brands like Unilever use Blockchain to improve the performance of digital ads. The technology will advance to complete production and will introduce a Blockchain marketing solution later in 2020 with IBM.

Preventing Deception

The Blockchain network authorizes the recording of certified digital sites and examines certified advertising methods in fraud prevention registers. These ratings can be safely shared with authorized participants only. There are potential sites such as digital advertising, bots, click-through farms, and ghost websites where fraud is possible.

Involving a third party may increase the risk of data breach and cyber security as well as personal error. Big brands like Toyota have been using Blockchain programs in digital advertising to reduce fraud in their digital marketing campaigns. They saw a 21% increase in website visitor volume.

Establish Trust and Confidence

Businesses choose why Blockchain is because they can safely store, store, and share information with multiple groups, ultimately gaining trust. Blockchain has indeed been shown to help build trust over the past few years.

It can be difficult for small businesses to mark in the market when there are already players in the industry. With Blockchain, business owners will prove where their products come from and showcase their sales to build resilience among their customers.

Encourage Openness

With online advertising, it is impossible to know if the statistics are accurate with a click of a site or instagram followers. Even bots used to increase ad statistics provide negative results. Research has shown that bots alone cost companies more than $ 7 billion in 2016. However, with Blockchain, this series is transparent and encrypted due to the digital system (Aumcore, 2018).

It is unavoidable for every product that goes through a supply chain. Organizations can save millions from advertising by ensuring that people who view their ads are their audience. Companies can be guaranteed to get advertising.

Strengthens Financial Performance

Content is one of the most important aspects of a business when it comes to advertising. Strong content is needed to promote products and services. Blockchain allows consumers, bloggers, and streamers to create authoritative content for a specific reward rather than third-party content platforms (Covetus, 2019).

By giving advertisers space, social media providers make millions as viewers view them while visiting the website. Many platforms eliminate third parties by rewarding users directly with crypto micropayments for content creation. For example, content sharing platforms like Steemit and PodMiners use Blockchain solutions and earn rewards in STEEM tokens and incentives.

SIGNIFICANT PLAYERS OF BLOCKCHAIN MARKETING MARKETS

Few companies use Blockchain for marketing purposes, which are described below (Curvearro, 2020).

Bitclave

BitClave is a marketing technology company. It uses Blockchain to remove the middle person using intelligent contracts rather than paying a lot of money to mediators like Google and Facebook.

A smart contract enables them to control the transfer of funds between two parties (Subramanian, H. 2018). Users handle entirely their data instead of the advertiser. They can sell that data to businesses or choose different advertising services.

Orioncoin

OrionCoin is the most reliable platform on the market, with many floors following. It uses loyalty and reward systems to increase the level of retention among its customers. It uses Blockchain to provide companies and their customers with loyalty points called "ORC". When more companies use OrionCoin, the most essential ORC will be available.

With ORC's unlimited acquisition, consumers will always be motivated to collect them. OrionCoin also handles the internal value of each "point". Customers can sell ORC for money and can spend on purchases they want.

Brave Browser

Courageous software is used to block unwanted advertisers and advertisers. The Basic Attention Token (BAT) has been introduced to bring back the digital advertising model behind a simple framework for users, advertisers, and publishers without taking the help of an object. Brave can anonymously track your sites of interest to you. With Blockchain, it acts as publishers who receive tokens when users view ads. Users can return passes to the publishers.

These are just some companies that have used Blockchain in their marketing strategy, making it private and reliable. All of these statistics and companies that make Blockchain marketing provide insight into the future of advertising.

THE FUTURE OF THE BLOCKCHAIN BUSINESS

Blockchain will help small businesses compete with larger companies in the coming years by reducing costs and increasing transparency and consumer confidence.

Gartner says Blockchain comes second in installation and machine learning technology as one of the most disruptive technologies in the future (Ertemel et al., 2019). Blockchain has benefited almost all sectors where it has been used from production to agriculture, banks, insurance, and many other industries.

Wrapping up with Blockchain, your marketing will benefit you the most. You will be targeted for what you intend to do, no wasted money wanting to be a Blockchain champion, thinking about where to start, coming to Grad, creating Blockchain right away, and building smart contracts and chain codes. If you are interested in becoming a blockchain engineer and making intelligent contracts and chain codes, check out the IIIT-B & upgrades PG Certification in Blockchain Technology.

BLOCKCHAIN: THE FUTURE OF DIGITAL MARKETING

Thanks to the adoption of state-of-the-art technology that enhances profitable customer engagement, the marketing climate is changing rapidly. Digital marketing helps attract and retain customers and works better for them on any social networking site (Adgully, 2020). But it has no flaws. Blockchain, a distributed ledger technology (DLT) technology that allows data to be stored globally on thousands of servers - while allowing anyone on the network to see everyone's entries in real-time rather than the best marketing apps. But before we examine its impact on digital marketing, let's take a look at the challenges in digital marketing that are harmful to retailers and consumers:

- **Ad Fraud:** Advertisers lose a large portion of their ad budget on fraud such as false appearances, false clicks, ad placement, domain interference, pixel insertion, and more. It is a significant challenge for active advertisers, leading to an increase in advertising spending but poor ROI.
- **Scheduled Contracts:** Digital marketing contracts are often the same, leading to a move between the parties involved due to changes in the industry and the confusion of T&C.
- **Wrong Monetization:** Research shows that consumers prefer to make money with their PIIs rather than lose the same control over third-party publishers who make money out of the user.
- **Limited Control Of Shared Data:** In many cases, end-users may not control their data if they provide it on an online platform. The data resides on the

application server, and users cannot control their usage or cannot consistently obtain permission to share information. Data breaches and other security concerns also exacerbate the problem.

- **Transparency:** Advertisers cannot always verify the ROI of their ad spend on one trustworthy source, which led to inefficiency and inefficiency and an utterly ineffective campaign.
- **Ad Saves:** Ad saves ad, disturbs, leads to ad fatigue, and, ultimately, creates a negative product image. Digital marketing is often at the risk of advertising savings, which causes campaigns to fail even though consumer interest stems from blockchain advertising. It aims to build a digital marketing plan on the pillars of transparency, power distribution in communities, and consensus. Blockchain allows transactions between two organizations without the need for third-party authentication. Technology can transform digital marketing by giving consumers the ability to manage their data and improve excellent product reliability.
- **Removal Of Mediators:** With Blockchain, advertisers can skip ad networks, and trade ads, and place ads directly on online platforms with ad spaces, without requiring the average person like Google to contact website owners and strengthen their credibility.
- **Reducing Ad Usage:** By eliminating middleware, products can reduce ad usage, ensuring more browsing of their revenue streams: Brands can now verify ad metrics themselves instead of going to third parties. Blockchain helps advertisers reach the right audience and ensures clicks by looking at whether a natural person has seen his or her ad instead of a bot.
- **Smart Contracts:** Unlike conventional contracts, traders can use the Blockchain to create smart contracts that secure transactions only after certain conditions are met, making price models more flexible, dynamic, and visible. This is used for solid marketing where both parties can be guaranteed 100% transparency and fulfilment of contract terms.
- **Extended Data Management:** Blockchain empowers consumers by placing them in charge of their data instead of ad platforms and data collection companies. It also creates an environment where consumers can be compensated for the amount of their data. For example, the BRAVE browser allows consumers to select the ads they see, determine who will receive their information, and in exchange, provides Basic Attention Token or BAT to users who choose to see ads. Advertisers pay consumers for their care more than any third-party network. Another third-party platform, Blockstack, uses the Blockchain to ensure that customer data is returned to the consumer once the seller has finished using it, thus giving users complete data ownership.

- **Consumer Transparency:** Consumers today know a lot and expect a lot of money. Blockchain helps them protect products and services, for example, if a beauty product is a fair trade or a 100% organic food item, leading to increased product reliability.
- **Accurate Consumer Information:** In addition to the integrated customer experience across all channels, advertisers can get accurate real-time data on customer preferences by looking at the ads they choose to engage with the customer.
- **Bottlenecks In Blockchain Advertising:** Blockchain is still not a widely accepted technology and will face competition from tech behemoths like Google and Facebook. For advertisers to rely solely on a blockchain, it may require many users to sign up for blockchain inequality. The inefficiency of blockchain transactions is a significant challenge, especially for social blockchains. The Ethereum blockchain network, for example, could handle 20 / second higher transactions compared to Visa, which could process more than 2000 / second. Blockchain transactions with the image problem due to its close association with cryptocurrency, which is currently illegal - evidence of many natural phenomena.

SOME AMAZING STATISTICS

The report estimates that spending on Blockchain solutions is expected to grow from 1.5 billion in 2016 to 15.9 billion by 2023. Almost every industry wants to take advantage of Blockchain technology (Xu et al. 2019). The financial sector alone holds more than 60 percent of the 2018 global blockchain market value.

DISSOLUTION OF GLOBAL BLOCKCHAIN SOLUTIONS 2017-2023

The year 2020 will prove global spending on Blockchain solutions to extend $ 4.3 billion. This is a much more prominent figure and almost 60 percent higher than last year. As the trend continues, predictions say the current global blockchain solutions will reach more than $ 14 billion by 2023.

DIGITAL MARKETING IS FRAGMENTED.

We've touched on this before, but let me jump right in on this sensitive topic. Advertisers can avoid the average person they currently trust. Let's use an ad as an example here. If your website ranks attractive ads, it will not make your site credible (Albrecht et al. 2020). It can lose credibility in all your digital marketing efforts. The same is true when your ads are posted on popular websites.

That's why businesses use a third-party platform like Google to act like a link. They monitor the ads delivered by their programs and keep the above example from happening. Sites that sell their place to advertisers will not have design companies that pollute their area, while companies displaying their ads should not worry that their content will be posted on the design website. Companies that make blockchain technology a part of their digital marketing base do not have to go through a mediator like Google because these systems can automatically authenticate companies.

Consumers Can Control Content

Right now, we are in danger of seeing a significant change in the world of digital marketing. With all the data breaches currently occurring, consumers are more concerned about feeling in control of their information. Blockchain technology affects the world in a way that we have never seen before. There are functions that users can use to gain complete control over their digital identity. Some countries even impose rules on businesses that require them to obtain a license from consumers before they can get their online identity.

Some experts even predict that they may need to start paying users to look at their marketing assets in the form of cryptocurrency sets. That probably won't happen. I feel that businesses will change their blockchain use strategies more than ever so that those consumers get complete control over their ownership. Perhaps the reward for consumers by giving them digital currency can be used for purchases made exclusively for them.

Look for Different Digital Marketing Methods

If you build the right blockchain programs, you will end up with a plan that looks like this. Ads are purchased using a platform like the BAT App. In these plans, the customer can decide what kind of ads they want to receive (Xu et al. 2019). The environment in which blockchain technology operates makes it a haven for both businesses and customers. Most transactions are all written in a public book, so everything is clear.

Identify Customer Customers with Blockchain Technology

Traditional programs rely on many external sources to learn about customers. They may collect their information on Facebook and their revenue from LinkedIn. Developed programs such as those used by Amazon will follow browsing and purchasing history to identify customers. Blockchain technology is taking this step forward. As blockchain performance is evident, we can discover what a particular segment of customers is doing without relying on another source for accuracy.

Data Security and Protection Benefits

With stricter information protection legal guidelines such as GDPR coming into impact in all principal markets, shops can use blockchain technological expertise to shop extra consumer data securely. In addition, the GDPR regulatory settlement will require retailers to achieve permission from their purchasers. The use of blockchain science ought to alternate the world of digital marketing as we recognize it. Blockchain presents many advertisers' advantages in phrases of security, transparency, and performance.

IS BLOCKCHAIN THE FUTURE OF DIGITAL MARKETING?

There is an ever-growing collection of online blocks that lead to altering digital ebook placement positions. It all commenced as primary technological expertise to aid protects transactions and improves monitoring with cryptocurrencies. But now, it has modified to a stage where it is used in ways that we no longer expect. Have you heard of current-day weddings "made in Blockchain"? This is the region the idea comes into play.

Digital advertising and marketing are altering in many techniques, which help companies restrict the massive and small expenses incurred in marketing campaigns. But for clients, this influences the internet searching experience. When you open any random internet web page, you may also be distracted by brilliant ads (Bons et al., 2020). There are limits to classified ads to assist you with this. But that does no longer exchange the reality that these ads are annoying. However, businesses can't help but appear for new strategies to put their merchandise in front of their goal market and win tracks. They are continually attempting to accumulate as many client statistics as possible. In the midst of all this, if there is a magic wand that can help create effective spelling and direct all conflicts in the advertising and marketing phase, it will is a massive success as one of the magic wands comes blockchain technology. Still, thinking how this technical information at the return of cryptocurrency is related to digital advertising in general?

Birth of Non-Public Ownership:

You browse the e-commerce site, depart some merchandise in your cart and forget about them. However, there is a magical advert on an entire web page with a direct hyperlink to the product page. These are steps that have been taken to tackle the trouble of automobile disposal and non-compliance issues. But some agencies quit up exaggerating this, and the entire gadget goes back. When a lot of cash is spent shopping for purchaser statistics, gathering customer records solely suggests how essential consumer statistics are. It would consequently make sense to provide person records real value via permitting customers to manipulate which facts are amassed and which information is shared, where it is used and how it is used. Blockchain makes this feasible by using introducing the thought of autonomous ownership. It is viable that customers will be asked for records and can also select to donate or no longer contribute. Customers will be paid less because they grant the essential facts wished in analytics.

Provide Get Information Entry:

Even the most high-priced and popular advertising and marketing campaigns will now not make a distinction if a commercial enterprise fails to obtain purchaser trust. If you would like customers to grant you dependable records, there should be transparency that will assist construct their confidence. When they recognize the place their data is going; they will be a little hesitant to furnish it. This will also help them realize that you have taken protection measures to keep their facts and prevent statistics leaks. Displaying this is one of the best commercials in any business.

The Most Excellent Way to Understand the Effectiveness of an Advert Campaign:

Blockchain is a fundamental obstacle for businesses. How do you music whether an online advert has acquired an excellent response? The number of clicks is one of the most accessible parameters. There are paid clicks that obtain advertisements from human users and bots. That would completely undermine the reason for line advertising. Blockchain, therefore, solves that trouble with the aid of putting the proper stage of transparency (Albrecht et al. 2020). Businesses will consequently obtain detailed statistics on the exact quantity of clicks received by bots and individuals.

And this will additionally assist determine whether the advert is nevertheless being targeted.

Au Revoir Middlemen

Speaking of the advantages that Blockchain presents in the economic region is one of the exceptional benefits of removing mediators. The same goes for digital advertising. Billions of dollars are spent on marketing. And of these billions of bucks, the largest share goes to the centre class. When outsourced, the prices determine out. For corporations, the benefits of cost-cutting objects are also there for customers to do. Customer records were once no longer heard, so it is feasible that facts loss has considerably reduced. Information is additionally reachable to companies very quickly.

IMPROVED REINFORCEMENT

Power is one of the most compelling features of Blockchain. It is about making records accessible however prevents permission to reproduce or delete data. Links in the collection can be delivered, but existing ones cannot be without problems confused with them. Use Blockchain in such a way that it will assist create a powerful advertising strategy that comes with data safety and records acquisition options.

Another location the place blockchain can drastically mirror a change in affects marketing. All communication and transactions with influencers and content creators are now commonplace. Without the well-known legal guidelines of this buy, it becomes challenging. Blockchain will help by offering clever contract systems that pave the way for an extra structured strategy to these processes. This can gain all stakeholders and avoid gaps that regularly cause delays and financial losses as well.

There are currently no policies governing Blockchain insurance policies, and it is easy to integrate them with the existing system. But there is no denying that adopting Blockchain ought to lead to principal and long-term trade-in processes. So this must happen gradually. The pace of integration will additionally range from one industry to another, from one enterprise to another.

KEY FEATURES OF BLOCKCHAIN ADVERTISING.

Some key blockchain indicators - namely transparency, security, and accessibility - may be set to disrupt almost the entire industry, including marketing and advertising. But what is blockchain marketing? “Blockchain Marketing has a vision for a completely new advertising and marketing space, where consumers can own and sell their information directly to advertisers and advertisers,". This means blocking platforms like Facebook and Instagram altogether, so there is a lot of reliance on consumer data usage.

Blockchain creates direct data exchanges between consumers and products as before. "Built from the ground up to emphasize the relationship between products and consumers," added Platz, "blockchain marketing exceeds the average person." This is important because platforms like Facebook tend to collect data based on user tracking, but the visual data is low quality. There is also consumer confidence in this type of surveillance.

HOW WILL BLOCKCHAIN AFFECT THE FUTURE OF DIGITAL MARKETING?

Blockchain technology is the backbone of Bitcoin and other cryptocurrencies. Many experts believe that technology can disrupt global finances, mainly because of its geographical location, which gives consumers more freedom.

Interestingly, Blockchain is transforming more than just finance. It transforms almost every economic sector, including agriculture, insurance, health, and digital marketing and advertising.

However, the focus of the Blockchain is essential in marketing and advertising technologies in their day-to-day operations.

Exciting Things about Blockchain Technology

- In 2016, the first Blockchain companies raised $ 290 million.
- The company's financial and technology companies have invested about 1.4 billion dollars in Blockchain (technology) (Rejeb et al., 2021).
- The average funding in blockchain initiatives was almost 1 million dollars in 2017.
- By 2024, the international blockchain market is estimated to be worth 20 billion dollars.

Relationship between Blockchain and Digital Marketing

So how will Blockchain affect digital marketing and advertising? Yes, consumers will eventually be able to control their purchase data and their details.

Technology will allow customers for managing the ads they want to see, which they hope will provide advertisers with more sophisticated and sophisticated ways to provide quality guidance. Blockchain agreements may affect purchases, delivery, ratings, and the number of promotions and promotional campaigns.

This can do because consumer data may be more expensive for retailers and advertisers, but it will give them new and improved investment benefits.

SOME BLOCKCHAIN TECHNOLOGIES WILL RADICALLY CHANGE THE FUTURE OF DIGITAL MARKETING.

Reliable Advertisement Purchases

Recent digital advertising strategies can be complicated. Digital advertisers are conscious that it is almost not possible to get correct information. Often they have to wonder how much of these click.

People hired with just a click on advertisements all day can log in and use facts and data to extend click-through rates. More significant than $ 7 billion has been misplaced due to bots. This has made digital marketing a challenge, and it is even more expensive to get an image of the advertisements you are buying.

Blockchain technology can be helpful to change all of this as protection and transparency are central to all blockchains, guaranteed, covered, and strengthened. How does this affect digital marketing? Experts at the Toronto-based digital marketing agency explain that since the series offers safe visibility and security, digital marketers can quickly target audiences; therefore, they can save millions every year. Chain, for example, is an open-source law in the Ethereum blockchain community. Provides digital retailers with a precise end-to-end tracker with white recorders and auditors.

Simplify the Advertisement Purchase Process

Everyday digital advertisement activities often involve mediators in the ad purchase process. Blockchain can somehow cut the average person free. Publishers who have removed the average person (with Blockchain or without Blockchain) can increase their costs per idea from $ 1 to $ 5. Ad purchase processes are simplified by clearing the middle ground, enabling digital marketers to reach their target audience directly as Brave Browser does (Rejeb et al. 2021). They can use primary attention tokens to make their digital advertising and advertising more advantageous and efficient.

The platform permits them to trade tokens between publishers, advertisers, and customers on the Blockchain. Digital entrepreneurs can earn tokens primarily based on consumer engagement ingenuity, therefore growing the advert through building higher connections with consumers.

Creating Customer Profiles at Once from Clients Easily

Blockchain can radically change the creation of a client profile for digital retailers. Instead of making them with bits and pieces from different sources, they can get all the information they need about Blockchain.

How is that possible? With blockchain transactions becoming more widespread, traditional user data capture methods are now obsolete. It may seem like bad news to digital marketers, but it is not. Instead of obtaining various information, advertisers and products can pay customers directly for their knowledge and purchase information. It can be costly, but one has to look at how much money is spent on bad ads and campaigns.

One of the great benefits that directly pay consumers is that they are willing to provide their information in a secure way that reflects their interest in the product, service, or organization being promoted. This gives digital marketers a real bullseye to profit from.

The Blockchain is Not Visible

Blockchain technology helps achieve consumer confidence, not just as a personal proposal but also as a history log with product/service data. This digital blockchain judge allows customers to get a clear view of the products from the manufacturer to the retailer. Some brands are using blockchain light to improve their marketing in new ways. Baby ghost has used blockchain technology recently to discuss product issues.

How Can Blockchain Impact Digital Marketing?

Many aspects of enterprise and verbal exchange can be affected with the aid of the Blockchain, but most of the conversations so some distance have been about their effect on banking and financial transactions. Although both sites are different, the impact of the Blockchain may additionally exceed the fees incurred by way of retailers of all products and services.

THE IMPACT OF BLOCKCHAIN ON DIGITAL ADVERTISING

Digital marketing is no longer locked away from the possible benefits of blockchain technology, says freelance author and digital advertising and marketing specialist Gem Franks. Franks looks at the services, and downsides, of Blockchain in digital markets (Adlibweb, 2020).

Here are three exquisite ways in which blockchain science will directly affect digital marketing.

Blockchain Science Opens Up International Markets

The first blockchain approach that can advantage digital retailers is again to its most popular use - cryptocurrency. If advertising and marketing efforts can include and promote crypto to purchase products and services using online bitcoin wallets, it opens up the international market. That is because crypto payments can be made across borders besides extra fees and except change rates. That will motivate more humans to purchase from foreign places groups, which outlets can use to make a profit.

Blockchain Will Increase Product Readability and Trust

Advertisers will additionally want to get into companies that use blockchains as service solutions. For example, suppose an entity uses the Blockchain to reveal the delivery of goods and allows each party to decide the vicinity of the package deal on its journey. In that case, it improves the client's assurance in the enterprise to deliver the item. Marketers will need to use this type of display to promote the product the usage of blockchains. In the early days, this was once the main USP for advertisers to advertise with a vehicle to appeal to a significant market phase. As many people are involved in how their data is handled, this can additionally be something that retailers need to spotlight when used with the aid of the businesses they sell.

Blockchain Helps Control Massive Data

The relationship between massive facts and blockchains has no longer been wholly explored. It is envisioned that huge facts could analyze the bitcoin blockchain to perceive trends and assist understand inflation and predict future prices. However, every other gain is that a giant quantity of statistics can be saved in blockchains to keep documents impervious and consistent, stop loss, and improve the accuracy of significant facts analysis between giant groups. There is no reason why this should now not be the case in marketing departments.

A giant marketing crew may desire to analyze client developments from facts set. By storing that fact within an internal blockchain, crew contributors can work successfully except for multiple versions of the identical data. That will amplify the accuracy of the result and record loss.

BLOCKCHAIN AND THE FUTURE OF DIGITAL MARKETING

No Extra Records Collection

Today, most human beings have access to the Internet, which may be Internet providers (ISPs) and net browsers. As you know, the companies that control these matters can look at all our data. They can promote facts to other groups about what we buy online, the websites we visit, and even the articles we read (UpGard 2020).

They can analyze citizens' performance, wants, and pastimes and promote facts about other groups or politicians. Extensive advertising and marketing businesses with authentic or informal patron information. They purchase the data and sketch their advertising strategy and choose the phrases they need in their advertising. They even devised strategies and approaches for content advertising to their customers based totally on this data, which may lead to the sale of substandard products and offerings to customers.

But what could be the position of a blockchain? Blockchain can resolve this misuse of information and statistics collection with a Blockstack browser. Blockstack is a computer-separated computer network that places users and functions in place to guard your digital rights and is enabled through a blockchain stack. In this way, no business enterprise can gather statistics and sell them to others.

There are no statistics breaches, and no one can abuse your data online. The Blockstack Browser lets you create and control Blockstack IDs and view disbursed applications.

No SEM Man or Woman in Between

According to wordstream.com, search engine marketing, or SEM, is one of the most advantageous methods to grow your business in an increasing number of competitive markets.

Search engine marketing is the practice of advertising an enterprise using paid ads from search engine consequences pages (or SERPs) (Rejeb et al. 2021). Advertisers enter vital phrases that customers like Google and Bing can enter when looking for specific products or services, giving the advertiser the chance to have their commercials appear close to the effects of those search queries. These ads, higher regarded as standard paid ads, come in a variety of forms.

As you can see, Google is a mediator between advertisers and hosted websites. With Blockchain, there is no need for conversation between advertisers and the advert internet hosting website.

Digital Advertising with Web Optimization and Content Material Marketing

Believe it or not, a world without nearby authorities is a quality region to live in. Your success relies upon your skills, and no one will pay to deliver your offerings and merchandise, and no one can abuse your online data and content.

But how can we use Blockchain to improve website positioning and content marketing? You can use the incomparable energy of digital marketing in a blockchain-focused on specific things.

Honesty is the Central Policy

You can share your fees with more than a few degrees of making your products blockchain, earning your clients more have faith than ever before.

As you know, all economic transactions are recorded on the Blockchain, reachable to everyone. In this way, clients can be sure of the fine and fee of the product.

CSR In Light

Corporate Commitment (CSR) in agencies is mirrored in the blockchain system. Blockchain provides clear documentation of the number of monetary institutions that make contributions to the crisis.

Commentary and Blockchain

Using Blockchain and cryptocurrencies in your business, you can import your merchandise and services in a new way. As you know, new companies have an excessive degree of branding.

One has to appear at the content strategy as well. You can use this approach to appeal to more customers today. Modern business has top-notch reliability amongst customers.

Content remains essential in the blockchain gadget as well. In the future, search engines will use blockchain records to make sure the exceptional of merchandise and services, creating a massive difference to the web optimization we recognize today.

Perhaps the satisfaction of the content is assured via the readers and no longer the inbound links and key phrases as the blockchain system has targeted at users. With Blockchain, faux products are known very rapidly, and as you can see, search engine optimization methods no longer work.

Is all of the above viable, or can it be observed one day with blockchain technology? No one knows how far this science will go in society. However, entrepreneurs need to view this rising science as a vital match that should affect their businesses shortly. Maybe it adjustments the lives of humans residing online in the online world.

FOR INSTANCE OF BLOCKCHAIN

What Are You Doing Now?

You are taking a clear route in front of you that is likely to share a record with a shared Google Drive hyperlink and between various pc networks where all people taking part in the assembly have to replica it (Eze et al. 2020).

About Blockchain

Data can be heard in blocks in a blockchain to connect them with different blocks in chronological order to structure a collection of blocks related together. The most prominent feature of blockchain science is that it lets in a shared conversation between extraordinary organizations, and all is written and verified. To access data, a character will have to signal to all statistics centres.

HOW DOES BLOCKCHAIN AFFECT ADVERTISING?

By 2020, the Blockchain is a panacea for all advertising problems. Ideas were quickly replaced by sound and tested solutions to problem-solving, efficiency, and fraud. Requests for ownership decisions become greater realistic (ThreeWindows 2021). Here we write down what the Blockchain has to provide the industry.

How to Share Rewards

Distributed ledger technology can pay off on any scale, enabling products to ship lower expenditures to consumers. This has a significant impact as it is used to transfer cash at once to financial institution accounts, including present cards and online credit with minimal redemption. This allows customers to have financial incentives, no be counted how small the connection.

Designed for Advertising Value Chain

One of the major focus areas of blockchain advertising and marketing is Adtech. Managing digital commercials is the key to spreading a distributed, secure, prominent, and responsive spreadsheet.

Ensures Purchaser Intelligence

Blockchain can collect, test, store, and robotically replace facts with minimal human intervention. This is believed to change the way customers understand. Blockchain is an entire platform for ideas because it prioritizes data-driven marketing.

Delivery of Targeted Content

Data can be linked to a custom object to generate appreciation alternatively than active technology for automatic identification.

Unused Functions

A small server builder is a higher way than usual cloud web hosting to deal with heaps of transactions as it allows shops to measure client demand. Blockchain permits products without delay to gain from restricted and indirect performance limits via going to the server because it will enable them to manage the campaigns they want.

Transparency and Trust

Blockchain helps advertisers pick the right publishers, evaluate marketing campaigns, construct trust, and protect against fraud. It reduces fees and speeds up transactions. Buyers know the entire system before the real estate can be identified.

REFERENCES

Adgully. (2020). *Blockchain: The Future of Digital Marketing*. https://www.adgully.com/blockchain-the-future-of-digital-marketing-98225.html

Adlibweb. (2020). *3 Ways Blockchain Technology Will Affect Digital Marketing*. https://www.adlibweb.com/3-ways-blockchain-technology-will-affect-digital-marketing/

Albrecht, S., Lutz, B., & Neumann, D. (2020). The behavior of blockchain ventures on twitter as a determinant for funding success. *Electronic Markets, 30*(2), 241–257. Advance online publication. doi:10.100712525-019-00371-w

Alt, R. (2020). Electronic Markets on blockchain markets. *Electronic Markets, 30*(2), 181–188. doi:10.100712525-020-00428-1

Atlam, H. F., Azad, M. A., Alzahrani, A. G., & Wills, G. (2020). A Review of Blockchain in Internet of Things and AI. *Big Data and Cognitive Computing., 4*(4), 28. doi:10.3390/bdcc4040028

Aumcore. (2018). *What Is Blockchain Technology and How Will It Impact Marketing?* https://www.aumcore.com/blog/2018/12/26/blockchain-technology-and-how-will-it-impact-marketing/

Blockchain Council. (2020). *Impact of Blockchain in Marketing and Advertising in 2020.* https://www.blockchain-council.org/blockchain/impact-of-blockchain-in-marketing-and-advertising-in-2020/

Bons, R. W., Versendaal, J., Zavolokina, L., & Shi, W. L. (2020). Potential and limits of Blockchain technology for networked businesses. *Electronic Markets, 30*(2), 189–194. doi:10.100712525-020-00421-8

Covetus. (2019). *5 Ways How Blockchain Technology Will Impact Digital Marketing.* https://www.covetus.com/blog/5-ways-how-blockchain-technology-will-impact-digital-marketing

Curvearro. (2020). *Some cons of using blockchain in digital marketing.* https://www.curvearro.com/blog/some-cons-of-using-blockchain-in-digital-marketing/

Digital Examiner. (2019). *What does blockchain mean for digital marketing?* https://www.digitalexaminer.com/blockchain-mean-digital-marketing/

ErtemelA. V. (2019) Implications of Blockchain Technology on Marketing. *Journal of International Trade, Logistics and Law, 4*(2), 35-44. https://ssrn.com/abstract=3351196

Eze, S. C., Chinedu-Eze, V. C. A., Okike, C. K., & Bello, A. O. (2020). Critical factors influencing the adoption of digital marketing devices by service-oriented micro-businesses in Nigeria: A thematic analysis approach. *Humanit Soc Sci Commun, 7*(1), 90. doi:10.105741599-020-00580-1

Kollmann, T., Hensellek, S., De Cruppe, K., & Sirges, A. (2020). Toward a renaissance of cooperatives fostered by Blockchain on electronic marketplaces: A theory-driven case study approach. *Electronic Markets*, *30*(2), 273–284. Advance online publication. doi:10.100712525-019-00369-4

MartechAdvisor. (2019). *What Is Blockchain in Marketing? Strategies, Best Practices, Benefits and Examples.* https://www.martechadvisor.com/articles/blockchain/what-is-blockchain-how-to-use-it-in-marketing/

News, B. D. A. (2020). *4 Important Ways Blockchain Will Change Digital Marketing and Advertising.* https://bigdataanalyticsnews.com/blockchain-change-digital-marketing-advertising/

PetersG.PanayiE. (2015) Understanding Modern Banking Ledgers through Blockchain Technologies: Future of Transaction Processing and Smart Contracts on the Internet of Money. Available at doi:10.2139srn.2692487

Rejeb, A., Keogh, J. G., & Treiblmaier, H. (2020). How Blockchain Technology Can Benefit Marketing. *Six Pending Research Areas. Front. Blockchain*, *3*, 3. doi:10.3389/fbloc.2020.00003

Rejeb, A., Rejeb, K., & Keogh, J. G. (2021). Cryptocurrencies in Modern Finance: A Literature Review. *Etikonomi*, *20*(1), 93–118. doi:10.15408/etk.v20i1.16911

Sihi, D. (2020). Impacts of Blockchain Technology in Marketing. In F. J. Martínez-López & S. D'Alessandro (Eds.), *Advances in Digital Marketing and eCommerce* (pp. 25–30). Springer. doi:10.1007/978-3-030-47595-6_4

Sihi, D. (2020). Impacts of Blockchain Technology in Marketing. In F. Martínez-López & S. D'Alessandro (Eds.), *Advances in Digital Marketing and eCommerce. Springer Proceedings in Business and Economics*. Springer. doi:10.1007/978-3-030-47595-6_4

Subramanian, H. (2018). Decentralized blockchain-based electronic marketplaces. *Communications of the ACM*, *61*(1), 78–84. doi:10.1145/3158333

Three 2 Five Marketing. (2021). *5 Crucial Ways Blockchain is Changing Digital Marketing.* https://3to5marketing.com/blockchain-is-changing-digital-marketing/

ThreeWindows. (2021). *10 Application Examples for Blockchain Technology in Digital Marketing.* https://threewindows.com/10-application-examples-for-blockchain-technology-in-digital-marketing/

UpGard. (2020). *Blockchain in Digital Marketing.* https://www.upgrad.com/blog/blockchain-in-digital-marketing/

Weking, J., Mandalenakis, M., Hein, A., Hermes, S., Böhm, M., & Krcmar, H. (2020). The impact of blockchain technology on business models – a taxonomy and archetypal patterns. *Electronic Markets*, *30*(2), 285–305. doi:10.100712525-019-00386-3

Xu, M., Chen, X., & Kou, G. (2019). A systematic review of blockchain. Financ. *Innovations: Technology, Governance, Globalization*, *5*(1), 27. doi:10.118640854-019-0147-z

Chapter 17
Motivating Antecedents and Consequences of Blockchain Technology in the Insurance Industry

Sumit Oberoi
Lovely Professional University, India

Pooja Kansra
Lovely Professional University, India

ABSTRACT

Quantum leaps in technology affect all phases of business models over numerous industries and are the fundamental characteristic of any technological revolution. Emerging technologies provide new avenues for industries to increase their competitive advantage and enhance the economic progression. The aim of this study is to advance a theoretical model on motivating antecedents and consequences of blockchain technology in insurance industry based on the evidence from past literature. This chapter is approached from the theoretical viewpoint, so it meticulously assesses and examines the prior literature to debate on the role of blockchain technology in the insurance industry. The outcome of the present study is dispassionate and corresponding to the conclusions of the prior literature. Blockchain helps in achieving innovation, augmenting transparency, refining data standards, and advancing an integrated approach for quality service. Thus, the espousal of blockchain in insurance is developing very quickly, and it has become the default platform for the complete insurance industry.

DOI: 10.4018/978-1-7998-8081-3.ch017

INTRODUCTION

Insuring risks has been a convoluted and multi-faceted responsibility which associates with innumerable aspects of lives. Consequently, the insurance sector acts as a major determinant in managing contemporary economies on their development pathway. According to Liedtke (2007), "*Scale of monetary investments, business size, number of individuals employed, possessions under management and the socio-economic role in embracing both personal and commercial risks, manifests the significance of insurance industry*". In 2017, the gross premium of global insurance industry was amounted to be $ 4.8 trillion (Crawford et al., 2018). Getting insurance is a requisite for majority of business activities or personal undertakings. Though, over the last couple of decades' numerous reforms have been introduced in the particular sector, still not much has been altered in business models and operations. Hence, intermediaries performed the most essential role in determining the needs and requirements of clients with explicit insurance solution (Grima et al., 2020).

Continuous transformations in the field of technology also alters the genre of risks, thereby, empowering the new start-ups to enter into markets and develop new ecosystems. Quantum jump in the field of technology touches all phases of businesses over numerous sectors and it's the essential trait of revolution in the area of technology. Inchoate technologies introduce new-fangled opportunities for businesses to augment their competitive lead and boost the economic evolution. According to Flovik et al. (2021, p. 665), "*Blockchain is a technology that supports tamper-resistant and transparent transaction recording. A block chain serves as a distributed database which maintains records secured by cryptography, and governed by a consensus algorithm*". Blockchain is the foremost "*Distributed Ledger Technology*", defining technology that gathers, accumulate, disseminate and simplify exchange of certain values amongst private and public operators. The true potential use of blockchain technology has been emphasized throughout an extensive variety of businesses activities and industries (Thake, 2018). Siyal et al. (2019, p. 1), "*Block-chain technology has acquired significant consideration and attention, ever-increasing inquisitiveness for plethora of various application, fluctuations from extraction of data or information, information management, pecuniary facilities, cyber impregnability, pre-requisite for healthcare sector and brain exploration*".

A momentous progression in research related to blockchain technology has been observed, but majority of it is concentrated to technological and advanced aspects of governance, which tends to overlook the snags related to blockchain technologies introduction in insurance industry (Janssen et al., 2020). Though, numerous platforms focussed upon developing blockchain technology environment has been set in motion for various categories *viz.* maritime indemnification, vehicle insurance, bancassurance, property protection, etc. The espousal of blockchain in insurance industry is developing very quickly and it has been putative to become the default platform for complete insurance industry (Crawford et al. 2018; Grima et al. 2020). Therefore, aim of this paper is to advance a theoretical model on motivating antecedents and consequences of blockchain technology in insurance industry based on the evidence from past literature. The present study is an endeavour to contribute to this discussion by advancing a conceptual model on blockchain.

The present study has been systematized into six different sections. Introduction is discussed in the Section 1, followed by an extensive literature review in Section 2 of the article. Section 3 of the study emphasize on the background of blockchain in insurance industry. Section 4 highlighted the mechanism linking motivating antecedents & consequences of blockchain technology. Discussion regarding various aspects of blockchain technology is examined in Section 5 of this paper. Lastly, implications and limitations of blockchain in insurance industry is debated in 6th Section (Oberoi and Kansra, 2019).

BACKGROUND OF BLOCKCHAIN TECHNOLOGY

An all-encompassing body of previous literature is available on blockchain technology. Blockchain technology was originally devised for its most desired application in the area of cryptocurrency and economics, but, presently it's utilization is escalating in numerous sectors, comprising the insurance industry. With the global progression and rising inquisitiveness for information and communication technology (ICT), one could easily foretell the future and prospects of Blockchain as an advancing technology of present time.

According to Lord (2016), Blockchain is a new-fangled and extensive platform which embrace distinctive software programs and know-hows together. Blockchain is a distributed ledger technology (DLT) used for keeping and maintaining records of all transactions accomplished among peers, exclusive of centralised influence. According to Hackett (2016), Verification of all digital records can be accomplished by either of the peer system on the same network, because they are connected to internet and each peer system has complete access to all digital records. Hence, blockchain technology is solely a sequence of blocks connected together by applying computational algorithms (Woodside et al., 2017). Thus, the process of chaining previous block information with new block is termed blockchain. The distributed digital ledger, as mentioned above is retained on personalized systems which are competent of connecting with each other, managing and cumulating data regarding transactions, inventories and finances. Hence, all the available data is stored cryptographically having a specific header, address of individuals associated in the transaction, the blocksize and timestamp, the chain is simultaneously updated at every node. Therefore, it is arduous for hackers to hack the digital data or records from any node or personalized system (Golosova and Romanovs, 2018).

BACKGROUND OF BLOCKCHAIN IN INSURANCE

Large number of propitious and heterogeneous blockchain applications are incessantly floating in the various areas *viz.* financial service industry, public administration/ govt. agencies, real-estate and health services (Johnson, 2017), therefore it's the need of an hour to develop or utilize blockchain technology in insurance industry for smoother and hassle free transactions amongst individuals or entities.

The present-time infrastructure of insurance industry is relatively apathetic and superfluous intermediaries make business operations costlier and lumbersome. Therefore, insurance industry is the utmost promising and propitious area for the utilization of blockchain technology (Johnson 2017; Grima et al., 2020). Blockchain technology could be used in distinctive sectors of insurance industry, thereby, permitting for speedier and uninterrupted data transfer, automation progressions, confirming prevention of frauds and lastly safeguarding audit trails. This will add value proposition in services to the customers/clients in addition to claim management and cost efficiency. Application of blockchain technology in insurance industry will also help in managing the subrogation and intercompany claims. According to PricewaterhouseCoopers (2016), work automation decreases the physical process, thereby, ensuring ineffaceable audit history and reports the acknowledgement of an agreement. This automation helps in removing barriers *viz.* data duplication, up-to-date information, data to be accurate & accessible at all time. Daley (2019), highlighted the application of blockchain technology in nine companies to revolutionize insurance sector. The study inferred that using blockchain technology benefits customers by giving an overview of insurance policy, notifying them about premium due dates, displaying history of policy, smart contracts, speeding up claim disputes and helps in removing inefficiencies. According to Bosisio et al. (2018), "Insurance industries are placed exclusively to get advantage from blockchain technology. Blockchain helps in achieving competitive lead, modernisation, limpidity, upgrading standards of data and developing an amalgamated tactic for quality facilities (Insights, 2019).

Henceforth this paper focusses upon the motivating antecedents of blockchain technology and their possible consequences which helps in transforming the insurance industry. Though, expectations are extraordinary, application of blockchain is still at nascent stages and not utilized to its fuller capacity (Pancetta, 2016; Olaf et al., 2017).

MECHANISM LINKING MOTIVATING ANTECEDENTS & CONSEQUENCES OF BLOCKCHAIN TECHNOLOGY

Understanding regarding motivational antecedents and consequences of blockchain technology is momentous for insurance industry business forecast and profitability. Therefore, to advance an integrated conceptual model, a meticulous examination of the previous literature was performed on blockchain technology and insurance industry (Figure 1).

Figure 1. A conceptual model on motivating antecedents and consequences of blockchain technology in insurance industry
Source: Author's compiled model based on literature review (Oberoi and Kansra, 2020)

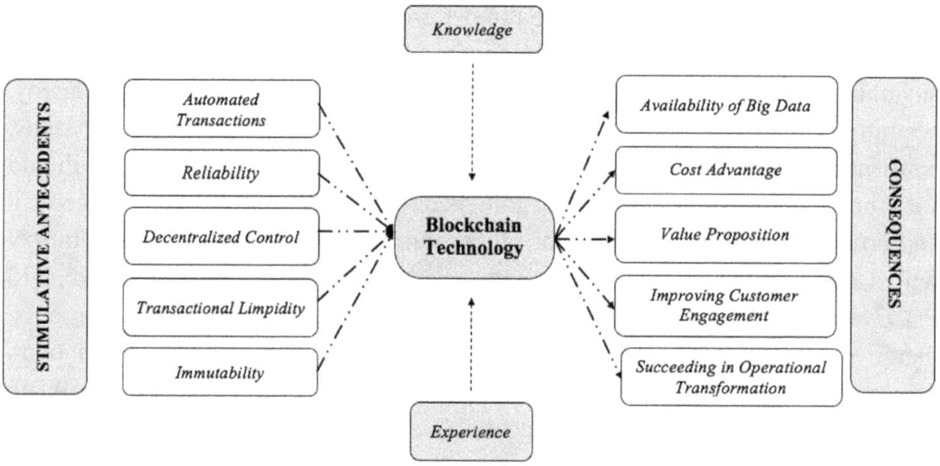

Motivating Antecedents of Blockchain Technology

The conceptual model of blockchain technology is grounded on various motivating antecedents *viz.* as automated transaction, reliability, decentralized control, transactional limpidity and immutability is indicated in Figure 1. Copious studies have acknowledged automated transaction as major driving force for blockchain technologies introduction in insurance industry (Beck et al., 2017; Hans et al., 2017; Lacity, 2018). Organizations of all genre are highly fascinated in use of blockchain technology because of its substantial commercial value. Blockchain technology delivers the potential to transact directly, reject reconciliations, monitor and detect assets, to safeguard the origin of data and transactional settlement speedily and economically (Lacity, 2018). Therefore, automation of transactions has significant influence on competition and efficiency. Reliability is another significant motivating antecedent acknowledged in previous literature highlighting the eminence of possessing a reliable system which works constantly (Schweizer et al., 2017; Hans et al., 2017; Gomber et al., 2018). Consequently, blockchain also holds the capability to deliver a reliable technique of data storing. Several studies by Beck et al. (2017); Glaser (2017); Schweizer et al. (2017), inferred that decentralized control yet another promising antecedent for blockchain implementation in insurance and various industry. According to Beck and Müller-Boch (2017), "*decentralization is mentioned as an important factor behind the initiative. Decentralization is expected to empower participants, moving trust from central parties to the network participants themselves*". Transactional limpidity and data immutability are the foremost and noteworthy antecedent of blockchain technology. Higher limpidity and immutability of transactional data is the utmost priority for insurance industry to halt the frauds, claim management and cost efficiency (Risius and Spohrer, 2017; Beck et al., 2018).

Preposition 1: - Motivating antecedents are positively related to the blockchain technology which in turn leads to progressive consequences in insurance industry.

Consequences of Antecedents on Blockchain Technology in Insurance Industry

Rising momentum of blockchain technology phenomenon has a massive consequence not just on consumers, but also leads to the value proposition for industry as well. Blockchain technology assist in shaping economic and operational goals. Application of blockchain technology in insurance sector will majorly benefit big companies with the availability of big data of customers by reformulating the policies, claim management criteria in accordance with peoples need. Moreover, blockchain technology will also succor insurance industries with cost efficiency, value proposition and operational transformation. Thus, with the use of blockchain in insurance industry it will advantageous on various grounds viz. subrogation, intercompany claims, removal of duplicate data, up-to-date information, data to be accurate & accessible at all time. The conceptual model also highlights two extremely significant moderator knowledge and experience. Both knowledge and experience holds direct and positive stimulus on the consequences reported in the model (Figure 1). Higher the level of knowledge and experience in the development and application of blockchain will be helpful for proper functioning of each node or personalized system, will easily observing the glictes and snags and lastly, rectifying the observed issue.

Preposition 2: - Motivating antecedents and both moderators (knowledge & experience) are positively and directly related to the blockchain technology in insurance industry which in turn leads to progression in insurance industry.

DISCUSSION

Quantum jump in the field of technology touches all phases of businesses over numerous sectors and it's the essential trait of revolution in the area of technology. Blockchain technology is contemplated as trending and niche technology, which could be applied on the numerous spheres of insurance industry. The purpose of this paper was to recognize the motivating antecedents of blockchain technology and their consequences on insurance industry and lastly, how these moderators *viz.* knowledge and experience are related to blockchain technology.

An all-encompassing review of the scholarly articles and different academic sources assisted in the development of conceptual model of blockchain technology in insurance industry and outlines how blockchain relates to the observed consequences. The outcome of the present study is dispassionate and corresponding to the conclusions of the prior literature. Blockchain helps in achieving competitive lead, modernisation, limpidity, upgrading standards of data and developing an amalgamated tactic for quality facilities. Therefore, the espousal of blockchain technology in insurance business is evolving swiftly and it has been putative to become the default platform for complete insurance industry (Crawford et al. 2018; Grima et al. 2020). Blockchain enabled compatible and interpretative health data could possibly become a prerequisite for insurers to amplify consumers experience and strengthening associations. Therefore, this particular type of alteration could help to develop the overall share of insured customers by convincing a greater proportion of prospects to start, moreover user-friendly application procedure, eventually increasing the statuses of those possessing life/health insurance and finally, refining the understanding of those spending for health insurance. Blockchain acts as a catalyst in restructuring health and life insurers access, thereby, influencing medical and other data. With the utilization of such technology, one could minimize the dissension in healthcare system by removing duplicate transactions between insurers and supplier, hence by providing multiple patient/provider credentials. Moreover, blockchain technology could help in the development of new and transparent relationship with policy-holder. Finally, incorporating blockchain technology increases the bottom line of insurer by saving capital, aggregating deals and boosting the retention.

IMPLICATIONS AND LIMITATIONS OF BLOCKCHAIN IN INSURANCE

Antecedents and moderators proposed in the study should be reviewed individually in order to understand, does each element deeply support to the usefulness of blockchain in insurance industry. The present study emphasises upon the potential implications of blockchain specific to the insurance industry. Electronic health records (HER) will reduce the prerequisite for customer to take new and extra lab test before applying for insurance policy. Thereby, providing benefits *viz.* reprice policy, easy claim reimbursement, agent information and non-monetary benefits grounded upon contemporary health status. Further, with the introduction of blockchain in insurance industry will ameliorate the back-office functioning such as swift dispensation of coverages, lesser overhead expenses, effortless accessibility to all-inclusive medical data and increases the reliability of data. Original, application of blockchain technology is to restrain fraudulent and help underwriters from those withholding crucial info regarding events, ailments and treatments. The immediate implication of this technology in insurance sector is to curtail fake claims, by strengthening additional data sources, exclusive of manual procedure. The only limitation of the present study is the empirical validation of the theoretical model. Thus, the future research should carefully emphasis on transforming the insurance industry with the extensive practice of blockchain technology.

Disagreement of Interest: Authors undoubtedly state no disagreement of interest.

Ethical Sanction: The present manuscript is grounded upon critical review, henceforth, it doesn't encompass any reports based on animals.

Funding: None

REFERENCES

Beck, R., Avital, M., Rossi, M., & Thatcher, J. B. (2017). *Blockchain technology in business and information systems research.* Academic Press.

Beck, R., & Müller-Bloch, C. (2017, January). Blockchain as radical innovation: a framework for engaging with distributed ledgers as incumbent organization. *Proceedings of the 50th Hawaii International Conference on System Sciences.* 10.24251/HICSS.2017.653

Beck, R., Müller-Bloch, C., & King, J. L. (2018). Governance in the blockchain economy: A framework and research agenda. *Journal of the Association for Information Systems, 19*(10), 1. doi:10.17705/1jais.00518

Bosisio, R., Burchardi, K., Calvert, T., & Hauser, M. (2018). *The first all-blockchain insurer.* Boston Consulting Group.

Crawford, S., Russignan, L., & Kumar, N. (2018). *Global insurance trends analysis 2018.* EY Report.

Daley, S. (2019). Nine companies using blockchain to revolutionize insurance. *Builtin.* Accessed on January 2021. https://builtin.com/blockchain/blockchain-insurance-companies

Flovik, S., Moudnib, R. A., & Vassilakopoulou, P. (2021). Determinants of Blockchain Technology Introduction in Organizations: An Empirical Study among Experienced Practitioners. *Procedia Computer Science, 181*, 664–670. doi:10.1016/j.procs.2021.01.216

Glaser, F. (2017, January). Pervasive decentralisation of digital infrastructures: a framework for blockchain enabled system and use case analysis. *Proceedings of the 50th Hawaii international conference on system sciences.* 10.24251/HICSS.2017.186

Golosova, J., & Romanovs, A. (2018, November). The advantages and disadvantages of the blockchain technology. In *2018 IEEE 6th workshop on advances in information, electronic and electrical engineering (AIEEE)* (pp. 1-6). IEEE. 10.1109/AIEEE.2018.8592253

Gomber, P., Kauffman, R. J., Parker, C., & Weber, B. W. (2018). On the fintech revolution: Interpreting the forces of innovation, disruption, and transformation in financial services. *Journal of Management Information Systems, 35*(1), 220–265. doi:10.1080/07421222.2018.1440766

Grima, S., Spiteri, J., & Romānova, I. (2020). A STEEP framework analysis of the key factors impacting the use of blockchain technology in the insurance industry. *The Geneva Papers on Risk and Insurance. Issues and Practice, 45*(3), 1–28. doi:10.105741288-020-00162-x

Hackett, R. (2016). *Wait, what is Blockchain?* Accessed on February 2021, http://fortune.com/2016/05/23/block chain-definition/

Hans, R., Zuber, H., Rizk, A., & Steinmetz, R. (2017). *Blockchain and smart contracts: Disruptive technologies for the insurance market.* Academic Press.

Insights, C. (2019). *Blockchain and Insurance: New Technology.* New Opportunities.

Janssen, M., Weerakkody, V., Ismagilova, E., Sivarajah, U., & Irani, Z. (2020). A framework for analysing blockchain technology adoption: Integrating institutional, market and technical factors. *International Journal of Information Management, 50*, 302–309. doi:10.1016/j.ijinfomgt.2019.08.012

Johnson, G.L. (2017). Planning the future. Blockchain technology and the insurance industry. Insurance law. *In-House Defense Quarterly*, 73–78.

Lacity, M. C. (2018). Addressing key challenges to making enterprise blockchain applications a reality. *MIS Quarterly Executive*, *17*(3), 201–222.

Liedtke, P. M. (2007). What's insurance to a modern economy? *The Geneva Papers on Risk and Insurance. Issues and Practice*, *32*(2), 211–221. doi:10.1057/palgrave.gpp.2510128

Lord, S. (2016). Bankchain & itBit: Settling on the blockchain. *Modern Trader, 16.*

Oberoi, S., & Kansra, P. (2019). Factors Influencing Medical Tourism in India: A Critical Review. *SAMVAD*, *17*, 9-16.

Oberoi, S., & Kansra, P. (2020). Economic menace of diabetes in India: A systematic review. *International Journal of Diabetes in Developing Countries*, *40*(4), 464–475. doi:10.100713410-020-00838-z PMID:32837090

Olaf, A., Hagen, H., & Hajj, J. (2017). *2017 Technology trends*. PwC. Accessed on February 2021. https://www.strategyand.pwc.com/ trend/2017-technology-trends

PricewaterhouseCoopers. (2016). *Blockchain in the insurance sector.* Accessed on January 2021, https://www.pwc.co.uk/financial-services/fintech/assets/blockchain-in-insurance.pdf

Risius, M., & Spohrer, K. (2017). A Blockchain Research Framework: What We (don't) Know, Where We Go from Here, and How We Will Get There. *Business & Information Systems Engineering*, *59*(6), 385–409. doi:10.100712599-017-0506-0

Schweizer, A., Schlatt, V., Urbach, N., & Fridgen, G. (2017, December). Unchaining Social Businesses-Blockchain as the Basic Technology of a Crowdlending Platform. ICIS.

Siyal, A. A., Junejo, A. Z., Zawish, M., Ahmed, K., Khalil, A., & Soursou, G. (2019). Applications of blockchain technology in medicine and healthcare: Challenges and future perspectives. *Cryptography*, *3*(1), 3. doi:10.3390/cryptography3010003

Thake, M. (2018). *What's the difference between blockchain and DLT?* Nakamo. To.

Woodside, J. M., Augustine, F. K. Jr, & Giberson, W. (2017). Blockchain technology adoption status and strategies. *Journal of International Technology and Information Management*, *26*(2), 65–93.

Compilation of References

8 Ways Cryptocurrency Is Changing Digital Marketing - Simpliv Blog. (n.d.). Retrieved March 11, 2021, from https://blog.simpliv.com/8-ways-cryptocurrency-is-changing-digital-marketing/

Abraham. (2021). *How an uncertain economic environment can be the biggest driver of innovation.* yourstory.com

Abuodha, K. (2020). *Factors Influencing Online Buying Behavior among University Students: A Case Study of United States International University Africa.* United States International University-Africa.

Accenture. (2017), *Banking on Block-chain – "A Value Analysis for Investment Banks".* New York: Accenture. www.accenture.com

Adgully. (2020). *Blockchain: The Future of Digital Marketing.* https://www.adgully.com/blockchain-the-future-of-digital-marketing-98225.html

Adlibweb. (2020). *3 Ways Blockchain Technology Will Affect Digital Marketing.* https://www.adlibweb.com/3-ways-blockchain-technology-will-affect-digital-marketing/

Agbo, C. C., & Mahmoud, Q. H. (2020). Blockchain in Healthcare. *International Journal of Healthcare Information Systems and Informatics, 15*(3), 82–97. doi:10.4018/IJHISI.2020070105

Ahram, T., Sargolzaei, A., Sargolzaei, S., Daniels, J., & Amaba, B. (2017). Blockchain technology innovations. *Proceedings of the 2017 IEEE Technology and Engineering Management Conference (TEMSCON)*, 8–10.

Ajzen, I. (1991). The theory of planned behavior. *Organizational Behavior and Human Decision Processes, 50*(2), 179–211. doi:10.1016/0749-5978(91)90020-T

Akben, İ., & Çinar, S. (2018). Lojistik ve tedarik zinciri yönetiminde Block- chain: Vaatler, uygulamalar ve engeller. Anadolu I. Uluslararasi Multidisipliner Çalişmalar kongresi, 2018, Diyarbakır.

Akkaya, G. C. (2020). *An Overview about Blockchain Technology Based Crowdfunding* (Unpublished Master's Thesis). Dokuz Eklül University, İzmir.

Alauthaman, M., Aslam, N., Zhang, L., Alasem, R., & Hossain, M. A. (2018). A P2P Botnet detection scheme based on decision tree and adaptive multilayer neural networks. *Neural Computing & Applications, 29*(11), 991–1004. doi:10.100700521-016-2564-5 PMID:29769759

Albrecht, S., Lutz, B., & Neumann, D. (2020). The behavior of blockchain ventures on twitter as a determinant for funding success. *Electronic Markets, 30*(2), 241–257. Advance online publication. doi:10.100712525-019-00371-w

Alladi, Chamola, Parizi, Kwang, & Choo. (2019). Blockchain Applications for Industry 4.0 and Industrial IoT: A Review. *IEEE Access*. doi:10.1109/ACCESS.2019.2956748

Alshura, M. S., Zabadi, A., & Abughazaleh, M. (2018). Big Data in Marketing Arena. Big Opportunity, Big Challenge, and Research Trends: An Integrated View. *Management and Economics Review, 3*(1), 75-84.

Alt, R. (2020). Electronic Markets on blockchain markets. *Electronic Markets, 30*(2), 181–188. doi:10.100712525-020-00428-1

Altunbaşak, T. A. (2018). Taxation with Blockchain Technology. *The Journal of Finance, 174*, 360–371.

Aluhairi. (2020). *Why COVID-19 makes a Compelling case for the Wider Integration of Blockchain*. World Economic Forum.

Alvarenga, I. D., Rebello, G. A., & Duarte, O. C. M. (2018, April). Securing configuration management and migration of virtual network functions using blockchain. In *NOMS 2018-2018 IEEE/IFIP Network Operations and Management Symposium* (pp. 1-9). IEEE. 10.1109/NOMS.2018.8406249

Ammous, S. (2018). Can cryptocurrencies fulfil the functions of money? *The Quarterly Review of Economics and Finance, 70*, 38–51. https://doi.org/10.1016/j.qref.2018.05.010

Amsyar, I., Christopher, E., Dithi, A., Khan, A. N., & Maulana, S. (2020). The Challenge of Cryptocurrency in the Era of the Digital Revolution: A Review of Systematic Literature. *Aptisi Transactions on Technopreneurship, 2*(2), 153–159. doi:10.34306/att.v2i2.96

Antoniadis, I., Kontsas, S., & Spinthiropoulos, K. (2019). Blockchain Applications in Marketing. *Proceedings of 7th ICCMI.*

Antoniadis, Kontsas, & Spinthiropoulos. (2019). Blockchain Applications in Marketing. *7th International Conference on Contemporary Marketing,* 1–7. https://www.researchgate.net/publication/337439697_Blockchain_Applications_in_Marketing

Antoniadis, I., Sariannidis, N., & Kontsas, S. (2018). The effect of bitcoin prices on US dollar index price. In *International Conference on Applied Economics* (pp. 511-521). Springer. 10.1007/978-3-030-02194-8_34

Antoniadis, I., Spinthiropoulos, K., & Kontsas, S. (2019). Blockchain applications in Tourism and Tourism marketing: A short review. *Proceedings of ICSIMAT.*

Antoniadis, I., Spinthiropoulos, K., & Kontsas, S. (2020). Blockchain Applications in Tourism and Tourism Marketing: A Short Review. In *Strategic Innovative Marketing and Tourism* (pp. 375–384). Springer. doi:10.1007/978-3-030-36126-6_41

Antonopoulos, A. M. (2017). *Mastering bitcoin: Programming the open blockchain*. O'Reilly Media, Inc.

Apelasyon. (2020). *Şarap Sektörü Değişen Tüketici Profilinin Farkında mı?* http://apelasyon.com/Yazi/267-sarap-sektoru-degisen-tuketici-profilinin-farkinda-mi

Ariffin, S. K., Mohan, T., & Goh, Y.-N. (2018). Influence of consumers' perceived risk on consumers' online purchase intention. *Journal of Research in Interactive Marketing*.

Armutlu, B. (2019). *Application of Blockchain in Apple Supply and Currency Exchange Offices Sector* (Unpublished Master's Thesis). Hacettepe University, Ankara.

Arora, N., & Aggarwal, A. (2018). The role of perceived benefits in formation of online shopping attitude among women shoppers in India. *South Asian Journal of Business Studies*.

Asian Development Bank (ADB). (2017). *Trade Finance Gaps, Growth, and Jobs Survey*. ADB Brief N. 83.

Atlam, H. F., Azad, M. A., Alzahrani, A. G., & Wills, G. (2020). A Review of Blockchain in Internet of Things and AI. *Big Data and Cognitive Computing.*, *4*(4), 28. doi:10.3390/bdcc4040028

Aumcore. (2018). *What Is Blockchain Technology and How Will It Impact Marketing?* https://www.aumcore.com/blog/2018/12/26/blockchain-technology-and-how-will-it-impact-marketing/

Bakan, İ., & Şekkeli, Z. H. (2019). Blockchain Technology and Its Applications in Supply Chain Managements. *International Journal of Society Researches*, *11*(18), 2848–2877.

Baralla, G., Ibba, S., Marchesi, M., Tonelli, R., & Missineo, S. (2018, August). A blockchain based system to ensure transparency and reliability in food supply chain. In *European conference on parallel processing* (pp. 379-391). Springer.

Baralla, G., Pinna, A., Tonelli, R., Marchesi, M., & Ibba, S. (2020). Ensuring transparency and traceability of food local products: A blockchain application to a Smart Tourism Region. *Concurrency and Computation*, *33*(1), e5857. doi:10.1002/cpe.5857

Barclays. (2016). *The Blockchain Revolution in Trade Finance*. Author.

Beck, R., Avital, M., Rossi, M., & Thatcher, J. B. (2017). *Blockchain technology in business and information systems research*. Academic Press.

Beck, R., Avital, M., Rossi, M., & Thatcher, J. B. (2017). Blockchain Technology in Business and Information Systems Research. *Business & Information Systems Engineering*, *59*(6), 381–384. doi:10.100712599-017-0505-1

Beck, R., & Müller-Bloch, C. (2017, January). Blockchain as radical innovation: a framework for engaging with distributed ledgers as incumbent organization. *Proceedings of the 50th Hawaii International Conference on System Sciences*. 10.24251/HICSS.2017.653

Beck, R., Müller-Bloch, C., & King, J. L. (2018). Governance in the blockchain economy: A framework and research agenda. *Journal of the Association for Information Systems*, *19*(10), 1. doi:10.17705/1jais.00518

Bell, A., & Hollander, D. (2018). *Blockchain and distributed ledger technology at travelport*, 1–12. Retrieved from https://www.travelport.com/sites/default/files/travelport-blockchain-whitepaper.pdf

Bell. (2019). Applications of blockchain in International Trade: An Overview. *The Romanian Economic Journal*.

Bentov, I., Gabizon, A., & Mizrahi, A. (2016). Cryptocurrencies Without Proof of Work. *International Conference on Financial Cryptography and Data Security*, 142-157.

Berg, A. (2020). The identity, fungibility and anonymity of money. *Economic Papers*, *39*(2), 104–117. doi:10.1111/1759-3441.12273

Bhardwaj. (2019). *How is blockchain disrupting supply chain management*. https://appinventiv.com/ blog/blockchain-in-supply-chain/#2,of

Bilgihan, A. (2016). Gen Y customer loyalty in online shopping: An integrated model of trust, user experience and branding. *Computers in Human Behavior*, *61*, 103–113. doi:10.1016/j.chb.2016.03.014

Billah, M. M. S., & Atbani, F. M. (2019). SWOT Analysis of Cryptocurrency an Ethical Thought. *Journal of Islamic Banking & Finance*, *36*(1).

Biswas, K., Muthukkumarasamy, V., & Tan, W. L. (2017). Blockchain based wine supply chain traceability system. *Future Technologies Conference*.

BitFury Group. (2015). *Public vs Private Blockchains*. White Paper.

Bitpanda. (2020). *How does a blockchain work?* Bitpanda Academy. https://www.bitpanda.com/academy/en/lessons/how-does-a-blockchain-work/ blockchain-in-aviation-white-paper.pdf

Black, A. (2017). *Using Blockchain for Supply Chain Transparency and Traceability*. https://medium. com/ blockchain-review/the-visible-supply-chain-ab73a80863fd

Blockchain Council. (2020). *Impact of Blockchain in Marketing and Advertising in 2020*. https://www.blockchain-council.org/blockchain/impact-of-blockchain-in-marketing-and-advertising-in-2020/

Blockchain. (2019a). *Blockchain, Çin şarap ticaretine şeffaflık getirdi*. https://bctr.org/blockchain-cin-sarap-ticaretine-seffaflik-getirdi-10284/

Blockchain. (2019b). *Merkle Tree*. https://tech-story.net/blockchain-merkle-tree/

Blockchain. (2019c). *Şarap Şişelerinde Blockchain Teknolojisi Kullanılacak.* https://bctr.org/sarap-siselerinde-blockchain-teknolojisi-kullanilacak-10273/

Blockchain. (2020). *Çiftçiden tüketiciye kahve takibi blokzinciri ile sağlanıyor.* https://bctr.org/ciftciden-tuketiciye-kahve-takibi-blokzinciri-ile-saglaniyor-17362/

Bodoni, S. (2019). *Mastercard Alerts Privacy Watchdogs After Loyalty Program Leak.* Bloomberg.Com. Available online at: https://www.bloomberg.com/news/articles/2019-08-23/mastercard-tells-belgian-german-privacy-watchdogs-ofbreach

Bogoch, I.I., Watts, A., Thomas-Bachli, A., Huber, C., Kraemer, M.U., & Khan, K. (2020). Potential for global spread of a novel coronavirus from China. *Journal of Travel Medicine, 27*(2).

Bohme, R., Christin, N., Edelman, B., & Moore, T. (2015). Bitcoin: Economics, technology, and governance. *The Journal of Economic Perspectives, 29*(2), 213–238. doi:10.1257/jep.29.2.213

Bond Brand Loyalty. (2020). *The Loyalty Report: State of Loyalty.* Author.

Bons, R. W., Versendaal, J., Zavolokina, L., & Shi, W. L. (2020). Potential and limits of Blockchain technology for networked businesses. *Electronic Markets, 30*(2), 189–194. doi:10.100712525-020-00421-8

Bontis, N., Janošević, S., & Dženopoljac, V. (2015). Intellectual capital in Serbia's hotel industry. *International Journal of Contemporary Hospitality Management, 27*(6), 1365–1384. doi:10.1108/IJCHM-12-2013-0541

Bosisio, R., Burchardi, K., Calvert, T., & Hauser, M. (2018). *The first all-blockchain insurer.* Boston Consulting Group.

Boston Consulting Group. (2017). *Digital Innovation in Trade Finance: Have We Reached a Tipping Point?* Author.

Boucher, P. (2017). How blockchain technology could change our lives, European Parliament Research Service. Academic Press.

Brauer, J., & Linnala Eriksson, B. (2020). *Blockchain's influence on digital marketing: An exploratory study examining blockchain in relation to big data and digital marketing.* Academic Press.

Breidbach, C. F., & Tana, S. (2021). Betting on Bitcoin: How social collectives shape cryptocurrency markets. *Journal of Business Research, 122*, 311–320. https://doi.org/10.1016/j.jbusres.2020.09.017

Breusch, T. S., & Pagan, A. R. (1979). A simple test for heteroscedasticity and random coefficient variation. *Econometrica, 47*(5), 1287–1294. doi:10.2307/1911963

Brosan, F. (2012). What works where in B2B digital marketing. *Journal of Direct, Data and Digital Marketing Practice, 14*(2), 154–159. doi:10.1057/dddmp.2012.29

Bu, N. (2018). The 22nd Session of the UNWTO General Assembly–Special Session on Smart Tourism: Chengdu, China, 14–15 September 2017. *Anatolia*, *29*(1), 143-145.

Burnham, K. P., & Anderson, D. R. (2004). Multimodel inference: Understanding AIC and BIC in model selection. *Sociological Methods & Research*, *33*(2), 261–304. doi:10.1177/0049124104268644

Business.com. (2020). *How Will Blockchain Impact Digital Marketing?* Available online at: business.com

Buterin, V. (2013). *Ethereum: The Ultimate Smart Contract and Decentralized Application Platform*. Ethereum's White Paper.

Buterin, V. (2015). *Visions part I: The value of blockchain technology*. https://blog.ethereum.org/2015/04/13/visions-part-1-the-value-of-blockchain-technology

Çağı, B. (2020). *Hash Fonksiyonu Nedir?* https://www.bilimcag.com/nedir/hash-fonksiyonu-ozetleme-fonksiyonu-nedir/

Calvaresi, D., Leis, M., Dubovitskaya, A., Schegg, R., & Schumacher, M. (2019). Trust in tourism via blockchain technology: results from a systematic review. In *Information and communication technologies in tourism* (pp. 304–317). Springer. (Original work published 2019)

Çarkacıoğlu, A. (2016). *Crypto-Currency Bitcoin*. Capital Markets Board of Turkey. https://www.spk.gov.tr/SiteApps/Yayin/YayinGoster/1130

Carreira, R., Pinto, P., & Pinto, A. (2020). In J. Prieto, A. Pinto, A. K. Das, & S. Ferretti (Eds.), *A Framework for On-Demand Reporting of Cryptocurrency Ownership and Provenance B.T. - Blockchain and Applications* (pp. 131–143). Springer International Publishing.

Casino, F., Dasaklis, T. K., & Patsakis, C. (2019). A systematic literature review of blockchain-based applications: Current status, classification and open issues. In *Telematics and Informatics* (Vol. 36, pp. 55–81). Elsevier Ltd., doi:10.1016/j.tele.2018.11.006

Castle, N. W., Combe, I. A., & Khusainova, R. (2014). Tracing social influence in responses to strategy change in an online community. *Journal of Strategic Marketing*, *22*(4), 357–375. doi:10.1080/0965254X.2013.876081

CB Insights. (2017). *The March Of Financial Services Giants Into Bitcoin And Blockchain Startups In One Chart*. Author.

Chaffey, D. (2010). Applying organisational capability models to assess the maturity of digital-marketing governance. *Journal of Marketing Management*, *26*(3-4), 187–196. doi:10.1080/02672571003612192

Chagas, E. (2019). *Blockchain: A Revolução Tecnológica e Impactos para a Economia*. Núcleo do Conhecimento. https://www.nucleodoconhecimento.com.br/tecnologia/blockchain

Chang, Y., Iakovou, E., & Shi, W. (2017). Blockchain in global supply chains and cross border trade: a critical synthesis of the state-of-the-art, challenges and opportunities. *International Journal Geodis*. https://geodis.com/sites/default/files/2019-03/170509_GEODIS_WHITE-PAPER.PDF

Chang. (2019). Exploring Blockchain Technology in International Trade: Business Process Re-engineering for Letter of credit. *Industrial Management and Data System, 119*(8).

Chapron, G. (2017). The environment needs cryptogovernance. *NATNews, 545*(7655), 403. PMID:28541332

Chartier-Rueg, T. C., & Zweifel, T. D. (2017). Blockchain, leadership and management: Business as usual or radical disruption? *EUREKA: Social and Humanities, 4*(4), 76–110. doi:10.21303/2504-5571.2017.00370

Chen, L. (2009). *Online consumer behavior: An empirical study based on theory of planned behavior*. The University of Nebraska-Lincoln.

Chen, Y., Li, Y., & Li, C. (2020). Electronic agriculture, blockchain and digital agricultural democratization: Origin, theory and application. *Journal of Cleaner Production, 268*, 122071. doi:10.1016/j.jclepro.2020.122071

Chowdhury, N. (2019). *Consensus Mechanisms of Blockchain. In Inside Blockchain, Bitcoin, and Cryptocurrencies*. Auerbach Publications. doi:10.1201/9780429325533

Christidis, K., & Devetsikiotis, M. (2016). Blockchains and smart contracts for the internet of things. *IEEE Access: Practical Innovations, Open Solutions, 4*, 2292–2303. doi:10.1109/ACCESS.2016.2566339

Coinmama. (2018). *What is the blockchain?* Retrieved February, 25, 2001, from https:// www.coinmama.com/guide/what-is-the-blockchain

Coita, D. C., Abrudan, M. M., & Matei, M. C. (2019). *Effects of the Blockchain Technology on Human Resources and Marketing: An Exploratory Study*. doi:10.1007/978-3-030-12453-3_79

Coleman, L. (2018). *American Express Gives Loyalty Program a Blockchain Upgrade*. https://www.ccn.com/american-expresstaps-hyperledger-blockchain-for-rewards-program-revamp

Colman, A. M. (2015). *A dictionary of psychology*. Oxford quick reference.

Corbitt, B. J., Thanasankit, T., & Yi, H. (2003). Trust and e-commerce: A study of consumer perceptions. *Electronic Commerce Research and Applications, 2*(3), 203–215. doi:10.1016/S1567-4223(03)00024-3

Corporate Finance Institute. (n.d.). *What is a supply chain?* CFI. https://corporatefinanceinstitute.com/ resources/knowledge/strategy/supply-chain/

Covetus. (2019). *5 Ways How Blockchain Technology Will Impact Digital Marketing*. https://www.covetus.com/blog/5-ways-how-blockchain-technology-will-impact-digital-marketing

Crawford, S., Russignan, L., & Kumar, N. (2018). *Global insurance trends analysis 2018.* EY Report.

Cryptocurrency: Social Media Influence and Digital Marketing Pitfalls. (n.d.). Retrieved January 31, 2021, from https://blog.influenceandco.com/cryptocurrency-social-media-influence-and-digital-marketing-pitfalls

Cuel, R., & Cangelosi, G. M. (2020). In Vino Veritas? Blockchain Preliminary Effects on Italian Wine SMEs. In R. Agrifoglio, R. Lamboglia, D. Mancini, & F. Ricciardi (Eds.), *Digital Business Transformation. Lecture Notes in Information Systems and Organisation* (Vol. 38). Springer. doi:10.1007/978-3-030-47355-6_20

Curvearro. (2020). *Some cons of using blockchain in digital marketing.* https://www.curvearro.com/blog/some-cons-of-using-blockchain-in-digital-marketing/

Cvitanovi´c, P. L. (2018). New technologies in marketing as competitive advantage. *2018 ENTRENOVA Conference Proceedings*, 294-302.

Cvitanović, P. L. (2018, September). New technologies in marketing as competitive advantage. *2018 ENTRENOVA Conference Proceedings.*

Dai, H. N., Zheng, Z., & Zhang, Y. (2019). Blockchain for Internet of Things: A Survey. *IEEE Internet of Things Journal*, *6*(5), 8076–8094. doi:10.1109/JIOT.2019.2920987

Daley, S. (2019). Nine companies using blockchain to revolutionize insurance. *Builtin.* Accessed on January 2021. https://builtin.com/blockchain/blockchain-insurance-companies

Danyal, D. (2020). *Farklı Sektörler İçin Blockchain Çözümleri.* https://medium.com/@devrimdanyal/farkl%C4%B1-sekt%C3%B6rler-i%CC%87%C3%A7in-blockchain-%C3%A7%C3%B6z%C3%BCmleri-c02815b609d9

DataReportal. (2020). *Digital 2020 in Vietnam.* Author.

Davidson, S., De Filippi, P., & Potts, J. (2016). *Economics of Block chain.* Academic Press.

Davies, R. (2015). *Industry 4.0 digitalisation for productivity and growth* (Vol. 1). European Parliamentary Research Service.

Davis, F. D. (1989). Perceived usefulness, perceived ease of use, and user acceptance of information technology. *Management Information Systems Quarterly*, *13*(3), 319–340. doi:10.2307/249008

De Meijer, C. R. W. (2019). *Blockchain and big Data: A great marriage.* Retrieved February, 22, 2021, from https://www.finextra.com/blogposting/16596/blockchain-and-big-data-a-great-mariage

Decons. (2020). *Tedarik Zinciri ve Lojistik'te Blockchain.* https://medium.com/@decons/tedarik-zinciri-ve-lojistikte-blockchain-1bd9e7b67669

Del Castillo. (n.d.). Blockchain toolkit to Fix broken Food Supply Chains. *Forbes.*

Deloitte. (2016). *Blockchain in Insurance*. Author.

Deloitte. (2017). *Blockchain & Cybersecurity*. Author.

Deloitte. (2018). *Blockchain, legal implications, questions, opportunities and risks*. Deloitte Legal.

DeMers, J. (2016). *New Technologies Shaping Online Marketing for the Better*. Academic Press.

DeVries, P. D. (2016). An analysis of cryptocurrency, bitcoin, and the future. *International Journal of Business Management and Commerce, 1*(2), 1–9.

Dey, P. P. (2019). Cryptocurrency: Its Implications and. Evincepub Publishing.

Di Vaio, A., & Varriale, L. (2020). Blockchain technology in supply chain management for sustainable performance: Evidence from the airport industry. *International Journal of Information Management, 52*, 102014. doi:10.1016/j.ijinfomgt.2019.09.010

Difference Between Digital Currency Vs Cryptocurrency. (n.d.). Retrieved March 13, 2021, from https://sourceessay.com/digital-currency-vs-cryptocurrency/

Digital Examiner. (2019). *What does blockchain mean for digital marketing?* https://www.digitalexaminer.com/blockchain-mean-digital-marketing/

Dogru, T., Mody, M., & Leonardi, C. (2018). *Blockchain technology & its implications for the Hospitality Industry*. Boston University.

Dudin, M. N., Burkaltseva, D. D., Tsohla, S. Y., Voronin, I. N., Yanovskaya, A. A., & Guk, O. A. (2017). Peculiarities of sustainable tourism development in the Russian Federation. *Journal of Environmental Management & Tourism, 8*(24), 1559–1566.

Dummies, C. (2016). *Bitcoin for Dummies*. John Wiley and Sons.

Durbilmez, S. E. (2018). *The Role and Applications of Blockchain Technology in Financial Services Sector* (Unpublished Master's Thesis). Marmara University, Istanbul.

Durbin, J., & Watson, G. S. (1971). Testing for serial correlation in least squares regression. III. *Biometrika, 58*(1), 1–19. doi:10.2307/2334313

Du, W., Pan, S. L., Leidner, D. E., & Ying, W. (2019). Affordances, experimentation and actualization of FinTech: A blockchain implementation study. *The Journal of Strategic Information Systems, 28*(1), 50–65. doi:10.1016/j.jsis.2018.10.002

Epstein, J. (2017). *Blockchain and the CMO.* Whitepaper. Availble online at: https://s3.us-east-2.amazonaws.com/brightline-website/downloads/reports/Brightline_Epstein_Blockchain-and-the-CMO_Blockchain-Research-Institute.pdf

Erbaş, S. (2019). New generation technology in marketing and advertising: Blockchain. *Journal of Gumushane University, 7*(2), 712–729.

Er-Rajy, L., El Kiram My, A., El Ghazouani, M., & Achbarou, O. (2017). Blockchain: Bitcoin wallet cryptography security, challenges and countermeasures. *Journal of Internet Banking and Commerce*, *22*(3), 1–29.

Ertemel, A. V. (2018). Implications of blockchain technology on marketing. *Journal of International Trade, Logistics and law*, *4*(2), 35-44.

Ertemel, A. V. (2018). Implications of blockchain technology on marketing. *Journal of International Trade, Logistics and Law*, *4*(2), 35-44.

ErtemelA. V. (2019) Implications of Blockchain Technology on Marketing. *Journal of International Trade, Logistics and Law*, *4*(2), 35-44. https://ssrn.com/abstract=3351196

Evans, D. (2014). *Economic aspects of Bitcoin and other decentralised public-ledger currency platforms*. Coase-Sandor Institute for Law and Economics working paper #685.

Eyal, I., Gencer, A. E., Sirer, E. G., & Van Renesse, R. (2016). Bitcoin-ng: A scalable blockchain protocol. In 13th USENIX symposium on networked systems design and implementation (NSDI 16) (pp. 45-59). USENIX.

Eze, S. C., Chinedu-Eze, V. C. A., Okike, C. K., & Bello, A. O. (2020). Critical factors influencing the adoption of digital marketing devices by service-oriented micro-businesses in Nigeria: A thematic analysis approach. *Humanit Soc Sci Commun*, *7*(1), 90. doi:10.105741599-020-00580-1

Felix, R., Rauschnabel, P. A., & Hinsch, C. (2017). Elements of strategic social media marketing: A holistic framework. *Journal of Business Research*, *70*(C), 118–126. doi:10.1016/j.jbusres.2016.05.001

Fernández-Caramés & Fraga-Lamas. (2018). A review on the use of blockchain for the internet of things. *IEEE Access, 6*.

Fernández-Caramés & Fraga-Lamas. (2019). A review on the application of blockchain to the next generation of cybersecure industry 4.0 smart factories. *IEEE Access, 7*.

Fernández-Caramés, T. M., Blanco-Novoa, O., Suárez-Albela, M., & Fraga-Lamas, P. (2018). A uav and blockchain-based system for industry 4.0 inventory and traceability applications. Multidisciplinary Digital Publishing Institute Proceedings, 4(1), 26. doi:10.3390/ecsa-5-05758

Fernández-Caramés, T. M., & Fraga-Lamas, P. (2018). A Review on the Use of Blockchain for the Internet of Things. *IEEE Access: Practical Innovations, Open Solutions*, *6*, 32979–33001. doi:10.1109/ACCESS.2018.2842685

Ferrag, M. A., Derdour, M., Mukherjee, M., Derhab, A., Maglaras, L., & Janicke, H. (2018). Blockchain technologies for the internet of things: Research issues and challenges. *IEEE Internet of Things Journal*.

Filimonau, V., & Naumova, E. (2020). The blockchain technology and the scope of its application in hospitality operations. *International Journal of Hospitality Management*, *87*, 102383. doi:10.1016/j.ijhm.2019.102383

Flovik, S., Moudnib, R. A., & Vassilakopoulou, P. (2021). Determinants of Blockchain Technology Introduction in Organizations: An Empirical Study among Experienced Practitioners. *Procedia Computer Science*, *181*, 664–670. doi:10.1016/j.procs.2021.01.216

Focalpoints. (2020). *The impact of blockchain in digital marketing.* Available online at: https://www.mediaupdate.co.za/marketing/147788/the-impact-of-blockchain-in-digital-marketing

Forbes Insights. (2018). *Logistics, Supply Chain and Transportation 2023 – Change at Breakneck, Speed.* http://info.forbes.com/rs/790-SNV-353/images/Penske_report-final- digital.pdf

Forbes. (n.d.). https://www.forbes.com/sites/jaysondemers/2016/

Forsythe, S., Liu, C., Shannon, D., & Gardner, L. C. (2006). Development of a scale to measure the perceived benefits and risks of online shopping. *Journal of Interactive Marketing*, *20*(2), 55–75. doi:10.1002/dir.20061

Fortuna, F., & Risso, M. (2019). Blockchain Technology in the Food Industry. *Symphonya. Emerging Issues in Management*, *2*(2), 151. doi:10.4468/2019.2.13fortuna.risso

Fraga-Lamas & Fernández-Caramés. (2019). A review on blockchain technologies for an advanced and cyber-resilient automotive industry. *IEEE Access, 7.*

Framingham. (2019). *Worldwide BlockChain Spending forecasts to Reach $2.9 Billion in 2019.* International Data Centre.

Gerdan, G. (2019). *Blockchain, Food Safety, Food Traceability, Supply Chain, Egg Production, User Interface Design* (Unpublished Master' Thesis). Marmara University, Istanbul.

Gerdan, D., Koç, C., & Vatandaş, M. (2020). Use of Blockchain Technology in Traceability of Food Products. *Journal of Agricultural Machinery Science*, *16*(2), 8–14.

Getz, D. (2000). *Explore Wine Tourism: Management, Development & Destinations.* Cognisant Communication Corporation.

Ghose, A. (2018). What blockchain could mean for marketing. *Harvard Business Review*, *5*, 2–5.

Gialis. (2018). Future challenges on the use of blockchain for food traceability analysis. *Trends Anal. Chem.*, *107*, 222–232. doi:10.1016/j.trac.2018.08.011

Gipp, B., Kosti, J., & Breitinger, C. (2016). Securing Video Integrity Using Decentralized Trusted Time stamping on the Bitcoin Blockchain. *Proceedings of the Mediterranean Conference on Information Systems (MCIS).*

Giudici, G., Milne, A., Vinogradov, D., Milne, A. K. L., & Milne, A. (123 C.E.). Cryptocurrencies: market analysis and perspectives. *Journal of Industrial and Business Economics, 47*, 1–18. doi:10.100740812-019-00138-6

Gjerding, K. (2017, March 28). *How blockchain technology will dominate the travel sector.* Retrieved from https://www.forbes.com/sites/forbesfinancecouncil/2017/03/28/how-blockchain-technology-will-dominate-the-travel-sector/#3b9dae4d9de5

Glaser, F. (n.d.). *Pervasive Decentralisation of Digital Infrastructures: A Framework for Blockchain enabled System and Use Case Analysis*. Retrieved February 16, 2021, from https://github.com/ethereum/wiki

Glaser, F. (2017, January). Pervasive decentralisation of digital infrastructures: a framework for blockchain enabled system and use case analysis. *Proceedings of the 50th Hawaii international conference on system sciences*. 10.24251/HICSS.2017.186

Goldin, M., Soleimani, A., & Young, J. (2017). *The Adchain Registry*. Whitepaper. Available online at: https://blockchain-x.eu/wp-content/uploads/2018/02/The_adChain_Registry_ENG.pdf

Golosova, J., & Romanovs, A. (2018, November). The advantages and disadvantages of the blockchain technology. In *2018 IEEE 6th workshop on advances in information, electronic and electrical engineering (AIEEE)* (pp. 1-6). IEEE. 10.1109/AIEEE.2018.8592253

Gomber, P., Kauffman, R. J., Parker, C., & Weber, B. W. (2018). On the fintech revolution: Interpreting the forces of innovation, disruption, and transformation in financial services. *Journal of Management Information Systems, 35*(1), 220–265. doi:10.1080/07421222.2018.1440766

Google & Temasek. (2020). *E-Conomy SEA 2019*. Author.

Görmez, B. (2017). *Finansal Sektörde Yıkıcı Yenilik: Dağıtılmış Defter Teknolojisi ve Türkiye Sermaye Piyasalarının Durumu (Distributed Ledged Technologies/Blokchain)*. Capital Markets Board of Turkey. https://www.spk.gov.tr/SiteApps/Yayin/YayinGoster/1136

Goudarzi, H., & Martin, J. I. (2018). *Blockchain in aviation*. Retrieved from International Air Transport Association website: https://www.iata.org/contentassets/2d997082f3c84c7cba001f50 6edd2c2e/ blockchain- in- aviation- white- paper.pdf

Goudarzi, H., & Martin, J. I. (2018). *Blockchain in aviation*. Retrieved from International Air Transport Association. https://www.iata.org/contentassets/2d997082f3c84c7cba001f506edd2c2e/

Greene, W. H. (2003). *Econometric analysis*. Pearson Education India.

Greenlow, M. (2018). *Marketing Security: The Phrase Every Executive Needs to Understand in 2019*. https://www.martechadvisor.com/articles/marketing-analytics/marketing-security-the-phrase-every-executiveneeds-to-understand-in-2019/

Gretzel, U., Sigala, M., Xiang, Z., & Koo, C. (2015). Smart tourism: Foundations and developments. *Electronic Markets, 25*(3), 179–188. doi:10.100712525-015-0196-8

Grima, S., Spiteri, J., & Romānova, I. (2020). A STEEP framework analysis of the key factors impacting the use of blockchain technology in the insurance industry. *The Geneva Papers on Risk and Insurance. Issues and Practice, 45*(3), 1–28. doi:10.105741288-020-00162-x

Grover, P., Kar, A. K., Janssen, M., & Ilavarasan, P. V. (2019). Perceived usefulness, ease of use and user acceptance of blockchain technology for digital transactions–insights from user-generated content on Twitter. *Enterprise Information Systems, 13*(6), 771–800. doi:10.1080/17 517575.2019.1599446

Gruschka, N., Mavroeidis, V., Vishi, K., & Jensen, M. (2018, December). Privacy issues and data protection in big data: a case study analysis under GDPR. In *2018 IEEE International Conference on Big Data (Big Data)* (pp. 5027-5033). IEEE. 10.1109/BigData.2018.8622621

Gujarati, D. N., & Porter, D. (2009). *Basic Econometrics. McGraw-Hill.*

Guo, X., & Donev, P. (2020). Bibliometrics and Network Analysis of Cryptocurrency Research. *Journal of Systems Science and Complexity, 33*(6), 1933–1958. https://doi.org/10.1007/s11424-020-9094-z

Güven, D. V., & Şahinöz, E. (2018). *Blokzincir- Kripto Paralar- Bitcoin / Satoshi Dünyayı Değiştiriyor.* Kronik Publishing, Istanbul.

Hackett, R. (2016). *Wait, what is Blockchain?* Accessed on February 2021, http://fortune.com/2016/05/23/block chain-definition/

Ha, M., Kwon, S., Lee, Y. J., Shim, Y., & Kim, J. (2019). Where WTS meets WTB: A Blockchain-based Marketplace for Digital Me to trade users' private data. *Pervasive and Mobile Computing, 59*, 101078. https://doi.org/10.1016/j.pmcj.2019.101078

Hans, R., Zuber, H., Rizk, A., & Steinmetz, R. (2017). *Blockchain and smart contracts: Disruptive technologies for the insurance market.* Academic Press.

Harvey, C. R., Moorman, C., & Toledo, M. (2018). *How blockchain can help marketers build better relationships with their customers.* https://hbr.org/2018/10/how-blockchain-can-helpmarketers-build-better-relationships-with-their-customers

Hawlitschek, F., Notheisen, B., & Teubner, T. (2018). The limits of trust-free systems: A literature review on blockchain technology and trust in the sharing economy. *Electronic Commerce Research and Applications, 29*, 50–63. doi:10.1016/j.elerap.2018.03.005

Helebrandt, P., Bellus, M., Ries, M., Kotuliak, I., & Khilenko, V. (2018, November). Blockchain adoption for monitoring and management of enterprise networks. In *2018 IEEE 9th Annual Information Technology, Electronics and Mobile Communication Conference (IEMCON)* (pp. 1221-1225). IEEE. 10.1109/IEMCON.2018.8614960

Herhausen, D., Miočević, D., Morgan, R. E., & Kleijnen, M. H. (2020). The digital marketing capabilities gap. *Industrial Marketing Management, 90*, 276–290. doi:10.1016/j.indmarman.2020.07.022

Hervey, A. (2017). *Blockchain is A new model that makes the existing model obsolete.* Retrieved January 30, 2021, from https://medium.com/future-crunch/blockchain-is-a-new-model-that-makes-the-existing-model-obsolete-8671ee6dd252

Hill, R. C., Griffiths, W. E., & Lim, G. C. (2018). *Principles of econometrics.* John Wiley & Sons.

Hjalager, A. M. (2010). A review of innovation research in tourism. *Tourism Management, 31*(1), 1–12. doi:10.1016/j.tourman.2009.08.012

Ho Lee, S., & Jung, K. S. (2018). Loyal customer behaviors: Identifying brand fans. *Social Behavior and Personality*, *46*(8), 1285–1303. doi:10.2224bp.6482

Hong, K., Park, K., & Yu, J. (2018). Crowding out in a dual currency regime? Digital versus fiat currency. *Emerging Markets Finance & Trade*, *54*(11), 2495–2515. doi:10.1080/1540496X.2018.1452732

How Cryptocurrency Will Affect Digital Marketing? (n.d.). Retrieved March 11, 2021, from https://www.qdexitechnology.com/how-cryptocurrency-will-affect-digital-marketing

How Does Cryptocurrency Work? (for Beginners) - CryptoCurrency Facts. (n.d.). Retrieved March 17, 2021, from https://cryptocurrencyfacts.com/how-does-cryptocurrency-work-for-beginners/

HTNG. (2018). *Blockchain for hospitality*. Retrieved from Hospitality Technology Next Generation. https://www.hospitalitynet.org/file/152008497.pdf

Humayun, M., Niazi, M., Jhanjhi, N. Z., Alshayeb, M., & Mahmood, S. (2020). Cyber security threats and vulnerabilities: A systematic mapping study. *Arabian Journal for Science and Engineering*, *45*(4), 3171–3189. doi:10.100713369-019-04319-2

Iansiti, M., & Lakhani, K. R. (2017). The truth about blockchain. *Harvard Business Review*, *95*, 118–127.

IBM. (2018). *Cybersecurity and Privacy Research*. IBM.

India will not “shut off” all Cryptocurrency, wants blockchain: Sitharaman | Business Standard News. (n.d.). Retrieved March 17, 2021, from https://www.business-standard.com/article/markets/india-will-not-shut-off-all-cryptocurrency-wants-blockchain-sitharaman-121031400754_1.html

Ingram, D., Panchadar, A., & Auchard, E. (2018). *Facebook Privacy Scandal Widens as Data Leak Hits 87 Million Users*. CIO. Available online at: https://www.cio.com.au/article/635768/facebook-privacy-scandal-widensdata-leak-hits-87-million-users/

Insights. (2018). *Blockchain startups absorbed 5X more capital via ICOs than equity financings in 2017*. Author.

Insights, C. (2019). *Blockchain and Insurance: New Technology*. New Opportunities.

İrak, G., & Topçu, Y. E. (2020). The effect of the implementation of blockchain technology in the supply chain cost. *International Journal of Management Economics and Business*, *16*(1), 171–185. doi:10.17130/ijmeb.700862

Irvin, C., & Sullivan, J. (2018). *Using blockchain to streamline airline finance*. Retrieved from Deloitte Development LLC website: https://www2.deloitte.com/us/en/pages/consulting/articles/airlines-blockchain-finance.html

İslam, A. (2019). *Blockchain technology and crypto currencies: Current situation, potantial and risk analysis* (Unpublished Master’s Thesis). Marmara University, Istanbul.

Jacobovitz, O. (2016). Blockchain for identity management. Technical Report, The Lynne and William Frankel Center for Computer Science Department of Computer Science, Ben-Gurion University, Beer Sheva, Israel.

Jadhav, V., & Khanna, M. (2016). Factors influencing online buying behavior of college students: A qualitative analysis. *Qualitative Report, 21*(1), 1.

Janssen, M., Weerakkody, V., Ismagilova, E., Sivarajah, U., & Irani, Z. (2020). A framework for analysing blockchain technology adoption: Integrating institutional, market and technical factors. *International Journal of Information Management, 50*, 302–309. doi:10.1016/j.ijinfomgt.2019.08.012

Jarvenpaa, S. L., Tractinsky, N., & Vitale, M. (2000). Consumer trust in an Internet store. *Information Technology and Management, 1*(1), 45–71. doi:10.1023/A:1019104520776

Jay, L., Moslem, A., & Jaskaran, S. (2019). A blockchain enabled cyberphysical system architecture for industry 4.0 manufacturing systems. *Manufacturing Letters, 20*, 34–39. doi:10.1016/j.mfglet.2019.05.003

Jensen. (2020). How Global Trade Digitization could Support COVID-19's Economic Rebound. *The Economic Times*.

Jesus, E. F., Chicarino, V. R., de Albuquerque, C. V., & Rocha, A. A. D. A. (2018). A survey of how to use blockchain to secure internet of things and the stalker attack. *Security and Communication Networks, 2018*, 2018. doi:10.1155/2018/9675050

Jiang, P., Guo, F., Liang, K., Lai, J., & Wen, Q. (2017). Searchain: Blockchain-based private keyword search in decentralized storage. *Future Generation Computer Systems*, (12), 1–12.

Johnson, G.L. (2017). Planning the future. Blockchain technology and the insurance industry. Insurance law. *In-House Defense Quarterly*, 73–78.

Jones, K. (2018). *How Much Will Blockchain Really Affect Digital Marketing?* https://www.forbes.com/sites/forbesagencycouncil/ 2018/10/04/how-much-will-blockchain-really-affect-digital-marketing/

Joshi, P. L., & Marthandan, G. (2019). The Hype of Big Data Analytics and Auditors. *Emerging Markets Journal, 8*(2), 1–4. doi:10.5195/emaj.2018.153

Juniper Research. (2020). *Online Payment Fraud: Emerging Threats, Segment Analysis & Market Forecasts 2020-2024*. Author.

Kamath, R. (2018). Food Traceability on Blockchain: Walmart's Pork and Mango Pilots with IBM. *The Journal of the British Blockchain Association, 1*(1), 1–12. doi:10.31585/jbba-1-1-(10)2018

Kamble, S., Gunasekaran, A., & Arha, H. (2019). Understanding the Blockchain technology adoption in supply chains-Indian context. *International Journal of Production Research, 57*(7), 2009–2033. doi:10.1080/00207543.2018.1518610

Kannan, P. K., & Li, H. A. (2017). Digital marketing: A framework, review and research agenda. *International Journal of Research in Marketing*, *34*(1), 22–45. doi:10.1016/j.ijresmar.2016.11.006

Karaarslan, E., & Akbaş, M. F. (2017). Blockchain based Cyber Security Systems. Blokzinciri Tabanlı Siber Güvenlik Sistemleri. *Uluslararası Bilgi Güvenliği Mühendisliği Dergisi.*, *3*(2), 16–21.

Kardaş, S. (2019). Blokzincir Teknolojisi: Uzlaşma protokolleri. *Journal of Dicle University Egineering*, *10*(2), 481–496.

Katta, R. M. R., & Patro, C. S. (2017). Influence of web attributes on consumer purchase intentions. *International Journal of Sociotechnology and Knowledge Development*, *9*(2), 1–16. doi:10.4018/IJSKD.2017040101

Kaur, N., & Sahdev, S. (2020). Fighting COVID-19 with technology and innovation, evolving and advancing with technological possibilities. *International Journal Of Advanced Research In Engineering & Technology.*, *11*, 395–405. doi:10.34218/IJARET.11.7.2020.039

Kaur, P., Sharma, M., & Mittal, M. (2018). Big Data and Machine Learning Based Secure Healthcare Framework. *Procedia Computer Science*, *132*, 1049–1059. doi:10.1016/j.procs.2018.05.020

Kelman, H. C. (1974). Social influence and linkages between the individual and the social system: Further thoughts on the processes of compliance, identification, and internalization. In J. Tedeschi (Ed.), Perspectives on social power. Academic Press.

Keybase. (2019). *Server*. https://keybase.io/

Khalifa, E. (2019). Blockchain: Technological Revolution in Business and Administration. *American Journal of Management*, *19*(2).

Khoi, B. H. (2021). *Factors Influencing on University Reputation: Model Selection by AIC. In Data Science for Financial Econometrics*. Springer.

Kim, D., Park, K., Park, Y., & Ahn, J. H. (2019). Willingness to provide personal information: Perspective of privacy calculus in IoT services. *Computers in Human Behavior*, *92*, 273–281. doi:10.1016/j.chb.2018.11.022

Kim, J. S., & Shin, N. (2019). The impact of blockchain technology application on supply chain partnership and performance. *Sustainability (Switzerland)*, *11*(21), 6181. Advance online publication. doi:10.3390u11216181

Kim, J. S., & Shin, N. (2019). The impact of blockchain technology application on supply chain partnership and performance. *Sustainability*, *11*(21), 6181.

King, S., & Nadal, S. (2012) *Ppcoin: Peer-to-Peer Crypto-Currency with Proof-of-Stake*, Self-Published Paper.

Kırbaç, G. (2020). *The evaluation of the Blockchain in supply chain at 3PL Companies with quality function deployment* (Unpublished Doctoral Thesis). İzmir Katip Çelebi University, İzmir.

Kırbaş, İ. (2018). Blockchain Technology and Its Application Areas in Near Future. *The Journal of Graduate School of Natural and Applied Sciences of Mehmet Akif Ersoy University*, *9*(1), 75–82.

Klinger, U., & Svensson, J. (2018). The End of Media Logics? On Algorithms and Agency. *Journals.Sagepub. Com*, *20*(12), 4653–4670. doi:10.1177/1461444818779750

Kollmann, T., Hensellek, S., De Cruppe, K., & Sirges, A. (2020). Toward a renaissance of cooperatives fostered by Blockchain on electronic marketplaces: A theory-driven case study approach. *Electronic Markets*, *30*(2), 273–284. Advance online publication. doi:10.100712525-019-00369-4

Konstantopoulos, G. (2017). *Understanding Blockchain Fundamentals: Proof of Work & Proof of Stake.* https://medium.com/loom-network/understanding-blockchain-fundamentals-part-2-proof-of-work-proof-of-stake-b6ae907c7edb9

Kosba, A., Miller, A., Shi, E., Wen, Z., & Papamanthou, C. (2016, May). Hawk: The blockchain model of cryptography and privacy-preserving smart contracts. In 2016 IEEE symposium on security and privacy (SP) (pp. 839-858). IEEE.

Kshetri, N. (2017). Blockchain's roles in strengthening cybersecurity and protecting privacy. *Telecommunications Policy*, *41*(10), 1027–1038. doi:10.1016/j.telpol.2017.09.003

Kshetri, N. (2018). 1 Blockchain's roles in meeting key supply chain management objectives. *International Journal of Information Management*, *39*, 80–89. doi:10.1016/j.ijinfomgt.2017.12.005

Kshetri, N., & Voas, J. (2019). Online advertising fraud. *Computer*, *52*(1), 58–61. doi:10.1109/MC.2018.2887322

Kumar, V., Ramachandran, D., & Kumar, B. (2021). Influence of new-age technologies on marketing: A research agenda. *Journal of Business Research*, *125*, 864–877. https://doi.org/10.1016/j.jbusres.2020.01.007

Kwok, A. O. J., & Koh, S. G. M. (2018). Is blockchain technology a watershed for tourism development? *Current Issues in Tourism*. Retrieved from https://www.tandfonline.com/doi/abs/10.1080/13683500.2018.1513460

Kwok, A. O., & Koh, S. G. (2019). Is blockchain technology a watershed for tourism development? *Current Issues in Tourism*, *22*(20), 2447–2452. doi:10.1080/13683500.2018.1513460

Lacity, M. C. (2018). Addressing key challenges to making enterprise blockchain applications a reality. *MIS Quarterly Executive*, *17*(3), 201–222.

Lane, M. (2007). The Visitor Journey: The new road to success. *International Journal of Contemporary Hospitality Management*, *19*(3), 248–254. doi:10.1108/09596110710739949

Langan, R., Cowley, S., & Nguyen, C. (2019). The State of Digital Marketing in Academia: An Examination of Marketing Curriculum's Response to Digital Disruption. *Journal of Marketing Education*, *41*(1), 32–46. doi:10.1177/0273475318823849

Larchet, V. (2017). *Blockchain: solution for the black market threat to the tourism industry*. Retrieved from SecuTix website: https://www.secutix.com/wp-content/uploads/2017/

Larivière, B., Joosten, H., Malthouse, E. C., Van Birgelen, M., Aksoy, P., Kunz, W. H., & Huang, M.-H. (2013). Value fusion: The blending of consumer and firm value in the distinct context of mobile technologies and social media. *Journal of Service Management*, *24*(3), 268–293. doi:10.1108/09564231311326996

Lee, J., Bagheri, B., & Kao, H. A. (2015). A cyber-physical systems architecture for industry 4.0-based manufacturing systems. *Manufacturing Letters*, *3*, 18–23. doi:10.1016/j.mfglet.2014.12.001

Lee, W. B., Chen, H. B., Chang, S. S., & Chen, T. H. (2019). Secure and efficient protection for HTTP cookies with self-verification. *International Journal of Communication Systems*, *32*(2), e3857. doi:10.1002/dac.3857

Lefroy, W. (2017, 9 November). *Blockchain: Changing Interaction in the F&A Supply Chain*. Rabobank: https://www.rabobank.com/en/raboworld/articles/blockchainchanging-interaction-in-the-fand-

Lemon, K. N., & Verhoef, P. C. (2016). Understanding customer experience throughout the customer journey. *Journal of Marketing*, *80*(6), 69–96. doi:10.1509/jm.15.0420

Lester, D. H., Forman, A. M., & Loyd, D. (2006). Internet shopping and buying behavior of college students. *Services Marketing Quarterly*, *27*(2), 123–138. doi:10.1300/J396v27n02_08

Leung, D., & Dickinger, A. (2017). Use of Bitcoin in online travel product shopping: The European perspective. In *Information and communication technologies in tourism* (pp. 741–754). Springer. (Original work published 2017)

Liao & Fan. (2020). *Supply Chain Have been Upended: how to make them more resilient?* World Economic Forum.

Liedtke, P. M. (2007). What's insurance to a modern economy? *The Geneva Papers on Risk and Insurance. Issues and Practice*, *32*(2), 211–221. doi:10.1057/palgrave.gpp.2510128

Liji, T. (2020), *Analysis of India's Battle with Covid-19*. https://www.news-medical.net/news/20200504/Analysis-of-Indias-battle-with-COVID-19.aspx

Liu, C. C., Xiao, Y. H., Javangula, V., Hu, Q., Wang, S., & Cheng, X. (2019). NormaChain: A blockchain-based normalized autonomous transaction settlement system for IOT-based E-commerce. *IEEE Internet of Things Journal*, *6*(3), 4680–4693. doi:10.1109/JIOT.2018.2877634

Longo, F., Nicoletti, L., Padovano, A., d'Atri, G., & Forte, M. (2019). Blockchain-enabled supply chain: An experimental study. *Computers & Industrial Engineering*, *136*(July), 57–69. doi:10.1016/j.cie.2019.07.026

Lord, S. (2016). Bankchain & itBit: Settling on the blockchain. *Modern Trader, 16*.

Lucidity. (2018). *Lucidity's Blockchain Pilot with Toyota Results in 21% Lift in Campaign Performance*. https://www.prnewswire.com/news-releases/luciditys-blockchain-pilot-with-toyota-results-in-21-lift-in-campaign-performance-300731983.html

Ludeiro, A. R. (2018, June). Blockchain technology for luggage tracking. In *International Symposium on Distributed Computing and Artificial Intelligence* (pp. 451-456). Springer, Cham.

Macrinici, D., Cartofeanu, C., & Gao, S. (2018). Smart contract applications within blockchain technology: A systematic mapping study. In Telematics and Informatics (Vol. 35, Issue 8, pp. 2337–2354). Elsevier Ltd. doi:10.1016/j.tele.2018.10.004

Magatef, S. G., & Tomalieh, E. F. (2015). The impact of customer loyalty programs on customer retention. *International Journal of Business and Social Science*, *6*(8), 78–93.

Malladi, R. K., & Dheeriya, P. L. (2021). Time series analysis of Cryptocurrency returns and volatilities. *Journal of Economics and Finance*, *45*(1), 75–94. https://doi.org/10.1007/s12197-020-09526-4

Mandolla, C., Petruzzelli, A. M., Percoco, G., & Urbinati, A. (2019). Building a digital twin for additive manufacturing through the exploitation of blockchain: A case analysis of the aircraft industry. *Computers in Industry*, *109*, 134–152. https://doi.org/10.1016/j.compind.2019.04.011

Manjunath, B. S. (2020, April 14). *Covid-19: 8 ways in which technology helps pandemic management*. Https://Cio.Economictimes.Indiatimes.Com/

Manzari, M., Kazemi, M., Nazemi, S., & Pooya, A. (2012). Intellectual capital: Concepts, components and indicators: A literature review. *Management Science Letters*, *2*(7), 2255–2270. doi:10.5267/j.msl.2012.07.018

Marsal-Llacuna, M. L. (2018). Future living framework: Is blockchain the next enabling network? *Technological Forecasting and Social Change*, *128*, 226–234. doi:10.1016/j.techfore.2017.12.005

MartechAdvisor. (2019). *What Is Blockchain in Marketing? Strategies, Best Practices, Benefits and Examples*. https://www.martechadvisor.com/articles/blockchain/what-is-blockchain-how-to-use-it-in-marketing/

Martin, K. (2018). The penalty for privacy violations: How privacy violations impact trust online. *Journal of Business Research*, *82*, 103–116. doi:10.1016/j.jbusres.2017.08.034

Mattiuzzi, C., & Lippi, G. (2020). Which lessons shall we learn from the 2019 novel coronavirus outbreak? *Annals of Translational Medicine*, *8*(3).

McAllister, M. P., & Turow, J. (2002). New media and the commercial sphere: Two intersecting trends, five categories of concern. *Journal of Broadcasting & Electronic Media*, *46*(4), 505–514. doi:10.120715506878jobem4604_1

McDermott, B. (2017). IBM's vice president of blockchain business development, interviewed by R. Kamath, June 23, 2017. Academic Press.

Medium. (2020). *Consensus mekanizmaları*. https://medium.com/@BlockchainIST/consensus-mekanízmalari-951c9c8d2a3e

Mehdi, B., & Ravaud, P. (2017). Blockchain technology for improving clinical research quality. *Trials*, *18*, 335.

Meixian, L. (2015). Convenience and online consumer shopping behavior: A business anthropological case study based on the contingent valuation method. *The Anthropologist*, *21*(1-2), 8–17. doi:10.1080/09720073.2015.11891788

Melewar, T. C., Foroudi, P., Gupta, S., Kitchen, P. J., & Foroudi, M. M. (2017). Integrating identity, strategy and communications for trust, loyalty and commitment. *European Journal of Marketing*, *51*(3), 572–604. doi:10.1108/EJM-08-2015-0616

Melkić, S., & Čavlek, N. (2020). The impact of blockchain technology on tourism intermediation. *Tourism (Zagreb)*, *68*(2), 130–143. doi:10.37741/t.68.2.2

Meng, W., Tischhauser, E. W., Wang, Q., Wang, Y., & Han, J. (2018). When intrusion detection meets blockchaintechnology: A review. *IEEE Access: Practical Innovations, Open Solutions*, *6*, 10179–10188. doi:10.1109/ACCESS.2018.2799854

Merkle, R. C. (1988). *Protocols For Public Key Cryptosystems*. www.merkle.com: http://www.merkle.com/papers/Protocols.pdf

Miles, J. (2014). Tolerance and variance inflation factor. *Wiley StatsRef: Statistics Reference Online*.

Mirzayi, S., & Mehrzad, M. (2017, October). Bitcoin, an SWOT analysis. In *2017 7th International Conference on Computer and Knowledge Engineering (ICCKE)* (pp. 205-210). IEEE. 10.1109/ICCKE.2017.8167876

Mohamed, N., & Al-Jaroodi, J. (2019). Applying blockchain in industry 4.0 applications. *2019 IEEE 9th Annual Computing and Communication Workshop and Conference (CCWC)*, 852–858. 10.1109/CCWC.2019.8666558

Mohamed, N., Al-Jaroodi, J., & Lazarova-Molnar, S. (2019). Leveraging the capabilities of industry 4.0 for improving energy efficiency in smart factories. *IEEE Access: Practical Innovations, Open Solutions*, *7*, 18008–18020. doi:10.1109/ACCESS.2019.2897045

Mohammad, H. J., Yuka, N., & Krishnan, D. (2019). Cryptocurrency, a successful application of blockchain technology. *Managerial Finance*, *46*(6), 715–733. https://doi.org/10.1108/MF-09-2018-0451

Mondragon, A. E. C., Mondragon, C. E. C., & Coronado, E. S. (2018). Exploring the applicability of blockchain technology to enhance manufacturing supply chains in the composite materials industry. *2018 IEEE International Conference on Applied System Invention (ICASI)*, 1300–1303. 10.1109/ICASI.2018.8394531

Montecchi, M., Plangger, K., & Etter, M. (2019). It's real, trust me! Establishing supply chain provenance using blockchain. *Business Horizons, 62*(3), 283–293. doi:10.1016/j.bushor.2019.01.008

Mouawi, R., Elhajj, I. H., Chehab, A., & Kayssi, A. (2019). Crowdsourcing for click fraud detection. *EURASIP Journal on Information Security, 2019*(1), 1–18. doi:10.118613635-019-0095-1

Mou, J., & Shin, D. (2018). Effects of social popularity and time scarcity on online consumer behaviour regarding smart healthcare products: An eye-tracking approach. *Computers in Human Behavior, 78*, 74–89. doi:10.1016/j.chb.2017.08.049

Mou, J., Shin, D.-H., & Cohen, J. F. (2017). Trust and risk in consumer acceptance of e-services. *Electronic Commerce Research, 17*(2), 255–288. doi:10.100710660-015-9205-4

Nabben, A., Wetzel, E., Oldani, E., Huyeng, J., Boel, M., & Fan, Z. (2016). Smart technologies in tourism: Case study on the influence of iBeacons on customer experience during the 2015 SAIL Amsterdam event. *International Tourism Student Conference*, 1-32.

Nakamoto, S. (2008). Bitcoin: A Peer-to-Peer Electronic Cash System. *Consulted*, 1–9.

Nakamoto, S. (2008). *Bitcoin: A peer-to-peer electronic cash system.* https://bitcoin.org/bitcoin.pdf

Nakamoto, S. (2008). *Bitcoin: a peer-to-peer electronic cash system.* Retrieved February 2, 2021, from https://bitcoin.org/bitcoin.pdf

Nakamoto, S. (2019). *Bitcoin: A peer-to-peer electronic cash system.* Manubot. https://git.dhimmel.com/bitcoin-whitepaper/

Nakamoto. (2008). *Bitcoin: A peer-to-peer electronic cash system.* Academic Press.

Nam, K., Dutt, C. S., Chathoth, P., & Khan, M. S. (2019). Blockchain technology for smart city and smart tourism: Latest trends and challenges. *Asia Pacific Journal of Tourism Research, 24*(5), 71–87. doi:10.1080/10941665.2019.1585376

Nasarre-Aznar, S. (2018). Collaborative housing and blockchain. *Administration, 66*(2), 59–82. doi:10.2478/admin-2018-0018

Nayak, P., & Debashish, S. (2017). Young consumers' online shopping decision influencers: A study on university students of Odisha. *Effulgence, 15*(1), 45–50. doi:10.33601/effulgence.rdias/v15/i1/2017/45-50

Newman, D. (2019). How Blockchain Is Changing Digital Marketing. *Forbes*. https://www.forbes.com/sites/danielnewman/2019/09/18/how-blockchain-is-changing-digital-marketing/?sh=5ed0b1d416eb

Newman. (2019). *How Blockchain Is Changing Digital Marketing.* Available online at: https://www.forbes.com/sites/danielnewman/2019/09/18/how-blockchain-is-changing-digital-marketing/?sh=7f60417816eb

News, B. D. A. (2020). *4 Important Ways Blockchain Will Change Digital Marketing and Advertising.* https://bigdataanalyticsnews.com/blockchain-change-digital-marketing-advertising/

Nieves, J., & Diaz-Meneses, G. (2016). Antecedents and outcomes of marketing innovation. *International Journal of Contemporary Hospitality Management, 28*(8), 1554–1576. doi:10.1108/IJCHM-11-2014-0589

Norbug. (2019). *Unblocking the Bottlenecks and making the Global Supply Chain Transparent: How Blockchain Technology Can update Global Trade.* The School of Public Policy Publication.

Norman, G., Pepall, L., Richards, D., & Tan, L. (2016). Competition and consumer data: The good, the bad, and the ugly. *Research in Economics, 70*(4), 752–765. doi:10.1016/j.rie.2016.09.002

Nowiński, W., & Kozma, M. (2017). How Can Blockchain Technology Disrupt the Existing Business Models? *Entrepreneurial Business and Economics Review, 5*(3), 173–188. doi:10.15678/EBER.2017.050309

Nuryyev, G., Wang, Y. P., Achyldurdyyeva, J., Jaw, B. S., Yeh, Y. S., Lin, H. T., & Wu, L. F. (2020). Blockchain Technology Adoption Behavior and Sustainability of the Business in Tourism and Hospitality SMEs: An Empirical Study. *Sustainability, 12*(3), 1256. doi:10.3390u12031256

Nussbaum, F. (1933). *A History of the Economic Institutions of Modern Europe: An Introduction of 'Der Moderne Kapitalismus' of Werner Sombart.* Crofts.

Oberoi, S., & Kansra, P. (2019). Factors Influencing Medical Tourism in India: A Critical Review. *SAMVAD, 17*, 9-16.

Oberoi, S., & Kansra, P. (2020). Economic menace of diabetes in India: A systematic review. *International Journal of Diabetes in Developing Countries, 40*(4), 464–475. doi:10.100713410-020-00838-z PMID:32837090

Oh, J.-S., & Jeong, D.-Y. (2015). The effects of consumers' beliefs about TV home shopping advertising on attitude and purchase intention. *Indian Journal of Science and Technology, 8*(14), 1.

Okan, Ş. (2018). *Nesnelerin İnterneti Blockchain Teknolojisiyle Buluşuyor.* https://magg4.com/nesnelerin-interneti-blockchain-teknolojisiyle-bulusuyor/

Olaf, A., Hagen, H., & Hajj, J. (2017). *2017 Technology trends.* PwC. Accessed on February 2021. https://www.strategyand.pwc.com/ trend/2017-technology-trends

Omran, Y., Henke, M., Heines, R., & Hofmann, E. (2017). *Blockchain-driven supply chain finance: Towards a conceptual framework from a buyer perspective.* Academic Press.

Önder, I., & Treiblmaier, H. (2018). Blockchain and tourism: Three research propositions. *Annals of Tourism Research, 72*(C), 180–182. doi:10.1016/j.annals.2018.03.005

onecoin-steps-to-protect-your-digital-currencies-9-638.jpg (638×479). (n.d.). Retrieved March 17, 2021, from https://image.slidesharecdn.com/tipstoprotectyourdigitalcurrencies-onecoin-171012101449/95/onecoin-steps-to-protect-your-digital-currencies-9-638.jpg?cb=1507803419

Onik, M. M. H., Miraz, M. H., & Kim, C. (2018). A recruitment and human resource management technique using blockchain technology for industry 4.0. *Smart Cities Symposium 2018*, 1–6. 10.1049/cp.2018.1371

Ovais, A. (2017). Block Chain Technology: Concept of Digital Economic. University Library of Munich.

Park, Y. J., Chung, J. E., & Shin, D. H. (2018). The Structuration of Digital Ecosystem, Privacy, and Big Data Intelligence. *The American Behavioral Scientist*, *62*(10), 1319–1337. doi:10.1177/0002764218787863

Pärssinen, M., Kotila, M., Cuevas Rumin, R., Phansalkar, A., & Manner, J. (2018). Is Blockchain Ready to Revolutionize Online Advertising? *IEEE Access: Practical Innovations, Open Solutions*, *6*, 54884–54899. doi:10.1109/ACCESS.2018.2872694

Partida, B. (n.d.). *APQC, Blockchain and its potential for supply chain innovation*. https://www.apqc.org/ System/files/K08553_APQC_Blockchain%20in%20Supply%20Chain%2,0Operations.pdf

Pavlou, P. A. (2003). Consumer acceptance of electronic commerce: Integrating trust and risk with the technology acceptance model. *International Journal of Electronic Commerce*, *7*(3), 101–134. doi:10.1080/10864415.2003.11044275

Pavlou, P. A., & Fygenson, M. (2006). Understanding and predicting electronic commerce adoption: An extension of the theory of planned behavior. *Management Information Systems Quarterly*, *30*(1), 115–143. doi:10.2307/25148720

Pawczuk, L., Massey, R., & Holdowsky, J. (2019). *Deloitte's 2019 Global Blockchain Survey: blockchain gets down to business* [Report]. Deloitte.

Penny, T. L. (2018). *Basic Attention Token & Brave: Digital Marketing on the Blockchain*. Academic Press.

PetersG.PanayiE. (2015) Understanding Modern Banking Ledgers through Blockchain Technologies: Future of Transaction Processing and Smart Contracts on the Internet of Money. Available at doi:10.2139srn.2692487

Philipp, G. J., Susanne, H.-B., & Jörg, H. (2020). Information technology and marketing: An important partnership for decades. *Industrial Management & Data Systems*, *121*(1), 123–157. https://doi.org/10.1108/IMDS-08-2020-0510

Pilkington, M. (2017). *Can blockchain technology help promote new tourism destinations? The example of medical tourism in Moldova*. Academic Press.

Pilkington, M., Crudu, R., & Grant, L. G. (2017). Blockchain and bitcoin as a way to lift a country out of poverty-tourism 2.0 and e-governance in the Republic of Moldova. *International Journal of Internet Technology and Secured Transactions*, *7*(2), 115–143. doi:10.1504/IJITST.2017.087132

Pingitore, G., Meyers, J., Clancy, M., & Cavallaro, K. (2013). *Consumer concerns about data privacy rising: What can business do*. Academic Press.

Pinmo. (2019). *How Pinmo Will Utilize Blockchain to Revolutionize the Advertising Industry*. https://pinmo.ca/

PN. (2020, August 5). *Role of Technology in the Era of COVID-19 Pandemic*. https://news.cleartax.in/role-of-technology-in-the-era-of-covid-19-pandemic/

Polasik, M., Piotrowska, A. I., Wisniewski, T. P., Kotkowski, R., & Lightfoot, G. (2015). Price fluctuations and the use of Bitcoin: An empirical inquiry. *International Journal of Electronic Commerce*, *20*(1), 9–49. doi:10.1080/10864415.2016.1061413

Pournader, M., Shi, Y., Seuring, S., & Koh, S. C. L. (2020). Blockchain applications in supply chains, transport and logistics: A systematic review of the literature. *International Journal of Production Research*, *58*(7), 2063–2081. doi:10.1080/00207543.2019.1650976

Prause, G. (2019). Smart contracts for smart supply chains. *IFAC-PapersOnLine*, *52*(13), 2501–2506. doi:10.1016/j.ifacol.2019.11.582

PricewaterhouseCoopers. (2016). *Blockchain in the insurance sector.* Accessed on January 2021, https://www.pwc.co.uk/financial-services/fintech/assets/blockchain-in-insurance.pdf

Puthal, D., Malik, N., Mohanty, S. P., Kougianos, E., & Das, G. (2018). Everything you wanted to know about the blockchain: Its promise, components, processes, and problems. *IEEE Consumer Electronics Magazine*, *7*(4), 6–14. doi:10.1109/MCE.2018.2816299

Ramos, C. M. Q., & Brito, I. S. (2020). The Effects of Industry 4.0 in Tourism and Hospitality and Future Trends in Portugal. In A. Hassan & A. Sharma (Eds.), *The Emerald Handbook of ICT in Tourism and Hospitality* (pp. 367–378). Emerald Publishing Limited. doi:10.1108/978-1-83982-688-720201023

Rashideh, W. (2020). Blockchain technology framework: Current and future perspectives for the tourism industry. *Tourism Management*, *80*, 104125. doi:10.1016/j.tourman.2020.104125

Rayome, A. D. (2019). *Top 10 Emerging Technologies of 2019*. TechRepublic.

Reagan, J. R., & Singh, M. (2020). Transportation, Travel, and Tourism Evolution. In *Management 4.0. Blockchain Technologies*. Springer.

Reinkrul. (2020). *Implementing a Merkle Tree in Go*. Academic Press.

Rejeb, A., & Karim, R. (2019). Blockchain Technology in Tourism: Applications and Possibilities. *Sustainable Technology eJournal*.

Rejeb, A., & Karim, R. (2019). Blockchain technology in tourism: Applications and possibilities. *World Scientific News*, *137*, 119–144.

Rejeb, A., Keogh, J. G., & Treiblmaier, H. (2020). How Blockchain Technology Can Benefit Marketing. *Six Pending Research Areas. Front. Blockchain*, *3*, 3. doi:10.3389/fbloc.2020.00003

Rejeb, A., Rejeb, K., & Keogh, J. G. (2021). Cryptocurrencies in Modern Finance: A Literature Review. *Etikonomi*, *20*(1), 93–118. doi:10.15408/etk.v20i1.16911

Rennock, M. J. W., Cohn, A., & Butcher, J. R. (2018). *Blockchain technology and regulatory investigations*. Academic Press.

Rios, R., Fernandez-Gago, C., & Lopez, J. (2018). Modelling privacy-aware trust negotiations. *Computers & Security*, *77*, 773–789. doi:10.1016/j.cose.2017.09.015

Rishel, T. D., & Burns, O. M. (1997). The impact of technology on small manufacturing firms. *Journal of Small Business Management*, *35*, 2–10.

Risius, M., & Spohrer, K. (2017). A Blockchain Research Framework: What We (don't) Know, Where We Go from Here, and How We Will Get There. *Business & Information Systems Engineering*, *59*(6), 385–409. doi:10.100712599-017-0506-0

Riva, G., Mantovani, F., & Wiederhold, B. K. (2020). Positive Technology and COVID-19. *Cyberpsychology, Behavior, and Social Networking*, *23*(9), 581–587.

Rodrigue, J. P. (2018). *Efficiency and sustainability in multimodal supply chains*. International Transport Forum Discussion Paper, No. 2018-17, Organisation form Economic Co-operation and Development (OECD), International Transport Forum.

Rohmah, D., Maharani, S., Kholis, M., Taqwa, S., & Setyaningrum, H. (2020).. . *Traceability and Tracking Systems of Halal Food Using Blockchain Technology to Improve Food Industry Competitiveness., c*. Advance online publication. doi:10.4108/eai.13-2-2019.2286199

Rungsrisawat, S., Joemsittiprasert, W., & Jermsittiparsert, K. (2019). Factors Determining Consumer Buying Behaviour in Online Shopping. *International Journal of Innovation. Creativity and Change*, *8*(8), 222–237.

S. Gupta and B. Gupta, "Securing Honey Supply Chain through Blockchain," in IoT Security Paradigms and Applications, CRC Press, 2020

S., S. (2017). Factors Influencing the Adoption of Cloud Computing by Saudi University Hospitals. *International Journal of Advanced Computer Science and Applications, 8*(1), 41–48. doi:10.14569/IJACSA.2017.080107

Saberi, S., Kouhizadeh, M., Sarkis, J., & Shen, L. (2019). Blockchain technology and its relationships to sustainable supply chain management. *International Journal of Production Research*, *57*(7), 2117–2135. doi:10.1080/00207543.2018.1533261

Sadhya, V., & Sadhya, H. (2018). Barriers to Adoption of Blockchain Technology. *Proceedings of the 24th Americas Conference on Information Systems*, 1–10.

Sahu. (2020). *Why is Blockchain the Future? Future Prospects, Expectations & Current Scenario*. Available online at: https://www.upgrad.com/blog/why-is-blockchain-the-future/#:~:text=According%20to%20Gartner%2C%20the%20world,with%20the%20data%20confidentiality%20enterprises

Saini, V., & Gupta, S. (2019). Blockchain in Supply Chain: Journey from Disruptive to Sustainable. *J. Mech. Contin. Math. Sci.*, *14*(2). Advance online publication. doi:10.26782/jmcms.2019.04.00036

Salman, T., Zolanvari, M., Erbad, A., Jain, R., & Samaka, M. (2018). Security services using blockchains: A state of the art survey. *IEEE Communications Surveys and Tutorials*, *21*(1), 858–880. doi:10.1109/COMST.2018.2863956

Sankar, L. S., Sindhu, M., & Sethumadhavan, M. (2017). Survey of consensus protocols on blockchain applications. In *4th international conference on advanced computing and communication systems* (pp. 653-657). Piscataway, NJ: Institute of Electrical and Electronics Engineers.

Santomier, J. (2008). New media, branding and global sports sponsorship. *International Journal of Sports Marketing & Sponsorship*, *10*(1), 9–22. doi:10.1108/IJSMS-10-01-2008-B005

Saturno, M., Pertel, V. M., Deschamps, F., & Loures, E. D. F. (2017). Proposal of an automation solutions architecture for industry 4.0. In *Proceedings of the 24th International Conference on Production Research*. Poznan: ICPR.

Schilling, L., & Uhlig, H. (2019). Some simple bitcoin economics. *Journal of Monetary Economics*, *106*, 16–26.

Schweizer, A., Schlatt, V., Urbach, N., & Fridgen, G. (2017, December). Unchaining Social Businesses-Blockchain as the Basic Technology of a Crowdlending Platform. ICIS.

Scope of Blockchain in Digital Marketing. (n.d.). Retrieved March 11, 2021, from https://www.blockchain-council.org/blockchain/scope-of-blockchain-in-digital-marketing/

Scott, M. (2017). *Bext360 and the World of Blockchain Traceable Coffee*. https://medium.com/@Theurbane journalist/bext360-and-the-world-of-blockchain-traceable-coffee-4ee1d9bba560

SDG. (2019). *Sustainable Development Goals (SDG)*. Retrieved from: https://sustainabledevelopment.un.org/

Shen & Pena-Mora. (2018). Blockchain for cities—a systematic literature review. *IEEE Access, 6*.

Sheth, J. N., Sisodia, R. S., & Sharma, A. (2000). The antecedents and consequences of customer centric marketing. *Journal of the Academy of Marketing Science*, *28*(1), 55–66. doi:10.1177/0092070300281006

Shih, D. H., Lu, K. C., Shih, Y. T., & Shih, P. Y. (2019). A simulated organic vegetable production and marketing environment by using Ethereum. *Electronics (Basel)*, *8*(11), 1341.

Shin, D. D. H. (2019). Blockchain: The emerging technology of digital trust. *Telematics and Informatics*, *45*(September), 101278. Advance online publication. doi:10.1016/j.tele.2019.101278

Shin, D. H. (2017). Conceptualizing and measuring quality of experience of the internet of things: Exploring how quality is perceived by users. *Information & Management*, *54*(8), 998–1011. doi:10.1016/j.im.2017.02.006

Shin, D., & Bianco, W. T. (2020). In Blockchain We Trust: Does Blockchain Itself Generate Trust? *Social Science Quarterly*, *101*(7), 2522–2538. doi:10.1111squ.12917

Shin, D., & Biocca, F. (2018). Exploring immersive experience in journalism. *New Media & Society*, *20*(8), 2800–2823. doi:10.1177/1461444817733133

Shin, D.-H. (2013). User experience in social commerce: In friends we trust. *Behaviour & Information Technology*, *32*(1), 52–67. doi:10.1080/0144929X.2012.692167

Shin, D., & Ibahrine, M. (2020). The socio-technical assemblages of blockchain system: How blockchains are framed and how the framing reflects societal contexts. *Digital Policy. Regulation & Governance*, *22*(3), 245–263. doi:10.1108/DPRG-11-2019-0095

Shrouf, F., Ordieres, J., & Miragliotta, G. (2014). *Smart factories in industry 4.0: A review of the concept and of energy management approached in production based on the internet of things paradigm. In 2014 IEEE international conference on industrial engineering and engineering management*. IEEE.

Sihi, D. (2020). Impacts of Blockchain Technology in Marketing. In F. J. Martínez-López & S. D'Alessandro (Eds.), *Advances in Digital Marketing and eCommerce* (pp. 25–30). Springer. doi:10.1007/978-3-030-47595-6_4

Siyal, A. A., Junejo, A. Z., Zawish, M., Ahmed, K., Khalil, A., & Soursou, G. (2019). Applications of blockchain technology in medicine and healthcare: Challenges and future perspectives. *Cryptography*, *3*(1), 3. doi:10.3390/cryptography3010003

Stalidis, G., Karapistolis, D., & Vafeiadis, A. (2015). Marketing decision support using Artificial Intelligence and Knowledge Modeling: Application to tourist destination management. *Procedia: Social and Behavioral Sciences*, *175*, 106–113. doi:10.1016/j.sbspro.2015.01.1180

Stickdorn, M., & Zehrer, A. (2009, November). Service design in tourism: Customer experience driven destination management. In *First Nordic conference on service design and service innovation* (pp. 1-16). Oslo: Academic Press.

Subramanian, H. (2018). Decentralized blockchain-based electronic marketplaces. *Communications of the ACM*, *61*(1), 78–84. doi:10.1145/3158333

Sullivan, J. (2018). *Using blockchain to streamline airline finance*. Retrieved from Deloitte Development LLC website: https://www2.deloitte.com/us/en/pages/consulting/ articles/airlines-blockchain- finance.html

Suveen, A., Krumholz, H. M., & Schulz, W. L. (2017). Blockchain technology: Applications in health care. *Circulation: Cardiovascular Quality and Outcomes, 10*, e003800.

Swan, M. (2015). *Block chain: Blueprint for a New Economy*. O'Reilly Media.

Swan, M. (2015). *Blockchain: Blueprint for a new economy*. O'Reilly Media, Inc.

Tabachnick, B. G., Fidell, L. S., & Ullman, J. B. (2007). *Using multivariate statistics* (Vol. 5). Pearson Boston.

Talas, D. (2020). *Bağcılık Nedir?* https://www.bilgiustam.com/bagcilik-nedir/

Tanadi, T., Samadi, B., & Gharleghi, B. (2015). The impact of perceived risks and perceived benefits to improve an online intention among generation-y in Malaysia. *Asian Social Science, 11*(26), 226. doi:10.5539/ass.v11n26p226

Tan, B., Yan, J., Chen, S., & Liu, X. (2018). The Impact of Blockchain on Food Supply Chain: The Case of Walmart. In M. Qiu (Ed.), Lecture Notes in Computer Science: Vol. 11373. *Smart Blockchain. SmartBlock 2018*. Springer. doi:10.1007/978-3-030-05764-0_18

Tan, B., Yan, J., Chen, S., & Liu, X. (2018, December). The impact of blockchain on food supply chain: The case of walmart. In *International Conference on Smart Blockchain* (pp. 167-177). Springer.

Tandon, U., Kiran, R., & Sah, A. N. (2016). Understanding online shopping adoption in India: Unified theory of acceptance and use of technology 2 (UTAUT2) with perceived risk application. *Service Science, 8*(4), 420–437. doi:10.1287erv.2016.0154

Tapscott, D., & Kaplan, A. (2019). *Blockchain Revolution in Education and LifeLong Learning: Preparing for Disruption, Leading the Transformation*. www.blockchainresearchinstitute.org/contact-us

Tapscott, D., & Tapscott, A. (2016). Blockchain revolution: how the technology behind bitcoin is changing money; business; and the world. New York: Academic Press.

Tapscott, D., & Tapscott, A. (2016). *Blockchain revolution: how the technology behind bitcoin is changing money, business, and the world*. Penguin.

Tasatanattakool, P., & Techapanupreeda, C. (2018, January). Blockchain: Challenges and applications. In *2018 International Conference on Information Networking (ICOIN)* (pp. 473-475). IEEE. 10.1109/ICOIN.2018.8343163

Thake, M. (2018). *What's the difference between blockchain and DLT?* Nakamo. To.

The Economist. (2015). *The Trust Machine – The Promise of the Blockchain*. Author.

The Impact of Cryptocurrency on Digital Marketing - Digiperform. (n.d.). Retrieved March 11, 2021, from https://digiperform.com/the-impact-of-cryptocurrency-on-digital-marketing/

The Ultimate Guide to Blockchain Marketing and Cryptocurrency - Blog - Creative Bear Tech. (n.d.). Retrieved March 17, 2021, from https://cbtemailextractor.com/blog/the-ultimate-guide-to-blockchain-marketing-and-cryptocurrency/

Thees, H., Erschbamer, G., & Pechlaner, H. (2020). The application of blockchain in tourism: Use cases in the tourism value system. *European Journal of Tourism Research*, *26*, 2602–2602.

Three 2 Five Marketing. (2021). *5 Crucial Ways Blockchain is Changing Digital Marketing.* https://3to5marketing.com/blockchain-is-changing-digital-marketing/

ThreeWindows. (2021). *10 Application Examples for Blockchain Technology in Digital Marketing.* https://threewindows.com/10-application-examples-for-blockchain-technology-in-digital-marketing/

Tiago, M. T. P. M. B., & Veríssimo, J. M. C. (2014). Digital marketing and social media: Why bother? *Business Horizons*, *57*(6), 703–708. doi:10.1016/j.bushor.2014.07.002

Tian, F. (2016). An agri-food supply chain traceability system for china based on RFID & Blockchain technology. In *Service Systems and Service Management (ICSSSM), 13th International Conference on*. IEEE.

Tian, F. (2016). An agri-food supply chain traceability system for China based on RFID & blockchain technology. *13th International Conference on Service Systems and Service Management (ICSSSM)*, 1-6.

Tipsinterview. (2018). *Blockchain technology and its impact on digital marketing in 2018 revealed.* Available online at: https://tipsinterviews.blogspot.com/2017/11/blockchain-and-its-impact-on-digital.html

Tiwari, T. (2016). *Profit alert: Walmart is adopting the blockchain right now*. Palm Beach Research Group. palmbeachgroup.com/content/palm-beach-daily/profit-alert- Walmart-is-adopting-the-blockchain-right-now/32499

Tönnissen, S., & Teuteberg, F. (2020). Analysing the impact of blockchain-technology for operations and supply chain management: An explanatory model drawn from multiple case studies. *International Journal of Information Management*, *52*, 101953. doi:10.1016/j.ijinfomgt.2019.05.009

Travizano, M., Minnoni, M., Ajzenman, G., Sarraute, C., & Della Penna, N. (2018). *Wibson: A decentralized marketplace empowering individuals to safely monetize their personal data.* White paper.

Treiblmaier, H. (2020). Blockchain and Tourism. Handbook of e-Tourism, 1-21. doi:10.1007/978-3-030-05324-6_28-1

Treiblmaier, H. (2018). The impact of the blockchain on the supply chain: A theory-based research framework and a call for action. *Supply Chain Management*, *23*(6), 545–559. doi:10.1108/SCM-01-2018-0029

Treiblmaier, H. (2019). Toward more rigorous blockchain research: Recommendations for writing blockchain case studies. *Front Blockchain*, *2*(3), 1–15. doi:10.3389/fbloc.2019.00003

Treiblmaier, H. (2020). Toward more rigorous blockchain research: Recommendations for writing blockchain case studies. In *Blockchain and Distributed Ledger Technology Use Cases* (pp. 1–31). Springer. doi:10.1007/978-3-030-44337-5_1

Tribis, Y., Bouayad, H., & El Bouchti, A. (2018). Supply chain management based on blockchain: A systematic mapping study. *MATEC Web of Conferences, 200*, 1-8. 10.1051/matecconf/201820000020

Tsai, W. T., Blower, R., Zhu, Y., & Yu, L. (2016). A system view of financial blockchains. *IEEE Symposium on Service-Oriented System Engineering (SOSE)*, 450–457. 10.1109/SOSE.2016.66

Twesige, R. L. (2015). *A Simple Explanation of Bitcoin and Blockchain Technology*. Available online at: https://www.researchgate.net/profile/Richard_Twesige/ publication/270287317

Ubex. (2019). *Artificial Intelligence in Advertising*. https://www. ubex.com

Underwood, S. (2016). Blockchain beyond bitcoin. *Communications of the ACM*, *59*(11), 15–17. doi:10.1145/2994581

UpGard. (2020). *Blockchain in Digital Marketing*. https://www.upgrad.com/blog/blockchain-in-digital-marketing/

Urquhart, A. (2016). The inefficiency of Bitcoin. *Economics Letters*, *148*, 80–82. doi:10.1016/j.econlet.2016.09.019

Urquhart, A. (2017). Price clustering in Bitcoin. *Economics Letters*, *159*, 145–148. doi:10.1016/j.econlet.2017.07.035

Usta, A., & Doğantekin, S. (2017). *Blockchain 101*. MediaCat Publishing.

Valeri, M., & Baggio, R. (2020). A critical reflection on the adoption of blockchain in tourism. *Information Technology & Tourism*, 1–12. doi:10.100740558-020-00183-1

van Hilten, M., Ongena, G., & Ravesteijn, P. (2020). Blockchain for Organic Food Traceability: Case Studies on Drivers and Challenges. *Frontiers in Blockchain*, *3*, 43.

Vassiliadis, S., Papadopoulos, P., Rangoussi, M., Konieczny, T., & Gralewski, J. (2017). Bitcoin value analysis based on cross-correlations. *Journal of Internet Banking and Commerce*, *22*(S7), 1.

Venkatesh, V., Morris, M. G., Davis, G. B., & Davis, F. D. (2003). User acceptance of information technology: Toward a unified view. *Management Information Systems Quarterly*, *27*(3), 425–478. doi:10.2307/30036540

Vidan, G., & Lehdonvirta, V. (2019). Mine the gap: Bitcoin and the maintenance of trustlessness. *Journals.Sagepub.Com, 21*(1), 42–59. doi:10.1177/1461444818786220

Villalmanzo, I. V. (2018). *Blockchain: Applications, Effects and Challenges in Supply Chains* (Unpublished Master's Thesis). Tampere Technology University.

Vinfolio. (2020). *Digital Provenance: How Wine Bottles Will Be Tracked Using Bitcoin*. https://blog.vinfolio.com/2014/10/06/the-future-of-wine-provenance-is-bitcoin/

Walker-Roberts, S., Hammoudeh, M., & Dehghantanha, A. (2018). A Systematic Review of the Availability and Efficacy of Countermeasures to Internal Threats in Healthcare Critical Infrastructure. *IEEE Access: Practical Innovations, Open Solutions*, *6*, 25167–25177.

Walmart. (2019). How Walmart brought unprecedented transparency to the food supply Chain with Hyperledger Fabric. *International Journal of Production Research.*

Wang, H. (2018). Anonymous Data Sharing Scheme in Public Cloud and Its Application in E-health Record. *IEEE Access: Practical Innovations, Open Solutions*, *6*, 27818–27826.

Wang, L., Luo, X., & Lee, F. (2019). Unveiling the interplay between blockchain and loyalty program participation: A qualitative approach based on Bubichain. *International Journal of Information Management*, *49*, 397–410. doi:10.1016/j.ijinfomgt.2019.08.001

Wang, S., & Lin, J. C. C. (2011). The effect of social influence on bloggers' usage intention. *Online Information Review*, *35*(1), 50–65. doi:10.1108/14684521111113588

Weber, I., Xu, X., Riveret, R., Governatori, G., Ponomarev, A., & Mendling, J. (2016.) Untrusted business process monitoring and execution using blockchain. In *International Conference on Business Process Management*. Springer.

Weking, J., Mandalenakis, M., Hein, A., Hermes, S., Böhm, M., & Krcmar, H. (2020). The impact of blockchain technology on business models – a taxonomy and archetypal patterns. *Electronic Markets*, *30*(2), 285–305. doi:10.100712525-019-00386-3

Wertheim, S. (2020). Tips for Fighting Off Cybercrime in 2020. *The CPA Journal*, *90*(3), 64–66.

Westlund, S., & Engström, R. P. (2019). *Increasing transparency in the supply chain with blockchain technology A case study of small and medium sized South African wine producers* (Unpublished Master's Thesis). Karlstad University, Sweden.

Weyer, S., Schmitt, M., Ohmer, M., & Gorecky, D. (2015). Towards industry 4.0-standardization as the crucial challenge for highly modular, multivendor production systems. *IFAC-PapersOnLine*, *48*(3), 579–584. doi:10.1016/j.ifacol.2015.06.143

What Cryptocurrency Means for Digital Marketers. (n.d.). Retrieved March 13, 2021, from https://www.waxmarketing.com/cryptocurrency-means-digital-marketers/

What is the Cryptocurrency Bill & What Happens to Those Holding Bitcoins in India? (n.d.). Retrieved March 17, 2021, from https://www.news18.com/news/business/what-is-the-cryptocurrency-bill-what-happens-to-those-holding-bitcoins-in-india-3432443.html

Williams, P. (2001). The Evolving Images of Wine Tourism Destinations. *Tourism Recreation Research, 26*(2), 3–10. doi:10.1080/02508281.2001.11081338

Willie, P. (2019). Can all sectors of the hospitality and tourism industry be influenced by the innovation of Blockchain technology? *Worldwide Hospitality and Tourism Themes, 11*(2), 112–120. doi:10.1108/WHATT-11-2018-0077

Wong, D. R., Bhattacharya, S., & Butte, A. J. (2019). Prototype of running clinical trials in an untrustworthy environment using blockchain. *Nature Communications, 10*(917), 917. Advance online publication. doi:10.103841467-019-08874-y PMID:30796226

Woodside, J. M., Augustine, F. K. Jr, & Giberson, W. (2017). Blockchain technology adoption status and strategies. *Journal of International Technology and Information Management, 26*(2), 65–93.

Worthington, R. L., & Whittaker, T. A. (2006). Scale development research: A content analysis and recommendations for best practices. *The Counseling Psychologist, 34*(6), 806–838. doi:10.1177/0011000006288127

Wu, H. T., & Tsai, C. W. (2018). Toward blockchains for health-care systems: Applying the bilinear pairing technology to ensure privacy protection and accuracy in data sharing. *IEEE Consum. Electron. Mag, 7*, 65–71.

Wüst, K., & Gervais, A. (2018). *Do you need a blockchain? In: 2018 Crypto valley conference on blockchain technology*. CVCBT. doi:10.1109/CVCBT.2018.00011

Xiao, Y., & Fan, Z. (2020, April 27). *10 technology trends to watch in the COVID-19 pandemic*. https://www.weforum.org/agenda/2020/04/10-technology-trends-coronavirus-covid19-pandemic-robotics-telehealth/

Xu, L. D., Xu, E. L., & Li, L. (2018). Industry 4.0: State of the art and future trends. *International Journal of Production Research, 56*(8), 2941–2962. doi:10.1080/00207543.2018.1444806

Xu, M., Chen, X., & Kou, G. (2019). A systematic review of blockchain. Financ. *Innovations: Technology, Governance, Globalization, 5*(1), 27. doi:10.118640854-019-0147-z

Yadav, S. P., Agrawal, K. K., Bhati, B. S., Al-Turjman, F., & Mostarda, L. (2020). Blockchain-Based Cryptocurrency Regulation: An Overview. *Computational Economics*. doi:10.100710614-020-10050-0

Yang, Q., Pang, C., Liu, L., Yen, D. C., & Tarn, J. M. (2015). Exploring consumer perceived risk and trust for online payments: An empirical study in China's younger generation. *Computers in Human Behavior, 50*, 9–24. doi:10.1016/j.chb.2015.03.058

Yang, R., Yu, F. R., Si, P., Yang, Z., & Zhang, Y. (2019). Integrated blockchain and edge computing systems: A survey, some research issues and challenges. *IEEE Communications Surveys and Tutorials, 21*(2), 1508–1532. doi:10.1109/COMST.2019.2894727

Yang, Y., Li, X., Qamar, N., Liu, P., Ke, W., Shen, B., & Liu, Z. (2018). MedShare: A Novel Hybrid Cloud for Medical Resource Sharing among Autonomous Healthcare Providers. *IEEE Access: Practical Innovations, Open Solutions*, *6*, 46949–46961.

Yanik, S., & Kiliç, A. S. (2018). A framework for the performance evaluation of an energy blockchain. In *Energy Management—Collective and Computational Intelligence with Theory and Applications* (pp. 521–543). Springer. doi:10.1007/978-3-319-75690-5_23

Yao, X., Lin, Y., Liu, Q., & Zhang, J. (2018). Privacy-preserving search over encrypted personal health record in multi-source cloud. *IEEE Access: Practical Innovations, Open Solutions*, *6*, 3809–3823.

Yener, E. (2020). *The role of blockchain Technologies in digital business and a model proposal: Blockchain based second hand vehicle trade platform* (Unpublished Master's Thesis). Istanbul Medipol University, Istanbul.

Yıldız, Ö. E. (2009). *Wine Tourism in Turkey – An Exemplary Product Development Model in Çeşme* (Unpublished Master's Thesis). Dokuz Eylül University, İzmir.

Yli-Huumo, J., Ko, D., Choi, S., Park, S., & Smolander, K. (2016). Where is current research on blockchain technology? - A systematic review. *PLoS One*, *10*(10), e163477. doi:10.1371/journal.pone.0163477 PMID:27695049

Yong, T., Jason, X., Rafael, B.-A., & Lakshmi, I. (2019). Ethics of blockchain: A framework of technology, applications, impacts, and research directions. *Information Technology & People*, *33*(2), 602–632. https://doi.org/10.1108/ITP-10-2018-0491

Zamani, E. D., & Giaglis, G. M. (2018). With a little help from the miners: Distributed ledger technology and market disintermediation. *Industrial Management & Data Systems*, *118*(3), 637–652. doi:10.1108/IMDS-05-2017-0231

Zhang, P., White, J., Schmidt, D. C., & Lenz, G. (2017). *Applying software patterns to address interoperability in blockchain-based healthcare apps.* arXiv:1706.03700.

Zhang, N., Zhong, S., & Tian, L. (2017). Using blockchain to protect personal privacy in the scenario of online taxi-hailing. *International Journal of Computers, Communications & Control*, *12*(6), 886–902. doi:10.15837/ijccc.2017.6.2886

Zhong, R. Y., Xu, X., Klotz, E., & Newman, S. T. (2017). Intelligent manufacturing in the context of industry 4.0: A review. *Engineering*, *3*(5), 616–630. doi:10.1016/J.ENG.2017.05.015

Zhou, K., Liu, T., & Zhou, L. (2015). Industry 4.0: Towards future industrial opportunities and challenges. *2015 12th International conference on fuzzy systems and knowledge discovery (FSKD)*, 2147–2152. doi:10.1109/FSKD.2015.7382284

About the Contributors

Rohit Bansal is working as Assistant Professor in Department of Management Studies in Vaish College of Engineering, Rohtak. He obtained Ph.D. in Management from Maharshi Dayanand University, Rohtak. With a rich experience of 13 years, he has achieved growth through robust and proactive academic initiatives. He has authored & edited 8 books as well as published 95 research papers in national and international journals of repute including chapters in edited books. He has also presented papers in 30 conferences and seminars. His area of interest includes marketing management, human resource management, organizational behaviour, services marketing and organizational development. He has proficiency in handling graduate and post graduate students by using interactive discussions and "hands-on" approaches to help them undergo experiential learning He is on Editorial Advisory Board as a member in 110 national and international peer reviewed journals. He is Managing Editor of International Journal of 360° Management Review & International Journal of Techno – Management Research.

Pacha Malyadri obtained Doctorate in Commerce in 1991 from Sri Venkateswara University. He rendered services in Government with 33 years of experience in Teaching, Research, Administration, Training, and consultancy. A prolific writer; Dr. Malyadri has authored 6 Books and 144 Research papers. He is a Peer Team member/Assessor, NAAC.. He is on the International Editorial advisory boards as a Member of 355 International Peer-reviewed journals. He carried out two Major Research Projects sponsored by the UGC, New Delhi. Under his guidance 13 Ph.D.'s and 14 M.Phil.'s are awarded.Dr Malyadri served as Principal for more than a decade in affiliated colleges of Osmania University and Rayalaseema University and also served as Director (Research & Development) in a JNTUH affiliated Engineering College. He got an award of Senior Fellowship from ICSSR, New Delhi. He is also serving as Inspecting Authorities (IAs) appointed by the Ministry of Minority Affairs, Govt. of India to conduct inspections of the NGOs/Institutions/Skill Development Centre across the country. Dr. Malyadri is a State level Best Teacher awardee in the year 2008, honored by the Government of Andhra Pradesh.

Amandeep Singh has done BIT MBA PhD and he is also UGC-NET qualified. Currently, he is working as Professor Chitkara Business School, Chitkara University, Punjab, India. He is having more than 14 years of teaching experience. He has served as Dean / Principal in various reputed Universities and colleges. He has published 28 research papers in various journals and conferences. He has also chaired many National and International Conferences. He is on the editorial board for 3 International Journals. He was awarded as the Best Teacher in 2008.

Asif Pervez is working as an Assistant Professor (management) in the Centre for Distance and Online Education, Jamia Millia Islamia. He got MBA (FM) and Ph.D from Department of Commerce, Aligarh Muslim University Aligarh. His research and teaching interest includes finance, Banking, Investment and Blockchain technology among others. He has published several papers in journals of repute. He has presented papers in various national and international conferences. Before joining the Centre for Distance and Online Education, JMI, he has Pursued Post doctorate (UGC) and has served in Department of Commerce and Women's College, AMU as Guest faculty.

* * *

Shradhha Awasthi is currently working as Associate Professor at Chitkara Business School. Possess 15+ years of work experience in the field of HR and OB besides a Doctorate in Management from Amity University.

Anil B. Malali, Associate Professor & Head of the Department of Commerce and Management, Acharya Institute of Graduate Studies. He has received his Ph.D., in Commerce from Alagappa University, Tamilnadu. He is known for his proficiency in Accounts and Finance. He is having 20 years of teaching experience in the field of Commerce and Management. He has published several research articles in the leading National as well as International Journals. His current research interests are Accounts and Finance.

Hanène Babay holds a PhD and a master's degree in marketing from the Faculty of Economics and Management of Tunis. She is currently professor of marketing at the Fashion Institute of Monastir, Tunisia. She is also the author / co-author of several marketing research works, particularly around social network marketing, consumer-brand relationship, e-learning, etc. Her areas of research interest are in relationship marketing, brand management, digital marketing, marketing and NTIC, consumer behavior, e-commerce, e-learning, etc. She is also a trainer and marketing consultant for Tunisian companies. She has provided numerous training and team building activities on behalf of several organizations and companies in Tunisia.

Devesh Bathla is an industry practitioner and a Business Analytics' Trainer to Working professionals and Management students who demand innovation & continuous improvement. Experienced in marketing analytics, consistently achieved business objectives, reduced marketing / operating costs and improved productivity.

Hardik Bhadeshiya is working in the capacity of Assistant professor in the Department of Commerce and Business Management under the faculty of Commerce in esteemed The Maharaja Sayajirao University of Baroda. He is the holder of prolific academic accolades like M.Com(Marketing), MBA(Finance & Marketing), M.A. (Economics), UGC-NET(Commerce), UGC-NET(Management), SLET(Commerce), Ph. D(Commerce) with rich academic, research and administrative experience of 10+ years. He has completed various faculty development programs from well-established institutions functioning under Pandit Madan Mohan Malaviya National Mission on Teachers and Teaching (PMMMNMT) on various themes like Managing Online Classes and Co-creating MOOCs, Moodle, use of statistical computer packages (SPSS & GRETL) in Research and Creation of google sites and OER. He has authored 5 books in the area of Economic Value Added, Indian Stock market, Performance appraisal of various Mutual fund schemes, Shareholders' Value Creation, and a study of investor's expected rate of return. In his account, he has a credit of 11 research papers published in well-known Scopus indexed/UGC Care Listed/Peer-Reviewed journals, 2 Research articles in peer-reviewed ISBN Journal proceedings, has attended 7 UGC Sponsored national Seminars, and presented 3 research papers in international conferences. One of his research papers published with the Indian journal of finance (Scopus Indexed) is honored as the Top 5 research papers having 7000+ views. He has rendered his expert services as a resource person in the various areas of management and research in the events/seminar/FDPs and students capacity building programs organized by various colleges/institutes/departments of the universities at the state and national level. He is a lifetime member of the Indian Accounting Association. He is having his active participation in various departmental, faculty, and university-level committees. He is an editor of a well-known international journal of creative research thoughts and giving his continuous contribution in the field of research.

Khoi Bui works at Industrial University of Ho Chi Minh City, Vietnam. His field is in Econometrics and Management.

Devi Parameswari C. received her B.Sc and M.Sc (Computer Science) from Madurai Kamaraj University in 2013 and 2018 respectively. Now, she is a Research Scholar in the Department of Computer Applications, Kalasalingam Academy of Research and Education, Krishnankoil, Tamilnadu, India. Her current research areas include block chain technology, security.

Nozha Erragcha holds a PhD and a master's degree in marketing from from the Faculty of Economics and Management of Tunis. She is currently assistant professor in marketing in the faculty of Faculty of Legal, Economic and Management Sciences of Jendouba. She is also the author of several marketing research works, particularly around social network marketing, consumer-brand relationship, e-learning, etc. Her areas of research interest are in relationship marketing, brand management, digital marketing, marketing and NTIC, consumer behavior, e-commerce, e-learning, consumer behavior, etc. She I was in 2013 and currently reviewer in the journal Computer in Human Behavior. She is expert in the field of eLearning, educational decoupage, Instructional design.

Bhoomi Gupta is a faculty at Maharaja Agrasen Institute of Technology at Delhi. She has completed her doctoral degree from IKGPTU. She has published numerous papers and chapters in international and national journals. She is a member of various committees and technical societies.

Pooja Kansra is working as an Associate Professor of Economics in Mittal School of Business, Lovely Professional University, Jalandhar. She has over eleven years of teaching experience and seven years of research experience. Her areas of interest include econometrics methods, microeconomics, macroeconomics, managerial economics, quantitative techniques and economics of health and education. She is a member of Indian Economic Association. Her research interests include health economics, insurance and service operation management. She is an avid researcher and presented papers in various national and international conferences. She has to her credit various research papers published in refereed national and international journals of repute.

Manminder Kaur is working as Associate Professor with GNKITMTC, Yamuna nagar since 2009. Her work experience includes teaching to UG and PG students of management. She has a number of good publications in her credit.

Hameed Khan is associated with Guru Ramdas Khalsa Institute of Science & Technology Jabalpur, MP.

Pawan Kumar has academic experience of 15 years and have done his PhD from Kurukshetra university, Kurukshetra. He have done 20 publications in national and international journals and had presented papers in 15 National & International seminars and conferences.

Ilayaraja M., Assistant Professor, Department of Computer Science & Information Technology, Kalasalingam University, Krishnankoil. He has completed his doctoral degree in the area of data mining. He has been very much interest in doing research in the area of data mining and network security. He was published various papers related to heart disease prediction and information security. He has been familiar in working with some of the data mining tools. He also developed some methods to predict the risk of heart diseases by analyzing large volume of medical datasets and also developed various methods to secure the information over public transmission medium.

Sudha M. is currently working as Associate Professor & Head of the Department of Management, Acharya Institute of Graduate Studies. She has received her Ph.D., in Management from Alagappa University, Tamilnadu. She is known for his proficiency in Marketing and Finance. She is having 14 years of teaching experience in the field of Commerce and Management, and three years of Industrial Experience. She has also received an Award from the GSN Publications for her Academic Excellence in the year 2021. She has published several research articles in the leading National as well as International Journals. Her current research interest is in the marketing field. She can be contacted through the email msudha@acharya.ac.in.

Sumathy Mohan, M.Com., M.B.A., (M) M.B.A., (F)., PGDCA., M.A(WS)., M.Phil., Ph.D. She served as Dean, School of Commerce, Professor, Assosicate Professor, Reader in Bharathiar University, Coimbatore and Currently working as Professor & Head, Department of Commerce Bharathiar University, Coimbatore, TamilNadu, has taught Commerce and Management Subjects for three decades. She guided 70 Post Graduate Commerce and Management Students, 51 M.Phil and 18 PhD Scholars have been awarded. She authored 15 Books including edited Volumes and text books and to name few “Banking Industry in India”, “Globalization and Consumerism-issues and Challenges”, “Consumer Awareness, Welfare and Protection Problems”, Research Paradigms in Social Sciences Research, Teaching of Commerce, A Hand book of e-governance in India etc., Her 188 research papers have been published in various National, International, Refereed, Peer Reviewed, Scopus, and Web of Science Journals with impact factor and also contributed 17 chapters for the edited book. She has participated and Chaired International and National Seminars/conferences and presented 163 research papers in the National and International Conference including Malaysia (2010), Sri Lanka(2011), Sharjah, UAE(2012), Singapore(2017), Thailand(2018) and Vietnam(2019).. During COVID 19 pandemic she participated 44 Online workshops/Training /Faculty Development Programmes and 15 Certificate Programmes including Leadership Programmes . She organized 27 Programmes like National Seminars, Research methodology workshops, Anveshan: Research Convention for faculty and Scholars including funded programmes with a tune of Rs. 15, 73,000/- from various National funding Agencies including the Ministry of Consumer Affairs and MHRD, GOI. Association of Indian Univesities, New Delhi(2010-20201) . She has completed Six Major Research Projects and Five Minor Research Projects.She has been registered three copyrights on the topics Perception of Women on New Economic Policy, Evaluative Model on Perception of Users towards E-Governance Practices, A Hand Book of e-Governance Practices in India, SWOT Analysis Model on e-Governance Practices. member of editorial board and Review Board for 15 National and International journals and the Life Member of various Academic Associations . She got Certificate of Appreciation Towards the Spread of Digital Financial Literacy in Effecting to Excel and Achieve Second Rank among top Best 20 Institutions out of 4896 Institutions and also towards meritorious service She is the Member of various academic and administrative committees. Her articles cited by 188 researchers with h-Index 6 and i10 index 4. Her current research interests include Finance, accounting Banking, Marketing, Consumer Issues, and Rural Development. In recognition of the outstanding contributions made, the Tamilnadu State Council for Science and Technology is privileged to confer her The Esteemed TANSA Award in Social Sciences Category for the year 2019.

Sumit Oberoi is a research scholar at Mittal School of Business, Lovely Professional University, Jalandhar. His areas of interest embrace health economics, international trade, Research methodology and Micro-economics. He has published paper in high indexed journals such as Economic & Political Weekly, Int. J. of Diabetes in Developing Countries, Springer, Int. J. of Commerce, Economics and Policy (IJCEP), Anvesha, etc. Sumit is also reviewer for various journal viz. International Journal of Emerging Markets (Emerald), Int. J. of Diabetes in Developing Countries, ClinicoEconomics and Outcomes Research, etc.

Jin Yong Park is a Professor of Marketing in the School of Business, Konkuk University, Seoul, Korea. He holds a Ph.D. from Yonsei University, Seoul, Korea. His research interests include channels of distribution, retailing management, online consumer behaviors, information quality in marketing channels, and e-business research. His papers appear in journals and proceedings of international conferences related to marketing, information technology, and management.

Kanthavel R. has 22 years' experience in teaching and research in the field of information and Communication Engineering. He has the credit of more than 100 research articles in peer reviewed international Journals. His areas of interests are computer networking, Machine Learning and AI, Cooperative communication, computing and mobile networks.

Kazi Turin Rahman is an MBA graduate from Coventry University, UK, with distinction. He has had the privilege of working in various reputed organizations such as BRAC University, BRAC Bank Ltd., and Kantar Research. Another key accolade of his is being a Bangladeshi Youth Delegation member to India in 2014. The delegation called on the then President of India, Pranab Mukherjee. The author's primary research interests include digital marketing, consumer behavior, human-technology interaction, etc.

Célia M. Q. Ramos graduated in Computer Engineering from the University of Coimbra, obtained her Master in Electrical and Computers Engineering from the Higher Technical Institute, Lisbon University, and the PhD in Econometrics in the University of the Algarve (UALG), Faculty of Economics, Portugal. She is Coordinator Professor at School for Management, Hospitality and Tourism, also in the UALG, where she lectures computer science. Areas of research and special interest include conception and development of information systems, tourism information systems, big data, etourism, econometric modeling and panel-data models. Célia Ramos has published in the fields of information systems and tourism, namely, she has authored a book, twelve book chapters, conference papers and journal articles. At the level of applied research, she has participated in several funded projects.

Minky Sharma has five years of academic experience teaching managerial subjects to undergraduate and postgraduate students. Having two publications one is national and another one is international. And pursuing her Ph.D. in Commerce.

Gopalakrishnan Subramaniyan, Associate Professor, Department of Commerce & Management, Head - Research and Development Cell, Acharya Institute of Graduate Studies, Bangalore. Executed a major research project on "Solid Waste Management" funded by ICSSR – New Delhi for the period of two years from January 2018 to December 2019. Has 25 years of experience including 12 years of industry and 13years of teaching Management and Commerce subjects.

Dhanabalan Thangam is presently working as an Assistant Professor in Commerce and Management at Acharya Institute of Graduate Studies, Banglore, India. Earlier he was worked as Post - Doctoral researcher in Konkuk School of Business, Konkuk University, Seoul, Korea South. He received his Ph.D. degree in Management from Alagappa University, Tamilnadu, India. His current research interests are marketing, small business management, and artificial intelligence in management fields. He has received a Seminar Grant of Rs.2,50,000 from the Indian Council of Social Science Research, New Delhi, and arranged Two National Conference on Artificial Intelligence and Robotics in Business and Employment: Opportunities and

Challenges in 2020. He has authored several books, research articles, and proceedings presented at many professional conferences and venues.

Cigdem Unurlu is a lecturer at Trakya University in the department of Tourism and Hotel Management. She holds a Bachelor's Degree in Tourism and Hotel Management from Abant İzzet Baysal University and a masters and Ph.D. in business administration from Trakya University. Her research interests include consumer behavior, destination marketing and branding.

Dhaya Vel has 16 years experience in teaching and research in the field of Computer Science and Engineering. She published more than 80 research papers in peer reviewed international Journals. She was the recipient of IEI Young women Engineer award. Her areas of interests are wireless sensor networks, embedded systems, Machine Learning, Communication Systems.

Chittipaka Venkataiah is an engineering graduate and completed his MBA from the National Institute of Technology, Warangal. He has obtained his doctorate from the Department of Business Management, Osmania University, and qualified in UGC-NET conducted by University Grants Commission, New Delhi. He has selected for "Summer Faculty Research Fellow (SFRF) – 2020 from IIT Delhi. He is a certified ZED Master Trainer from the Quality Council of India and National Monitoring & Implementation Unit (NMIU) for the Zero Defect and Zero Effect (ZED) scheme of the Ministry of Micro, Small and Medium Enterprise (MSME). He has been conferred with the "Best Professor in Project Management" award by Business School Affaire & Dewang Mehta National Education Awards. Has over 18 years of experience in Teaching and Research in the area of Operations, Quality, Project Management, Logistics & Supply Chain Management. He is having professional membership in the 'Production and Operations Management Society (POMS)', 'All India Management Association (AIMA)', 'Quality Circle Forum of India (QCFI)', and the life member in 'National HRD Network (NHRD)'. He is also an executive committee member of the NHRD – Visakhapatnam chapter. He was an editorial member of the International Centre of Economics, Humanities, and Management (ICEHM). His area of teaching and research includes Operations, Quality, logistics, Supply Chain Management, and Project Management. He has presented several papers at various National and International conferences.

Harsh Yadav is a B.Tech scholar currently working on projects based on blockchain and full stack projects under MERN stack. He has previously worked on developing mapping software using Java and Spring boot.

Index

www.ingramcontent.com/pod-product-compliance
Lightning Source LLC
LaVergne TN
LVHW081341300926
849161LV00008B/2043